The Paulist Liturgy Planning Guide

For the Readings of Sundays and Major Feast Days, Year C

The Paulist Liturgy Planning Guide

For the Readings of Sundays and Major Feast Days, Year C

Edited by Lawrence Boadt, CSP, and Celine M. Allen

SCRIPTURE COMMENTARY
by Lawrence Boadt, CSP

HOMILY HELPS
by Roland Faley, TOR

LITURGICAL NOTES
by Ronald Hayde

MUSIC CONNECTION
by Kenneth Meltz

CATECHETICAL SUGGESTIONS
by Margaret Nutting Ralph

PAULIST PRESS
New York/Mahwah, N.J.

Cover design by Lynn Else

Book design by Celine M. Allen

Nihil Obstat: Rev. Msgr. James M. Cafone, M.A., S.T.D.
          Censor Librorum

Imprimatur: + Most Rev. John J. Myers, J.C.D., D.D.
          Archbishop of Newark

Library of Congress Cataloging-in-Publication Data

The Paulist liturgy planning guide : for the readings of Sundays and major feast days, year C / edited by Lawrence Boadt and Celine M. Allen.
     p. cm.
  Includes bibliographical references and index.
  ISBN 0-8091-4414-X (alk. paper)
  1. Public worship—Catholic Church—Planning. 2. Catholic Church—Liturgy. 3. Liturgical preaching. 4. Catholic Church. Lectionary for Mass (U.S.). Year C. I. Boadt, Lawrence. II. Allen, Celine.
  BX1970.P343 2006
  264'.02—dc22

                                        2006006624

Published by Paulist Press
997 Macarthur Boulevard
Mahwah, New Jersey 07430

www.paulistpress.com

Printed and bound in the
United States of America

CONTENTS—YEAR C

INTRODUCTION

The Paulist Liturgy Planning Guide for Year C continues the insights and
suggestions found in the books for Years A and B. It is written by the same
competent authors who contributed to the earlier volumes, and so it is a
completion and fulfillment of their overview of the Lectionary as a whole.
Year C especially highlights the insights of the wisdom tradition found in
the Old Testament selections. These readings were chosen by the Church
because they fit so well the particular approach of the Gospel of Luke that
stresses Jesus' use of parables and wisdom sayings in his teaching. A key
theme in both the wisdom tradition and Luke is the concern for the lowly
and despised. This theme and related topics are reflected in the various
resources contained in this volume for planning Sunday liturgies throughout the year. Whether the subject is exegesis, or homily suggestions, or
liturgical themes, or music, or catechetical topics, it is important that the
weekly celebration of the Eucharist for the local Catholic community be
carefully planned and connect all its important parts to the central themes
of the particular Sunday. *The Paulist Liturgy Planning Guide* has been prepared with that in mind, to make it easier and more convenient to find in
one place all the materials necessary for planning eucharistic celebrations.

Following the development of the liturgical and Lectionary themes
from week to week throughout the year provides a faith community with
its richest source of growth and understanding of the mystery of God's
grace at work in salvation history and in the present moment. This volume covers not only all the Sundays of the year but also all the major
holy days, Ash Wednesday, and the Holy Week Triduum. How often
Holy Week is neglected in our liturgical catechesis! The considerable
body of reflections on the central week of our liturgical year available
here constitutes one of the unique features of this book.

The layout of *The Paulist Liturgy Planning Guide* is designed to clearly
mark out each subject for a given Sunday so that the different planners
and ministers can study it and get ideas to share with all the others on the
liturgy planning committee or, if there is only one liturgical coordinator, so
that he or she can obtain all the information that would be helpful in as
simple a manner as possible. One of our greatest hopes is that this book
will become a useful tool for each person in a parish who participates in
liturgical or catechetical ministry. We have designed it primarily so that
each individual can have a personal copy. He or she can mark it up, use it
to make marginal notes, and keep it as a resource for prayer during the
year, for reflecting on the exegesis of the various scripture passages, especially the continuous reading of the gospel in Ordinary Time, and for the
insights presented under the various subjects. This kind of tool has wonderful potential for deepening our understanding and love of the scriptures in

the liturgy and for all our worship and prayer. With the various resource materials that are provided here, other services during the week can be developed as a continuation of the scriptural themes of Sunday.

We encourage all who use this book to do so with the Lectionary or a missalette at hand. To make the book as usable as possible and keep the costs reasonable, we have made two choices that will draw the reader to the Lectionary proper.

First, some Sundays offer the option of longer or shorter readings. For the sake of space, we have sometimes found it necessary to print the shorter reading in this book, so you will need to look at the Lectionary for the longer form. Note, though, that all the exegesis and homiletic suggestions are based on the longer reading.

Second, we have not printed the responsorial psalm and Alleluia verses. These are often treated elsewhere as musical interludes, with little attention given to anything other than following the musical settings for the antiphons printed in standard missalettes. Here we want the reader to take up and examine some central theme from the entire psalm or other biblical hymn from which the few verses of the responsorial psalm or Alleluia have been drawn. In this way, the reader will come to a greater appreciation of the psalms and grow in an awareness of how they echo the theology of the covenant and express biblical spirituality.

Thus, instead of printing the full text of the psalm response and Alleluia verse for each Sunday in this guide, we provide the following:

1. the standard antiphon assigned to the responsorial psalm of the day;

2. a verse selected from the psalm as a whole (and not necessarily from the verses used in the responsorial) that captures the theme of the entire psalm and also resonates with the major theme of the gospel reading of the day; and

3. a short exegesis that discusses the psalm's meaning in the context of the entire Psalter.

We have chosen to do this in order to encourage liturgical planners to look at the psalms as complete poems of divine inspiration and not just limit themselves to a few verses selected for the day's celebration without confronting the beauty and message of the full psalm.

As with any new project, there may be important and useful areas that are not covered here and that you would find valuable in next year's edition. Please feel free to write us at the Paulist Press or e-mail your suggestion to info@paulistpress.com. We value your comments.

Lawrence Boadt, CSP, Publisher

SCRIPTURE AND THE LITURGY

 In the liturgy, scripture not only forms the basis for the prayers of the Mass, especially the narrative prayers of the prefaces and the eucharistic prayers, but also, as proclaimed during the liturgy of the word, governs weekly themes and shapes catechesis.

All of the readings contained in the Lectionary were selected by the International Consilium charged with finding suitable texts after the close of the Second Vatican Council. Consilium members were aware that the texts selected needed to convey the most important teachings of the Old and New Testaments and that each selection had to be a complete and self-contained artistic unit that would have dramatic impact when heard by the congregation. At the Eucharist we do more than share the body of the Lord; we are transformed and grow spiritually by hearing his word.

The art of interpreting a biblical text involves not only noting and establishing an accurate translation from the original Hebrew or Greek but also discovering the larger meaning of the passage, both for the author and for us today. Our translation is not in question, since the Lectionary uses a superb translation, the New American Bible that was carefully prepared by members of the Catholic Biblical Association of America. That leaves the exegete to help the modern reader unlock the original sense of the text as well as point out ways in which it still speaks to the modern world thousands of years after it was written.

Even though inspired by the Holy Spirit, the biblical authors were fully human writers, limited in their modes of expression by their cultures and languages. Their ways of thinking and their views of the world were shaped by what they experienced. It follows that every time we read a scripture passage, we need to ask the questions: Where did this text come from? What was its original sense? How did an ancient audience (e.g., Jesus' disciples) hear it in their day? For us to understand the nature of the situation described in, say, the parable of the workers in the vineyard, we need to find out something about the customs of the time. How did one go about hiring workers? What were they really paid? Was it unusual for an owner to pay the last-hired workers first? An understanding of the literal meaning of a text gives us a firm foundation for discovering its spiritual meaning.

The Scripture Commentary section of this guide has three major tasks to perform. First, it points out how the three readings—especially the first reading and the gospel—resonate with each other. Second, it discusses the historical background of each text and what the passage meant in its original cultural setting. At times this involves presenting information on ancient events as we know them from archaeology and from written tablets and monuments. (Amazingly enough, the responses of biblical writers to the situations of their day readily match our own responses to contemporary experiences.) Finally, the third task is to apply the theological vision contained in the passage to our own century's concerns. The hope is that the reader will come to a deeper understanding of and appreciation for the Church's use of each text in the liturgy of the day.

Lawrence Boadt, CSP

THE "WHY" OF HOMILY HELPS

 A good homily is not simply an exercise in exegesis. Nor is it a relevant presentation, only loosely connected with the text. As I see it, good exegesis is the background to the homily. It is vitally important to know what the author intended. Once that is accomplished, a number of ideas will ordinarily emerge from the text.

On Sundays of the year, the dominant theme appears in the first reading and the gospel. But this is not to restrict the homilist who may wish to develop secondary themes that appear on that day. The important thing is to let the text speak for itself.

In my Homily Helps, I generally picked one or two themes for development by the homilist. These are rooted in the Sunday or feast day texts. What I wished to avoid at all costs was suggesting that the text could be an appendage or a peg on which to hang one's own ideas. I see any form of "eisegesis" as alien to the true spirit of the liturgy. The message must spring from the text itself. Should it occasionally occur that the preacher feels the need to speak on an extraneous topic, he should make it clear to his hearers that this is what he is doing and then set the text aside. Needless to say, in the spirit of the liturgy, this should happen only rarely.

Once the theme is decided upon and the text elucidated, the homilist then passes to the life of his congregation. He must ask himself: How does the message that I see as important today touch the lives of the people whom I serve? Generally in my commentary I make one or two applications of the text. This is meant to assist the homilist, but it is not intended to be exhaustive. The homilist may well see other applications that are equally valid, and he should not hesitate to bring the message to bear in his own way.

In short, the Homily Helps are meant to facilitate personal thoughts and reflections. And this work is paramount. My own experience comes from my days of teaching in a Protestant seminary. There the primacy of the word was an overarching principle. In preaching class, the professor stringently demanded that the text be grappled with and its sense delivered. Repeatedly the question was asked of the young preacher: "Is that what the text says?" The next step was to apply the text in a way that was clear and relevant. I was deeply impressed with the reverence that was given the word.

Preaching should not be seen as a difficult task, but it is a disciplined one. It is wholly concerned with the text and life. Fidelity to both is the central demand.

Roland Faley, TOR

ABOUT LITURGICAL NOTES

 Each Sunday the gathered assembly hears God's word proclaimed through the cycles of the three-year Lectionary. However, this word is not heard in a vacuum. The liturgy and the liturgical year are the lens through which the scriptures are heard, seen, and experienced by the Sunday assembly. They provide the context in which the Sunday assembly will hear each week the message of salvation so that they can go forth and live it. The Liturgical Notes are designed for use by liturgy committees and liturgy planning teams in planning and preparing both for individual Sunday liturgies and for the seasons of the liturgical year as well as catechesis on and for the liturgy and the ongoing renewal of liturgical ministers.

In some cases the Liturgical Notes outline the legitimate options that may be used on a particular Sunday; in other cases they suggest a specific prayer or blessing that is appropriate for a particular day. They also recognize the other events that occur on Sundays, such as Mother's Day, and suggest how these events might be acknowledged and celebrated in the Sunday liturgy. The suggestions are designed to move the team beyond the primary liturgical books, the Lectionary and the Sacramentary, to the other approved ritual books of the church and the options that can be found within them.

There is another aspect to the Liturgical Notes that moves them beyond a guide to the nuts-and-bolts tools for preparing the liturgy. Taking their cue from the Sunday readings, the Liturgical Notes also make recommendations for particular aspects of catechesis that can be incorporated into the ongoing formation of the Sunday assembly. For example, when the scripture readings speak of sickness and healing, the user will find suggestions for catechesis from sections of the Rite of Pastoral Care of the Sick. When the scripture readings turn our attention to death and resurrection, the user will find suggestions for catechesis from the Order of Christian Funerals. In the course of the three-year cycle of the Lectionary, major aspects of liturgical and sacramental catechesis are covered.

Using the readings as a springboard, the Liturgical Notes also suggest times when a particular ministry or a particular part of the liturgy might become the subject of reflection, evaluation, and ongoing catechesis. It is not necessarily intended that such evaluation and reflection actually take place on these particular Sundays. Rather, the Sunday scriptures can bring to light a particular ministry and provide a way to begin the process of evaluation and reflection.

The user of the Liturgical Notes will clearly find a considerable amount of repetition. This repetition is intentional. Too often we have made the mistake of believing that, because we have catechecized the assembly or a group of ministers, the catechesis has been heard and internalized. Quite the contrary is true. It is the very repetition of the catechesis, in a variety of forms, that allows the information to take root in both head and heart and bear abundant fruit not only in full, conscious, and active participation in the celebration of the Eucharist but also in the whole of life.

Ronald Hayde

Many years ago Jesuit liturgist John Gallen offered a three-stage developmental model of the interrelationship between music and worship. The first stage Gallen referred to as "Music in the Liturgy," wherein music was a nice addition to the ritual but not particularly necessary. The next stage he referred to as "Liturgical Music," wherein the connective tissue between ritual and music was fleshed out more coherently through responses and acclamations, which were ideally sung by all at *every* Mass. Included here would be the responsorial psalm, the Gospel Acclamation, the eucharistic acclamations, and the Communion hymn/processional, which had begun to reclaim its position as one of the most ancient and revered times for Christian singing. In the last stage, which Gallen hoped would be the main agenda for the future, we would be in the realm of "Musical Liturgy," where the nature of ritual as poetic and musical would become apparent by the fulsome, conscious, and active participation of all in musical prayer.

As we stand early in this new millennium, it is apparent that we still have a way to go in realizing this vision. Most of us know that, for the majority of Catholic communities, we are still in the early stages of birthing Gallen's insightful and prophetic vision. There are no magic potions, no *deus ex machina* interventions that will overnight solve the problem of nonexistent, lackluster, and sporadic musical participation, but here are a few suggestions that might help us all along.

1. Accompany well. I am a firm believer that the "song leader" in worship is and should be the accompanist, whether that is on organ, piano, or guitar. When congregations are kept guessing as to when the hymn or acclamation begins, it is a sure way to defeat full participation. This also means that the accompanist needs to be aware of and respond to the congregation's vocal range, which can vary from place to place, not to mention times of day.

2. Lead, but don't dominate. The congregation is not an audience. Congregations need to hear themselves sing but, too often, all one can hear is the cantor/song leader or choir. It may be time to turn down the microphones and to embrace our congregations as the primary musicians of Catholic worship.

3. Select music that is rooted in the readings of the day, the motifs of the season, or the ritual action of the service. All three of these are fertile soil for musical choices and arrangement and are considerations in the suggestions offered in this volume.

4. Balance the new with the old. We are blessed with composers who provide many beautiful and fitting hymns, psalms, and Mass settings. Integrating newer pieces (which keep a music program interesting and growing) without jettisoning older pieces (which give a congregation confidence) is a delicate balancing act.

5. Remind yourself and all who collaborate in your music program that this is a ministry, a service to enable the larger Church to participate more fully. The litmus test for the success of any music ministry is not the sound that goes out from the cantor or choir but the sound that comes back from the congregation.

With these few thoughts in mind, I wish all of us well as we continue to "sing a new song to the Lord."

Kenneth Meltz

ABOUT CATECHETICAL SUGGESTIONS

 The purpose of including catechetical suggestions in a Liturgy Planning Guide is to encourage parish catechists to consider Lectionary-based catechesis. Lectionary-based catechesis is designed to help all those who participate in the liturgy see an obvious connection between how we pray, what we teach, and how we live.

When I first became acquainted with Lectionary-based catechesis, I found myself resistant to it. Having been an in-school teacher, I wanted a syllabus that would cover all the topics I considered important. I wanted to make sure people learned all they needed to know. I raised this concern to a friend who responded, "Do you know everything you need to know?" Of course, I don't. Growing in faith and in our knowledge of our faith is a lifelong process.

While Lectionary-based catechesis may not address every topic under the sun, it will address those topics most important to our growth in faith. Why? Because the Lectionary is designed to help us name and celebrate the core mysteries of our faith over the course of one liturgical year. Over the course of three liturgical years we probe and celebrate those mysteries three times and hear the biblical witness behind our beliefs from many different voices: many Old Testament authors, many letters, and all four gospels.

You may notice that the catechetical topics suggested often include a scripture topic. This is because we Catholics are taught that we should be "nourished and ruled" by scripture (see *Dei Verbum*, 21). We are nourished by scripture in many ways at our Sunday celebration. If we are also going to be ruled by scripture, that is, if we are going to give scripture authority over the way we live our lives, we need to correctly understand what the biblical authors intended to say. To accomplish this, we must become biblical contextualists, understanding the biblical passages not only in the context of the Lectionary but also in the contexts in which they appear in the Bible.

As you read the catechetical suggestions, remember that they are just that: suggestions. The ideal way to choose Lectionary-based catechetical topics is to gather your catechists and brainstorm together over appropriate topics that are related to the readings. This method will build on the interests and talents of each parish's particular catechists. It will also make it possible for catechetical programs offered for different age levels to address the same topics in age-appropriate ways. This will result in families having very interesting conversations around the dinner table about what was celebrated and discussed each Sunday.

Perhaps a topic will be suggested that interests your parish catechists but no one feels equipped to address it. A good parish library with print resources and a good search engine such as Google should help solve this problem.

We have included catechetical suggestions in this Liturgy Planning Guide because we believe that Lectionary-based catechesis will help your parishioners understand and live the truths that we celebrate in our liturgy.

Margaret Nutting Ralph

First Reading:
Jeremiah 33:14–16

The days are coming, says the Lord, when I will fulfill the promise I made to the house of Israel and Judah. In those days, in that time, I will raise up for David a just shoot; he shall do what is right and just in the land. In those days Judah shall be safe and Jerusalem shall dwell secure; this is what they shall call her: "The LORD our justice."

SCRIPTURE COMMENTARY

We are entering Year C of Lectionary passages. The major readings this year will turn on the gospel passage of the day taken from the Gospel of Luke. (The few exceptions are the celebration days of great biblical events not recorded in Luke, such as Epiphany.) The selections for our first Sunday share the common theme of waiting for the day when the Lord will return to bring his righteousness to the earth. We read first a passage from Jeremiah where the prophet foresees a coming age when Jerusalem and Judea will no longer remain under punishment for their past unfaithfulness and injustice. Instead they will see a restoration of the dynasty of King David as of old. The new king will do what is just and right, not just any old way but in direct obedience to God's own demand for justice. He will be so faithful and lead his people to such obedience that the whole people will simply be called by a name identifying them with God himself: "The LORD our justice [righteousness]." It is a pun. The last king before the Babylonian exile was Zedekiah, whose name means "The LORD is righteous," but he hardly lived accordingly! God has a better king and better role model in mind in the ages to come.

Use of God's Name. *From long tradition going back to Jewish usage before the time of Jesus, Jews do not pronounce God's proper name, "Yahweh," but out of reverence replace this word in biblical texts with "Adonai," which means "the LORD." Modern Catholic translations respect this tradition and usually use "the LORD," as does the Lectionary.*

HOMILY HELPS

It is helpful to see Advent as our annual "wake-up" call. When the tsunami disaster struck southern Asia with such catastrophic force, some people thought of it as the end of the world. The gospel today speaks of the "end time"—or the "final days"—in apocalyptic terms. The sea roars in tsunami-like fashion; the heavens are shaken; people are enveloped in dreadful fear. Finally there is the return of Christ on the clouds of heaven. There is an underlying lesson here. When we speak of the end, we do so in vague, figurative language; we simply don't know the "when" and the "how."

But the message is clear enough: Be alert.

Personal experience shows us the countless ways in which life can come to an end. A dreadful car accident; the abduction of a child; a person leaving for work and never returning. We have all known or heard of these or similar events. But how quickly we put them out of our mind. They don't directly relate to our own personal end, and so it is back to business as usual. The gospel description today may not be too far off the mark. Self-indulgence, carousing, worldly cares. While we may not go as far as all that, daily interests consume us once more as they move to center stage. Still, our own end is no less inevitable for its being forestalled.

Yet, as always, we are reminded that there is a bright side to this picture. The first reading from Jeremiah is full of end-time hope as it speaks of the royal descendant of David, a future king of justice and right. According to many scholars, this was written after centuries of disappointing kings, in the post-exilic era, when there was no Davidic king. But the hope was still alive for a new and brighter future.

This is precisely the message that Paul extends to the Thessalonians. Paul readily admits that he cannot fix the date of Christ's return, but he does indicate the way to prepare for it. There should be an alertness that expresses itself in love for one

PSALM REFLECTION

"Discovering the ways of God" summarizes the major theme of Psalm 25. It returns over and over to various ways of expressing God's teaching as a guide for life. His "paths" are learning the truth; his "ways" reveal goodness; his guidance is by means of justice; his teaching makes us humble; and his friendship is with those who believe in and reverence God in their lives. As in the first reading to which it responds, the emphasis falls on the close relationship established between those who declare their faithfulness to God's teaching in the scriptures for their life, and God himself. One never obeys God without also becoming God's friend. And this is because God himself has taught us his "ways" by establishing a covenant relationship with his people. As the book of Exodus, the prophets, and several psalms express it, "He is our God and we are his people" (Exod 6:7).

Psalm Response
Psalm 25:4–5, 8–9, 10, 14

Antiphon
To you, O Lord, I lift my
    soul.

Verse for Reflection
No one who attends to you
    is ever made ashamed
    for it;
Only those who act treach-
    erously are put to
    shame. (v. 3)

CATECHETICAL SUGGESTIONS

Covenant: Old Testament and New Testament
Examination of conscience
Apocalyptic literature
The season of Advent in the liturgical year
Jesus' "end times" statements
Prophecy and fulfillment

---

another and "for all." We are to live in accord with conscience on a daily basis.

The eventualities of life are uncertain. Our mortality is rooted in our fragility. But to return to faith and prayer is to live with constant awareness. Advent is a period of longing and waiting, a time for our attention to be directed toward the future. None of us knows what form the end will take. But with a faith-based life and a love for prayer, we need not fear. The psalmist today has it right: "The paths of the LORD are kindness and constancy toward those who keep his covenant."

LITURGICAL NOTES

Around this time of year, everyone feels it in one way or another. The days are shorter; darkness comes even sooner. The green of Ordinary Time gives way to the rich purples of Advent.

On the Sundays of Advent, the Gloria is omitted. The first Sunday of Advent focuses on the second coming of Christ at the end of time in judgment, and in power and glory, at a hour we least expect. The prophet Jeremiah reminds us that the time is coming when God will fulfill the promise made to our ancestors. Paul tells the Thessalonians to allow their love to strengthen one another so

that they might be "blameless in holiness" at the coming of the Lord. As we begin this "year of Luke," we are reminded not to fear the signs of the end of time, because our "redemption is at hand." We are also exhorted to "be vigilant." The preface invites us to "watch for the day, hoping that the salvation promised us will be ours when Christ our Lord will come again in his glory."

One of the symbols of our joyful expectation is the Advent wreath, with its circle of evergreens and four candles. When the Advent wreath is used in church, it should be large enough to be visible but should not compete with altar, ambo, font, or chair. It should serve to remind

**Second Reading:
1 Thessalonians 3:12—4:2**

Brothers and sisters: May the Lord make you increase and abound in love for one another and for all, just as we have for you, so as to strengthen your hearts, to be blameless in holiness before our God and Father at the coming of our Lord Jesus with all his holy ones. Amen.

Finally, brothers and sisters, we earnestly ask and exhort you in the Lord Jesus that, as you received from us how you should conduct yourselves to please God—and as you are conducting yourselves—you do so even more. For you know what instructions we gave you through the Lord Jesus.

SCRIPTURE COMMENTARY

St. Paul adds still another dimension to the theme of waiting for the Lord by staying close to his teachings and his ways. He asks the Thessalonians to go beyond simply accepting his instructions on Christ's teaching into their lives, to grow by increasing in love for each other. Paul has shown them through his example how to live a life of complete dedication to the Lord Jesus. They must learn that God invites each and every one of them to do likewise. And how are they to do this? Only by entering into a closer relationship with Jesus himself! They must learn to follow Christ by living with the awareness that Christ himself is always present with them. Note how even in this very short excerpt from his letter, Paul uses the expression "the Lord Jesus" three times to reinforce his point.

About Advent. Advent has a twofold character: as a time to prepare for Christmas, when Christ's first coming among us is remembered, and as a time when that remembrance directs the mind and heart to await Christ's second coming at the end of time. Advent is thus a period for devout and joyful preparation (GNLYC, 49).

the assembly of our time spent watching and waiting.

The Advent wreath can be blessed at every Mass on the first Sunday of Advent; the texts can be found in the *Book of Blessings.* The prayer of blessing calls attention to the purpose of the wreath and its relation to the assembly gathered for worship. When the wreath is blessed during Mass, the blessing takes place at the conclusion of the General Intercessions, replacing the concluding collect or prayer. After the wreath has been blessed, the first candle is lit.

Many families maintain the custom of having an Advent wreath in their homes. *Catholic Household Blessings and Prayers*

provides a short order of service for the blessing and lighting of the Advent wreath in the home. This service would help people extend the celebration of Advent from the church to their homes.

The texts, words, sounds, symbols, and colors of Advent are rich. Jesse trees, giving trees, angels for Christmas, and the like also compete for our attention. Liturgy planners should exercise care not to bring too many additions to the Sunday Eucharist. Less is most definitely more. And while Advent is a time of preparation, there is often a tendency to compete with the mall, a place that has looked like Christmas since Halloween. Restraint is in order.

Crowds tend to grow on the Sundays leading up to Christmas. This would be a good time for liturgy planners to examine the parish ministry of hospitality. While members of the ministry of hospitality might say, "We did this last year!" our efforts at hospitality can always be improved. How will the stranger, returning after months or years, be greeted when arriving at church? How will the regular churchgoer be prepared to fit yet another person at the table of word and sacrament? We need to be reminded that we should always conduct ourselves in ways that are pleasing to God.

SCRIPTURE COMMENTARY

Luke's vision of the end of time is chosen as the first passage from his gospel to be read this year. It sets a theme as we begin the yearlong exploration of his entire gospel. By examining the end, we are better able to understand the beginning. What are we waiting for? In what do we place our hope? Since Advent means the period of waiting for the birth of Christ, the Church chooses passages of the gospel that explain why this birth will mean salvation for the whole world. The *Son of Man* who is one day going to return in heavenly glory to bring our ransom from sin and the power of evil in the world first came as the *son* of human origin in Bethlehem. This child will teach us how to live so that we in turn will be strong and eager for his final return. Luke stresses the upright and ethical life lived by all true followers of Jesus right up to that common moment when the whole world will face God's final judgment. Christians possess an inner peace and confidence built on a personal relationship of prayer with God that gives them courage to stay the course to the end—and it comes not from our doing but from God's sending his own Son to be "our way, our truth, and our life."

Gospel: Luke 21:25–28, 34–36

Jesus said to his disciples: "There will be signs in the sun, the moon, and the stars, and on earth nations will be in dismay, perplexed by the roaring of the sea and the waves. People will die of fright in anticipation of what is coming upon the world, for the powers of the heavens will be shaken. And then they will see the Son of Man coming in a cloud with power and great glory. But when these signs begin to happen, stand erect and raise your heads because your redemption is at hand.

"Beware that your hearts do not become drowsy from carousing and drunkenness and the anxieties of daily life, and that day catch you by surprise like a trap. For that day will assault everyone who lives on the face of the earth. Be vigilant at all times and pray that you have the strength to escape the tribulations that are imminent and to stand before the Son of Man."

MUSIC CONNECTION

Neither the homilist nor the musician needs to "reinvent the wheel" when it comes to repetitive seasons such as Advent and Lent. Indeed, it is the very repetition of ritual seasons throughout our lifetime that allows us to ponder the meaning of those seasons in ever new and vibrant ways. In Year C we are treated to the distinctive qualities of Luke's gospel as the primary filter through which to view our Christian narrative. Today's pericope borrows from standard apocalyptic imagery to address our need to "be on guard" for the day of the Lord. There is no dearth of traditional hymns to keynote this season. These include *O Come, O Come, Emmanuel; Wake, O Wake and Sleep No Longer; The King Shall Come;* and *Come Thou Long Expected Jesus.* In a more contemporary vein, one should mention Mattingly's *On That Holy Mountain* and Grayson Brown's *When He Comes.* There is much to be said for a consistent musical opening for the Advent liturgies, and Chepponis's *Advent Gathering Song* provides a good example. Another offering in this vein is *Advent Gathering* by Rory Cooney and Gary Daigle. The responsorial, Psalm 25, has many excellent settings, including that of Marty Haugen from GIA and Steve Janco in the very fine collection *Psalms and Ritual Music* from World Library.

First Reading:
Genesis 3:9–15, 20

After the man, Adam, had eaten of the tree, the LORD God called to the man and asked him, "Where are you?" He answered, "I heard you in the garden; but I was afraid, because I was naked, so I hid myself." Then he asked, "Who told you that you were naked? You have eaten, then, from the tree of which I had forbidden you to eat!" The man replied, "The woman whom you put here with me—she gave me fruit from the tree, and so I ate it." The LORD God then asked the woman, "Why did you do such a thing?" The woman answered, "The serpent tricked me into it, so I ate it."

Then the LORD God said to the serpent:
"Because you have done this, you
     shall be banned
     from all the animals
     and from all the wild creatures;

SCRIPTURE COMMENTARY

From the earliest days of Christian faith, the Old Testament provided a whole range of prophetic texts that helped believers understand the meaning of the Incarnation. If God sent his own divine Son to be our Savior while accepting our human estate, as Paul says in Philippians 2:6, how could the all-holy one be part of our sinful condition? The doctrine of the "hypostatic union" answers this by saying that the human and divine natures were united but also kept separate. Jesus lived as a holy and sinless person, who yet shared the basic qualities of both natures. Genesis 3:15 prophesies an ongoing battle between the serpent as a symbol of Satan and the children of Adam and Eve. Since the word "offspring"—"her seed"—is singular, it was natural to apply it to Jesus as the messiah who would conquer Satan and his power. But without the mother descended from Eve, there would

HOMILY HELPS

Today our thinking turns to the age-old conflict between good and evil. Even after two thousand years of Christianity, there is still a limitless residue of sin. Why is such the case? Why this insistent separation from God's will? But evil does not end there. We have widespread disaster—hurricanes, earthquakes, floods. Is God in some way involved in all of this?

We shall never have a totally satisfying answer. There is no civilization or religion in the history of the world that has not wrestled with the problem of evil, and with limited success. One

ancient Near Eastern belief explained evil as the capriciousness of the gods themselves.

While the answers may be incomplete and not wholly satisfying, Christian tradition provides us with important insights. Sin is never due to God. According to the Genesis narrative read today, it is human beings who introduce sin into the world. In his conversation with God, Adam points to the origin of sin in an initial triumvirate—man, woman, and the serpent. With the natural world closely allied with humanity, it too pays a price. It becomes antagonistic to human designs and responds in terms of pain and hardship. There is a biblical link between sin and natural disaster.

But there is a bright light at the end of the tunnel. Where sin abounds, grace abounds even more. The goodness of God in creation and redemption dwarfs all other considerations. We are gifted. Mary's acceptance of God's plan as recounted in today's Lucan reading makes this clear. Where Eve had given a resounding "No" to God, Mary's response is an unqualified "Yes." Thus begins a new era of grace. The child to be born of her will one day take the mystery of pain and undeserved suffering upon himself. He also gives his "Yes" to God in achieving our salvation.

Today we celebrate the sinlessness of Mary. From the first moment of her existence, she

SCRIPTURE COMMENTARY, CONTINUED

be no son born to be messiah. To early biblical interpreters, the role of the mother was an integral part of God's plan, thus making this reading a very suitable passage to emphasize the Immaculate Conception as intended by God from the beginning.

on your belly shall you crawl,
and dirt shall you eat
all the days of your life.
I will put enmity between you and the woman,
and between your offspring and hers;
he will strike at your head,
while you strike at his heel.''

The man called his wife Eve, because she became the mother of all the living.

PSALM REFLECTION

Psalm 98 is part of the series of great psalms (Psalms 95–100) acclaiming God's eternal rule over the world. All of them accent God's goodness proclaimed joyfully by everything in creation, and especially they laud his saving will that restores and renews the whole earth. Since Psalm 98 directs our praise to the wonderful works of God that are totally new, or at least being done in a totally new way, it is a good psalm for declaring the wonder of God's saving plan revealed in the Incarnation. The psalmist doesn't want an actual new song to be composed, but wants us to praise the new work of God happening now in our sight.

Psalm Response
Psalm 98:1, 2–3ab, 3cd–4

Antiphon
Sing to the Lord a new song, for
he has done marvelous deeds.

Verse for Reflection
He [the Lord] has remembered
his love and fidelity
To the house of Israel! (v. 3)

was "graced," our "tainted nature's solitary boast." As we said at the beginning, we shall never have all the answers to the problem of evil. But the glass is more than half full. We now belong to Christ. Paul tells us today that we were chosen in him before the world began. Mary was the first chosen; we follow in her wake. Our prayer today is that she show us the way to be "holy and blameless in his sight."

LITURGICAL NOTES

In the midst of Advent, the Church celebrates the Solemnity of the Immaculate Conception. For Americans, Mary, under the title of the Immaculate Conception, stands as the patroness of our country.

Today's solemnity is often confusing to people, since some believe that it celebrates the conception of Jesus. This mistaken notion is often underscored by the gospel for the day, which is the account of the annunciation to Mary. What this day in fact commemorates is the conception of Mary, free from original sin. Free from sin, she stands as a sign of hope to people in every age as they journey to the kingdom.

Although it is still Advent, white vestments are worn, and

Second Reading:
Ephesians 1:3–6, 11–12

Brothers and sisters: Blessed be the God and Father of our Lord Jesus Christ, who has blessed us in Christ with every spiritual blessing in the heavens, as he chose us in him, before the foundation of the world, to be holy and without blemish before him. In love he destined us for adoption to himself through Jesus Christ, in accord with the favor of his will, for the praise of the glory of his grace that he granted us in the beloved.

In him we were also chosen, destined in accord with the purpose of the One who accomplishes all things according to the intention of his will, so that we might exist for the praise of his glory, we who first hoped in Christ.

SCRIPTURE COMMENTARY

St. Paul often speaks of God having planned our salvation from the first moment of creation. In this passage Paul says that even before the first human being was created, God desired to have Christ save us. He *planned* it so that if we sinned, he could reveal himself to us more fully in his own Son! He chose us to be holy, and then predestined us to be accepted as his own children so we would be entitled to his heavenly inheritance. He chose us to receive all of this in Christ, and for those who now believe in Jesus as the Christ, praise for God's saving goodness becomes our destiny. Are Paul's words not fittingly also said of Mary, who was chosen and predestined to holiness for the sake of Christ and who most truly could be said to be united to her Son? The Church thinks so, and takes Paul's deep insight into the way God works from the beginning to bring about lasting salvation and links it with his special favor to Mary.

Gospel: Luke 1:26–38

The angel Gabriel was sent from God to a town of Galilee called Nazareth, to a virgin betrothed to a man named Joseph, of the house of David, and the virgin's name was Mary. And coming to her, he said, "Hail, full of grace! The Lord is

SCRIPTURE COMMENTARY

This is the account of the annunciation, and it is also read more properly for that feast on March 25. Why would it be suitable for this feast celebrating Mary born free from the effects of original sin? Luke in his gospel constructed the scene of the annunciation to emphasize two

the Gloria makes a brief return. There might be a tendency to celebrate this solemnity in isolation from Advent, but when we join it to our Advent vigilance of watching, waiting, and preparing, we see that Mary is the very model of Advent: listening, waiting, obeying.

The basic Advent environment remains the same, although it would be appropriate to place flowers at Mary's shrine. Her example of faithful obedience to God's will, of simple trust in all that God asks, ought to be reflected in the General Intercessions. Since she is patroness of our nation, it would also be fitting to include prayers for our country in the General Intercessions.

CATECHETICAL SUGGESTIONS

The story of Adam and Eve in its biblical context
Original sin
Mary as the model for all Christians
The development of doctrine
The joyful mysteries of the Rosary
Mary in the gospels

SCRIPTURE COMMENTARY, CONTINUED

essential points about the Incarnation, namely, that (1) Jesus was not just another child born into this world but was sent by God to fulfill the prophets' hopes for a messiah—a messiah who had a special mission from God to bring God's own salvation to the world, and (2) he would be not just another human prophet but, having been conceived by the power of the Holy Spirit, he would rightly be called "Son of God." We don't know directly from Luke's wording whether he knew what the councils have since defined (and what was perceived more sharply by John's gospel a little after Luke's time), that Jesus shared in God's divine nature. The title "Son of God" has a range of meanings in the Old Testament and is most often used of the king as God's chosen and appointed regent for Israel. Luke certainly is telling us that the birth of Jesus will be miraculous, brought about by God's Spirit, and that the child to be born will be the messiah. What sinful human being can worthily bear such a child and be of the same flesh? The Church reflected on this all through her history and, based on the language of Luke about Mary as one who had "found favor with God" and was "blessed among women," came to the conclusion that Mary was free from the effects of original sin. Mary was given special graces to enable her otherwise sinful humanity to be united with the divine nature in this unique and never-repeated miracle of God. If the Holy Spirit enabled her to be the virgin mother of Jesus, the Spirit also purified her for the task. But, of course, such purity is not just freedom from the power of original sin. Mary must have lived her "Yes" to God all her life to have been suitably holy for her task. Thus the Church recognizes that the grace of the Immaculate Conception was given by God from the first moment of Mary's coming into this world.

with you." But she was greatly troubled at what was said and pondered what sort of greeting this might be. Then the angel said to her, "Do not be afraid, Mary, for you have found favor with God. Behold, you will conceive in your womb and bear a son, and you shall name him Jesus. He will be great and will be called Son of the Most High, and the Lord God will give him the throne of David his father, and he will rule over the house of Jacob forever, and of his Kingdom there will be no end." But Mary said to the angel, "How can this be, since I have no relations with a man?" And the angel said to her in reply, "The Holy Spirit will come upon you, and the power of the Most High will overshadow you. Therefore the child to be born will be called holy, the Son of God. And behold, Elizabeth, your relative, has also conceived a son in her old age, and this is the sixth month for her who was called barren; for nothing will be impossible for God." Mary said, "Behold, I am the handmaid of the Lord. May it be done to me according to your word." Then the angel departed from her.

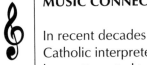

MUSIC CONNECTION

In recent decades Catholic interpreters have attempted to view the distinctively Marian theological symbols within the larger context of the Church and all creation. This is certainly applicable today when we celebrate the fact that Mary, like the Church and, indeed, all of God's creation, is saved and made holy through the grace of Christ. The first reading from Genesis recounting the fall of Adam depicts the repercussions of Adam's transgression. From such a situation we long to be freed and saved, as the Wesley hymn *Come, O Long Expected Jesus* forcefully states. Owen Alstott's setting of Psalm 98 delivers the text well, and Bedford's setting from WLP effectively employs a contemporary refrain with the traditional Tone 5 in the verses. The Haas/Haugen collaboration *All the Ends of the Earth* erupts musically with feeling and great joy. Marian hymnody is certainly appropriate today, whether Landry's *Hail Mary, Gentle Woman,* Haas's *Holy Is Your Name,* Joncas's *My Soul Rejoices,* or the Bach/Gounod or Schubert *Ave Maria.* The so-called Lourdes hymn, *Immaculate Mary,* should surely be considered today given the nature of the feast we celebrate. Since the Immaculate Conception is part of the Advent season, other hymns composed for the season such as *O Come, O Come Emmanuel,* Parker's *Be Consoled My People,* and Joncas's *A Voice Cries Out* should also be considered.

First Reading: Baruch 5:1–9

Jerusalem, take off your robe of mourning and
    misery;
    put on the splendor of glory from God
      forever:
wrapped in the cloak of justice from God,
    bear on your head the mitre
    that displays the glory of the eternal name.
For God will show all the earth your splendor:
    you will be named by God forever
    the peace of justice, the glory of God's
      worship.

Up, Jerusalem! stand upon the heights;
    look to the east and see your children
gathered from the east and the west
    at the word of the Holy One,
    rejoicing that they are remembered by God.
Led away on foot by their enemies they left
    you:
    but God will bring them back to you
    borne aloft in glory as on royal thrones.
For God has commanded
    that every lofty mountain be made low,
and that the age-old depths and gorges
    be filled to level ground,

SCRIPTURE COMMENTARY

The book of Baruch is often associated with the prophet Jeremiah's message, since Baruch was the name of Jeremiah's assistant. But the words of Baruch sound much closer to the words of Isaiah. Today's selection illustrates the point. The message echoes the words of Isaiah 40–43 and 60–62. The book of Baruch was probably a meditation on the message of hope in Isaiah (and Jeremiah), written sometime after the exile in Babylon had ended but while people were still in despair that their situation had not improved and God had not yet answered their longing for a new age of prosperity. Baruch is so visionary and excited about the glories of a coming new age that he almost seems to be not much more than an unrealistic dreamer. The end of the seventy-year exile was indeed a moment of huge expectations for some Judeans who were willing to go home to Judea, but many of the captives had lived all their lives in Babylon and refused to face an uncertain future by leaving the place where they were comfortable. Baruch calls for everyone

HOMILY HELPS

The city of God and the city of man. The struggle between the two is centuries old, and from the time of St. Augustine both have played a key part in Christian history. There are those who see everything in terms of the city of God, with little attention paid to the human city, which is seen as passing away. Others are so immersed in the swirl of the earthly city that they give scant attention to the city of God. As is true in most of life, the answer lies somewhere in the middle.

The city that is dominant in the pages of scripture is unquestionably Jerusalem. It not only had national prominence; when the monarchy was at its height, it had international stature. On the level of faith, it was God's chosen city, the place where he dwelt, sacred as a place of worship. If Jerusalem fell prey to foreign invaders, it was due to the moral failure of its citizens. When restored to its former glory, it was a symbol of divine fidelity and forgiveness. The book of Baruch, written only a few centuries before Christ, sings of Jerusalem's restored splendor, with its new names of "peace" and "glory" and the definitive return of its exiles. The scene is eschatological, yet it is rooted in the historical city. With every road leveled and every mountain lowered, Jerusalem will know again its former splendor.

The great irony of modern history is that Jerusalem, so central in the sacred text, is today largely a center of conflict, hatred, and endless unrest. God is marginalized in a city sacred to the three great monotheistic faiths. A war-torn Jerusalem is a sad reflection of the spiritual state of our times.

History is prominent in today's gospel as well. John the Baptist announces the inbreaking of heaven in a historical context, with the text naming the emperor as well as the local civil and religious authorities. It is worth noting also that Luke's gospel centers on the city of Jerusalem in its opening and closing chapters. Today John announces the coming of the redeemer; the city of God engages the city of man. Salvation

SCRIPTURE COMMENTARY, CONTINUED

to risk a wild hope that will give them the courage to make the journey back to Jerusalem. It becomes a perfect first reading to prepare for the gospel's announcement that Jesus will bring about just such a world-shattering new age!

> that Israel may advance secure in the glory of God.
> The forests and every fragrant kind of tree have overshadowed Israel at God's command;
> for God is leading Israel in joy by the light of his glory,
> with his mercy and justice for company.

PSALM REFLECTION

In the spirit of the first reading, Psalm 126 is a postexilic psalm that celebrates God as the savior who restored Israel to its home. It was probably sung as pilgrims went up to Jerusalem to celebrate the annual feasts of Pentecost or Booths at the time of the spring and fall harvests. Its language echoes the experience of the exile, when people were conquered, taken forcibly into exile, and suffered much but were later able to return home to begin again. It reflects the constant theme of all biblical texts that no matter how low we seem to have gone, and no matter how angry God seems to have been, God always returns to his people with salvation in a new way. In turn, Israel constantly acknowledges the graciousness of God with joyful celebrations of his goodness.

Psalm Response
Psalm 126:1–2, 2–3, 4–5, 6

Antiphon
The Lord has done great things for us; we are filled with joy.

Verses for Reflection
They said before the peoples:
The Lord did great things for them!
The Lord did great things for us—
we are glad! (vv. 2–3)

---

is woven into a tapestry of specific time and place. Our experience of God is refracted through our human experience. Our life in the God who is Other is circumscribed by a human birth and death. We walk with God in manmade shoes.

There is a tension here that is all too real. As our gaze is directed toward the heavenly Jerusalem, our sight is often impaired by the somber clouds of disbelief, so much a part of the secular city. But as Paul tells the Philippians today, our faith life is a process of growth. What God has begun in us he will bring to completion. As we grow in charity, we will move inexorably toward that city on the hill which is our final home.

LITURGICAL NOTES

As we begin the second week of Advent, we light two candles on the Advent wreath, asking that God might "open our hearts in welcome" and "remove the things that hinder us from receiving Christ with joy." The first reading from the prophet Baruch announces God's activity: "leading Israel in joy by the light of his glory, with his mercy and justice for company." The gospel announces the preaching of John the Baptist, proclaiming a baptism of repentance for the forgiveness of sins. The words of Baruch state clearly that the activity being accomplished is God's activity: God is being faithful to the prom-

ises made. John the Baptist appears, announcing not so much the coming of the messiah as how we must be prepared to recognize him when he comes.

Much time will be spent in planning and arranging the liturgies of Christmas. In addition, people will be busier than usual with holiday preparations. However, this is not a time to slack off. These days of "preparing" provide an excellent opportunity to reexamine some of the basics that may not have been looked at since last year. Liturgy planners could make good use of this time by examining those aspects of our worship life that hinder our full, conscious, and active participation. The first few weeks of the new church year provide a

Second Reading: Philippians 1:4–6, 8–11

Brothers and sisters: I pray always with joy in my every prayer for all of you, because of your partnership for the gospel from the first day until now. I am confident of this, that the one who began a good work in you will continue to complete it until the day of Christ Jesus.

God is my witness, how I long for all of you with the affection of Christ Jesus. And this is my prayer: that your love may increase ever more and more in knowledge and every kind of perception, to discern what is of value, so that you may be pure and blameless for the day of Christ, filled with the fruit of righteousness that comes through Jesus Christ for the glory and praise of God.

SCRIPTURE COMMENTARY

Second readings in our Lectionary generally take the major theme found in the Old Testament reading and the gospel reading and extend it from the words and lifetime of Jesus to the life of the early Church. Paul can take the message of a God of salvation who returns to his people after exile and suffering and say that the joy of realizing this is exactly the same attitude the Philippian Christians must maintain as they wait for the end of the world and the second coming of Christ in glory. Their spirit must be one of joyful awareness of the great things the Lord has done by bringing them salvation in Jesus. They must be filled with joyful hope that they will grow more and more richly in the way of Christ right up to that final day—a way of love and blameless conduct that is indeed the fruit of the justice (or justification, as Paul says elsewhere) that Christ has won for them.

good opportunity to take stock— to look again at how our gatherings and our places of gathering are experienced by the men and women who constitute our worshiping assemblies. From the welcome and environment the people experience as they enter the church, to the cleanliness of the building, to the ability of the assembly to see, to respond, to listen, and to sing, what obstacles stand in the way? The strong scripture readings of the season provide an excellent opportunity to see and hear how effectively the word is proclaimed in the liturgical assembly. How is the word heard in various parts of the church building? How good are the microphones? Some excellent readers will clearly

shine; others might need help with preparation, diction, pace, articulation. While the season of Advent might be a busy time for people, it might also be an ideal time to plan some additional training sessions for readers after the Christmas holidays. Too often we make the mistake of thinking that the training of readers and the maintenance of sound systems are one-time tasks. Nothing could be further from the truth. Both the objects that assist in the proclamation of the word and the persons who proclaim the word need regular and ongoing care and attention.

It is also not too early to plan for the upcoming liturgies of Christmas to make sure that readers are clear about their

assignments and the particular readings that will be proclaimed at each Mass.

If the Advent wreath is made of real evergreens, and even if it is made of artificial greens, it will need some maintenance during the season, so that it continues to stand as a powerful symbol of our Advent waiting. The worship environment should remain simple. While many parish communities engage in the Advent activity of the "Giving Tree" or a similar program where members of the parish are able to purchase Christmas gifts for the poor and return them to the parish for distribution, the presence of these gifts ought not to overwhelm the worship space and distract from the Advent focus.

SCRIPTURE COMMENTARY

In St. Luke's gospel, John the Baptist plays a very important role in preparing for the coming of Jesus as the world's Savior. Much of the gospel will focus on Jesus' reaching out to pagans and instructing his disciples on their mission to those beyond the chosen people. But first he gives special attention to Jesus as the fulfillment of Israel's own hopes for salvation. Today's reading reflects the tradition in Matthew, Mark, and Luke alike that John the Baptist took the first public step to open Jesus' ministry by fulfilling the prophet Isaiah's promise that God would send a *herald* before coming himself with salvation (Isa 40:3–4). Note that Luke, alone among the gospels, specifies an exact moment in the time of the empire of Rome. Prophets in the Old Testament almost always spoke to rulers and priestly leaders. John's words are directed to every individual, but clearly foresee a world-changing message that leaders must heed. Moreover, while Luke says that John's prophetic word is a call to repent and receive forgiveness, his quotation of Isaiah does not mention forgiveness of sin but a victorious arrival of the mighty king of kings, which will transform the earth itself. The two can be connected, however, because for Luke the battle is between God and Satan, the ruler of evil over human hearts. When God comes, it will be a victory over the power of sin, bringing with it a forgiveness we could never achieve on our own merits.

Gospel: Luke 3:1–6

In the fifteenth year of the reign of Tiberius Caesar, when Pontius Pilate was governor of Judea, and Herod was tetrarch of Galilee, and his brother Philip tetrarch of the region of Ituraea and Trachonitis, and Lysanias was tetrarch of Abilene, during the high priesthood of Annas and Caiaphas, the word of God came to John the son of Zechariah in the desert. John went throughout the whole region of the Jordan, proclaiming a baptism of repentance for the forgiveness of sins, as it is written in the book of the words of the prophet Isaiah:

A voice of one crying out in the desert:
"Prepare the way of the Lord,
  make straight his paths.
Every valley shall be filled
  and every mountain and hill shall
    be made low.
The winding roads shall be made
    straight,
  and the rough ways made smooth,
and all flesh shall see the salvation of
    God."

MUSIC CONNECTION

As noted in previous years, Advent progresses gradually in a steady crescendo toward the celebration of Christmas and Epiphany. It is John the Baptist who moves center stage for the second and third Sundays of Advent. The prophet Baruch, often eclipsed in our appreciation by his better-known colleagues Jeremiah and Isaiah, rises to the occasion in the first lesson. Baruch's note of joy permeates both the psalm and the second reading and undergirds the gospel pericope. Parker's ever-popular *Be Consoled My People*, Deiss's *Sion Sing*, and the traditional *On Jordan's Bank* highlight the message of today's readings. Cooney's *Walk in the Reign* is a fervent addition to the traditional repertoire, as is Browning's *Lead Us to Your Light*. *People Look East* and Dufford's pulsating *Every Valley* also merit consideration for today. The responsorial, Psalm 126, vibrant with joy at the return from exile, finds wonderful expression in the settings by Haugen, Gelineau/Proulx, and Marchionda. There are numerous hymns titled *Maranatha,* from the ancient Aramaic for "Come, Lord," fitting for this season, including those by Deiss, Meltz, Powell, and O'Brien.

CATECHETICAL SUGGESTIONS

The Catholic canon
Israel during and after the Babylonian exile
The fruits of the Holy Spirit
The role of John the Baptist in the gospels
The sacrament of reconciliation
Ways in which we can prepare for the coming of the Lord

First Reading:
Zephaniah 3:14–18a

Shout for joy, O daughter Zion!
   Sing joyfully, O Israel!
Be glad and exult with all your heart,
   O daughter Jerusalem!
The LORD has removed the judgment
   against you
   he has turned away your enemies;
the King of Israel, the LORD, is in
   your midst,
   you have no further misfortune to
   fear.
On that day, it shall be said to
   Jerusalem:
   Fear not, O Zion, be not
   discouraged!
The LORD, your God, is in your midst,
   a mighty savior;
he will rejoice over you with
   gladness,
   and renew you in his love,
he will sing joyfully because of you,
   as one sings at festivals.

SCRIPTURE COMMENTARY

So far in Advent, we have had the joyful proclamations of Jeremiah 33 and Baruch 5, and today we hear a soaring message from Zephaniah. This prophet lived at the end of the seventh century BC, at the moment when the Assyrian Empire was collapsing. He proclaims that the fall of this nation of tyranny is the working of divine favor to God's people. Because God dwells in their midst, they should not have feared that Assyria could destroy them—see, now the oppressors themselves are being conquered! Zephaniah would have welcomed Babylon, the conqueror, as a gift of God. But ironically, Babylon will turn out within twenty years to be a worse conqueror yet, finally destroying Jerusalem and taking most of the people into exile. As we read Zephaniah today, knowing how time-conditioned his joy was, we realize that God often uses prophets to declare a message of salvation good for one moment that God will make much greater and more significant at a later time. We now link Zephaniah to the message of John the Baptist in the gospel that the messiah is coming in an entirely new way.

HOMILY HELPS

The Christian moral life goes beyond a basic catalogue of "dos" and "don'ts." We are called to a standard higher than a simple observance of the ten commandments. Yet this is not to say that moral fundamentals have no role to play. They represent the outer limits; to disregard them places us "out of bounds." We can never score a goal without observing the boundaries.

In a pre-Christian setting, John's questioners in today's gospel are concerned with the basics. The man with two coats needs only one; thus, the extra one can go to someone in need. In a person's professional life, honesty should prevail. In exacting the payment of debt, excess is to be avoided. In the maintenance of civil order, undue physical force has no place.

These basic norms of conduct fall short of the higher Christian standard yet are not to be ignored. But the facts of life today clearly indicate that they are frequently ignored. We see this in the propensity for dishonesty in the corporate business world. How often we are reminded that our streets are not safe at night. There is also the flouting of sexual morality in pornography and licentious behavior from the Internet to daytime sitcoms. There can be little doubt that while we keep our eye on the greater good, we must never forget the basic norms of conduct. The mores of our time place us and our children in considerable jeopardy.

But John also has his eyes riveted on the future, on Christ's baptism of the Holy Spirit and fire. With it will come a moral life that is spelled out in the Sermon on the Mount: turn the other cheek, walk the extra mile, give both your jacket and your shirt. We are to forgive every injury, promote the good, and turn aside from the first lustful stirrings.

Yet is this possible? Jesus himself tells us that it is. The words of Zephaniah, read today, are truly fulfilled. "The Lord is in your

PSALM REFLECTION

The prophet Isaiah's name means "The LORD is savior." Isaiah lived from 740 to 700 BC and left us a rich collection of words about God's judgment on evil behavior, the stubborn rebellion of Judah's kings, and the enduring, trustworthy presence of God as protector of Israel. The response today is taken from his great hymn of praise of God as savior in chapter 12 that caps his announcement in chapters 7–11 that God will send a new messianic king. God will show his power and love not through a storm or a war but through the birth of a new and more faithful servant king. Isaiah calls this hoped-for Savior Emmanuel, a name meaning "God is with us." Thus the hymn glorifies God for his presence in the midst of his people in his temple, from which he will bring about salvation through his messiah.

Psalm Response
Isaiah 12:2–3, 4, 5–6

Antiphon
Cry out with joy and gladness:
    for among you is the great
    and Holy One of Israel.

Verse for Reflection
The Lord God is my strength
    and my song;
He has become my savior!
    (v. 2)

CATECHETICAL SUGGESTIONS

Psalms of praise
Prayers of petition
The role of the laity
Baptism
Merciful and *just*: compatible attributes of God?
Universal invitation to covenant love

---

midst." Ours is not an ideal imposed from above. Christ is not a sideline coach; he is in our hearts and minds by reason of the Holy Spirit. Paul states today that the peace of Christ removes all fear and anxiety. The first words of Christ to the apostles at Easter were "Peace be with you," words echoed by Francis of Assisi in his constant greeting: *Pace e bene*—"Peace and all good."

In our embrace of the greatest commandment, the love of God and neighbor, we also embrace all other goods. We are called to the holiness of God, as members of his family, and we must never lose sight of the fact that it is his love which makes it possible.

LITURGICAL NOTES

We light three candles on the Advent wreath as we begin the third week of Advent, acknowledging that we "look forward to the birthday of Christ." On this Sunday, two purple and one rose candle are lit, and rose vestments may be worn, symbolizing our joy that our waiting is halfway over. The color for this Sunday is an often-debated point among liturgy planners. A strong case can be made for the use of rose-colored vestments and hangings, as they mark a kind of midpoint in our Advent waiting. The con-

tinued use of violet vestments and hangings on this Sunday can provide continuity to the season.

This Sunday, often referred to as Gaudete Sunday, receives its name from the first Latin word of the entrance antiphon, "Rejoice." The liturgy moves our attention away from the second coming and begins to focus it on the coming of Christ in the flesh at Christmas.

The prophet Zephaniah announces, "Shout for joy . . . sing joyfully . . . be glad and exult with all your heart." Paul writes to the Philippians, telling them to "rejoice in the Lord always. I shall say it again: rejoice!" In the

Second Reading: Philippians 4:4–7

Brothers and sisters: Rejoice in the Lord always. I shall say it again: rejoice! Your kindness should be known to all. The Lord is near. Have no anxiety at all, but in everything, by prayer and petition, with thanksgiving, make your requests known to God. Then the peace of God that surpasses all understanding will guard your hearts and minds in Christ Jesus.

SCRIPTURE COMMENTARY

The theme of this third Sunday of Advent is clearly one of rejoicing. From Zephaniah to Isaiah 12 to Paul, the repeated calls to rejoice control the spirit of the readings. It is not an accident that we also heard from Paul's letter to Philippi last week also. Of all Paul's letters, this one reverberates most with Paul's sense of gratitude for a city of converts that really embraces the gospel and puts it into practice every day. Not only are they people of prayer and confidence in God's salvation, but they express their faith in generosity to each other and to outsiders, even sending Paul regular donations to support his work as a traveling missionary! He has nothing but good to say of the Philippians, and they become, in Paul's thinking, a model for all of the rest of the churches to imitate.

Gospel: Luke 3:10–18

The crowds asked John the Baptist, "What should we do?" He said to them in reply, "Whoever has two cloaks should share with the person who has none. And whoever has food should do likewise." Even tax collectors came to be baptized

SCRIPTURE COMMENTARY

Today's gospel continues the special treatment of John the Baptist's mission that we read about last Sunday. Just as last week John announced a salvation that would fulfill the messianic hopes of Isaiah the prophet for the Jewish people but still spoke to the Roman world as well, today's message also includes both Jew and Gentile alike. Wondering what it would mean to receive John's water baptism as a sign of being repentant, the people ask him about

gospel, the crowds ask John what they should do. People from various walks of life ask: "How ought we to prepare? How ought we to live?" And John responds to each with the values of the kingdom: do justice, act with mercy, live in love. The people then wonder if John could be the messiah, and he declares that "one mightier than I is coming."

Joyous anticipation is a hallmark of today's liturgy, yet the restraint exercised throughout Advent ought to continue. While floral arrangements may have been scarce or absent for the first two weeks of Advent, a variety of purple, rose, and pink arrangements could make a subtle appearance today, as a visual expression both of joy and of our continuing movement through Advent.

The General Intercessions can fittingly include references to living, in whatever walk of life a person might be in, the values of the kingdom: justice, mercy, and love. Any number of writers have remarked that Christians often do not look like very happy people. If we are living the values of the kingdom, we will be joyful people.

This might be a good Sunday to examine how our liturgical ministers appear to the assembly. The issue here is not the inner state of the liturgical ministers but rather how they are perceived by the assembly. Are their joy, their hope, their faith evident as they minister at the altar, as they sing God's praises, as they show forth the hospitality of Christ himself, as they distribute the Eucharist? Do they look like people who share in the redemption won by Christ? Do they act like people who share in the redemption won by Christ?

SCRIPTURE COMMENTARY, CONTINUED

what they will have to do afterwards. He addresses the wealthy, those who serve the Romans as tax collectors, and even Roman soldiers themselves—quite a collection of the kinds of people that ordinary folks resented! He asks of them all to treat everyone fairly and equally, a message that echoes the constant proclamation of the prophets. Isaiah and other prophets pictured a world under God's future rule where every person lived in mutual concern and love and avoided all unjust behavior. John announces that this age is about to begin when the messiah comes. John emphasizes that the new Savior will baptize with the Holy Spirit and with fire. Since these are qualities associated with God himself as the divine judge of the world, John is assuring the people that this new messiah comes directly in the name of God to rescue the righteous and bring divine salvation. While the language in this passage seems very harsh, it is in reality the normal way in which Old Testament prophets reassured a suffering and victimized people that God would restore a new world of justice.

and they said to him, "Teacher, what should we do?" He answered them, "Stop collecting more than what is prescribed." Soldiers also asked him, "And what is it that we should do?" He told them, "Do not practice extortion, do not falsely accuse anyone, and be satisfied with your wages."

Now the people were filled with expectation, and all were asking in their hearts whether John might be the Christ. John answered them all, saying, "I am baptizing you with water, but one mightier than I is coming. I am not worthy to loosen the thongs of his sandals. He will baptize you with the Holy Spirit and fire. His winnowing fan is in his hand to clear his threshing floor and to gather the wheat into his barn, but the chaff he will burn with unquenchable fire." Exhorting them in many other ways, he preached good news to the people.

MUSIC CONNECTION

While in the past Gaudete Sunday was often seen as a time of joyful reprieve from the dreariness of the rest of Advent, we now realize that the entire season should be one of joyful expectation, which builds in a crescendo-like effect. Zephaniah sets the tone not only for this Sunday but also for the entire season: "Shout for joy, O daughter Zion! Sing joyfully, O Israel!"

This joy finds a thunderous echo in Philippians: "Rejoice in the Lord always! I say it again: rejoice!" If our music selections today do not deliver that message, we are doing something wrong. Be sure to consider *Wake, O Wake and Sleep No Longer; O Come, Divine Messiah; When He Comes; Proclaim the Joyful Message; Awake, Awake and Greet the New Morn;* and *A Voice Cries Out. Soon and Very Soon,* a spiritual, makes a wonderful closing hymn to use today

and throughout this *joyful* season. The responsorial from Isaiah 12 is a fixture of the Easter Vigil and has several fine settings by Guimont, Batastini/Gelineau, Meltz, and the late priest and composer Don Reagan. Whatever hymns are selected for today's liturgy ought to convey the deep-seated joy at the heart of this season. This is the sublime challenge for all pastoral musicians—to deliver not merely the text and the melody but the *feeling* as well.

First Reading: Micah 5:1–4a

Thus says the LORD:
You, Bethlehem-Ephrathah
  too small to be among the clans
    of Judah,
from you shall come forth for me
  one who is to be ruler in Israel;
whose origin is from of old,
  from ancient times.
Therefore the Lord will give them
  up, until the time
  when she who is to give birth has
    borne,
and the rest of his kindred shall
    return
  to the children of Israel.
He shall stand firm and shepherd his
    flock
  by the strength of the LORD,
  in the majestic name of the LORD,
    his God;
and they shall remain, for now his
    greatness
  shall reach to the ends of the
    earth;
he shall be peace.

SCRIPTURE COMMENTARY

Micah was born and lived in Moresheth, a town not very far from Bethlehem. Although he prophesied at the same time as did Isaiah, the great prophet of Jerusalem, and may well have known Jerusalem well because of his visits to the temple, he never seems to have been a great fan of the vision that Jerusalem was everything. Instead, he alone among the prophets emphasizes that the Davidic messiah will come not from Jerusalem but from the town of David's family, Bethlehem. We hear the story, told fully in the book of Ruth, of how Ruth married Boaz, an elder of the town, and three generations later, David was born into their family. They had land and raised sheep, probably putting them among the better-off families of the area. But certainly they were not related to the royal circles of the capital. As a result, Micah chooses to proclaim a messiah not so much as a rich or resplendent king but as a shepherd, much like the shepherds he knew so well. But he is also connecting the messiah to the oldest traditions of Near Eastern kingship, in which kings saw themselves as delegates of God's own care, humbly caring for their people. It is a fitting reading to prepare for the gospel of the visitation.

HOMILY HELPS

The readings for this last Sunday of Advent move us rapidly forward toward the great solemnity of the nativity of Christ. There are three speakers who draw our attention: the Lord God, Jesus, and Elizabeth. A reflection on each of them will help us to internalize the Christmas message.

The first reading's prophet Micah, dating from the eighth century, gives us a concise but well-defined portrait of the ideal future king. He will be of the line of David, here identified with the monarch's birthplace, Bethlehem. He is not spoken of as a warrior or conqueror but rather as a caring and solicitous shepherd, with a territory that is not geographically circumscribed but has the widest possible extension. Military exploits ill befit him who is designated simply "peace." The picture is as striking as it is unusual: a king, firm but gentle, who has a concern for all people, with a spirit that conveys harmony and well-being.

And what is to be said of the worship and ritual of this new era? The letter to the Hebrews makes clear that there is now only one priest and one sacrifice, a single offering to last forever and never to be repeated. Centered in the person of Christ, son of David and prince of peace, it is a sacrifice rooted in his total acceptance of the Father's will. All other sacrifices are now obsolete. A sinful humanity now made holy has its heavenly intercessor whose unqualified "Yes" to God overturns the "No" of Adam.

As Mary passes through the portals of Elizabeth's home in the Lucan visitation narrative, she is extolled for her trust in the Lord's

PSALM REFLECTION

This psalm has been chosen as the response because it is one of the few references in the psalms to God as the shepherd of Israel (see Psalm 23 as well). In fact, it combines the image of God as a loving shepherd, Israel as a chosen people, and the king as God's son, a rich mixture of themes that is used for Jesus by the New Testament writers. The psalm is in love with its images—indeed it mixes its metaphors without shame, moving from the shepherd to the farmer in the field. But both shepherd and farmer are characterized by their caring, and the psalm actually applies this directly to the person of the king ("the man of your right hand," "the son of man"). Israel's kings are to be God's delegates, caring for the nation as God himself would. They are not to serve themselves but those given into their care.

Psalm Response
Psalm 80:2–3, 15–16, 18–19

Antiphon
Lord, make us turn to you; let
   us see your face and we
   shall be saved.

Verse for Reflection
Let your arm be with the man
   at your right hand;
The son of man to whom you
   gave your own strength.
   (v. 16)

CATECHETICAL SUGGESTIONS

Discernment: how do we discern God's will?
Christology
Mary in Luke's gospel
Birth narratives
Joyful mysteries of the Rosary
The promise of a messiah: expectations and fulfillment

---

word. She will shortly deflect the praise in attributing all to God's favor. But the words of Elizabeth remind us that Mary remains the first of the disciples, the one who trusted in God's providence, the one who, like her son, made God's will her own. Her *Fiat* at the annunciation remains the model of the Christian response.

One idea that emerges clearly in today's readings is the centrality of the gift of peace. Because we are Christians, words of war should not fall easily from our lips. War is always a tragedy, regardless of the cause; it brings in its wake nothing but horror

and destruction. Catholic tradition has allowed it only in very limited cases. As Christians we must support every measure that seeks peace. In the simple terms of Micah, the Lord himself is our "peace."

The second idea that appears clearly is the importance of obedience and trust. This is the lesson of Christ and Mary, a lesson not simply enshrined in words but one lived by its two exemplars. We pray with the psalmist today that our lives will always remain firmly directed by the One who is our strength and our deliverer.

LITURGICAL NOTES

We light four candles on the Advent wreath as we begin the fourth week of Advent, praying that God might "lift our minds in watchful hope to hear the voice that announces his glory."

On this Sunday, the first reading is from the book of the prophet Micah, where the Lord—who continues to surprise—announces that it is from obscure Bethlehem that the ruler will come forth. The gospel is the story of the visitation: the pregnant Mary going to visit and

Second Reading: Hebrews 10:5–10

Brothers and sisters:
When Christ came into the world, he said:
"Sacrifice and offering you did not desire,
but a body you prepared for me;
in holocausts and sin offerings you took no delight.
Then I said, 'As is written of me in the scroll,
behold, I come to do your will, O God.'"

First he says, "Sacrifices and offerings, holocausts and sin offerings, you neither desired nor delighted in." These are offered according to the law. Then he says, "Behold, I come to do your will." He takes away the first to establish the second. By this "will, " we have been consecrated through the offering of the body of Jesus Christ once for all.

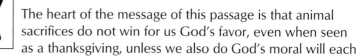

SCRIPTURE COMMENTARY

The heart of the message of this passage is that animal sacrifices do not win for us God's favor, even when seen as a thanksgiving, unless we also do God's moral will each day. This was one of the most frequent themes of Jesus' teaching as reported in the gospels, and the author of Hebrews emphasizes it in his letter. External worship in not as important as is the will of the heart. Jesus himself was following the lead of the prophets who regularly emphasized this theme (Hosea 6, Amos 5, Micah 6), as did the psalms (Pss 40 and 51). Very specially here, Hebrews argues that Jesus took a human body to replace animal sacrifices with his own death as the only acceptable sacrifice, a sacrifice that was the culmination of a whole life lived in obedience to the Father's will. The new covenant is to live in obedience to God's will as Jesus himself did.

Connecting the liturgy with what happens at home. Catholic *Household Prayers and Blessings provides a Blessing of a Christmas Tree in the home, along with a Blessing of a Christmas Crèche or Manger scene. Copies of these blessings could be given out on this Sunday, or printed in the bulletin, since many families will be doing their home Christmas decorating in the coming days.*

---

assist her cousin, Elizabeth, who is also pregnant. The passage concludes with a blessing given not only to Mary but to believers in every age: "Blessed are you who believed that what was spoken to you by the Lord would be fulfilled." While our Advent focus has shifted to the coming of Christ at Christmas, the second Advent preface continues to keep both "comings of Christ" alive in our prayer.

As our Advent waiting draws to a close, elements of the closeness of Christmas might be added to the environment, such as undecorated trees, unadorned wreaths, and the like. If our Advent is about vigilance, waiting, and preparing, our church building can also exhibit the preparations we are making for the great solemnity of Christmas. These additions can easily get out of control, so we need to be reminded about restraint.

Times for the celebration of the sacrament of penance ought to be announced, along with opportunities for Communal Celebrations of Penance with Individual Confession and Absolution (Rite II).

The people of our parishes have experienced the rush, the tension, and the crowds in stores and malls, on streets and parkways; virtually everywhere they go, they can be guaranteed a line and a wait. This might be a good time to prepare them for the Christmas crowds they will experience in church during the coming days, and to remind them of our responsibility to offer a gracious welcome to both the regular churchgoer and the stranger. This often seems almost too obvious to mention, but after-Christmas stories of inhospitable welcome continue to abound.

SCRIPTURE COMMENTARY

St. Luke's gospel has more material on the circumstances of Jesus' birth than any other gospel. Most of it is quite unique, and very little is found even in Matthew's own collection of birth traditions about Jesus. Luke focuses attention on the people whose hearts were ready and so welcomed the good news of Jesus' coming. He also links John the Baptist as closely to the person of Jesus as he can—they are actually cousins! Luke sees the mothers as the key: Elizabeth, the mother of the prophet, and Mary, the mother of the Savior. Today, in the story of the visitation to Elizabeth, Luke tells us that already the mothers recognized the presence of the Holy Spirit with their sons. John's prophecy in Luke 3 that the messiah will come with the Holy Spirit and fire was already revealed in the events surrounding Jesus' birth. It has been traditionally believed that Mary met Elizabeth in Ain Karem, a town just outside Jerusalem. A church of the house of John the Baptist and a church of the visitation at the town well are both standing today. Mary, the girl of Nazareth, travels far to bring Jesus to where John is found—just as Jesus will later travel to the Jordan to meet John and receive his acknowledgment as the messiah. Luke again has already prepared the reader for that moment with this first encounter in the womb between the two, in which the Holy Spirit inspires John to recognize Jesus as the one greater than he.

Gospel: Luke 1:39–45

Mary set out and traveled to the hill country in haste to a town of Judah, where she entered the house of Zechariah and greeted Elizabeth. When Elizabeth heard Mary's greeting, the infant leaped in her womb, and Elizabeth, filled with the Holy Spirit, cried out in a loud voice and said, "Blessed are you among women, and blessed is the fruit of your womb. And how does this happen to me, that the mother of my Lord should come to me? For at the moment the sound of your greeting reached my ears, the infant in my womb leaped for joy. Blessed are you who believed that what was spoken to you by the Lord would be fulfilled."

MUSIC CONNECTION

The Advent crescendo reaches its climax with the introduction of Mary on this fourth Sunday of Advent. The prelude is found in the first reading from Micah, with its prediction that Bethlehem, "too small to be among the clans of Judah," will bring forth a preeminent ruler of Israel whom Christians understand to be Jesus. Psalm 80 obviously connects to the shepherd imagery of Micah and is well expressed in settings by Guimont, Alstott, Gelineau, and Schaffer. Advent hymns previously mentioned are certainly fitting today, but the introduction of Mary as a key actor in this scene of salvation history also suggests Marian hymns. The Gregorian *Ave Maria* is within the abilities of many congregations. Lacking that, an expressive soloist can render the hymn beautifully and make it a signpost for this wonderful season. While it is many years old, Carey Landry's moving arrangement *Hail Mary, Gentle Woman* has earned a place in the pantheon of contemporary Marian pieces. Also, be sure to explore three more contemporary pieces by the prolific and talented Michael Joncas: *Magnificat, Mary's Song,* or *My Soul Rejoices.* David Haas's *Holy Is Your Name* is a favorite of many congregations and delivers the classic text of the Magnificat with power and beauty. Nearing the close of this season, *People Look East; Come, Thou Long Expected Jesus;* and *Maranatha* can also be considered.

VIGIL—First Reading: Isaiah 62:1–5

For Zion's sake I will not be silent,
    for Jerusalem's sake I will not be quiet,
until her vindication shines forth like the
    dawn
    and her victory like a burning torch.

Nations shall behold your vindication,
    and all the kings your glory;
you shall be called by a new name
    pronounced by the mouth of the LORD.
You shall be a glorious crown in the hand
    of the LORD,
    a royal diadem held by your God.
No more shall people call you "For-
    saken,"
    or your land "Desolate,"
but you shall be called "My Delight,"
    and your land "Espoused."
For the LORD delights in you
    and makes your land his spouse.
As a young man marries a virgin,
    your Builder shall marry you;
and as a bridegroom rejoices in his bride
    so shall your God rejoice in you.

SCRIPTURE COMMENTARY

The themes of Advent have been *prophetic.* God did not send his Son into the world unannounced or without a preparation. Instead, God *prepared* a background so that, when we needed to ask "Why did this happen?" or "What does it mean?" or "How are we to understand this?" we could search the scriptures and begin to understand. Isaiah 62 was probably uttered prophetically for the generation of Jews who came home from exile to a ruined Jerusalem. The prophet reassures them that God will not be silent or forgetful of his city but will reestablish her in glory and in the covenant bond of union that they enjoyed of old. The theme of God taking his nation or his city as a bride goes back at least to the prophet Hosea (Hosea 1–3) in the eighth century and was strongly emphasized by Jeremiah. Now, seventy years after Jeremiah, the Isaian voice gives it the fullest expression that we can find in the Old Testament. The sense of complete reversal from utter desolation and abandonment to the love of spouses dominates this passage and sets the tone of awe and wonder needed to receive the birth of the messiah.

HOMILY HELPS

"The Word was made flesh and pitched his tent among us." So reads the literal translation of the passage from John read in the third Mass of Christmas Day. It says a great deal, but it is Luke in his account of the birth of Jesus who speaks in concrete terms about what that "tent pitching" meant.

Luke goes out of his way to mention Caesar Augustus and Quirinius, the civil authorities of that historical period. As Luke presents it, the journey of Jesus' family from Nazareth to Bethlehem was at the order of the civil authority. The birth of Jesus is related to the highest echelons of world government as well as to the most menial members of the working class, the sheep herders. Jesus belongs to the rich and the poor, and while his predilection always tended toward the poorer class, the wealthy were never excluded from his saving mission.

The letter to Titus today reminds us that we are saved by no merits of our own but by God's mercy. That mercy is repeatedly extended during Jesus' ministry, and not solely to the poor. He calls tax collectors from their desks, heals the daughter of a synagogue official, and encourages a rich young man to avoid entanglements and to focus on the reign of God.

None of us is a stranger to civil authority and wealthy people. To government we owe the obedience of citizens, and we maintain that we have no intention of imposing a set of beliefs on our citizenry. But we do raise our voice in support of those basic values on which our civilization is based. These include the sacredness of all human life, the welfare of the family, and the right of all people to worship according to their conscience. We see war as a grave evil and make every effort to avoid it. As for the wealthy, we recognize that they are indeed loved by God, and we know that conversation, rather than confrontation, can lead to the salutary and beneficial use of wealth.

But the shepherds too are part of the story of God among us. The blue-collar worker, the

PSALM REFLECTION

Psalm 89 shares much of the same confidence manifested in Isaiah 62. It proclaims that God will reverse the fortunes of Israel and restore its Davidic king who has gone into exile and perhaps even been executed. It bases this confident hope on the testimonies of the scriptures that were proclaimed at covenant festivals. God has made an everlasting pledge and will not renege. In this psalm, the king, speaking in the name of each Israelite individually, declares his total trust in the promises of God. And he trusts despite the fact that hope for a king is not promising on an international level. The psalmist's words, however, echo the promise of 2 Samuel 7 that God would establish David's throne to stand firm forever. This psalm, more than any other, expresses the conviction that God will establish a new David for the future.

VIGIL—Psalm Response
Psalm 89:4–5, 16–17, 27, 29

Antiphon
For ever I will sing the goodness of the Lord.

Verses for Reflection
I found David my servant,
with my holy oil I anointed
    him.
Truly then my hand will stay
    with him,
my arm will strengthen him!
    (vv. 21–22)

CATECHETICAL SUGGESTIONS

Luke's and Matthew's genealogies
    Significance of Jesus being of the house of David
Annunciations in Luke and in Matthew
Isaiah's messianic prophecies
Midrash in Luke's and Matthew's infancy narratives
What is the good news of Jesus Christ?

immigrant laborer, those who work for the minimum wage (and sometimes less)—these are the people who play a vital part in our society but are often voiceless. They are the shepherds of modern society for whom the good news is also destined. We are required to be concerned about the less fortunate among us. In the face of the evident needs of people, a voiceless Christianity is an inexcusable anomaly. This is what the shepherd story means today.

Christmas touches so many aspects of our life. Because the Word became flesh and pitched his tent among us, we have a grave responsibility. Our Christmas joy is complete only when it is all-embracing.

LITURGICAL NOTES

The Church defines the Christmas season as that "most sacred memorial of Christ's birth and early manifestations." The season runs from Christmas until the Feast of the Baptism of the Lord.

The Sacramentary provides four sets of texts for the liturgies of Christmas: vigil, midnight, dawn, and day. The prayers are constructed to fit the particular time of the celebration.

The Gloria, absent since the beginning of Advent, returns, sung with joy. In the Profession of Faith, all genuflect at the words that recall the Incarnation. The 2004 *Sacramentary Supplement* for the dioceses of the

United States also provides the Liturgical Proclamation of the Birth of Christ. This proclamation might be used to introduce the Mass on Christmas Eve or at midnight. When it is used, it replaces the Penitential Rite.

The *Lectionary for Mass* provides four sets of readings: vigil, midnight, dawn, and day. The Lectionary permits that the midnight, dawn, and day readings may be interchanged. The readings of the vigil presume an actual vigil, with people returning to celebrate the Christmas Eucharist on Christmas Day. It would be important for readers and psalmists to know which readings will be used at each Mass.

The church building, virtually bare during the Advent season, is

VIGIL—Second Reading: Acts 13:16–17, 22–25

When Paul reached Antioch in Pisidia and entered the synagogue, he stood up, motioned with his hand, and said, "Fellow Israelites and you others who are God-fearing, listen. The God of this people Israel chose our ancestors and exalted the people during their sojourn in the land of Egypt. With uplifted arm he led them out of it. Then he removed Saul and raised up David as king; of him he testified, 'I have found David, son of Jesse, a man after my own heart; he will carry out my every wish.' From this man's descendants God, according to his promise, has brought to Israel a savior, Jesus. John heralded his coming by proclaiming a baptism of repentance to all the people of Israel; and as John was completing his course, he would say, 'What do you suppose that I am? I am not he. Behold, one is coming after me; I am not worthy to unfasten the sandals of his feet.'"

SCRIPTURE COMMENTARY

This sermon of St. Paul is provided by Luke in his Acts as a typical type of proclamation of the *kerygma*, the mission of preaching with a view to winning converts to Christ. The word *kerygma* comes from the Greek verb for "to announce [good news]." Paul emphasizes the key promises of the Old Testament and their fulfillment. One is that God chose a people to be great in his service and then raised up David as a king obedient in every way to lead that people. Paul leaves out the loss of kingship and nationhood and immediately jumps to the fulfillment in this age, when God sent Jesus to fulfill the promise anew. By citing the words of a fiery prophet such as John the Baptist in testimony to Jesus' power and status, Paul is assuring the audience that Jesus comes with a glory and mission that transcends those of just ordinary national rulers. God has personally sent him, and we need to repent and humble ourselves to receive him.

now filled with the colors and smells of Christmas. Careful consideration of the entire environment, not just the sanctuary area, is in order. In some places the custom has developed of keeping the Advent wreath and lighting a white candle in its center at Christmas. Another variation on this theme is to replace the purple and rose candles with white candles. While this is a noble attempt to bridge seasons, the Christmas season has more than enough richness already. Before the first Christmas liturgy begins, the Advent wreath should be retired until next year.

One of the most powerful signs will be the crèche, or Christmas manger. If the crèche is located inside the church, it should not be in competition with the altar, ambo, or font. The crèche may be blessed at one or all of the Masses, using the texts provided in the *Book of Blessings*, chapter 48.

While many parishes experience their greatest crowds at the vigil Masses, Masses on Christmas Day are still crowded. Liturgy planners need to be prepared. Extra programs will be needed, and they should be "user friendly" for those who only occasionally come to worship. Ushers and ministers of hospitality might need to have additional numbers added to their ranks, so that it can be evident that we are a church that welcomes all into our sacred assemblies. The ministers might

also need some special preparation, since the large numbers can cause potential jams during the collection and during the Communion procession. It is also important to check the church building after each Mass to bring the space back into order for the next Mass.

Children are a prominent feature of Christmas, and while in many parishes a Christmas pageant is part of the parish tradition, it does not belong at the liturgies of Christmas Eve or Day. The *Lectionary for Masses with Children* reminds us that "the Mass is not an historical reenactment of the events of salvation history, and care should be taken not to give the impression that the liturgy of the word is a

SCRIPTURE COMMENTARY

The gospel for the Vigil of Christmas has to be both one of the most exhilarating and most frustrating of gospels to proclaim. Matthew has prefaced the birth of Jesus with a prophetic opening, citing the generations that prepared the way. In his three sets of fourteen ancestors, he divides the world into three ages of readiness. From Abraham to David is the period of the preparation for statehood. The great ancestors of this period looked for God's promise of a great nation in terms of land and descendants. The second age, from David to the exile, was the period of the royal

VIGIL—Gospel: Matthew 1:1–25 (or Matthew 1:18–25)

The book of the genealogy of Jesus Christ, the son of David, the son of Abraham.

Abraham became the father of Isaac, Isaac the father of Jacob, Jacob the father of Judah and his brothers. Judah became the father of Perez and Zerah, whose mother was Tamar. Perez became the father of Hezron, Hezron the father of Ram, Ram the father of Amminadab. Amminadab became the father of Nahshon, Nahshon the father of Salmon, Salmon the father of Boaz, whose mother was Rahab. Boaz became the father of Obed, whose mother was Ruth. Obed became the father of Jesse, Jesse the father of David the king.

David became the father of Solomon, whose mother had been the wife of Uriah. Solomon became the father of Rehoboam, Rehoboam the father of Abijah, Abijah the father of Asaph. Asaph became the father of Jehoshaphat, Jehoshaphat the father of Joram, Joram the father of Uzziah. Uzziah became the father of Jotham, Jotham the father of Ahaz, Ahaz the father of Hezekiah. Hezekiah became the father of Manasseh, Manasseh the father of Amos, Amos the father of Josiah. Josiah became the father of Jechoniah and his brothers at the time of the Babylonian exile.

After the Babylonian exile, Jechoniah became the father of Shealtiel, Shealtiel the father of Zerubbabel, Zerubbabel the father of Abiud. Abiud became the father of Eliakim, Eliakim the father of Azor, Azor the father of Zadok. Zadok became the father of Achim, Achim the father of Eliud, Eliud the father of

---

play.... Care should be taken especially at Christmas ... not to stage the various liturgies as plays. The Christmas Mass should not be presented as a birthday party for Jesus, nor should secular notions of Santa Claus be introduced into the Christmas liturgy" (LFMWC, 52). The rubrics of the *Lectionary for Masses with Children* present a unique challenge to parishes. The mystery of the Incarnation cannot be contained in one liturgy. A Christmas pageant held the week before Christmas can serve as a wonderful opportunity for children to be engaged in the Christmas mystery and a wonderful preparation for children and families for the celebration of the Christmas Eucharist.

 ## MUSIC CONNECTION

Regardless of our age, Christmas grips our religious imagination like no other feast in the liturgical cycle. There is certainly no dearth of carols and hymns that can help us probe the depths of the Incarnation, the mystery we celebrate this day. The time-honored familiar pieces—*Silent Night, The First Noel, Hark the Herald, Joy to the World* and *O Come, All Ye Faithful*—deserve yearly repetition as they evoke memories and draw generations together. Choral anthems from *Messiah* can stir a congregation, but so can contemporary lullabies such as Rutter's *Candlelight Carol* and Kantor's *Night of Silence.* Particularly note-

worthy is Mack Wilberg's arrangement of *The First Noel,* which has a rather predictable beginning but swells in surprising ways to highlight atonement theology in a textual and musical climax. Be sure to have a festive and joyous *Gloria* to sing today and throughout this season. Alex Peloquin's *Gloria of the Bells* and Mike Joncas's *Gloria* from his John Carroll Mass are both wonderful possibilities. For fitting psalm settings, be sure to check either the Howard Hughes or Gelineau setting of Psalm 96 for the Mass at midnight, the Gelineau or Kreutz Psalm 97 for the Mass at dawn, and Haugen's *All the Ends of the Earth* [Psalm 98] or Marchionda's arrangement for the Mass during the day.

Eleazar. Eleazar became the father of Matthan, Matthan the father of Jacob, Jacob the father of Joseph, the husband of Mary. Of her was born Jesus who is called the Christ.

Thus the total number of generations from Abraham to David is fourteen generations; from David to the Babylonian exile, fourteen generations; from the Babylonian exile to the Christ, fourteen generations.

Now this is how the birth of Jesus Christ came about. When his mother Mary was betrothed to Joseph, but before they lived together, she was found with child through the Holy Spirit. Joseph her husband, since he was a righteous man, yet unwilling to expose her to shame, decided to divorce her quietly. Such was his intention when, behold, the angel of the Lord appeared to him in a dream and said, "Joseph, son of David, do not be afraid to take Mary your wife into your home. For it is through the Holy Spirit that this child has been conceived in her. She will bear a son and you are to name him Jesus, because he will save his people from their sins." All this took place to fulfill what the Lord had said through the prophet:

> Behold, the virgin shall conceive and bear a son,
>   and they shall name him Emmanuel,
> which means "God is with us."

When Joseph awoke, he did as the angel of the Lord had commanded him and took his wife into his home. He had no relations with her until she bore a son, and he named him Jesus.

SCRIPTURE COMMENTARY,
CONTINUED

covenant with David, and it too had generations of those who were faithful, even though the sins of some and the idolatry of many condemned the people to punishment under the Babylonians. The final period, from exile to Joseph, was the period of the *anawim*, the meek of heart and lowly of status who hoped in God, not in kings and empires. The period of preparation was now complete for the coming of Jesus, lowliest of the lowly in human terms, greatest of the human race in his divine sonship.

MIDNIGHT—First Reading: Isaiah 9:1–6

The people who walked in darkness
    have seen a great light;
upon those who dwelt in the land of gloom
    a light has shone.
You have brought them abundant joy
    and great rejoicing,
as they rejoice before you as at the harvest,
    as people make merry when dividing spoils.
For the yoke that burdened them,
    the pole on their shoulder,
and the rod of their taskmaster
    you have smashed, as on the day of Midian.
For every boot that tramped in battle,
    every cloak rolled in blood,
    will be burned as fuel for flames.
For a child is born to us, a son is given us;
    upon his shoulder dominion rests.
They name him Wonder-Counselor, God-Hero,
    Father-Forever, Prince of Peace.
His dominion is vast
    and forever peaceful,
from David's throne, and over his kingdom,
    which he confirms and sustains
by judgment and justice,
    both now and forever.
The zeal of the LORD of hosts will do this!

SCRIPTURE COMMENTARY

The reading from the original prophet Isaiah is just as visionary as the later oracle from Isaiah 62 that we read at the vigil Mass. Both of them foresee the same *kind* of action by God: taking the limited hope of the present and picturing a time to come in which God will do even greater things. In the case of Isaiah 9, scholars point to similar language about the king as father to his people, worker of wonders, divine hero, giver of peace. These are the phrases idealizing the king on the day of his coronation. It is almost a prayer: "May the king be thus and so!" The sad truth of kings who almost always fell short of such hopes gave rise to the widespread expectation that God was preparing a future day when he would actually send the ideal king to institute a new age of peace and prosperity. This passage begins with Isaiah's anger at the disobedience of King Ahaz of Judah, and Isaiah's prediction that disaster would come upon Ahaz and Jerusalem because he did not trust in God as his protector. But Isaiah also predicts that God will replace Ahaz with a better king who will be obedient and God will bless the kingdom in that day. Later still, Christians see that the fulfillment of the prophecy comes with Jesus.

PSALM REFLECTION

Psalm 96 is one of the psalms extolling God's divine kingship over the entire universe. The psalm combines the idea of divine salvation with universal human acknowledgement of God's greatness. Now the saving work of God will not just touch Israel but will affect all the peoples of the world. The psalmist is surely optimistic in hoping that the pagan nations will praise the Lord and accept him as king of the universe, but he is longing for the day beyond any present world politics when this indeed *shall come*. Such cosmic hymns give special emphasis to the fact that God governs every movement of every creature in the universe and therefore our sight is limited when we look only to what we get from God. His plan of salvation is made known in a unique way to Israel, but it extends far beyond Israel's borders to all nations.

MIDNIGHT—Psalm Response Psalm 96:1–2, 2–3, 11–12, 13

Antiphon
Today is born our Savior, Christ the Lord.

Verses for Reflection
Give to the Lord, all families of nations,
Give to the Lord glory and praise,
Give to the Lord the glory due his Name! (vv. 7–8)

SCRIPTURE COMMENTARY

Even though we are celebrating the first moments of Jesus in the world as its Savior, Paul's letter to Titus already looks beyond the earthly ministry of Jesus to picture his return in glory at the end of time. To keep us from the sentimental attitude that focuses on admiring cute babies in our celebration of Christmas, the Church reminds us that this child was destined for rejection and death and a cosmic victory over the power of evil. He is the divine Savior who has taken on our state of human existence to wage a mighty battle against Satan and the universal fate of death for sin. While Christmas may be a warm and fuzzy moment in modern culture, the birth of Christ should be seen as an awe-inspiring event that leads us to bow down in humble adoration.

MIDNIGHT—Second Reading: Titus 2:11–14

Beloved: The grace of God has appeared, saving all and training us to reject godless ways and worldly desires and to live temperately, justly, and devoutly in this age, as we await the blessed hope, the appearance of the glory of our great God and savior Jesus Christ, who gave himself for us to deliver us from all lawlessness and to cleanse for himself a people as his own, eager to do what is good.

SCRIPTURE COMMENTARY

The story of Jesus' birth would never make it into one of the great epics of heroes, people born into great families and with knightly destinies to fulfill. Jesus was born among the very poor and humble, was first recognized in joy by one of the lowliest of such groups, shepherds, and lived all of his life as a teacher with no school appointment to pay his bills. But despite the lowliness of the setting, a hay trough in a barn rather than a bed in a house, a great heavenly drama is unfolding around the moment of Jesus' birth. First of all, God guides the decisions of the mighty Roman Empire to decree the census that brings about this birth in a distant city, Bethlehem. And the humble shepherds learn of the child

MIDNIGHT—Gospel: Luke 2:1–14

In those days a decree went out from Caesar Augustus that the whole world should be enrolled. This was the first enrollment, when Quirinius was governor of Syria. So all went to be enrolled, each to his own town. And Joseph too went up from Galilee from the town of Nazareth to Judea, to the city of David that is called Bethlehem, because he was of the house and family of David, to be enrolled with Mary, his betrothed, who was with child. While they were there, the time came for her to have her child, and she gave birth to her firstborn son. She wrapped him in swaddling clothes and laid him in a manger, because there was no room for them in the inn.

Now there were shepherds in that region living in the fields and keeping the night watch over their flock. The angel of the Lord appeared to them and the glory of the Lord shone around them, and they were struck with great fear. The angel said to them, "Do not be afraid; for behold, I proclaim to you good news of great joy that will be for all the people. For today in the city of David a savior has been born for you who is Christ and Lord. And this will be a sign for you: you will find an infant wrapped in swaddling clothes and lying in a manger." And suddenly there was a multitude of the heavenly host with the angel, praising God and saying:

"Glory to God in the highest
and on earth peace to those on whom his favor rests."

SCRIPTURE COMMENTARY, CONTINUED

through exalted angelic choirs in the heavens. By so guiding events, God also brings about the fulfillment of Micah's prophecy that the messiah will come from Bethlehem. Luke may have re-created the details of this story from some old memories of those who heard bits and pieces from shepherds or friends or even Mary, as earlier writers thought. But above all these, he gives detail after detail based on the words of the prophets who looked forward to the messiah coming in lowliness rather than in military might. This child was destined to fulfill God's promises to Israel and to all nations as the psalmist had declared.

DAWN—First Reading:
Isaiah 62:11–12

See, the LORD proclaims
    to the ends of the earth:
say to daughter Zion,
    your savior comes!
Here is his reward with
    him,
    his recompense before
    him.
They shall be called the
    holy people,
    the redeemed of the
    LORD,
and you shall be called
    "Frequented,"
    a city that is not
    forsaken.

SCRIPTURE COMMENTARY

The second Mass for Christmas proper at dawn picks up the same chapter of Isaiah 62 as did the Mass for the vigil. The chapter opened with the joyous proclamation that the desperate state of the exiles returning to a desolated Jerusalem would be reversed because of God's love. In verses 11–12, the prophet now announces that the savior is indeed coming. The message is directed not just to Jerusalem but to all nations. The combination of a people who are to be called holy with a city that is called fully populated suggests a richness in the promise that is not limited to the troubled moment of time in which the prophet spoke, but envisions a greater future moment when it shall really come to fulfillment. This was typical of prophetic language of hope in general. The actual words are addressed to the specific moment in history in which the prophet lived, but the language is so expansive and visionary that later readers always expected that a time would come when an even greater blessing would be bestowed. We Christians certainly read these prophecies in this manner.

DAWN—
Psalm Response
Psalm 97:1, 6, 11–12

Antiphon
A light will shine on us
    this day: the Lord is
    born for us.

Verse for Reflection
Light dawns for the
    righteous,
And joy for the upright of
    heart! (v. 11)

PSALM REFLECTION

Psalm 97 expresses the same mood as the preceding Psalm 96. The three Masses on Christmas Day each use one of the divine kingship psalms, Psalms 96, 97, and 98. Since they all highlight the rule of God over all nations and extol his greatness, they make a fitting expression of praise for the triple celebration of the birth of Christ. Christmas Day is very unusual in that we have three separate sets of readings. The repetition of the same psalm themes forms a unifying thread to hold them all in harmony. The special note we saw in Psalm 96 was the joy expressed by all of nature as well as human societies; in Psalm 97, the special emphasis falls on the interior state of the human recipients. To hear the great news of a saving God, one must be just and upright of heart, for no one who is harboring sinful intentions or has gotten away with evil can welcome God's coming. Salvation restores justice and blessing to those who live by justice.

SCRIPTURE COMMENTARY

The second Mass of Christmas continues the message of the letter of Titus that we saw in the Mass at midnight. In chapter 2, the letter speaks of those who await happily for Christ's coming again because they are already living in the commandments of Christ. They have no fears of judgment but see the fulfillment and completion of what they have already experienced as joy and deliverance in their lives. In this following chapter, the author reminds his audience that this salvation is not won by our great human effort or goodness but by the mercy and love of God and the life and death of Jesus for us. We experience that gift of God's salvation and power for the good now in the action of the Holy Spirit within us. It confirms that we can expect everlasting life because it doesn't depend on us but on the gift of God.

DAWN—Second Reading: Titus 3:4–7

Beloved:
When the kindness and generous love
   of God our savior appeared,
not because of any righteous deeds
      we had done
   but because of his mercy,
He saved us through the bath of
      rebirth
   and renewal by the Holy Spirit,
whom he richly poured out on us
   through Jesus Christ our savior,
so that we might be justified by his
      grace
   and become heirs in hope of eternal
      life.

SCRIPTURE COMMENTARY

By itself, this small section of the story of the shepherds coming to see the newborn child cannot stand on its own and make sense. It depends on our knowing the whole Christmas story or having attended the earlier midnight Mass to hear the first half of the scene. But if we take it as a small vignette of what the birth of Christ *means* among all the births of this world, we can say that the shepherds, like us, learned of the child through the grace of revelation from heaven, and they somehow intuited that despite very humble beginnings, this child was destined for a greater mission. Mary, too, must have wondered what her child would become and what his heavenly origins were going to mean. But she was not ambitious or fearful. She treasured all these events in her heart to wait on God's fulfillment later in life. In Luke's vision, both shepherds and Mary were models for all those who have enough space in their hearts for God to come and dwell there. Those full of themselves will never recognize their Savior in this Galilean peasant.

DAWN—Gospel: Luke 2:15–20

When the angels went away from them to heaven, the shepherds said to one another, "Let us go, then, to Bethlehem to see this thing that has taken place, which the Lord has made known to us." So they went in haste and found Mary and Joseph, and the infant lying in the manger. When they saw this, they made known the message that had been told them about this child. All who heard it were amazed by what had been told them by the shepherds. And Mary kept all these things, reflecting on them in her heart. Then the shepherds returned, glorifying and praising God for all they had heard and seen, just as it had been told to them.

SCRIPTURE COMMENTARY

Like all the earlier Masses for Christmas, this final Mass also opens with the prophet Isaiah. The imagined background of a Mass "during the day" is bright sunlight, so the selection is Isaiah's vision of the herald who climbs to the highest peak to announce the tidings of the day. The image of this messenger is taken from royal courts, where there was an official herald of the king. The herald would announce that the king was coming to take

DURING THE DAY—First Reading: Isaiah 52:7–10

How beautiful upon the mountains
   are the feet of him who brings glad tidings,
announcing peace, bearing good news,
   announcing salvation, and saying to Zion,
   "Your God is King!"

Hark! Your sentinels raise a cry,
   together they shout for joy,

for they see directly, before their
    eyes,
  the LORD restoring Zion.
Break out together in song,
  O ruins of Jerusalem!
For the LORD comforts his people,
  he redeems Jerusalem.
The LORD has bared his holy arm
  in the sight of all the nations;
all the ends of the earth will
    behold
  the salvation of our God.

SCRIPTURE COMMENTARY, CONTINUED

possession of his kingdom and restore its peace and prosperity. Suddenly the image reverses to the viewpoint of the hearers of the announcement—their watchmen shout that God is in sight, approaching the city, and as they see his power and invincible advance, they break out into cheers and praise that salvation has come to them. The prophecy was uttered to announce the end of the Babylonian exile and the time of liberation to return the people to their homeland. But it is heard anew as the announcement of the new Savior, who comes not just for Israel but for all nations.

**DURING THE DAY—
Psalm Response
Psalm 98:1, 2–3, 3–4, 5–6**

Antiphon
All the ends of the earth have seen
  the saving power of God.

Verse for Reflection
All the ends of the earth
Have seen the salvation of God!
    (v. 3)

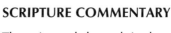 **PSALM REFLECTION**

The third of the great royal psalms celebrating God as king of the world mentions God's power to save, the miraculous acts of deliverance, and the recognition of his glory by the pagan nations that are mentioned in the other psalms we have used for Christmas Day (Pss 96 and 97). But this psalm depicts the *response* of the peoples—musical instruments abound and the sound of songs and hymns rises to God. As in the other psalms, the theme is not so much that of God as a warrior smashing enemies into nothingness as of his constant divine compassion and mercy that have been given to those who follow his commandments and live in his justice.

**DURING THE DAY—
Second Reading: Hebrews 1:1–6**

Brothers and sisters: In times past, God spoke in partial and various ways to our ancestors through the prophets; in these last days, he has spoken to us through the Son, whom he made heir of all things and through whom he created the universe,
  who is the refulgence of his
      glory,
    the very imprint of his being,
  and who sustains all things by
      his mighty word.
  When he had accomplished
      purification from sins,
  he took his seat at the right
      hand of the Majesty on
      high,
  as far superior to the angels
  as the name he has inherited is
      more excellent than theirs.

SCRIPTURE COMMENTARY

There is a subtle truth in the approach of the letter to the Hebrews to the true meaning of revelation, a truth that is often overlooked by modern people. Too often we attribute divine truth to words and their meanings, and we lose sight of the fact that words can begin to contradict one another as people express ideas in different ways in different cultures over many centuries. Ambiguities creep in, and we become uncertain as to exactly how literally we should take any individual thought. But when we have the life and example of the speaker as well, we learn much of the meaning of the words from his or her example and character. Old Testament revelation comes from encountering the living God as did Abraham, Jacob, Moses, and others. The human authors express in their words the truth of that God and what he did for them and what he would want, but what they express is drawn from the many appearances God granted his people. As Christians we first know we are freed from sin, share

SCRIPTURE COMMENTARY, CONTINUED

in Jesus' divine inheritance, and have been raised with him because he has shared our life, then passed through death to risen life, and finally has taken his throne in heaven to bestow his Spirit on us. Our New Testament words capture this in various ways, but none as powerfully as experiencing the living Lord in the works of the Spirit and in the Eucharist.

> For to which of the angels did God ever say:
> *You are my son; this day I have begotten you*?
> Or again:
> *I will be a father to him, and he shall be a son to me*?
> And again, when he leads the firstborn into the world, he says:
> *Let all the angels of God worship him.*

SCRIPTURE COMMENTARY

Where the two earlier Masses of Christmas Day have taken the story of Jesus' birth from the Gospel of Luke, the last Mass of the day turns instead to the Gospel of John for an entirely different view of Jesus' coming. This gospel never mention the birth or childhood of Jesus at all. Rather, it begins with the moment of creation. When God made the universe, the Son was already with God in eternity. The fact that John calls Jesus the "Word" coming into the world refers us back to the words of Isaiah 40:8, "The Word of God stands forever," or Isaiah 55:11, "My word never returns to me empty but accomplishes what I intend, and succeeds in the work for which I sent it." This divine "Word" shapes all that is true. Genesis 1:3 says that "God spoke, and there was light." Creation was formed by the Word of God spoken as good. But once human sin had broken that goodness and harmony, God worked to bring humans back to himself in reconciliation. The vision in John's Prologue expresses all of this. Jesus was sent as light into the human situation darkened by sin. He was not fully accepted by those in darkness, but those with faith saw the light! Faith to know Jesus as the messiah and divine Son is a gift from God, not a product of our great wisdom and understanding. The true followers of Christ recognize that in his life and mission he brought about the completion of the divine reconciliation of the world. John rarely views the story of Jesus as that of a human rabbi. Instead, in John's gospel, Jesus is always revealing his divine nature.

DURING THE DAY—
Gospel: John 1:1–18 (or John 1:1–5, 9–14)

In the beginning was the Word,
and the Word was with God,
and the Word was God.
He was in the beginning with God.
All things came to be through him,
and without him nothing came to be.
What came to be through him was life,
and this life was the light of the human race;
the light shines in the darkness,
and the darkness has not overcome it.

A man named John was sent from God. He came for testimony, to testify to the light, so that all might believe through him. He was not the light, but came to testify to the light. The true light, which enlightens everyone, was coming into the world.

He was in the world,
and the world came to be through him,
but the world did not know him.
He came to what was his own,
but his own people did not accept him.

But to those who did accept him he gave power to become children of God, to those who believe in his name, who were born not by natural generation nor by human choice nor by a man's decision but of God.

And the Word became flesh
and made his dwelling among us,
and we saw his glory,
the glory as of the Father's only Son,
full of grace and truth.

John testified to him and cried out, saying, "This was he of whom I said, 'The one who is coming after me ranks ahead of me because he existed before me.'" From his fullness we have all received, grace in place of grace, because while the law was given through Moses, grace and truth came through Jesus Christ. No one has ever seen God. The only Son, God, who is at the Father's side, has revealed him.

First Reading: Sirach 3:2–6, 12–14

God sets a father in honor over his children;
  a mother's authority he confirms over her
    sons.
Whoever honors his father atones for sins,
  and preserves himself from them.
When he prays, he is heard;
  he stores up riches who reveres his
    mother.
Whoever honors his father is gladdened by
  children,
  and, when he prays, is heard.
Whoever reveres his father will live a long
  life;
  he who obeys his father brings comfort to
    his mother.

My son, take care of your father when he is
  old;
  grieve him not as long as he lives.
Even if his mind fail, be considerate of him;
  revile him not all the days of his life;
kindness to a father will not be forgotten,
  firmly planted against the debt of your
    sins
  —a house raised in justice to you.

> *Note that in Year C the following readings may be used:*
> *First Reading: 1 Samuel 1:20–22, 24–28*
> *Psalm Response: Psalm 84:2–3, 5–6, 9–10*
> *Second Reading: 1 John 3:1–2, 21–24*

SCRIPTURE COMMENTARY

The Old Testament insists on great reverence for parents. A stubborn and consistently disobedient son could be stoned to death. Because there were no hospitals or permanent hospices for the care of a sick, infirm, and aged father or mother, this responsibility was considered the most sacred of familial duties. This sacred obligation is found not just in the Bible but in every known law code from the ancient world. Wisdom literature gives special attention to the relationship of children to their parents as a model of what wisdom really means. Today, from the great teacher Jesus ben Sirach, we have an excellent example of such praise of the dutiful son (and daughter). This and similar passages had a very strong influence on the early Church as well: note the similar list of values in the letters of 1 and 2 Timothy and Titus.

HOMILY HELPS

In our times much is said about family values and their importance for our society. But as often happens, we may spend more time talking about these values than we do putting them into practice. Today's readings are eminently practical in addressing husbands, wives, and children.

Weddings are universally happy occasions. At a wedding everything is so positive; it is a match, we say, made in heaven. However, the glow of the honeymoon soon grows dim, and we are back to the course of everyday life. The daily commute still means the traffic headache; the laundry and housecleaning never seem to end; the evening meal has to be prepared and served on time. There is a monotonous rhythm to life, a rhythm that brings frayed nerves dangerously close to the surface. That is where the hard work begins.

Today's epistle reminds us of the effort to be expended in building the edifice of married life, the cultivation of a love beyond the romantic. It all centers on the infused virtue of charity, that life in the Spirit which makes all things possible. Nothing is of greater importance to a Christian marriage than a spiritual and sacramental life, supported by quality time alone for the married couple and an occasional time of retreat for renewal and rededication. Colossians speaks of mutual forgiveness for those inevitable misunderstandings and conflicts that arise, as well as a genuine concern for the well-being of the other. The Eucharist shared together; an occasional dinner out; sufficient time for rest and relaxation. Above all, there is the primary importance of a faith-centered life.

The Old Testament reading from Sirach has very practical norms for young people in responding to their parents' needs. Obedience is coupled with honor, which makes the former far more palatable. As children mature, they should come to a deeper awareness of indebtedness. Abraham Lincoln once remarked that at twelve he was amazed at how unintelligent his

PSALM REFLECTION

Psalm 128 echoes the spirit of harmony and rejoicing that characterizes a household in which parents and children live in mutual love and respect. It is written from the husband and father's point of view, but the Church proposes it to us for every member of the family to learn to cherish one's family as a true gift from God. Only the family that gives praise to the loving God of all goodness in creation recognizes the strength and blessing that being part of a family gives us in "good times and in bad, until death do us part."

> **Psalm Response**
> **Psalm 128:1–2, 3, 4–5**
>
> *Antiphon*
> Blessed are they who dwell in your
>   house, O Lord.
>
> *Verse for Reflection*
> May you see your children's
>   children!
> Peace be upon Israel! (v. 6)

SCRIPTURE COMMENTARY

The key to the selection of Colossians is not just the mechanical connection to Holy Family Sunday of the mention of husbands, wives, and children at the end—it is in Paul's astounding, almost lyrical, vision of a man, woman, or child of God who is metaphorically "clothed" in the very qualities that make a person fully mature in God's purposes for us. If God himself witnesses to perfect love and creativity, to the generosity of giving himself to his entire creation, of joy in all that exists, we are at our fullest when we accept God's qualities as the behavior and conduct of our

> **Second Reading:**
> **Colossians 3:12–21**
> **(or Colossians 3:12–17)**
>
> Brothers and sisters: Put on, as God's chosen ones, holy and beloved, heartfelt compassion, kindness, humility, gentleness, and patience, bearing with one another and forgiving one another, if one has a grievance against another; as the Lord has forgiven you, so must you also do. And over all these put on

father was, but by the time he was nineteen, he was amazed at how much his father had learned in seven years! Special mention is made in Sirach of the parent whose mental ability is fading with the passing of years. Children are often asked to bear the burden of a parent with Alzheimer's or dementia. It is a heavy cross, but a labor of love.

The story of Jesus' separation from his parents in Jerusalem, taken from Luke's infancy narrative, has a post-Easter ring. Jesus was lost for three days, just as in death he was three days in the tomb. He is now seated in the heavenly temple where his

Father presides. On more than one occasion during his earthly ministry, Jesus indicated that his first allegiance was to his mission from the Father and all human relationships were secondary. "Who are my mother and my brothers? Those who do the will of my Father." This is precisely the message depicted in the Lucan story. In the interests of his God-directed mission, Jesus had to bypass his human parents. And they acceded in the interests of a greater good, that gift of the Spirit which the risen Jesus sends from the Father. It is that gift which makes Christian marriage enduring and edifying.

LITURGICAL NOTES

The celebration of Christmas continues with the feast of the Holy Family of Jesus, Mary, and Joseph, which makes clear that Jesus was born into our human condition, sharing in all that it means to be human. It was in the context of family that Jesus grew in age and wisdom.

The *Lectionary for Mass* provides specific gospel readings for this feast in each of the three cycles, and optional cycle B and cycle C readings that may be used. Liturgy planners need to

love, that is, the bond of perfection. And let the peace of Christ control your hearts, the peace into which you were also called in one body. And be thankful. Let the word of Christ dwell in you richly, as in all wisdom you teach and admonish one another, singing psalms, hymns, and spiritual songs with gratitude in your hearts to God. And whatever you do, in word or in deed, do everything in the name of the Lord Jesus, giving thanks to God the Father through him.

Wives, be subordinate to your husbands, as is proper in the Lord. Husbands, love your wives, and avoid any bitterness toward them. Children, obey your parents in everything, for this is pleasing to the Lord. Fathers, do not provoke your children, so they may not become discouraged.

SCRIPTURE COMMENTARY, CONTINUED

own lives. We "put on" divine virtues as we grow spiritually day by day. For Paul, the fully committed Christian is indeed clothed with the life of God in imitation of Christ, who showed us the human face of fully living God's ways while in our earthly home. But Paul never honors the perfect individual who achieves his or her perfection—we do this in mutuality, helping one another, supporting the good in each other, and building a family that mirrors the divine Trinity in its fully familial love.

Gospel: Luke 2:41–52

Each year Jesus' parents went to Jerusalem for the feast of Passover, and when he was twelve years old, they went up according to festival custom. After they had completed its days, as they were returning, the boy Jesus remained behind in Jerusalem, but his parents did not know it. Thinking that he was in the

SCRIPTURE COMMENTARY

This small scene is unique to the Gospel of Luke and may seem strange to us. It is not that unbelievable if we imagine Jesus receiving from his parents the special gift of going to Jerusalem for his bar mitzvah upon reaching his twelfth birthday. Every Jewish male leaves his childhood, a time with no special responsibilities for religious practice, and is solemnly received into the community as an adult bound to keep the Torah in all its obligations. Luke emphasizes that Jesus has faithfully prepared for this

check with presiders, preachers, and readers so the correct readings can be prepared. The readings place the life and love of the believer in the context of the community or family that supports the growth of all.

The gospel for cycle C presents the story of Joseph and Mary journeying with the child Jesus to Jerusalem for the feast of Passover, and the child Jesus remaining behind. Once found, Jesus asks them, "Did you not know that I must be in my Father's house?" Luke follows this curious question with the narrative that Jesus "went down

with them . . . and was obedient to them . . . and advanced in wisdom, age, and favor."

The liturgical texts reflect the mystery of the Word made flesh and the implications for believers in every age who call upon the name of Jesus. This liturgy can become an occasion to celebrate "family" and the obedience we owe to one another out of love. Liturgy planners should keep in mind that families come in a variety of shapes and sizes.

This feast, coming so close to Christmas, often suffers from neglect due to simple exhaustion

on the part of planners and liturgical ministers. Awareness of our human condition in the days immediately after Christmas invites us to ensure that some members are charged with the liturgy planning, with the coordination of ministers, and with maintenance of the worship environment, specially for this Sunday.

Some parishes plan an extra liturgical service, such as a Christmas carol sing or Christmas pageant, that can bring together families of all shapes and sizes in the family of the Church.

SCRIPTURE COMMENTARY, CONTINUED

moment by thoroughly studying the law and is ready to discuss its meaning with the learned teachers who used to make themselves available in the temple for the public during the Passover celebrations. Luke does not say that Jesus put the teachers down or was superior to them but that he listened and questioned with great insight and wisdom. His humility is shown by his immediate willingness to return and be obedient to his parents. Nor are his parents irresponsible. Most large groups that traveled the three days or more it took to go from Galilee to Jerusalem would get the women under way earlier in the day because they traveled more slowly. The men would leave together later and all would meet at the end of the first day at the appointed stopping place. In this case, Mary and Joseph each would have assumed that Jesus was with the other group—but as soon as they realized he was not with the group, they immediately went back to Jerusalem. As in the first two readings, this scene makes the essential point of discipleship of Jesus—one lives in full harmony with one's human father and mother, but the true father is God who makes all family blessing possible. One must dwell in his house above all other households.

caravan, they journeyed for a day and looked for him among their relatives and acquaintances, but not finding him, they returned to Jerusalem to look for him. After three days they found him in the temple, sitting in the midst of the teachers, listening to them and asking them questions, and all who heard him were astounded at his understanding and his answers. When his parents saw him, they were astonished, and his mother said to him, "Son, why have you done this to us? Your father and I have been looking for you with great anxiety." And he said to them, "Why were you looking for me? Did you not know that I must be in my Father's house?" But they did not understand what he said to them. He went down with them and came to Nazareth, and was obedient to them; and his mother kept all these things in her heart. And Jesus advanced in wisdom and age and favor before God and man.

MUSIC CONNECTION

It is misleading and too facile to view this feast as an enthronement of the nuclear family and a rallying point for "traditional" family values. As Walter Cuenin, a Catholic pastor, once wrote: "We should not overload this day with our concerns for the American family or the stability of married life. The purpose of the feast is to center on the Incarnation and then, by extension, on the family." The hymn *Once in Royal David's City* is a good example of a text that pinpoints the majesty of the Incarnation in the ebb and flow of the Christ child's growth and how that example is meant to encourage and challenge us as disciples. The West Indian carol *The Virgin Mary Had a Baby Boy* resonates with the same mystery by its skillful and rhythmic repetition of the phrase "baby boy." Today's responsorial, Psalm 128, is well treated by Haugen, Meltz, and Gelineau. Finally, Alan Hommerding's *Come, Sing a Home and Family* is a truly wonderful and thought-provoking text set to a familiar Mozart melody. It conveys the meaning of this feast with tender realism and is a recommended way to conclude today's feast of the Holy Family.

CATECHETICAL SUGGESTIONS

The family as the domestic church
Intergenerational catechesis
A contextualist's understanding of the letter to the Colossians
Vocations
Hannah's prayer (1 Samuel 2:1–10) and Mary's *Magnificat*
A parent's love as an image of God's love in scripture

MARY, MOTHER OF GOD

First Reading:
Numbers 6:22–27

The LORD said to Moses: "Speak to Aaron and his sons and tell them: This is how you shall bless the Israelites. Say to them:

The LORD bless you
and keep you!
The LORD let his face
shine upon you, and
be gracious to you!
The LORD look upon
you kindly and give
you peace!

So shall they invoke my name upon the Israelites, and I will bless them."

SCRIPTURE COMMENTARY

In the Old Testament, the priests were charged with regularly blessing the congregation gathered for the celebration of the great feast days of the year. They spoke the blessing as the word of God himself to his children, much as Isaac spoke the blessing over his son Jacob in Genesis 27. Blessing was intimately connected with the very nature of the covenant bond between God and Israel. In typical ancient treaties between peoples, the great king, or overlord, bestowed a promise of protection and favor to the lesser party, while the subject promised faithfulness and obedience to the commands and laws of the overlord. Thus, blessing is essentially the divine promise of care and protection for us. It is pronounced over the people whenever the covenant is celebrated in any way. This includes the great pilgrim feast days such as Passover or Pentecost, but also covenant renewal gatherings as described in Deuteronomy 27–28 or in Joshua 24. God blesses his children with care, just as a human father would promise care for his children. On the other hand, when we bless God, we are really giving thanks and praise for the care and love he has given to us. There are many examples of blessings in the Bible, but none comes close to the beauty of the language of this priestly blessing in Numbers 6.

HOMILY HELPS

At the start of a new year, Mary, a key player in the infancy narratives, stands at the center of our liturgy. Today's gospel presents her as a reflective person as she takes to heart the plan of God that is unfolding.

Many of us would admit that prayerful reflection should be more a part of our life than it is. Prayer time is often not a high priority. So many things seem to restrict us, whether at home or at work. Distractions seem omnipresent—the task at hand, concern for the children, the shopping that cannot be put off. It is not easy to find quality time to reflect on our life and simply to pray. But it is indispensable if we do not want to find ourselves running on empty. A personal acquaintance, who was a doctor, was distraught by the daily traffic snarls in his commute until he decided to pray the Rosary. He recited it daily on his way to work for years and found it a great help. A woman acquaintance decided to forego one of her daily "soaps" in the interest of spiritual reading. It is well to remember that in every Mass we are reminded to lift up our hearts to the Lord!

The blessing of Aaron, our first reading today, speaks of God's turning his face to his people. The same metaphor applies to life today. When people are upset with us, they are said to turn their back. Engagement

PSALM REFLECTION

The second verse of psalm 67 is the closest parallel anywhere in the Bible to the wording given in our first reading. The whole psalm is set in a covenant context. Israel prays that God may be recognized as the overlord of all the earth and that all peoples may come to acknowledge his name and rule over them. When Israel came to know and obey their God, they did not see him as merely some local divinity with power in Palestine; they understood that the emperor of the universe had entrusted them with a special role and blessed them with his special care. But in all of their worship they included the hope and awareness that all peoples were subject to him.

Psalm Response
Psalm 67:2–3, 5, 6, 8

Antiphon
May God bless us in his
    mercy.

Verse for Reflection
God has truly blessed us,
And may all the ends of
    the earth
        reverence him!
    (v. 8)

A Psalm for New Year's Day. Psalm 67 may have been sung on the annual New Year's feast, when Israel celebrated God's kingship over the world. It calls on the nations to join in giving God praise and thanks for his goodness. It makes an ideal psalm for New Year's Day.

---

means to turn our face toward someone with a kindly spirit. But our understanding of the priestly blessing points to God's kindness in a much more forceful sense because it is centered in Jesus.

One of our major concerns today is with the human face of the Church. Scandal has badly tarnished the image of the Church. There is added disappointment with leaders, both religious and political, in a country strongly divided along ideological lines. In the face of the continual "spin," people find it increasingly difficult to know what to believe.

But people still cherish their faith. It is prayer and reflection, like that exemplified in Mary, which serves us so well. The Church ultimately is Jesus Christ, who touches each of us in word and sacrament. It is in him that we are nourished and encouraged. Ultimately it is with Christ we stand. And when we cross the Rubicon to the land beyond, it is Christ who will bring us home. That may come during the year that begins today or sometime down the road. The truth is that yesterday is history, today is gift, and tomorrow is mystery.

LITURGICAL NOTES

New Year's Day is significant both in the church community and in the culture. The new year begins under the patronage of Mary, Mother of God; Pope Paul VI designated this day as a day of prayer for world peace. Liturgy planners will need to make some decisions on the texts and readings for this day. While some Masses may be that of the solemnity and others for peace, many have found that both themes can be very easily integrated into the same celebration.

SCRIPTURE COMMENTARY

While the first reading and psalm focused on blessings for the year that is just beginning, the second reading and gospel emphasize the special place we have in God's plan as adopted brothers and sisters of God's own Son. God had planned from all eternity to send his Son to redeem humanity. By being fully human and obedient to the covenant relationship with God, Jesus could teach and lead others to have faith in him and to be his followers. In turn he gave them his own Holy Spirit so that they would no longer act on their own but with the power of Christ and his Spirit. Thus they would be entitled to share in the same inheritance as the Son deserved for his obedience, namely, an eternal place with the Son in his Father's house. Paul is using the analogy of the family and the rights of all members within it, so this reading is particularly fitting for the celebration of Mary as the mother who brought Jesus into our human family.

CATECHETICAL SUGGESTIONS

Family prayers and blessings
The theological significance of the title "Mother of God"
Christology
Mary in the gospels
Mary's titles
Lumen Gentium, The Dogmatic Constitution of the Church (Vatican II), Chapter 8

The liturgical texts invoke Mary's intercession and remind us of the effectiveness of that intercession in our lives. The scripture readings for the solemnity present the Aaronic blessing, "The LORD look upon you kindly and give you peace." The gospel shows Mary keeping "all these things and reflecting on them in her heart."

It is still the Christmas season, although Masses on this day are not as well attended as at other times. This could prompt committees to examine the schedule of vigil Masses and Masses during the day.

The General Intercessions should include several intentions for peace and justice, especially in those parts of our world torn apart by violence, war, and terrorism. It is also an excellent opportunity to pray for those who work for peace—from the members of the Peace Corps to the United Nations. The concluding collect for the Intercessions could be taken from Masses and Prayers for Various Need and Occasions: For Peace and Justice or Beginning the Civil Year. There is also a special solemn blessing for the beginning of the new year.

New Year's Day can also be a time for families to gather and invoke God's blessing on the new year. *Catholic Household Blessings and Prayers* provides a blessing for the new year, placing our prayer in the context of both the Christmas season and our quest for peace.

Those charged with the environment should remember that live trees need water; evergreen branches might need to be sprayed or even replaced. The Christmas environment will need some maintenance throughout the season.

SCRIPTURE COMMENTARY

The gospel opens with a continuation of the Christmas night event of the shepherds rushing to see the child after the angels announced this astounding news to them. Luke alone tells us that shepherds were the first to hear and believe in the promise of a new Savior being born. It is Luke's way of emphasizing that only the lowly and humble will be able to recognize and understand the divine status of Jesus. But Luke immediately continues by noting that both Mary and the shepherds treasured this moment, Mary ready to know what this might signify for the future, and the shepherds rejoicing that they had received such a special notice and hoping it would come true for them one day. Luke roots the birth of Jesus solidly in the historical moment. This is no angelic illusion. To confirm this, Luke tells us that Jesus completely fulfills the law as any Jewish family would expect, by receiving his name on the eighth day and by being circumcised painfully in the flesh. As the firstborn son, he would also be consecrated to the Lord as required by Exodus 13. The Incarnation may be filled with the grace of the supernatural and achieved by divine power alone, but the evangelist insists that this in no way takes away from the full humanity of Jesus.

Gospel: Luke 2:16–21

The shepherds went in haste to Bethlehem and found Mary and Joseph, and the infant lying in the manger. When they saw this, they made known the message that had been told them about this child. All who heard it were amazed by what had been told them by the shepherds. And Mary kept all these things, reflecting on them in her heart. Then the shepherds returned, glorifying and praising God for all they had heard and seen, just as it had been told to them.

When eight days were completed for his circumcision, he was named Jesus, the name given him by the angel before he was conceived in the womb.

MUSIC CONNECTION

The octave of Christmas falls on January 1 and is celebrated as a Marian feast, the Solemnity of Mary, the Mother of God. This continues a decidedly Marian theme that began in Advent and, understandably, has permeated the celebrations of Christmas and Holy Family. Certainly, Christmas carols and anthems are appropriate today, especially those that highlight Mary. Among these could be mentioned *Angels We Have Heard on High*; *Silent Night*; *O Little Town of Bethlehem*; *Virgin-born, We Bow before You*; *What Child Is This*; *Once in Royal David's City*; and *Sing of Mary*. Haugen's *Child of Our Dreams* is a beautiful complement to the traditional seasonal repertoire and merits some attention. Today's Psalm 67 is treated well by both Guimont and by the Batastini/Gelineau endeavor. Other pieces one might consider are Foley's *The Beautiful Mother*; Deiss's *Sleep My Sweet Jesus*; *Come, Sing a Home and Family*; and *Go Tell It on the Mountain*. The desire for peace and well-being certainly permeates New Year's Day in most cultures, including our own, and so one should not overlook the power and appropriateness of the Miller/Jackson classic *Let There Be Peace on Earth*. Since shepherds are mentioned in the gospel pericope, the spiritual *Rise Up, Shepherd, and Follow* would contribute musically to today's celebration.

EPIPHANY OF THE LORD

First Reading: Isaiah 60:1–6

Rise up in splendor, Jerusalem! Your light has
    come,
    the glory of the Lord shines upon you.
See, darkness covers the earth,
    and thick clouds cover the peoples;
but upon you the LORD shines,
    and over you appears his glory.
Nations shall walk by your light,
    and kings by your shining radiance.
Raise your eyes and look about;
    they all gather and come to you:
your sons come from afar,
    and your daughters in the arms of their nurses.

Then you shall be radiant at what you see,
    your heart shall throb and overflow,
for the riches of the sea shall be emptied out before
        you,
    the wealth of nations shall be brought to you.
Caravans of camels shall fill you,
    dromedaries from Midian and Ephah;
all from Sheba shall come
    bearing gold and frankincense,
    and proclaiming the praises of the LORD.

SCRIPTURE COMMENTARY

In the ancient Near East, the image of overwhelming bright light was identified with the splendor that radiated from the divine "being" of a god. When a god appeared to humans, he or she was accompanied by a blaze of light that blinded the eyes, much as when we try to look directly at the sun. Indeed, above all, sun imagery was most often used for describing God's glory. In today's vision expressed by a disciple of the prophet Isaiah, solar references abound throughout the poem. Just as ancient travelers and traders always moved by daylight in order to both navigate directions and ensure safety, so the prophet sees a time coming when God will be the compass and source of direction for Israel. She will have prosperity not just in business but as a witness to and model of God's blessing, attracting all nations. In a nationalistic sense, God is pictured moving like the sun from east to west to direct the caravans toward Israel—and the fabled wealth of the Orient, the spices from Arabia and India, will flow into their merchants' hands, and not those of strangers. In a more universal sense, just as the sun's rays reach even the farthest corners of the world, God extends the goodness he has given to Israel to all other peoples as well.

HOMILY HELPS

Polarization. It's a word that is used a lot today. People cluster around an issue or an interpretation and quickly divide into camps.

The coming of the messiah was a polarizing issue. Today's gospel makes that very clear. The story of the magi is a cameo presentation of what became later a much larger issue. Most of the Jewish religious leaders did not recognize Jesus as messiah. The peripheral Gentiles, on the other hand, flowed toward him in great numbers and eventually made of Christianity a universal faith.

The magi (who were neither kings nor designated as three) anxiously followed the star's lead. King Herod and the chief priests and scribes were reluctant to follow the travelers' lead. They chose to stay behind. What the king and his retinue missed was the greatest story ever told. The author of this engaging narrative says far more than meets the eye. The single truth to be learned is that the tender embrace of God excludes no one. There are no exceptions. Polarization means only division. That division is not of God is seen clearly in Christ's repeated prayer for unity.

Today, unfortunately, polarization and division are part of daily life, part of both church and society. Polarization may have existed in the past, but in the present it is front and center. The Second Vatican Council, with all its riches, also triggered a reaction and proved to be a flashpoint for many. The council moved too far or did not move far enough. The result is that on the right and the left there are contentious issues that refuse to go away.

Nothing divides a country more than war. We have seen it is Korea, Vietnam, and Iraq. The picture is aggravated by the fact that much of the citizenry feels that it has no voice or that the small voice it has is reduced to a whisper.

In all of this, there is one rule of thumb that proves helpful. We need to prevent issues from growing to a point of polarization. If a worthy point of difference arises, then it is worthy of discussion.

39

PSALM REFLECTION

Psalm 72 echoes many of the themes of Isaiah 60. It is a psalm composed for the coronation of a king, and it is a prayer for God's blessings on the king as he begins to rule over the nation. Yes, part of the blessing will be riches offered by the kings of other peoples, and the psalmist, like Isaiah, uses the famous wealth of the spice trade as an example. But more than that, the psalm is a prayer that God will bestow the qualities of good kingship on this new ruler: the ability to judge wisely and fairly, to render impartial judgment, to care for the poor and the least of his kingdom, to be compassionate and sympathetic to the complaints of victims and the afflicted, and to seek peace and harmony for all in the nation.

Psalm Response
> Psalm 72:1–2, 7–8, 10–11, 12–13

Antiphon
Lord, every nation on earth will adore you.

Verse for Reflection
May all kings bow down before him,
May all the nations serve him! (v. 11)

CATECHETICAL SUGGESTIONS

3 Isaiah's prophecies of hope
Royal Psalms
Universal effect of Christ's redeeming acts
The two-thousand-year process of revelation in the Bible
Interreligious dialogues
Matthew's infancy narrative

Many a virtual conflagration has been neutralized or diminished by reaching a moral consensus.

Ephesians today sees nothing but good in the mystery that has now been revealed. In Christ Jesus both Jew and Gentile have become coheirs. Even though God had a long engagement with the Jewish people, that engagement ultimately extends to all. Every step that brings "Jew and Greek" closer together is a blessing. The lesson is well learned. It is better to discuss issues than to fight over them. It is even possible to disagree in peace and friendship. Epiphany means a universal embrace. If this is what God wills, who are we to turn away?

LITURGICAL NOTES

Our Christmas celebration continues with the Solemnity of the Epiphany. As we acknowledge that God revealed the "Son to the nations by the guidance of a star," so may we be led to "glory in heaven by the light of faith." This is a season of light, and this day calls for a suitable and increased display of lights (cf. *Ceremonial of Bishops,* 240). The opening procession could include liturgical ministers or members of the assembly bearing candles that could then be placed around the altar, around the ambo, around the crèche (with great care), and in any other place where they might

safely be placed for the duration of the liturgy. If the parish has dedication candles on the walls, these too could be lighted. The use of these candles can be very effective—and will necessitate careful planning and even rehearsal—but the results will be worth the efforts.

Gold vestments can be worn, and gold ribbons might be placed in the Christmas trees or wreaths. Incense would be appropriate in the entrance procession. Lights and incense ought to accompany the gospel procession. At the conclusion of the gospel, a deacon or other minister could chant (or read) the Proclamation of the date of Easter. This text, which announces the date of Easter, and all those feast days that depend

**Second Reading:
Ephesians 3:2–3a, 5–6**

Brothers and sisters: You have heard of the steward-ship of God's grace that was given to me for your benefit, namely, that the mystery was made known to me by reve-lation. It was not made known to people in other generations as it has now been revealed to his holy apostles and prophets by the Spirit: that the Gentiles are coheirs, members of the same body, and copartners in the promise in Christ Jesus through the gospel.

SCRIPTURE COMMENTARY

The reading from Isaiah and the gospel story of the magi highlight foreigners streaming toward Israel, drawn there by the light of God's presence. One of the central points in Jesus' teaching was that the "kingdom of God" that he proclaimed would include not just the chosen people of Israel but the pagan nations as well. How could this be? How could there be a chosen people or an Israel under Torah if outsiders and nonobservant peoples were also allowed to receive God's blessings that came because of the covenant relationship? Paul wrestled with this new dimension of the mystery of salvation and concluded that it was not known to any of the Old Testament prophets or writers. It was revealed only by the death and resurrection of Jesus. Throughout his letters, Paul tells us that because Jesus' death conquered sin and broke its power over all humanity, all people subject to mortality will be raised up because of his resurrection. Jews already had received the promise of salvation, but now Gentiles too would be included in God's salvation. Jews hear the promise through the Torah; Gentiles learn it through the preaching of the gospel.

Gospel: Matthew 2:1–12

When Jesus was born in Bethlehem of Judea, in the days of King Herod, behold, magi from the east arrived in Jerusalem, saying, "Where

SCRIPTURE COMMENTARY

Matthew's version of the magi from the East is unknown in other gospels. It has the character of a *midrash*, a story that has a number of events each built around a biblical prophecy. The notable scholars or aristocrats from

on Easter, would be proclaimed in a manner similar to the procla-mation of the gospel, with incense and light. While this prayer might sound strange to some ears, it provides an excel-lent opportunity for liturgical cate-chesis. The text of this Proclamation can be found in the 2004 *Sacramentary Supplement.*

In some places the custom has developed of bringing up gold, frankincense, and myrrh along with the gifts of bread and wine for the Eucharist. This custom is similar to attempts at bringing up "symbolic gifts" during the pro-cession. The gifts that are brought forward from the assem-bly are the gifts needed by the Church: the bread and wine for the Eucharist, and the gifts for the

poor. It is helpful to recall that all the gifts brought forward will be transformed: the bread and wine will be transformed into the body and blood of Christ, to be given back to God's holy people as their food and drink. The mone-tary offerings will be transformed into the works of mercy that the Church engages in every day. Other gifts brought forward will not be changed or transformed; they will remain the same. A good rule of thumb might be that if what is brought forward will not be changed, then it ought not to be brought forward.

Incense could also be used during the preparation of the gifts, tying in with the prayer over the gifts, which says, "Accept the offerings of your Church, not

gold, frankincense, and myrrh, but the sacrifice and food they symbolize, Jesus Christ."

While the Christmas decora-tions may be gone from stores and malls, we are still unfolding the mystery of Christmas. Keep the music alive, the prayers focused on the wonder of the Incarnation, and the environment fresh and attractive.

The Epiphany is a traditional day for the blessing of homes. The *Book of Blessings* provides an order for the blessing of homes during the Christmas season; *Catholic Household Blessings and Prayers* provides a simpler rite that could be done by the mem-bers of the family. Providing some of these texts in the bulletin will encourage their use.

SCRIPTURE COMMENTARY, CONTINUED

the East bearing gifts reflect both Isaiah 60 and Psalm 72, which we have just read; the location of the birthplace in Bethlehem combines Micah 3:1–2 with the offer of kingship to David in 2 Samuel 5:2. The star comes from the promised vision of Numbers 24:17. As a result, Matthew does not intend for us to take the narrative to be historically accurate in all of its details. He affirms (1) that Jesus fulfilled all the prophetic signs that revealed him to be the messiah, (2) that King Herod refused to accept any messiah and sought to kill all possible claimants, and (3) that the mission of Jesus was recognized instead by foreign wise men who eagerly looked for the signs of God's coming. What all the prophetic sources have in common is that they each originally referred to King David (or Solomon in the case of Psalm 72). We usually think of David as the messianic hope mostly for Jewish restoration, but the universal aspects of his empire extending over other nations (e.g., in 2 Samuel 10) became the basis for Israel's hopes that all nations would come to acknowledge God and his Torah for themselves as well. Matthew emphasizes this meaning from the beginning of his gospel. In its understanding of God's saving plan it is similar to Paul's ideas in today's reading from Ephesians.

is the newborn king of the Jews? We saw his star at its rising and have come to do him homage." When King Herod heard this, he was greatly troubled, and all Jerusalem with him. Assembling all the chief priests and the scribes of the people, he inquired of them where the Christ was to be born. They said to him, "In Bethlehem of Judea, for thus it has been written through the prophet:

And you, Bethlehem, land of Judah,
  are by no means least among the rulers of
    Judah;
since from you shall come a ruler,
  who is to shepherd my people Israel."

Then Herod called the magi secretly and ascertained from them the time of the star's appearance. He sent them to Bethlehem and said, "Go and search diligently for the child. When you have found him, bring me word, that I too may go and do him homage." After their audience with the king they set out. And behold, the star that they had seen at its rising preceded them, until it came and stopped over the place where the child was. They were overjoyed at seeing the star, and on entering the house they saw the child with Mary his mother. They prostrated themselves and did him homage. Then they opened their treasures and offered him gifts of gold, frankincense, and myrrh. And having been warned in a dream not to return to Herod, they departed for their country by another way.

MUSIC CONNECTION

This solemnity, originating in the East, underscores the manifestation of God to the world in Jesus Christ. It is this emphasis on the revelation of God in Christ that is the theological point of the gospel and the centerpiece of today's celebration. The memorable details of the magi serve well to highlight the universality of God's revelation. The Lord has come to manifest and reveal God's self to all peoples and every nation—a thought that

should cauterize our often parochial and narrow salvific instincts. The theme of light breaking into the darkness permeates the first reading from Isaiah, suggesting hymns such as Haugen's *Awake, Awake and Greet the New Morn,* Deiss's *Sion Sing,* and *Brightest and Best.* Psalm 72 is well treated by Alstott, Joncas, and Gelineau. The pericope from Matthew suggests pieces for the feast including *We Three Kings, As with Gladness Men of Old, Songs of Thankfulness and Praise,* and

What Star Is This. A recent text by Fran O'Brien wedded to the ever versatile melody *Beach Spring* provides a good contemporary hymn named *Epiphany Carol.* Finally, one of the season's favorites, *What Child Is This,* deserves special consideration as we close out this year's Advent/Christmas season. Its final verse with reference to gold, frankincense, and myrrh ties in wonderfully with Matthew's account of the journey of the mysterious magi bringing their opulent gifts to the newborn son of Mary.

First Reading: Isaiah 62:1–5

For Zion's sake I will not be silent,
 for Jerusalem's sake I will not be
 quiet,
until her vindication shines forth
 like the dawn
 and her victory like a burning
 torch.

Nations shall behold your
 vindication,
 and all the kings your glory;
you shall be called by a new name
 pronounced by the mouth of the
 LORD.
You shall be a glorious crown in the
 hand of the LORD,
 a royal diadem held by your God.
No more shall people call you
 "Forsaken, "
 or your land "Desolate, "
but you shall be called "My
 Delight,"
 and your land "Espoused."
For the LORD delights in you
 and makes your land his spouse.

SCRIPTURE COMMENTARY

This chapter is part of "Third Isaiah," composed after the return from exile in the period between 539 and 516 BC. It was a time of great hope and great frustration, the end of a period during which the land of Judah had been lost and an entire generation had been captured and carried off to Babylon. We cannot overestimate the vital importance of possessing the hereditary land of one's ancestors and serving one's God in one's own homeland, where he rules and has special power to bestow prosperity on his worshipers. Gods were considered to be weakened and not fully able to help you if their territorial land had been conquered by a nation with another and more powerful god. So the poet announces that Yahweh, God of Israel, is about to restore his full blessing on the land of Judah. Gods are often pictured in ancient sculpture with their walled capital cities as a crown on their head. Isaiah uses such an image here. God will guarantee the rebuilding of Jerusalem and its walls, and he will rename his city with new names of promise. The original prophet Isaiah had once warned king Ahaz of doom by naming his own child "Speedy the spoil, quick the Plunder" (Isaiah 8:1–3). Once the idea is spoken, it will certainly happen! Today's passage it is very similar to Hosea 2, in which God

HOMILY HELPS

We are living in a graced moment. This is the end time, the greatest moment in the history of salvation. That may be hard for us to believe at times as our cares and worries close in on us. Yet it is a fact that today's liturgy makes eminently clear.

The Old Testament speaks frequently of God's definitive intervention in history but gives expression to it in a variety of images. At times it is seen as a marriage between God and his people, as is the case in today's reading from Isaiah. At other times it is depicted as a great banquet, replete with the best meats and the choicest wines.

Both these images appear in the account of the Cana wedding in today's gospel. It is a time when the Church makes intercession for the needs of her children as does Mary—here called "Woman" (as in Genesis) or the new Eve—requesting of her Son the wine of the new age. It is a time of feasting, of good cheer, the time of a people no longer referred to as "Desolate" or "Abandoned" but now God's "Delight," his spouse.

The Christian life is not a life of gloom and doom. Long faces are inappropriate in the place of word and sacrament. Our spiritual needs are addressed at every turn. We are members of the body of Christ and are fed on his sacramental body daily if we so desire.

There is no doubt that the going is rough at times, but we have every reason to be encouraged. We are truly the beloved of God.

Yet Paul reminds the Corinthians today that we are not simply devout believers. We are not only cared for; we are today the caring. We are not only fed; we do the feeding. According to our ability and calling, we are to be engaged in the upbuilding of the Church. There is no more striking sign of the successful outcome of Vatican II than the involvement of the laity in the strengthening of the Church. Statistics show that the number of Catholics involved in church ministry today is counted in the tens of thousands. They serve as extraordinary ministers of Holy Communion, they care for

SCRIPTURE COMMENTARY, CONTINUED

promises to take back his wayward bride and renew his vows with her. It is a passage bursting with optimism based on echoing wildly hopeful oracles from the great prophets of Israel's past.

> As a young man marries a virgin,
> your Builder shall marry you;
> and as a bridegroom rejoices in his
>   bride
> so shall your God rejoice in you.

PSALM REFLECTION

As one of the psalms sung in honor of God's kingship at the annual festival of Tabernacles (or actually on New Year's Day itself) to pray for divine blessing on the land for the coming year, Psalm 96 focuses on God's rule over all of creation, not just over his own people Israel. A god who guides the destinies of the sun and stars as well as the fates of mighty nations such as Egypt or Babylon is a god from whom we can expect great goodness and blessing. Israel was firmly convinced that the special relationship that God had granted to them did not tie God to being merely a local patron for this particular people or piece of geography. No, the miracle was that the almighty ruler of the universe cared enough to reveal his name and his plans to such a small nation. As God had given them blessing and his personal care, they in turn were to give God a constant worship filled with glory and praise and joyful song, proclaiming and declaring to every other nation how great was their blessing that God was their ruler as well.

Psalm Response
Psalm 96:1–2, 2–3, 7–8, 9–10

Antiphon
Proclaim his marvelous deeds to all the
   nations.

Verse for Reflection
Great is the Lord and greatly to be
   praised;
Awesome is he beyond all gods! (v. 4)

---

the sick, they teach Christian doctrine. Some are involved in outreach programs for the poor and the needy; others assist the bereaved. This is the age of parish councils and finance councils, called to work with the pastor in making the parish a more effective witness in today's world.

We are a unified Church with a singular set of beliefs. But we are not marked by uniformity. As a Church we are blessed with a variety of gifts and talents. No two people serve in the same way, and no one's gifts are superior to another's, for it is the one Spirit who guides and directs the Church in different ways. No one is fit for every task, yet every contribution is valuable. That is the beauty of our end-time life.

LITURGICAL NOTES

The white and gold of the Christmas season is replaced by the green of Ordinary Time. "Apart from those seasons having their own distinctive character, thirty-three or thirty-four weeks remain in the yearly cycle that do not celebrate a specific aspect of the mystery of Christ. Rather, they are devoted to the mystery of Christ in all its aspects. This period is known as Ordinary Time" (GNLYC, 43).

We should make sure that the green does not return before we have had some evaluation of, and notes on, both the purple of Advent and the white of Christmas. The evaluation not only will

become the basis for planning for next Advent and Christmas but may also provide some insight into the next "big" seasons of Lent and Easter. We need to be able to identify those aspects of our celebrations that were effective. Why were they effective? What aspects of our planning and celebration fell short of our expectations? Again, we need to ask why. This also becomes an ideal opportunity to offer correctives for the future. Comments from the liturgy committee should come freely, but they also need to be as specific as possible, for by next year memories may fade.

The General Intercessions should include mention of the Week of Prayer for Christian

**Second Reading:
1 Corinthians 12:4–11**

Brothers and sisters: There are different kinds of spiritual gifts but the same Spirit; there are different forms of service but the same Lord; there are different workings but the same God who produces all of them in everyone. To each individual the manifestation of the Spirit is given for some benefit. To one is given through the Spirit the expression of wisdom; to another, the expression of knowledge according to the same Spirit; to another, faith by the same Spirit; to another, gifts of healing by the one Spirit; to another, mighty deeds; to another, prophecy; to another, discernment of spirits; to another, varieties of tongues; to another, interpretation of tongues. But one and the same Spirit produces all of these, distributing them individually to each person as he wishes.

SCRIPTURE COMMENTARY

Now that we are beginning the Sundays of Ordinary Time, the second reading will follow sections from the different letters of Paul for several weeks in a row. From now until the beginning of Lent we are about to explore chapters 12 to 15 of Paul's first letter to Corinth. Paul will treat two major subjects in these chapters: the interaction between the spiritual gifts given to individuals by the Holy Spirit, and the significance for Christians of the resurrection of the Lord. What these two subjects have in common is that both are given to us because we are united to Christ as his body, and that union is itself the work of the Holy Spirit. Today's reading opens with the insight that all of us have unique gifts to bring to the Church to make that body stronger. All gifts have the same source: God's outpouring of the Holy Spirit. The Holy Spirit infuses us with supernatural grace to share Christ's risen life and sends the particular active graces that enable each member of Christ's body to perform his or her gift for the good of all. While the lesson here is not quite the same as that of today's gospel, both the gifts of the Spirit and the miracle of the water turned to wine share the same purpose: they are done not for the glory of the doer but for the welfare of the community.

Unity, along with intentions for those called to the priesthood, diaconate, consecrated life, and other ministries within the Church.

This Sunday's reading from John's gospel shows the miracle at the wedding feast in Cana, the final "epiphany" of Jesus (the first two were the manifestation to the magi and the baptism of Jesus in the Jordan). Because this gospel reading is also found in the Lectionary for the conferral of the sacrament of marriage, some might tend to use this Sunday as an opportunity to reflect on marriage and even to have a renewal of marriage vows. While celebrating the gift of marriage within the Christian community should never be discouraged, focusing exclusively on marriage limits the potential of the scriptures set before us on this day. As the "delight" of the Lord, the Christian community is given a variety of the Spirit's gifts that the body of the Church might be built up in holiness. But it is that same body that needs to listen to the voice of its head, Christ the Lord, so that we, like the servers in the gospel, can follow Mary's instruction to "do whatever he tells you." This return to Ordinary Time can be the first occasion in the new year to pray and to listen to the voice of God, who calls each of us to build up the body. What areas, ministries, or groups might benefit from our concern and attention? This might be the Sunday to watch and listen to discover the work ahead.

CATECHETICAL SUGGESTIONS

The Babylonian exile and the return
Apostolic exhortation *Evangelii Nuntiandi,* Evangelization in the Modern World (Pope Paul VI)
The gifts of the Spirit
The charismatic movement
Ecumenism
John's allegorical method

SCRIPTURE COMMENTARY

In John's gospel, this is the first action Jesus takes apart from associating with the disciples of John the Baptist, inviting them to come and discover where he "stayed," and promising them they would witness his coming as Son of Man in the end of times (all in chapter 1). Clearly, the occasion of a wedding feast to open Jesus' ministry is highly symbolic. Not only is the kingdom of heaven regularly described by Jesus himself as a wedding feast (see Matt 22:1–14 and 25:1–13), but the setting on the third day after promising his new disciples they would see him coming on the clouds of heaven is a direct parallel to death and resurrection as the last act of his ministry. It is common for commentators to note that beginning with water for purification and ending with wine better than the best the earth can offer can be nothing else than an allusion to both baptism and the Eucharist. It also matches the final note in John in 19:34 that, at Jesus' death, blood and water flowed forth from him. And like that scene, where John continues in the next verse to tell us that he has witnessed this and that his testimony is true, John ends his Cana scene by saying it was the "beginning of his signs" given to Jesus' disciples to convince them of his promise. Finally, as Jesus begins his work at Mary's word, so on the cross John has Jesus give Mary to the disciples. Thus this entire Cana gospel contains the vision of the Church community after Jesus' departure: seeing their Lord in the signs of the water and the wine, knowing how he turns failure and sin into victory through his word, and promising a banquet unlike anything they have ever known. The best is yet to come if we have faith in Jesus.

Gospel: John 2:1–11

There was a wedding at Cana in Galilee, and the mother of Jesus was there. Jesus and his disciples were also invited to the wedding. When the wine ran short, the mother of Jesus said to him, "They have no wine." And Jesus said to her, "Woman, how does your concern affect me? My hour has not yet come." His mother said to the servers, "Do whatever he tells you." Now there were six stone water jars there for Jewish ceremonial washings, each holding twenty to thirty gallons. Jesus told them, "Fill the jars with water." So they filled them to the brim. Then he told them, "Draw some out now and take it to the headwaiter." So they took it. And when the headwaiter tasted the water that had become wine, without knowing where it came from—although the servers who had drawn the water knew—, the headwaiter called the bridegroom and said to him, "Everyone serves good wine first, and then when people have drunk freely, an inferior one; but you have kept the good wine until now." Jesus did this as the beginning of his signs at Cana in Galilee and so revealed his glory, and his disciples began to believe in him.

MUSIC CONNECTION

The reading from Isaiah revels in the promise of a restored Jerusalem after a long captivity. The delight of God in the restoration is compared to the delight experienced by a young bridegroom with his bride. That marriage imagery connects this first lesson to the wonderful scene from John usually referred to as the wedding of Cana. This "first" of Jesus' signs in the fourth gospel is replete with rich drama, and its symbolism anchors the Idle/Krisman hymn *Jesus, Come! For We Invite You.* The traditional *Songs of Thankfulness and Praise* masterfully connects the dots among numerous "manifestations" of Jesus from the star of Bethlehem to Jesus' baptism by John in the Jordan to this "first" sign at Cana and, indeed, throughout the public ministry of Jesus. Its recurrent refrain, "God in flesh made manifest," is really a summary of the message and meaning of the fourth gospel. The second reading from Corinthians, with its focus on "different gifts but the same Spirit," has given rise to numerous wonderful hymn texts including *One Bread, One Body; We Are Many Parts; Many Are the Lightbeams;* and *There Is One Lord.* In this vein, Larry Rosania's *As Grains of Wheat* is one of the best. Today's responsorial, Psalm 96, has many fine settings, including those by Janco, Haas, Gelineau, and Alstott.

First Reading: Nehemiah 8:2–4a, 5–6, 8–10

Ezra the priest brought the law before the assembly, which consisted of men, women, and those children old enough to understand. Standing at one end of the open place that was before the Water Gate, he read out of the book from daybreak till midday, in the presence of the men, the women, and those children old enough to understand; and all the people listened attentively to the book of the law. Ezra the scribe stood on a wooden platform that had been made for the occasion. He opened the scroll so that all the people might see it—for he was standing higher up than any of the people—; and, as he opened it, all the people rose. Ezra blessed the LORD, the great God, and all the people, their hands raised high, answered, "Amen, amen!" Then they bowed down and prostrated themselves before the LORD, their faces to the ground. Ezra read plainly from the book of the law of God, interpreting it so that all could understand what was read. Then Nehemiah, that is, His Excellency, and Ezra the priest-scribe and the Levites who were instructing the people said to all the people: "Today is holy to the LORD your God. Do not be sad, and do not weep"—for all the people were weeping as they heard the words of the law. He said further: "Go, eat rich foods and drink sweet drinks, and allot portions to those who had nothing prepared; for today is holy to our LORD. Do not be saddened this day, for rejoicing in the LORD must be your strength!"

SCRIPTURE COMMENTARY

The book of Nehemiah narrates how Jerusalem was restored after the exile by the work of two great leaders, Ezra the priest and Nehemiah the governor. Both were high-level officials in the court of the king of Persia who were sent back to Judah, which had failed to prosper. In fact, the people were mostly in despair about their future. With royal support, Nehemiah got the walls rebuilt and the city fortified and safe to live in again, but this of course was not enough. Without a religious revival, the effort would simply collapse.

In today's passage Ezra brings forth the completed Torah to be read to every adult and child of responsible age. The people's reaction of weeping and sorrow suggests that they recognized they had not been living according to this law. It would mean a radical conversion of their ways for most people, but Ezra encouraged them to see it as a new outpouring of God's blessing and to celebrate. To be God's people would not be easy, but it would be made possible by becoming a holy people, living the law fully while worshiping and reverencing God in awe.

HOMILY HELPS

There was a time when the understanding of scripture was seen as a largely Protestant endeavor. To arrive at Sunday Mass after the readings but before the gospel was at most a venial sin. Much of this has been abandoned in the contemporary Church, largely because of our understanding of the importance of God's word. This is a point underscored in today's first reading, about Ezra's proclamation of the law in the presence of the assembled crowd, and in the gospel, with its account of Jesus' reading of Isaiah in the Capernaum synagogue. As a Jewish layman, Jesus was within bounds in reading and interpreting the scriptures during the Sabbath gathering.

An encouraging sign in today's Church is the laity's interest in a better appreciation of God's word. It stands at the center of continuing education in the post-conciliar Church. In many cases, the Bible no longer collects dust on the living room shelf but is kept close at hand. Scripture offers the opportunity for an unmatched conversation with the Lord, since it is he who addresses us in his word. It is well worth the effort to give ourselves fifteen to thirty minutes a day for scripture reading. If we attend Mass during the week, the readings are different each day. They should be seen as integral to the Eucharist,

not simply an adjunct. Since God is addressing us, we should be particularly attentive.

Two examples of applying today's readings come readily to mind. Paul speaks of the one body and many members. Our unity as Christians is found in our adherence to the person of Christ; our diversity is found in the variety and complementarity of our many gifts. In parishes today this is immediately evident in the various ministries: teaching, care of the sick and homebound, assisting the bereaved, to mention but a few. There is place for all of us in lending our talents and inspiration to building up the body of Christ.

The second example is to be found in those to whom Jesus

PSALM REFLECTION

In the first part of this psalm, the poet praises God for his laws of nature by which the world is run with a regularity and good order. In the second part of the psalm, the psalmist turns to the way of life given by God in the Torah. He extols each commandment and rule as *perfect*, that is, each one *perfects* the one who practices it. Each regulation governs part of a well-ordered life in imitation of God's ways. We can see the central role that Torah plays in the life of Judaism by noting the second half of each couplet: refreshing the soul, giving wisdom to the simple, rejoicing the heart, enlightening the eye, enduring forever, being true and just! God's law is the strength on which we can rely, and the psalm ends with the psalmist's heartfelt acknowledgement that God is indeed the rock of our life.

Psalm Response
Psalm 19:8, 9, 10, 15

Antiphon
Your words, Lord, are
Spirit and life.

Verse for Reflection
Day pours out the word
to day,
And night to night
imparts knowledge!
(v. 2)

SCRIPTURE COMMENTARY

Paul continues his discussion of the gifts given by the Spirit. He turns his attention to his central metaphor: that we are the body of Christ. A body acts as a single individual, with all the parts coordinated and acting together. Although in shape and function fingers are far different from a liver, both make possible the body as a living, acting agent. Some may seem more important than others, but in Paul's reasoning, God intends each one for its unique contribution and so all are equally worthy of

**Second Reading: 1 Corinthians 12:12–30
(or 1 Corinthians 12:12–14, 27)**

Brothers and sisters: As a body is one though it has many parts, and all the parts of the body, though many, are one body, so also Christ. For in one Spirit we were all baptized into one body, whether Jews or Greeks, slaves or free persons, and we were all given to drink of one Spirit.

Now the body is not a single part, but many. If a foot should say, "Because I am not a hand I do not belong to the body, " it does not for this reason belong any less to the body. Or if an ear should say, "Because I am not an

---

was sent—the poor, the imprisoned, and the handicapped. In America there is one very affluent city that advertises the fact that "here we have no poor." But there is a poverty in the claim itself—a poverty of lack of awareness. We are all poor in one way or another and therefore in need of a helping hand. We are not to be complacent in our abundance but rather accommodating in our sensitivity. Jesus avoided the title "messiah" because of its worldly implications. He preferred to be seen as the servant extending himself to others, especially those on the fringes of society. In what ways can we do the same?

LITURGICAL NOTES

The gospel passage begins with the opening verses (1–4) of Luke's gospel, stating Luke's intentions in compiling this narratives of the events "that have been fulfilled among us." The Jesus of Luke's gospel will be one who identifies with the poor and the outcast, the marginalized and the neglected. This notion, joined with the images from the first letter to the Corinthians concerning the many parts forming one body, can give planners the opportunity to reflect on those groups who might be neglected in our Sunday assemblies. The focus of our attention could

begin with children and young people.

Children and young people are often referred to as "the future of the Church"—as if they were not already part of the Church. But they are part of the Church, and their particular needs, along with their particular gifts, need to be recognized and celebrated. Many parishes have a weekly or monthly family Mass, a children's Mass, or a teen Mass. These celebrations can cause planners to believe children and young people have been successfully "addressed" in the liturgy. That would be a mistake. In many places where these celebrations do exist, the other liturgies, almost without knowing it, can tend to

eye I do not belong to the body, " it does not for this reason belong any less to the body. If the whole body were an eye, where would the hearing be? If the whole body were hearing, where would the sense of smell be? But as it is, God placed the parts, each one of them, in the body as he intended. If they were all one part, where would the body be? But as it is, there are many parts, yet one body. The eye cannot say to the hand, "I do not need you, " nor again the head to the feet, "I do not need you." Indeed, the parts of the body that seem to be weaker are all the more necessary, and those parts of the body that we consider less honorable we surround with greater honor, and our less presentable parts are treated with greater propriety, whereas our more presentable parts do not need this. But God has so constructed the body as to give greater honor to a part that is without it, so that there may be no division in the body, but that the parts may have the same concern for one another. If one part suffers, all the parts suffer with it; if one part is honored, all the parts share its joy. Now you are Christ's body, and individually parts of it. Some people God has designated in the church to be, first, apostles; second, prophets; third, teachers; then, mighty deeds; then gifts of healing, assistance, administration, and varieties of tongues. Are all apostles? Are all prophets? Are all teachers? Do all work mighty deeds? Do all have gifts of healing? Do all speak in tongues? Do all interpret?

SCRIPTURE COMMENTARY, CONTINUED

honor and respect. The range of Paul's distinctions, which he seems to belabor somewhat, are all to emphasize clearly for the Corinthians not only that every member of the community must receive respect but that they must all work together. Paul is very concerned about this point, for the Corinthians have shown that they do not find unity easy. They are always dividing into camps and attacking each other as less important members of the community. Apparently they claim the authority of this apostle or that evangelist to put down the claims of others. Paul lists the significant roles in the Church that are due to spiritual gifts and reminds us to do as well as possible with what we have been given, and not to seek to have what others have been given. The main point is that *in Christ* we are a single community that must act with the mind of Christ—we must act as though we were Christ acting, we must act as his spiritual body!

CATECHETICAL SUGGESTIONS

Covenant renewal ceremonies
Consensus decision making
The law in the Old Testament and in the New Testament
How our present-day gospels came into existence
Jesus' use of scripture as a living word

MUSIC CONNECTION

The Lucan pericope in which Jesus, returning to Nazareth, reads from the book of the prophet Isaiah in the synagogue is clearly the centerpiece of today's lessons. The reading from Nehemiah parallels this Lucan story with that of Ezra reading aloud from the Torah to all the people. The word of God proclaimed by both Ezra and Jesus is lovingly displayed in one of the most poignant of the Lectionary psalms, Psalm 19. "The precepts of the Lord are right, rejoicing the heart; the command of the Lord is clear, enlightening the eye." This psalm has many fine settings, including those of

isolate those very groups. The liturgical celebration should reflect the needs of the community and the unique gifts and abilities of each person, rather than their ages. Young people and even children should be seen as readers, servers, psalmists, gift bearers, and greeters at all liturgies, not just at those designated as a "children's Mass" or a "youth Mass."

The planning team might begin examining the presence and the role of children and young people at the Sunday celebrations of the Eucharist in the parish. The team's observations might be aided by some informal conversation with these very age groups concerning their participation, or lack thereof, in the Sunday Eucharist.

SCRIPTURE COMMENTARY

The passage we read today is the first public appearance of Jesus recorded in Luke's gospel. He returns to his hometown to visit the synagogue in which he had prayed and learned as a child. His fellow townspeople now recognize that he is no longer a student but a teacher, a rabbi, and they offer him the honor of being the teacher of the day by explaining the reading. It is part of Sabbath worship to read a portion of the Pentateuch and a selection from one of the prophetic books. Jesus reads Isaiah 61:1–2 at the reading stand and then sits down, because the rabbis always taught seated. The message of Isaiah was aimed at giving hope to the exiles that God was coming to release them from their poverty and imprisonment. That hope is fulfilled in Jesus. God will manifest his Spirit in the words and works of Jesus, and the new age will come about for those who hear and commit themselves to him, as the assembly in the reading from Nehemiah had done on hearing the words of the law read by Ezra.

Gospel: Luke 1:1–4; 4:14–21

Since many have undertaken to compile a narrative of the events that have been fulfilled among us, just as those who were eyewitnesses from the beginning and ministers of the word have handed them down to us, I too have decided, after investigating everything accurately anew, to write it down in an orderly sequence for you, most excellent Theophilus, so that you may realize the certainty of the teachings you have received.

Jesus returned to Galilee in the power of the Spirit, and news of him spread throughout the whole region. He taught in their synagogues and was praised by all.

He came to Nazareth, where he had grown up, and went according to his custom into the synagogue on the sabbath day. He stood up to read and was handed a scroll of the prophet Isaiah. He unrolled the scroll and found the passage where it was written:
> The Spirit of the Lord is upon me,
>   because he has anointed me
>   to bring glad tidings to the poor.
> He has sent me to proclaim liberty to captives
>   and recovery of sight to the blind,
>   to let the oppressed go free,
>   and to proclaim a year acceptable to the Lord.

Rolling up the scroll, he handed it back to the attendant and sat down, and the eyes of all in the synagogue looked intently at him. He said to them, "Today this Scripture passage is fulfilled in your hearing."

Haugen, Haas, Gelineau, and Meltz. Hearing, understanding, appropriating, and living the word are worthwhile trajectories for homilist and musician alike. The GIA hymn *Good News* captures the setting of the Lucan narrative as well as the poignancy of the message "to bring glad tidings to the poor, to proclaim liberty to captives." Other hymns in this vein include *The Voice of God Goes Out through All the World, God Has Spoken by His Prophets, The Church of God in Every Age,* and Christopher Walker's *Take the Word of God with You.* Since the second reading from Corinthians continues the discussion of the "body of Christ" begun last week, the hymns *One Bread, One Body; We Are Many Parts;* and *Many Are the Lightbeams* are certainly fitting for today. Also highly recommended is Walker's *One In Body, Heart and Mind,* a wonderful blending of contemporary text and ancient Celtic melody.

> **The Jubilee Year.** In the selection from Isaiah read by Jesus, the final phrase about a "year acceptable to the Lord" refers to the commands about the Jubilee year in Leviticus 25. Every fifty years, all debts were to be forgiven, all lands were to be restored to their original owners, and all slavery was to be cancelled. Jesus is not talking about a national decree that would be enacted by the Sanhedrin or Roman authorities—instead he refers to the work of the Spirit in himself as the messiah.

First Reading:
Jeremiah 1:4–5, 17–19

The word of the LORD came to me, saying:
Before I formed you in the womb I
knew you,
before you were born I dedicated
you,
a prophet to the nations I appointed
you.

But do you gird your loins;
stand up and tell them
all that I command you.
Be not crushed on their account,
as though I would leave you crushed
before them;
for it is I this day
who have made you a fortified city,
a pillar of iron, a wall of brass,
against the whole land:
against Judah's kings and princes,
against its priests and people.
They will fight against you but not prevail over you,
for I am with you to deliver you,
says the LORD.

SCRIPTURE COMMENTARY

Today we read of Jeremiah's call to be a prophet. Next week we will hear of Isaiah's call. The two are proposed to us with different purposes. Isaiah is a model for the call of disciples, but Jeremiah is the model for Jesus' own understanding of his mission as one sent by God. Jeremiah's call has many unique features. He is designated from the womb for his work; that is, he is designated from before his birth. In this sense, the gospel writers saw Jesus to be a new Jeremiah—God had intended his coming from the beginning of time. Jeremiah would face constant and terrible opposition as Jesus too was to experience. It might look as though opponents have crushed Jeremiah, but God reassures the prophet that in the end his enemies will not be able to prevail against him. Even more pointedly, among the most deter-mined opponents of Jeremiah are the priests and rulers—the same group that will oppose Jesus. But Jeremiah was honored by the Babylonians for his efforts to convince Judah not to rebel against their rule. In the same way, Jesus will at times be more appreciated by foreigners than by his own people. In all of this, the call of Jeremiah makes a perfect preparation for today's gospel story of how Jesus is opposed by his closest associates from the beginning.

HOMILY HELPS

The message is often the cause of the mes-senger's rejection. Neither Jeremiah nor Jesus was rejected as a malefactor, guilty of serious crimes. Both of them pro-voked their contemporaries with an annoying message, more easily rejected than embraced.

The point of both the Jeremiah and the Jesus story in today's readings is that, despite opposi-tion and rejection, God was pres-ent to see them through. There is a strong pro-Gentile reference—a reference to the Gentiles being open to God's message—present in the gospel's mention of both Naaman the Syrian and the widow of Zarephath. It must be remembered that by the time Luke's gospel was written, Chris-tianity was well on its way to becoming a Gentile religion.

Both Jeremiah and Jesus had to preach God's word to ears that were deaf. What was true in biblical times is no less true today. People are so convinced of their point of view that they become militant in defending it. There is no room for fruitful dis-cussion. There seems to be an inherent fear of being drawn to the opposite side. It is well to remember that it was people's preconceptions and hardness of heart that brought Jesus to his death. "Lord, give me a willing heart and an open ear lest I miss you as you pass by."

Paul's great ode to love is appropriately read today. Love makes all things possible and strikes down division. It was the love of a sinful woman that broke with all convention in anointing the feet of Jesus. And there is the oft-told love of an offended father, expressed in his embrace of a prodigal son. It was a hated Samaritan who brought a

PSALM REFLECTION

This psalm expresses the positive counterpoint to the story of Jeremiah's rejection by his own people and their leaders, and to the story of Jesus' rejection at Nazareth. If you have nowhere on earth among your family and closest friends to find support, where do you turn? The constant answer in the psalms is that you turn to God, who is your only sure rock, refuge, stronghold, and fortress. Psalm 71 is a treasure chest of expressions for trust in God alone. It is a particularly fitting psalm to follow Jeremiah's call story because it too suggests that God has called the psalmist to learn this lesson from before his birth and summoned him to proclaim God's salvation and justice to the nations. Certainly Jesus himself must have meditated on both these passages as a youth and come to realize that they expressed so well the very mission that his Father had sent him to perform. One can imagine the many Sabbaths on which Jesus had recited Psalm 71 as he slowly grew in awareness of his mission.

Psalm Response
Psalm 71:1–2, 3–4, 5–6, 15–17

Antiphon
I will sing of your salvation.

Verse for Reflection
I will speak of the mighty works of the Lord
And, God, tell of your wonderful justice!
(v. 16)

CATECHETICAL SUGGESTIONS

Call stories
Go and Make Disciples (NCCB document)
The theological virtues
The fruits of the Spirit
The role of a prophet
Elijah and Elisha in the Old Testament and in the New Testament

broken and bruised man to an inn on the road.

Paul speaks of love today in three ways. First, love gives meaning to all the other virtues. Good actions can be performed for a variety of reasons. But when framed in love, their meaning becomes distinct and clear.

Second, love is positive. It is kind, patient, generous, forthright, enduring, and full of trust. It rejoices in the truth.

Finally, love surpasses all other virtues, even though it plays a part in all of them. Among the three theological virtues of faith, hope, and love, it is love that is in first place. Augustine put it well: "Love God and do what you will."

At times the Church appears all too human. It suffers from the same kinds of polarization that mark society as a whole. But how sad it is—and what a poor witness to the world we are—when we let issues divide us. It was once said, "Behold these Christians, how they love one another." Today it is all too frequently, "Behold, these Christians are at it again."

Angry people brought Jesus to the edge of a cliff in order to throw him over. It is love that brings people today from the brink of disaster to an embrace of love and concern. There is a worthy motto: "Seek unity; end division."

LITURGICAL NOTES

The people are amazed that this Jesus from Nazareth teaches with authority. Even the unclean spirits obey him. Their amazement comes in part from low expectations. Anyone who works with children or young people could assure you that low expectations will certainly lead to insignificant results. As the planning team continues to reflect on the place of children and young people, its members should be aware that low expectations can stifle or kill any potential for involvement and engagement.

In every parish there are children and young people with

**Second Reading: 1 Corinthians 12:31—13:13
(or 1 Corinthians13:4–13)**

Brothers and sisters: Strive eagerly for the greatest spiritual gifts. But I shall show you a still more excellent way.

If I speak in human and angelic tongues, but do not have love, I am a resounding gong or a clashing cymbal. And if I have the gift of prophecy, and comprehend all mysteries and all knowledge; if I have all faith so as to move mountains, but do not have love, I am nothing. If I give away everything I own, and if I hand my body over so that I may boast, but do not have love, I gain nothing.

Love is patient, love is kind. It is not jealous, it is not pompous, It is not inflated, it is not rude, it does not seek its own interests, it is not quick-tempered, it does not brood over injury, it does not rejoice over wrongdoing but rejoices with the truth. It bears all things, believes all things, hopes all things, endures all things. Love never fails. If there are prophecies, they will be brought to nothing; if tongues, they will cease; if knowledge, it will be brought to nothing. For we know partially and we prophesy partially, but when the perfect comes, the partial will pass away. When I was a child, I used to talk as a child, think as a child, reason as a child; when I became a man, I put aside childish things. At present we see indistinctly, as in a mirror, but then face to face. At present I know partially; then I shall know fully, as I am fully known. So faith, hope, love remain, these three; but the greatest of these is love.

SCRIPTURE COMMENTARY

In the readings of the last two Sundays, Paul has developed at some length his idea of the ordinary range of spiritual gifts. Many of them, such as tongues and prophetic utterance, are expressed only as parts of liturgical worship. Others are practical tasks of leadership in small church communities: preachers, teachers, apostles, and evangelists. Now Paul turns to love as a unique gift of the Spirit, a gift that can be developed by every single member of the community. This greatest of the gifts is not for the few. It is the common gift given to all believers, as are its partners, faith and hope. All three of these last beyond the practical moment because they directly tie us to the covenant relationship with God—we know him, we love him, we trust and rely fully upon him. When we do good things, they last for a time, but they gradually fade away and we must do more. But as we develop a deeper oneness with God through the love of Christ, we can share and support our unity with each other primarily through mutual love—that is why it is the greatest of the gifts. Love never values what it gets for itself but only what it can give to others; it never breaks down relationships but always builds more.

extraordinary gifts and talents, coupled with a tremendous desire to use those gifts for the service of others. These gifts and talents need to be not only recognized but cultivated. A visit to any local school will demonstrate the breadth of talent and ability in young people: from music, to drama, to all the arts, to huge, welcoming smiles. Those who work with children or young people readily attest to the fact that there is more than a willingness to learn, but there is also an equal expectation that there will be a willingness to listen. Perhaps the youth minister or one of the catechetical leaders could assist in bringing forward the initial round of children/young people

to be involved in various ministries, along with providing suggestions regarding time, approaches, and methods of training.

While the Sunday assembly will welcome the presence of these "younger ministers," the reception they will receive from the other ministers might not be as welcoming. While training and formation are taking place for the young, those already engaged in the various ministries should also be catechized and prepared to welcome new members to their ranks.

This week begins the celebration of Catholic Schools Week. The liturgy guides and notes, available from the United States

Conference of Catholic Bishops in Washington, DC, integrate the mission and ministry of the Catholic school into the Sunday liturgy. Care should be taken that the theme of Catholic schools does not overtake the liturgy, nor should this be a weekend on which planners surrender the Sunday celebrations of the Eucharist to a particular "theme." In many places, the occurrence of Catholic Schools Week and its liturgical celebrations will provide planners with ideal opportunities to see children engaged in prayer and worship, to see them actively participate in a variety of ministries, and to allow them to become connected to the larger ministry within the parish.

SCRIPTURE COMMENTARY

The gospel today continues the drama that began in the synagogue at Nazareth in last Sunday's reading when Jesus announced that he would himself fulfill the promise of Isaiah 61 that a new messianic age had come. Had the story stopped where we ended last week, we could imagine that the audience would have been delighted with Jesus' words, seeing that he might push a plan for liberation from the Romans or at least intend a career ahead as a faith healer and miracle worker. But the continuation that Luke reports in today's reading stands in stark contrast to Isaiah's optimism. Jesus announces that he cannot do miracles in Nazareth because they will reject him as a prophet, and that his mission is really to the pagans. He cites the stories of Elijah and Elisha, who worked their major miracles not for Israelites but for Phoenicians and Arameans. The congregation is furious. When Jesus announces he will do more for outsiders than for his own people, they realize that he is not going to answer their dreams. And they certainly will not accept his. As a result, in his very first preaching of his "good news," he stirs up serious opposition. His very own circle of friends and perhaps relatives are ready to kill him now, and he has just begun his work. For Luke, the crucifixion is already the certain end when Jesus' own town will not receive him even at the beginning.

Gospel: Luke 4:21–30

Jesus began speaking in the synagogue, saying: "Today this Scripture passage is fulfilled in your hearing." And all spoke highly of him and were amazed at the gracious words that came from his mouth. They also asked, "Isn't this the son of Joseph?" He said to them, "Surely you will quote me this proverb, 'Physician, cure yourself,' and say, 'Do here in your native place the things that we heard were done in Capernaum.'" And he said, "Amen, I say to you, no prophet is accepted in his own native place. Indeed, I tell you, there were many widows in Israel in the days of Elijah when the sky was closed for three and a half years and a severe famine spread over the entire land. It was to none of these that Elijah was sent, but only to a widow in Zarephath in the land of Sidon. Again, there were many lepers in Israel during the time of Elisha the prophet; yet not one of them was cleansed, but only Naaman the Syrian." When the people in the synagogue heard this, they were all filled with fury. They rose up, drove him out of the town, and led him to the brow of the hill on which their town had been built, to hurl him down headlong. But Jesus passed through the midst of them and went away.

MUSIC CONNECTION

Both Jeremiah and Luke deal with the vocation of the prophet. From Jeremiah we learn that the prophet is chosen by God from the first moments of life—a conviction voiced in settings of Psalm 139, including Schutte's popular *You Are Near* and Farrell's moving *O God, You Search Me.* Luke's pithy phrase that "no prophet is accepted in his own native place" points to the struggle of all prophetic voices to announce God's will while suffering the indignation and rejection of close friends and relatives. Hymns such as *God Has Spoken by His Prophets, The Church of Christ in Every Age, What Is This Place,* and *Take the Word of God with You* highlight that the prophetic call is not a past event but an ever-recurring vocation for all disciples. Psalm 71 finds good expression in settings by Marchionda and Currie. There are few passages in the New Testament better recognized than the paean to love from Paul's letter to the Corinthians. Almost de rigueur at Christian weddings, this passage creates another rich trajectory for the homilist and musician at today's liturgy. Hopson's *The Gift of Love* and Dudley-Smith's *May Love Be Ours* grow directly out of Corinthians while other hymns such as *What Wondrous Love, No Greater Love,* and *Love Is His Word* strive to convey the centrality of love in the Judeo-Christian message.

First Reading:
Isaiah 6:1–2a, 3–8

In the year King Uzziah died, I saw the Lord seated on a high and lofty throne, with the train of his garment filling the temple. Seraphim were stationed above.

They cried one to the other, "Holy, holy, holy is the LORD of hosts! All the earth is filled with his glory!" At the sound of that cry, the frame of the door shook and the house was filled with smoke.

Then I said, "Woe is me, I am doomed! For I am a man of unclean lips, living among a people of unclean lips; yet my eyes have seen the King, the LORD of hosts!" Then one of the seraphim flew to me, holding an ember that he had taken with tongs from the altar.

He touched my mouth with it, and said, "See, now that this has

SCRIPTURE COMMENTARY

Isaiah inserts the account of his call to be a prophet in chapter 6, just before beginning the story of his encounter with King Ahaz. The king will refuse to receive the prophetic message of Isaiah that he must disarm and trust that God will deliver him from the hands of his enemies. Isaiah will appear to be badly defeated in fulfilling God's task, but instead of simply going away, he will have the courage to threaten the end of Ahaz in favor of a better king whom God will raise up and who will heed God's word in every way. This helps us make sense of this vision. God himself directly intervenes in Isaiah's life to commission him. Isaiah is apparently in the temple court facing the temple doors and can see the smoke of the incense and the gleam of the golden vessels in the dark interior. He suddenly has a vision of the throne of God within, as though transported to the heavenly throne room itself. The terrible and mighty seraphim angels are thundering the divine praises, and Isaiah realizes he cannot stand on his own power in the divine presence. This humbling moment also makes him recognize his own sinfulness and unworthiness. However, his role is not to be determined by his abilities or power or self-worth but by God's summons—and so he is purified by holy fire from the altar of offerings itself and God gives him the spirit that

HOMILY HELPS

"Do not be afraid; from now on you will be catching men." At one time, during Sunday Mass, I decided to broaden the personal reference: "…you will be catching men and women." It sounded awkward, but at least it was inclusive. After Mass, a woman who was an English professor promptly insisted that my good intentions had been misdirected. The expression was hardly good form, and a very traditional expression was distorted.

There is another problem. There are those who feel distinctly uncomfortable in being

compared to fish, or, for that matter, sheep. However, in their Palestinian context, such expressions have a striking validity. A fishing trip is, in fact, an ingathering, a bringing together. It points to the fact that we have a faith to be shared—not by coercion or proselytism but by extending this greatest proof of God's love to others, always with the hope that it will make a difference to them. Fishing, in this sense, is nothing more than faith sharing.

What is the heart of this fishing expedition? What do we have to share? In Paul's message to the Corinthians we are presented with the fundamental truth of the Christian life. Christ died for us, was buried, rose on

the third day, and appeared to Peter, then to the Twelve, and others. It was the faith acceptance of this truth that was central; everything else was secondary and subsequent. In this summary, it should be noted that Paul makes mention of both the Twelve and other apostles, showing conclusively that there were apostles beyond the Twelve. The Pauline criterion for apostleship was to be commissioned by the risen Christ, whether or not one had been with him during his earthly ministry.

Whether those in ministry in the Church are called fishermen or shepherds makes little difference. Like Isaiah in the first reading, they are called and are

SCRIPTURE COMMENTARY, CONTINUED

enables him to say, "Yes! I will go!" He will need all the strength God will bestow in order to face the task ahead when his words will be rejected, yet he must continue to challenge the king and people to change their ways.

touched your lips, your wickedness is removed, your sin purged."

Then I heard the voice of the Lord saying, "Whom shall I send? Who will go for us?" "Here I am," I said; "send me!"

PSALM REFLECTION

This psalm describes the typical worship scene in the Jerusalem temple. The psalmist comes with his prayer to God, whether it is a plea for health or help or is a thank offering required for purification or at the birth of a child. When he receives the priest's blessing or perhaps just feels that God is answering him positively, he gives thanks and sings hymns of praise and presents whatever the required offerings would be in the situation. This moment of gratitude leads the psalmist to praise God for all the benefits he bestows on the earth and its peoples and to call upon all the pagan rulers to join him in praising God's goodness. The psalm ends with a statement of absolute confidence in God. The praises of God's glory shining forth from the temple link this psalm to the same setting as the first reading.

Psalm Response
Psalm 138:1–2, 2–3, 4–5, 7–8

Antiphon
In the sight of the angels I will sing
 your praises, Lord.

Verse for Reflection
The Lord will complete what he has
 done for me;
Your kindness, O Lord, endures forever. (v. 8)

expected to give that willing answer, "Here I am, send me." One of their tasks is to take biblical images and bring them to life in a modern context. The basic idea of the shepherd, for example, is to care and provide for others in the sharing of the gospel message.

But there is another important message in the fishing narrative. It was Jesus who brought success to the mission. We succeed and sometimes we seem to fail. But it is the Lord's work that we are doing, and the outcome depends on him. God directs things in ways that we often do not understand. In difficult moments we

should entrust ourselves to the Lord and leave the outcome to him. If we act in faith, we never really fail.

There are many truths of our faith, but not all things are of equal importance. The truths advanced by Paul today are truly fundamental, admitting of neither compromise nor dilution. They express succinctly the heart of Christ's mission. At times we are so lost in secondary issues that we "lose sight of the forest for the trees." Paul's summary, which appears also elsewhere in the New Testament, stands at the very heart of our relationship with the living Christ.

LITURGICAL NOTES

The scriptures all speak, in one way or another, of the call of God to follow, to do God's will, to listen to God's voice. Those who are called are not always those whom we might expect to be called; in some cases, their talents and abilities have yet to come to light. But they are present, and God will use them. Doubt, fear, unworthiness, sinfulness—none of these can stand in the way of the call of God.

As members of the planning team look for additional liturgical

**Second Reading: 1 Corinthians 15:1–11
(or 1 Corinthians 15:3–8, 11)**

I am reminding you, brothers and sisters, of the gospel I preached to you, which you indeed received and in which you also stand. Through it you are also being saved, if you hold fast to the word I preached to you, unless you believed in vain. For I handed on to you as of first importance what I also received: that Christ died for our sins in accordance with the Scriptures; that he was buried; that he was raised on the third day in accordance with the Scriptures; that he appeared to Cephas, then to the Twelve. After that, Christ appeared to more than five hundred brothers at once, most of whom are still living, though some have fallen asleep. After that he appeared to James, then to all the apostles. Last of all, as to one born abnormally, he appeared to me. For I am the least of the apostles, not fit to be called an apostle, because I persecuted the church of God. But by the grace of God I am what I am, and his grace to me has not been ineffective. Indeed, I have toiled harder than all of them; not I, however, but the grace of God that is with me. Therefore, whether it be I or they, so we preach and so you believed.

SCRIPTURE COMMENTARY

After three weeks of hearing about the spiritual gifts, we now turn to Paul's treatment of the resurrection of Jesus. We can see how differently he treats this topic and how he considers it to be of grave importance because of the way he changes his line of argument. Up to now he has discussed the existence and the role of the different spiritual gifts bestowed by the Holy Spirit by arguing that we all experience these gifts at the present moment in the Church. There is no need to prove they are important; we can each know them directly in some way *now*. But when Paul turns to the resurrection, he lays out all the historical evidence he has at his disposal. He traces all the witnesses that he has heard about and adds his own testimony to theirs. Usually Paul takes his stand directly on what God has revealed to him, but here he associates himself closely with the tradition of the Church as the basis of his authority. We will hear in the weeks ahead of how he understands the power of the resurrection for *our* lives, but in this first part of his enormous chapter (58 verses long!), he lays out three points of major importance about the fact of Jesus' resurrection: (1) Paul did not originate this teaching but is passing on what is taught by all the apostles; (2) the death of Christ was not just another good man's end—it was the fulfillment of God's salvation promised by the prophets to heal the guilt of our sins; and (3) this is verified by the testimony of the most credible of all witnesses, the apostles that Jesus himself chose—of which Paul is just the last and least!

---

ministers or people to assist in some of the "behind the scenes" preparation work for the celebration, be careful not to narrow the field too much. Search out those hidden talents; be specific in voicing needs or the particular kind of assistance that is sought.

Team members ought to be mindful of the fact that there are many hidden treasures within our assemblies. It might be easier to find people who have the gifts to read, to sing, to minister to the liturgical assembly within the liturgical assembly. But there are other gifts that are also needed to ensure the full, conscious, and active participation of all within the liturgy.

For example, many young people are more adept at the computer than some adults could ever be. They could certainly place their talents at the service of parish worship in the design and layout of participation aids and booklets, of flyers, of information that can regularly and attractively be posted on the parish website. Specific advertising, conversation with youth ministers, catechists, and others who work with young people can certainly help both broaden the search and yield good results.

Since today's liturgy speaks so clearly to the call to follow, there ought to be specific mention in the General Intercessions of the call to follow in the priesthood, the consecrated life, the diaconate, and all ministries within the Church. Not only should there be mention of an increase in those ministries; there should also be an intention for those currently engaged in those ministries. This Sunday also provides an opportunity for recruitment for ministries and an explanation of how these various ministries can be a concrete response to the call of Christ.

SCRIPTURE COMMENTARY

Many of the small scenes in this story of the call of the first apostles from among the fishermen on the Sea of Galilee remind us of Isaiah's call. In both, an event that could easily be miraculous makes the person realize his unworthiness when called. But he is reassured that God will guide him and strengthen him, and he accepts the call. Before this moment (in chapter 4 with its stories of Jesus' first public works), Jesus moved about largely alone, preaching in different synagogues. But he must already have known Simon and his friends, for he had cured Simon's mother-in-law as one of those early acts. Peter does not seem to have any objection to Jesus' using his boat as a pulpit to preach to the crowds. Indeed, the three fishermen, Peter, James and John, must have been deeply enough impressed to obey without question the request by Jesus that they go back to fishing. As a result, the astounding catch makes them permanent believers in Jesus. From this moment on, these three will become his core witnesses and partners, whom Jesus will keep close to him at critical moments such as at the transfiguration and on his last night in the garden of Gethsemane. Opposition to him in the synagogues was already strong, as we saw in last week's gospel, so Jesus decides to work in a new way to reach people directly on the roads and village squares where they are eager to hear his message. The apostles will need all the strength God grants to them so that they can accompany Jesus.

Gospel: Luke 5:1–11

While the crowd was pressing in on Jesus and listening to the word of God, he was standing by the Lake of Gennesaret. He saw two boats there alongside the lake; the fishermen had disembarked and were washing their nets. Getting into one of the boats, the one belonging to Simon, he asked him to put out a short distance from the shore. Then he sat down and taught the crowds from the boat. After he had finished speaking, he said to Simon, "Put out into deep water and lower your nets for a catch." Simon said in reply, "Master, we have worked hard all night and have caught nothing, but at your command I will lower the nets." When they had done this, they caught a great number of fish and their nets were tearing. They signaled to their partners in the other boat to come to help them. They came and filled both boats so that the boats were in danger of sinking. When Simon Peter saw this, he fell at the knees of Jesus and said, "Depart from me, Lord, for I am a sinful man." For astonishment at the catch of fish they had made seized him and all those with him, and likewise James and John, the sons of Zebedee, who were partners of Simon. Jesus said to Simon, "Do not be afraid; from now on you will be catching men." When they brought their boats to the shore, they left everything and followed him.

CATECHETICAL SUGGESTIONS

The Bible in liturgical prayers
Isaiah: call, setting, theme
Angels in the Old Testament and in the New Testament
Psalms of thanksgiving
The kerygma
Peter's preeminence in Luke and Acts

MUSIC CONNECTION

The classic theophany recounted by Isaiah in the first reading has given rise to several hymns as well as the acclamation embedded in our eucharistic prayers. The most celebrated setting is, for sure, the text by Heber in the hymn *Holy, Holy, Holy*. Schutte's *Here I Am, Lord* has become a staple of contemporary hymnody in focusing on Isaiah's faith-filled response to God's invitation: "Here I am, send me." This classic passage of call and response directs our gaze to the Lucan gospel account of Jesus' calling of Simon and his fishing colleagues at the Sea of Galilee. The totality of commitment evidenced by Isaiah is echoed in the response of Simon, James, and John, who "brought their boats to shore … left everything and followed him." The Lucan phrase "Do not be afraid" finds musical expression in Dufford's *Be Not Afraid* and Haas's *You Are Mine*. The shoreline setting and exchange are aptly conveyed by Dunston in *You Walk along Our Shoreline*, Toolan in her *Two Fishermen*, and Gabaraín in *Pescador de Hombres*, which appears in bilingual fashion in most hymnals. Finally, the responsorial, Psalm 138, is well presented by Bolduc, Carroll/ Gelineau, and Guimont.

First Reading: Jeremiah 17:5–8

Thus says the LORD:
　Cursed is the one who trusts in
　　human beings,
　　who seeks his strength in flesh,
　　whose heart turns away from the
　　　LORD.
　He is like a barren bush in the
　　desert
　　that enjoys no change of season,
　but stands in a lava waste,
　　a salt and empty earth.
　Blessed is the one who trusts in the
　　LORD,
　　whose hope is the LORD.
　He is like a tree planted beside the
　　waters
　　that stretches out its roots to the
　　　stream:
　it fears not the heat when it comes;
　　its leaves stay green;
　in the year of drought it shows no
　　distress,
　　but still bears fruit.

SCRIPTURE COMMENTARY

Jeremiah 17 as a whole is a fierce polemic against idolatry, that is, the worship of the gods of foreign nations. The covenant is engraved on the hearts of the Israelites with a diamond-tipped pen—so it cannot be erased! They must never forget their loyalty belongs to God alone. In this context, there is a stark contrast between the person who relies on the Lord alone for his or her strength and the one who relies on personal human achievements and honor and his or her own strength. The first is blessed, the second cursed; one will flourish even in bad times with God's favor; the other will be barren and fruitless. The imagery is drawn from the harsh desert landscape of Judea itself. Dry tumbleweed is scattered across the dead, hard hills, contrasting with the stately and lonely great tree that stands near one of the few springs or permanent wadis. Although we don't read them today, verses 9–10, which conclude this section, sum up the lesson well: "More twisted than anything is the human heart—beyond healing, who can understand it? Just I, the Lord, who probe the heart and test the heart, to reward each person according to his or her deeds!"

HOMILY HELPS

Today, as much as at any time in history, the world is divided into the "haves" and "have-nots." This is seen clearly in the stark difference between the affluent West and the poverty of much of Africa. There are some cities in the world that are little more than giant slums. There are rural communities that make their livelihood with farming tools that were in use in biblical times. This is all compounded by droughts, wars, and racial massacres. In India there are people subsisting on one bowl of rice a day, while in the affluent countries, shopping malls multi-ply with merchandise that far surpasses moderate needs. There are whole sections of supermarkets that carry a vast variety of pet foods. It is possible to spend as much on a dinner party as some fellow humans earn in a year.

The scriptures today center on antitheses. Luke's beatitudes differ from Matthew's inasmuch as they look to very concrete human and social categories and are less given to spiritual elaboration. The Lucan Jesus speaks of those who are the real poor, hungry, and sorrowful and contrasts them with the rich, the well fed, and the merrymakers. The former are favored by God, while the latter face a bleak future.

Jeremiah has his own antithesis, using plant life as imagery for the human condition. The tree in its verdant splendor is close to the river with an ample supply of water; the bush, on the other hand, is planted in a wasted and arid desert with no sustenance to assure growth. It is clearly illustrative of human choices, with some placing their whole trust in God, and others, in human pursuits.

A careful reading of Paul's message today helps us bridge these antitheses. It is the resurrection of Christ that makes all the difference. No resurrection, no Holy Spirit. A risen Christ means a Spirit-filled Christian. To believe in the risen Christ and to place

PSALM REFLECTION

The psalm uses the same metaphor as did Jeremiah 17 in the first reading. But here the subject is not the idolater but the broader contrast between those who live according to God's Torah and those who disobey and refuse to follow God's commands. The just person does not only keep the commandments in daily living but goes further, meditating on the law in his or her heart as a way of knowing God more deeply and growing in divine love. The law establishes a relationship of mutual love and respect between God and ourselves. Like the tree that stands for decades in its strength because it constantly draws on the waters of the stream, so the one who lives in God's presence and guards his thinking always finds the strength that is needed for life.

Psalm Response
Psalm 1:1–2, 3, 4 and 6

Antiphon
Blessed are they who hope in the Lord.

Verse for Reflection
The Lord watches over the way of the just;
But the way of the wicked perishes. (v. 6)

CATECHETICAL SUGGESTIONS

Parallelism in Hebrew poetry
Beatitudes in the Old Testament
The resurrection: core Christian belief
Ramifications of the resurrection for Christian life and choices
The commandments compared to the beatitudes
The kingdom of God: present and future

---

our trust in him is to be the tree planted near living water. This means that we are outfitted to bridge the gap between rich and poor. We are ill at ease with social inequality and find ways, even though modest, to bring about a just society both at home and abroad. Examples abound today that are more than ample proof of this. A group of Christian people fund, support, and sustain a private school for underprivileged minority children in a large city, with remarkable results. In another case, a prominent artist volunteers each week to teach gifted poor children how to paint.

There are "big brothers" and "big sisters" who give of their time generously to help seriously disadvantaged youth. Some major pharmaceutical companies have worked to overcome barriers to bringing important medical drugs, in a cost-effective way, to needy countries.

Christ reminds us that the poor we will have always with us. They are the beloved of God. But blessed are those who seek to bridge the gap. They reach out to the poor, the hungry, and the weeping. The truth is that prayers are said not only on one's knees. To touch the neediest is also to pray.

LITURGICAL NOTES

The reading from the book of the prophet Jeremiah and the Lucan beatitudes present us with a series of blessings and curses. Those who cling to the Lord, who allow nothing to stand in their way, are the ones who are truly blessed.

Our ministries are not designed for our own edification but rather to build up the body of Christ. Too often ministers and potential ministers, young or old, allow all the reasons "not to serve" to stand in their way. Reg-

Second Reading:
1 Corinthians 15:12, 16–20

Brothers and sisters: If Christ is preached as raised from the dead, how can some among you say there is no resurrection of the dead? If the dead are not raised, neither has Christ been raised, and if Christ has not been raised, your faith is vain; you are still in your sins. Then those who have fallen asleep in Christ have perished. If for this life only we have hoped in Christ, we are the most pitiable people of all.

But now Christ has been raised from the dead, the first-fruits of those who have fallen asleep.

SCRIPTURE COMMENTARY

Again this week we continue to read Paul's chapter on the resurrection and its effects on us as Jesus' followers even after his leaving us. Paul reflects on the eternal meaning of the resurrection, not just for Jesus being raised but for its real meaning as the conquest of the power of death itself. Paul makes the link to us very tight: if Jesus rose, then it is certain that we will rise with him one day. He argues that God would have had no purpose in raising Jesus back to our life were it not for our sake, to deliver us from death to life. Indeed, Paul says, if we cannot believe in the resurrection and its power over death for us, then we will not be convinced of the second reality, the forgiveness of our sins. Only God can forgive our sins to make us able to be united with him through the resurrection of his Son. Our faith does not free us from the powerful effects of sin and death while we cope in this life, but it gives us the certainty to know that we will truly pass from death to life with Christ, now in the life of faith and someday in our very bodies.

ular encouragement ought to be given to remain open to God's workings within each of us.

The children and young people who may have surfaced as potential ministers will no doubt need some special attention and some special training. But their training and ongoing formation should not be so separate from that of the other ministers that they seem in a class by themselves. The idea is not to create a separate track of ministers but to see these younger people as coworkers in building up the kingdom.

Lent is only two weeks away. Preparations should be in order, and the bulletin ought to contain ample information about the opportunities that the Lenten discipline sets before us for prayer, fasting, and works of charity. It is always helpful to repeat the norms concerning fasting and abstinence during the season of Lent.

Lent is a period of preparation for Easter. The question of how we will use this season of preparation to renew our baptismal promises at Easter looms large. Many of the Lenten practices of our tradition could serve as a fitting subject for catechesis. In what ways should we pray? How do we pray? Why fast? What ought we to fast from? What might be some concrete examples of works of charity that we could perform?

Parishes might find it helpful to provide suggestions on how individuals and the community can celebrate the season of Lent. Some parishes hold a Friday evening soup supper, followed by Stations of the Cross. Others choose to have every parish activity begin in the church with prayer. There ought to be both personal and communal opportunities to celebrate this season. It will also be helpful to provide

SCRIPTURE COMMENTARY

Today's gospel is Luke's parallel to the beatitudes in the Sermon on the Mount in the Gospel of Matthew (Matt 5:1–12). Matthew makes the sermon three chapters long and concentrates many of Jesus' basic demands for true discipleship in one place. Luke breaks these up and spreads them through different parts of his gospel, but he does preserve the same type of setting for the giving of the beatitudes, namely, that Jesus saw the crowds were hungry for teaching about God and willing to be challenged. In Matthew, Jesus insists they take the extra step and go beyond bare obedience to the law to excel in mercy and compassion as God himself does. Luke makes this an even more radical demand: disciples must give up all hope of satisfaction in this life and accept persecution as their fate, knowing that God will reward them in the life to come. Moreover, those who choose wealth or honor in this life will not receive the blessings of God's kingdom to come. Those who give up all things as Jesus did, however, will be richly blessed. In this, the starkness of Jesus' message as presented by Luke is similar to that in the message of Jeremiah in today's first reading.

Gospel: Luke 6:17, 20–26

Jesus came down with the twelve and stood on a stretch of level ground with a great crowd of his disciples and a large number of the people from all Judea and Jerusalem and the coastal region of Tyre and Sidon.

And raising his eyes toward his disciples he said:
"Blessed are you who are poor,
for the kingdom of God is yours.
Blessed are you who are now hungry,
for you will be satisfied.
Blessed are you who are now weeping,
for you will laugh.
Blessed are you when people hate you,
and when they exclude and insult you,
and denounce your name as evil
on account of the Son of Man.
Rejoice and leap for joy on that day! Behold, your reward will be great in heaven. For their ancestors treated the prophets in the same way.
But woe to you who are rich,
for you have received your consolation.
Woe to you who are filled now,
for you will be hungry.
Woe to you who laugh now,
for you will grieve and weep.
Woe to you when all speak well of you,
for their ancestors treated the false
prophets in this way."

materials for use during Lent to the extraordinary ministers of Holy Communion who bring the Eucharist to the sick and homebound.

Liturgy committees might consider asking people to bring last year's palms to church next Sunday so that they can be burned and used as ashes on Ash Wednesday. Even when people are not part of the actual burning of the palms, bringing them back to church helps people make a connection with the liturgical year and their participation in it.

MUSIC CONNECTION

The biblical imagery from Jeremiah ties directly into the responsorial psalm's tree "planted near running water." The image is meant to convey steadfastness and faithfulness. Psalm 1 finds good expression in settings by French, Gelineau, and Alstott. The second reading from Corinthians, with its reasoned discussion of Christ's resurrection, suggests certain Easter hymn texts such as *I Am the Bread of Life, Jesus Christ Is Risen Today,* and *Jesus Is Risen.* The Pauline stress on faith suggests Alford's classic text *We Walk by Faith,* and Haugen's setting is accessible and stirring. The gospel reading, sometimes referred to as Jesus' sermon on the plain, with its parallel structure of blessings and woes, complements the first reading's juxtaposition of "Cursed is the man…" and "Blessed is the man…" Haas's setting of the beatitudes from Matthew, *Blest Are They,* is certainly appropriate today, as is Becker's pulsating and popular *Lead Me, Lord.* The prolific composer Richard Proulx also provides a slightly more difficult setting of the Matthean pericope in his *O Blessed Are the Poor in Spirit.*

First Reading:
1 Samuel 26:2, 7–9, 12–13, 22–23

In those days, Saul went down to the desert of Ziph with three thousand picked men of Israel, to search for David in the desert of Ziph. So David and Abishai went among Saul's soldiers by night and found Saul lying asleep within the barricade, with his spear thrust into the ground at his head and Abner and his men sleeping around him.

Abishai whispered to David: "God has delivered your enemy into your grasp this day. Let me nail him to the ground with one thrust of the spear; I will not need a second thrust!" But David said to Abishai, "Do not harm him, for who can lay hands on the LORD's anointed and remain unpunished?" So David took the spear and the water jug from their place at Saul's head, and they got away without anyone's seeing or knowing or awakening. All remained asleep, because the LORD had put them into a deep slumber.

Going across to an opposite slope, David stood on a remote hilltop at a great distance from Abner, son of Ner, and the troops. He said:

SCRIPTURE COMMENTARY

The dramatic story of how David gets the better of King Saul takes up all of chapter 26 in the first book of Samuel. In our reading we get the highlights only. If we had the whole chapter before us, we would see just how relentlessly Saul hunted David down, and how, through his resourcefulness, David always stayed one step ahead. Saul's considerable army is now deep in the Judean wilderness. David invites Abishai, the brother of his loyal general Joab, to make a bold effort to convince Saul that David really was a loyal servant. They go down in the middle of the night, get close enough to kill the king, but only take his most precious sign of authority, his very spear to defend himself, and get up to a hill far enough away to be safe. By managing this act, David has shamed Saul and shown he has God's blessing. But David had also spared the king when he could have killed him, and Saul realizes no enemy would have been that merciful. David is proven a person of justice

HOMILY HELPS

The ten commandments and what they require are basic to normal life in society. Stealing and cursing are forbidden; fidelity in marriage is basic to well-founded family life. Respect for parents and for the rights of others is normative and clearly understandable. Recognition of God and neighbor is basic to a well-ordered society. In our first reading today, David's respect for the king excludes any form of violence while he sleeps. The king is, after all, the first in the realm; even if he is an avowed enemy, he is worthy of respect.

The Christian ethic builds on this form of morality and carries it further. The sermon on the plain, read in part today, parallels Matthew's Sermon on the Mount. Both sermons cite examples of the Christian response to situations of daily life. Enemies are not simply to be tolerated; they are to be loved. Our response to insult is not retaliation. In short, evil is to be overcome not by distancing oneself but by using the power of love.

When it comes to personal assets, society safeguards our interests. This is the meaning of debts, loans, or other forms of restitution. But the Christian has a certain disinterest and should give out of love, with little concern for the "pound of flesh." In the Christian vision, everything we have is on loan, and none of

SCRIPTURE COMMENTARY, CONTINUED

and righteousness, and is certainly loyal to the king. Although it is left out of the reading, Saul confesses his wrong and asks David's forgiveness in the final verse of the chapter.

"Here is the king's spear. Let an attendant come over to get it. The LORD will reward each man for his justice and faithfulness. Today, though the LORD delivered you into my grasp, I would not harm the LORD's anointed."

PSALM REFLECTION

Psalm 103 is a psalm of divine glory that soars to heights of praise for God's faithfulness in love, his *hesed*, a word we often translate as "enduring love." The first half of the psalm that we read today piles up attributes of God that reveal his love for us. In the first four verses God is said to bestow prosperity, forgive sins, heal wounds, save from death, and treat us with compassion. In the next six verses, the psalmist repeats these things all over again in new ways. Throughout, the key word is *hesed*. It is usually associated with the obligation to love someone, as fathers or mothers or children or spouses or good friends have. It relates to our love of God because God freely chose to enter into a love relationship with us through the covenant he made. The covenant is a bond of relationship that obligates both sides to act in love. God remains faithful in his care and mercy; we remain faithful (hopefully) in doing justice and in being faithful and obedient to his law. These are the very qualities said of David in the first reading!

Psalm Response
Psalm 103:1–2, 3–4, 8, 10, 12–13

Antiphon
The Lord is kind and merciful.

Verse for Reflection
The Lord is merciful and kind;
Slow to anger and rich in faithful
    love. (v. 8)

---

us is a real proprietor. Therefore we should be generous and willing to give without measure.

In the face of misconduct, we are to leave justice to the courts. The Christian response is always to be one of compassion. In the face of moral failure, we are to let God be the judge. In the face of personal hurt, hostility is not an appropriate response; forgiveness and pardon are.

Christian ethical demands are not difficult to comprehend. They are, in fact, almost too clear. And in our examination of conscience, we realize that we fall

short. The letter to Corinth reminds us today that the children of Adam have to live within the bounds of a society ordered by basic moral values. But the descendants of the second Adam, the risen Christ, must live by higher standards. Why? Because we are empowered by a Spirit that makes all things possible. But do our lives make this evident? Of the early Christians it was said: "Behold how they love one another." The world will be far better off when the same can be said of us.

LITURGICAL NOTES

As we stand on the threshold of Lent, the scripture readings invite us to do more than that which is required. To walk the extra mile seems to be the task of the Christian.

In the past few weeks of working with children and young people, their generosity has been obvious. Their willingness to "go that extra mile" is apparent in their willingness to want to do the right thing and to do it well. Young people can and will continue to stand

**Second Reading:
1 Corinthians 15:45–49**

Brothers and sisters: It is written, *The first man, Adam, became a living being*, the last Adam a life-giving spirit. But the spiritual was not first; rather the natural and then the spiritual. The first man was from the earth, earthly; the second man, from heaven. As was the earthly one, so also are the earthly, and as is the heavenly one, so also are the heavenly. Just as we have borne the image of the earthly one, we shall also bear the image of the heavenly one.

SCRIPTURE COMMENTARY

Paul moves beyond his declaration in last Sunday's section of chapter 15 where he insisted that Jesus rose from death to deliver us from death and sin in our lives. He now addresses the logical question his audience would have asked: If this is true, then how come so many have died already in the past before Christ came? Paul argues that God did indeed make all humans to have his image in this life so we could live in God's ways, but that was not enough to get us out of the results of our sin in this natural world. We need the life-giving Spirit that Christ gives us so that we can be transformed from natural persons to *spiritual* persons united with Christ through possession of his Holy Spirit. The power of this gift of the eternal Spirit of God touches all human beings in all times. In the Spirit, in Christ, we live not in the power of our natural souls but in the grace of divine life.

CATECHETICAL SUGGESTIONS

Kingship in Israel
The sacrament of reconciliation
Forgiveness
Our penal system: punishment or rehabilitation?
The Truth and Reconciliation Commission in South Africa
Debt forgiveness in the Jubilee years and now

---

as a sign of openness and vitality in our liturgical ministries.

General Intercessions should contain mention of young people, of the challenge to go that extra mile, and of the approaching Lenten season. The fourth Eucharistic Prayer, "Jesus, the Compassion of God" (contained in *Eucharistic Prayer for Masses for Various Needs and Occasions*), with its reference to the compassion of Jesus in the welcoming of the sick and sinner, would be appropriate on this Sunday. "He was moved with

compassion for the poor and the powerless, for the sick and the sinner; he made himself neighbor to the oppressed. By his words and actions he proclaimed to the world that you care for us as a father cares for his children."

Lent begins this Wednesday. Plans for the celebration of the season should be firmed up. Whatever resources might be needed should be on hand. Bulletin announcements concerning the season of Lent should make their appearance once again this week.

While it is not yet Lent, many in our assemblies will find it useful to hear of some of the opportunities or various ways in which they might engage as individuals, or as part of the parish church, in the discipline of Lent. While such mention is helpful in the parish bulletin, a mention in the context of the homily is also in order. It is during this Lent that God will do in each of us a new thing. It is during this Lent that God will once again heal and restore us, raising us to life.

SCRIPTURE COMMENTARY

In this passage, Luke includes several more of the teachings of Jesus that also occur in Matthew's Sermon on the Mount, especially in Matthew 6 and 7. Luke had drawn a strong contrast between those who give up this world's wealth for the riches of the kingdom of God. Now Luke emphasizes that Jesus went beyond the teaching common to all great religions, that we love one another, to demand that we love even our enemies. Jesus passes over the ordinary words used for erotic love and the love between friends to insist on *agape*, a love that seeks only the good and the best for the other, no matter how good or bad that person is. It is the equivalent of *hesed* in the Old Testament, where one must love out of the bond God has established with all humans as his creatures. We need not consider our enemies to be our friends, but we must still see them as valuable in God's eyes and wish for the positive work of grace in their lives. The golden rule is to treat others with the love you desire. Jesus says that, by so doing, you will follow God's own example of love. God loves you unconditionally even when you sin, and always offers compassion and forgiveness. When you act in this manner, you are truly disciples not just of Jesus but of his Father also.

Gospel: Luke 6:27–38

Jesus said to his disciples: "To you who hear I say, love your enemies, do good to those who hate you, bless those who curse you, pray for those who mistreat you. To the person who strikes you on one cheek, offer the other one as well, and from the person who takes your cloak, do not withhold even your tunic. Give to everyone who asks of you, and from the one who takes what is yours do not demand it back. Do to others as you would have them do to you. For if you love those who love you, what credit is that to you? Even sinners love those who love them. And if you do good to those who do good to you, what credit is that to you? Even sinners do the same. If you lend money to those from whom you expect repayment, what credit is that to you? Even sinners lend to sinners, and get back the same amount. But rather, love your enemies and do good to them, and lend expecting nothing back; then your reward will be great and you will be children of the Most High, for he himself is kind to the ungrateful and the wicked. Be merciful, just as your Father is merciful.

"Stop judging and you will not be judged. Stop condemning and you will not be condemned. Forgive and you will be forgiven. Give, and gifts will be given to you; a good measure, packed together, shaken down, and overflowing, will be poured into your lap. For the measure with which you measure will in return be measured out to you."

MUSIC CONNECTION

The centerpiece of today's readings is the mercy of God as noted in the psalm refrain: "The Lord is kind and merciful." The mercy shown to us by God is to be our example of how to relate to others, as the gospel makes clear: "Be merciful, just as your Father is merciful." Certainly, David's mercy to his sworn enemy Saul in the selection from the first book of Samuel is a model for all of us. Numerous hymn texts, such as *There's a Wideness in God's Mercy; Awake O Sleeper, Rise from Death; Beloved, Let Us Love;* and *A Simple Command,* well serve today's liturgy. There are numerous settings of *Ubi Caritas* that could be used today, but Larry Rosania's manages to blend the old and the new in a masterful and singable arrangement of the ancient text. Steve Janco's setting of the Quinn text *A New Commandment* is a worthy addition to songs that extol God's love and compassion and our collaboration in that love through our words and actions. While Gelineau is a good choice for Psalm 103, be sure to take a look at settings by Marty Haugen and Jeanne Cotter as well.

First Reading: Joel 2:12–18

Even now, says the LORD,
   return to me with your whole
     heart,
   with fasting, and weeping, and
     mourning;
Rend your hearts, not your gar-
     ments,
   and return to the LORD, your God.
For gracious and merciful is he,
   slow to anger, rich in kindness,
   and relenting in punishment.
Perhaps he will again relent
   and leave behind him a blessing,
Offerings and libations
   for the LORD, your God.

Blow the trumpet in Zion!
   proclaim a fast,
   call an assembly;
Gather the people,
   notify the congregation;
Assemble the elders,
   gather the children
   and the infants at the breast;

SCRIPTURE COMMENTARY

The most striking expression of the covenant relationship between God and Israel was the declaration in God's own voice on Mount Sinai as recorded in Exodus 34:5–6: "The Lord, the Lord! A merciful and gracious God, slow to anger, rich in kindness and fidelity, continuing that kindness to a thousand generations, and forgiving wickedness and crime and sin; yet not declaring the guilty guiltless, but punishing the children and grandchildren to the third and fourth generation." Note that compassion is a quality of God's very nature, but so is maintaining justice and right in the world. Joel's ringing words today clearly reflect this beautiful description of God's covenant faithfulness, but Joel emphasizes that the God of mercy often overrules the just sentence that sinners deserve from the divine judge. Instead, God relents and forgives them by lessening or even foregoing the punishment. In turn, Joel asks that people show they have indeed repented of their evil and changed their ways by concretely showing their humility and dependence on God's mercy. Fasting, weeping for sin, even tearing one's garments or putting ashes on

HOMILY HELPS

Is there any term that captures the heart of the Christian message? One word may not be enough, but two are. They are *reconciliation* on God's part and *gratitude* on ours.

It is not accidental that the short reading from Corinthians is part of the Ash Wednesday liturgy. Paul speaks of himself and other believers as ambassadors. In diplomatic terms, an ambassador is one who speaks for a higher authority before another agency (e.g., one government before another). And what is our message as God's ambassador? The Lord's reconciling love as clearly seen in Christ Jesus. God's overarching intention through all of the scriptures is to bring us home, to free us from the shackles of evil and house us in the dwelling of the Lord. Christ took upon himself the wages of sin that we might become holy in the "holiness of God," which is life in the Holy Spirit.

Many ministers of the Church will tell us that there is nothing more rewarding than engaging the unreconciled. This may mean restoration to a life of faith or bringing alienated and disaffected persons together. This is truly the work of God in the world.

The second half of the essential Christian message is gratitude, a term that epitomizes our Christian stance. Gratitude says it all. It underlies, or should, every moral step we take, every observance or good work that we perform. It gives meaning to our Lenten response of fasting, almsgiving, and prayer. If gratitude is not our central motive, then we are servile task fulfillers, often open to self-deception. As followers of Jesus, we do not fast to obtain God's favor or practice good works to be seen. Today's

SCRIPTURE COMMENTARY, CONTINUED

one's forehead were all common ways of seeking forgiveness and mercy in times of suffering. But Joel is clear—we must turn our hearts and wills away from sin and toward God, not depend on the external symbols. Yes, they are important expressions of our internal attitude, but the heart of the covenant relationship is our prayer of trust and dependence on the God of mercy and kindness.

> Let the bridegroom quit his room
>   and the bride her chamber.
> Between the porch and the altar
>   let the priests, the ministers of the LORD, weep,
> And say, "Spare, O LORD, your people,
>   and make not your heritage a reproach,
>   with the nations ruling over them!
> Why should they say among the peoples,
>   'Where is their God?'"

Then the LORD was stirred to concern for his land and took pity on his people.

PSALM REFLECTION

The psalm that most reflects the attitude of which Joel speaks is Psalm 51. It is rightly considered the great penitential psalm of the Church because of its intense conviction that God certainly forgives us if we have confessed our sins and converted our hearts. The verses chosen for the response today are indeed the central verses of the psalm and place this message before us in all of its power. It is not, however, a straight exchange between two equals. "If you do this, I will do that...!" No, it requires us not only to realize that have we sinned and desire God's forgiveness but also to acknowledge that only God can change our hearts and give us the ability to live the renewed life we seek to have. The divine spirit must dwell in us. In the mention of the Holy Spirit in verses 12–13, we have the first key prophetic understanding of the role of the Holy Spirit in the doctrine of the Trinity that Jesus will reveal.

Psalm Response
Psalm 51: 3–4, 5–6ab,
  12–13, 14, 17

Antiphon
Be merciful, O Lord, for we
  have sinned.

Verse for Reflection
Truly you are pleased with a
  sincere heart,
In my soul you teach me wisdom. (v. 8)

---

gospel reminds us that such thoughts should be far from our mind. We do not seek God's recognition, since we are already recognized.

We walk the path of holiness because we are grateful, not because we are trying to achieve something. Our actions flow from the fact that we have been touched by love; we are incredibly gifted. In the words of Joel, it is all a matter of the heart; external observance is secondary. The forty days of Lent are our moment of "thank you" to God. We are not asking for his love; we are grateful that it is already ours.

LITURGICAL NOTES

The green of Ordinary Time gives way to the purple of Lent and the call of the prophet Joel to "return to me with your whole heart." Today ashes are blessed and distributed after the homily. Apart from Mass, a service of the word precedes the blessing and distribution of ashes, which concludes with General Intercessions, the Lord's Prayer and a hymn (see *Book of Blessings*, 1656–1678). The ordinary minister for the distribution of ashes is a priest or deacon; other ministers (extraordinary ministers of Holy Communion, ministers to the

homebound) can assist with the distribution of ashes where there is a need.

At Mass, the penitential rite is omitted. The preface of Lent IV is the recommended preface. It is also appropriate to use one of the Eucharistic Prayers for Masses of Reconciliation. It is unfortunate that the present Sacramentary does not provide a scripted introduction to this day as it does on the feast of the Presentation of the Lord or Passion Sunday. One could be carefully scripted outlining the purpose of our gathering, and the Church's Lenten journey. Such an example can be found in the *Book of Occasional Services* (New York:

68

**Second Reading:
2 Corinthians 5:20—6:2**

Brothers and sisters: We are ambassadors for Christ, as if God were appealing through us. We implore you on behalf of Christ, be reconciled to God. For our sake he made him to be sin who did not know sin, so that we might become the righteousness of God in him.

Working together, then, we appeal to you not to receive the grace of God in vain. For he says:

*In an acceptable time I
    heard you,
    and on the day of sal-
        vation I helped you.*
Behold, now is a very acceptable time; behold, now is the day of salvation.

SCRIPTURE COMMENTARY

This passage from St. Paul to the Corinthians is one of the most important texts in the New Testament on the nature of divine reconciliation brought by the death of Christ. We shall see part of it repeated on the fourth Sunday of Lent when we read verses 17–21. The overlap that we repeat, rightly, is that "we are ambassadors for Christ." Paul is speaking of himself, who brings them the good news of Jesus' death and resurrection. But he is also applying the title to the Corinthians as well. He tells them that now is the acceptable time to receive salvation, but he means also that now is the time to give witness to what we have received. Once we hear of the mercy of God to forgive sins and bring the world back into harmony with himself, the only possible response is to rejoice and accept the great gift of divine graciousness by renouncing our sins and receiving forgiveness.

CATECHETICAL SUGGESTIONS

An overview of Lent: history and purpose
The theological rationale for fasting and almsgiving
Evangelization programs for alienated Catholics
Individual conversion and the social mission of the Church
What is sin? Old Testament and New Testament understandings
What is the good news of redemption?

Church Hymnal Corporation). In most churches, this is a day that draws significant crowds. While ministers need to be conscious of the large numbers of people, they ought not to shortchange the power of the liturgy by reducing it to its bare minimum.

Ash Wednesday and the beginning of Lent lie deep within the fiber of all Christians, even those who do not regularly participate in the life of the Church. Pastoral ministers should keep in mind that this day is also an opportunity for evangelization and conversion. Ministers of hospitality should be on hand to welcome all who enter the church. There should be additional copies

outlining the Church's Lenten discipline, the parish's Lenten activities, and ways in which individuals and families can celebrate the season of Lent. There ought to be information on the celebration of the sacrament of penance—not only when services will occur but how an individual could prepare through an examination of conscience and how the sacrament itself is celebrated.

Several parish practices that have emerged since introduction of the RCIA bear reexamination. One such practice is "fasting from baptism" during Lent. While the tradition provides examples of such a fast, infant baptism ought not to be unreasonably delayed

simply because it is the season of Lent. Another practice is removing all holy water from the church and placing sand or rocks in the font. This attempts to extend the notion of the church's "fasting from baptism." However, holy water is a sacramental, a reminder of our own baptism. And even during Lent, we stand as baptized into the risen life of Christ. Lent is a call not to forget our baptism but rather to discover how far we have moved away from our baptismal dignity. The regular use of holy water, and reminders as to why we use it, will help to serve the members of the Church on this Lenten journey.

SCRIPTURE COMMENTARY

The gospel comes from the center of Jesus' Sermon on the Mount found in Matthew 5–7. Jesus addresses three of the most common religious practices that the rabbis commended as signs of true piety for Jews: almsgiving, prayer, and fasting. In each of these, Jesus warns his followers not to be misled by external observance but to focus on the interior attitude that gives these practices their value. In almsgiving, the danger is that we do it to look good ourselves or to help those we like over those we don't. Jesus asks that all almsgiving be simply given to anyone without regard for who receives it or how much praise we get for doing it. In prayer, he warns against appearing regularly in church or temple while the prayer never comes from our hearts. We have great capacity to fool ourselves as well as others by saying all the right words and talking about such things as honesty and compassion while failing to put them into practice. Prayer from the heart, however, must confess humbly and seek God's strength to live faithfully what we believe. Fasting looks great—what self-denial and humility and sense of sacrifice that person has! But how often do we give up the food but not the evil thoughts and ways of our hearts? External fasting is the bodily partner of our interior decision to reject and deny our sinful ways and thoughts.

Gospel: Matthew 6:1–6, 16–18

Jesus said to his disciples: "Take care not to perform righteous deeds in order that people may see them; otherwise, you will have no recompense from your heavenly Father. When you give alms, do not blow a trumpet before you, as the hypocrites do in the synagogues and in the streets to win the praise of others. Amen, I say to you, they have received their reward. But when you give alms, do not let your left hand know what your right is doing, so that your almsgiving may be secret. And your Father who sees in secret will repay you.

"When you pray, do not be like the hypocrites, who love to stand and pray in the synagogues and on street corners so that others may see them. Amen, I say to you, they have received their reward. But when you pray, go to your inner room, close the door, and pray to your Father in secret. And your Father who sees in secret will repay you.

"When you fast, do not look gloomy like the hypocrites. They neglect their appearance, so that they may appear to others to be fasting. Amen, I say to you, they have received their reward. But when you fast, anoint your head and wash your face, so that you may not appear to be fasting, except to your Father who is hidden. And your Father who sees what is hidden will repay you."

MUSIC CONNECTION

As we once again enter this holy season, we do well to remind ourselves that Lent has a bifocal agenda. On the one hand, it is a time of initiation as catechumens are brought into their final period of preparation for the Easter sacraments through the Rite of Election on the first Sunday of Lent. Through such practices as prayer, fasting, scrutinies, and presentations, the "elect" are readied for the saving water bath, the copious anointing and gift of the Spirit, and the generous banquet of the Easter Vigil. On the other hand, there is a penitential dimension to the season as the rest of us, already initiated, yearly renew ourselves through prayer, fasting, and good works (almsgiving)—all traditional works of penance. There are lots of choices for the responsorial Psalm 51, including settings by Gelineau, Haugen, Guimont, Haas, Bedford, and Alstott. Brian Wren's probing text *Dust and Ashes* artfully set to music by David Haas is a wonderful keynote for the season. Tom Conry's *Ashes* yearly calls many North American congregations to renewal and penance. The seasonal use of a sung penitential rite is worth considering. The Taizé (Jacques Berthier) *Kyrie* is eminently singable and engaging for this purpose. Finally, both James Chepponis's *This Is the Time of Fulfillment* and Alan Hommerding's *From Ashes to the Living Font* are great additions to the Lenten repertoire.

First Reading: Deuteronomy 26:4–10

Moses spoke to the people, saying: "The priest shall receive the basket from you and shall set it in front of the altar of the LORD, your God. Then you shall declare before the LORD, your God, 'My father was a wandering Aramean who went down to Egypt with a small household and lived there as an alien. But there he became a nation great, strong, and numerous. When the Egyptians maltreated and oppressed us, imposing hard labor upon us, we cried to the LORD, the God of our fathers, and he heard our cry and saw our affliction, our toil, and our oppression. He brought us out of Egypt with his strong hand and outstretched arm, with terrifying power, with signs and wonders; and bringing us into this country, he gave us this land flowing with milk and honey. Therefore, I have now brought you the firstfruits of the products of the soil which you, O LORD, have given me.' And having set them before the LORD, your God, you shall bow down in his presence."

SCRIPTURE COMMENTARY

The background of this reading is the command of Moses that all the Israelites must give back a portion of their first harvests each year as thanksgiving to the God who provided the fruit of the soil. It is also an acknowledgment that God is the real owner of the land and has granted it as a gift to Israel. This is an important commandment and is closely regulated here and in other passages such as Exodus 22:29, 23:19, 34:26 and Numbers 18:8–14. In the days of the kingdom, the offering had to be given to the priests to be presented to God on the altar in the temple. Then part was reserved to feed the priests, part was sacrificed only to God, and the remainder was given to the family to have a feast in thanksgiving to God. The remarkable note in Deuteronomy is the confession of faith to be said while the gifts are handed over. It records all the great events of the Pentateuch, such as Jacob's going down to Egypt, his family flourishing there, slavery under the pharaoh, the cry for help to God, the exodus liberation, and the journey to the Promised Land. It is perhaps the earliest version of the Pentateuch story we have. It lacks only the section on the giving of the covenant on Mount Sinai. Thus, giving of the harvest honors not just God's blessing to farmers but his salvation of his people as a whole.

HOMILY HELPS

Jerusalem is both the geographical and the theological center of Luke's gospel. It is important because it points up the continuity between the two Testaments, the Old and the New. The continuity between the two covenants reminds us of the close bonds we have with our Jewish brothers and sisters. We are reminded of the enlightened statement of Pius XI: "We are all spiritually Semites."

In the account of Jesus' three temptations, Luke reverses the order found in Matthew. The parapet of the temple in Jerusalem is climactic in Luke. As spectacular as this triptych may seem, it should be remembered that this was the type of temptation that Jesus faced, in a less dramatic fashion, from his contemporaries during his earthly ministry, namely, the temptation to become a miraculous "bread god," the temptation to manifest himself as king, and the temptation to presume on God's protection.

As we reflect on this gospel passage, we need to ask: To what extent am I inordinately attached to material things? To the pursuit of status? To believing that God will see me through regardless of my attitude and my behavior?

The major thrust of Jesus' temptations was to abandon God and his mission. We too are often tempted to abandon God and set off on our own course. But to reflect on Jesus' answer is to steer our course correctly.

The first reading today, from Deuteronomy, reminds us of our total dependence on God, significantly illustrated in the harvest offerings. One of the drawbacks of modern times is the great temptation to take everything for granted. Perhaps if we had less, we would be more grateful.

Do we believe in our hearts and profess with our lips the lordship of Jesus? This can work in one of two ways. It may be that we believe, but our faith is not apparent in our daily life. It costs little to say that our hearts are in the right place, but our lives may not be. Or it may be that we "talk a good game" but there is

PSALM REFLECTION

The whole of Psalm 91 is a medley of the ways in which God provides protection and security for those who place their trust in him, those who "dwell in the shadow of God." The first half of the psalm talks about the dangers of pestilence, the fears of unknown diseases, and evils that seem to come with no reason. These are passed over today to concentrate on the second half of the psalm, which provides resonances of the story of the temptation of Jesus. (The gospels indeed quote Psalm 91:11–12 in the temptation scene.) The psalmist emphasizes that those who put their trust in God are taken into the company of God's angels. The language used is covenantal, stressing God speaking directly to us and receiving glory when we stand under God's name in all that we do. This psalm is the clearest source for the role of guardian angels in God's plan—he provides his own assistants to watch over his human partners in the covenant.

Psalm Response
Psalm 91:1–2, 10–11, 12–13, 14–15

Antiphon
Be with me, Lord, when I am
  in trouble.

Verses for Reflection
Because you made the Lord
  your refuge,
The Most High your
  dwelling,
No evil will happen to you.
  (vv. 9–10)

CATECHETICAL SUGGESTIONS

God's covenant with Abraham and Moses
Scripture as a living word
Nostra Aetate, Declaration on the Relation of the Church to
  Non-Christian Religions (Vatican II)
An examination of conscience
The Stations of the Cross
Jesus' temptations and ours

---

very little depth behind our words. We might be very active and give little time to prayer. We must do both—believe in our hearts and confess with our lips.

In the passage from Romans today there is a strong emphasis on Christian equality. No more division, no more intolerance. No Jews or Greeks. We have found our common bond in Christ Jesus.

Lent has begun. There is no better time of the year to reassess our life in God. The readings today offer some interesting points for our examination of conscience.

LITURGICAL NOTES

The Church begins its Lenten journey, which "is a period of preparation for the celebration of Easter. For the Lenten liturgy disposes both catechumens and the faithful to celebrate the paschal mystery: catechumens, through the several stages of Christian initiation; the faithful, through reminders of their own baptism and through penitential practices" (GNLYC, 27). Lent is a journey to baptism: for the catechumens, it is their forty-day

retreat before baptism; for the already baptized, it is a journey back to the font, back to baptismal innocence through prayer, fasting, and works of charity.

Our Lent begins in the desert. The environment ought to be barren; let the absence of color, of additional symbols, of extra decorations speak to those making the Lenten journey. With the exception of the fourth Sunday of Lent, the use of flowers is prohibited throughout the season of Lent. Lent is an appropriate time to sing the Penitential Rite. Whether form A or C is used, the people's

Second Reading: Romans 10:8–13

Brothers and sisters: What does Scripture say?

The word is near you,
in your mouth and in your
heart

—that is, the word of faith that we preach —, for, if you confess with your mouth that Jesus is Lord and believe in your heart that God raised him from the dead, you will be saved. For one believes with the heart and so is justified, and one confesses with the mouth and so is saved. For the Scripture says,

No one who believes in him will
be put to shame.

For there is no distinction between Jew and Greek; the same Lord is Lord of all, enriching all who call upon him. For "everyone who calls on the name of the Lord will be saved."

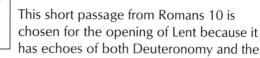

SCRIPTURE COMMENTARY

This short passage from Romans 10 is chosen for the opening of Lent because it has echoes of both Deuteronomy and the gospel story of the temptation. The point of the offerings to God in Deuteronomy 26 was to give thanks and praise to God for his goodness. Paul sees the greatest goodness of God in his forgiveness of our sins and in the resurrection that provides us everlasting life. But having faith also means we must confess the saving power and mercy of God publicly so that all will receive the good news. In the gospel that follows, Jesus refutes Satan's temptations by praising only God for his goodness and as the sole source of trust. So Paul's thinking fits this well—the great revelation above all others is that God's goodness and salvation are open to all human beings and that in Jesus we recognize this gift as given to us all.

response can easily be sung. The Gloria is omitted and the word "Alleluia" is not used in the Gospel Acclamation or any hymnody.

The "return to our baptism" call is imaged in the first reading, when the chosen people are called to confess their faith, and echoed in the second, where Paul speaks of believers in Christ confessing their faith. Luke's gospel deals with the devil's temptations of Jesus in the desert.

Today (or during this week) the catechumens will celebrate the Rite of Election. At this rite, the bishop, in the name of the whole Church, will elect them for the Easter sacraments. If there are candidates in addition to catechumens, they, too are sent to the bishop for recognition. While this rite is usually celebrated in the cathedral or some other large regional church, the American adaptations to the RCIA provide a parish Rite for Sending Catechumens for Election and Candidates for Recognition by the Bishop (RCIA, 530). While the use of this rite is optional, it does assist the wider parish community with their connection and involvement with the catechu-

mens and candidates. It simply acknowledges what will happen later on this day (or week) and asks the continued prayer of the community. Even if there are no catechumens or candidates in a particular parish, mention should be made of them in the General Intercessions.

The proper text provided in the Sacramentary for the Solemn Blessing is for the Passion of the Lord. The simpler form of the Prayer over the People might be used, particularly number four (avoiding evil) or number six (cleansing our hearts).

SCRIPTURE COMMENTARY

The temptation scene in Luke's gospel immediately follows Jesus' reception of the Holy Spirit at his baptism in chapter 3. In turn, the baptism followed the story of Jesus lost in the temple at the age of twelve, when he was learning and discussing the law with the great rabbis. There, Luke tells us, Jesus discovered his role as the Son of the Father, not as a disciple of some famous rabbi. Thus Jesus acknowledges his unique Sonship, receives the Spirit to strengthen him at his baptism, and then proves his trust in God alone before the efforts of Satan to seduce him. The temptation story reveals two commitments Jesus makes at the very beginning of his ministry: (1) he will follow only the will of his Father and no other ruler or power; (2) he will forego wealth and earthly fame and power to choose the way of lowliness, humility, suffering and—if necessary—even persecution. Jesus emerges from this scene strong and confident in his mission. In the rest of his ministry he will never waver in insisting on the truth of this way to all of his followers.

Gospel: Luke 4:1–13

Filled with the Holy Spirit, Jesus returned from the Jordan and was led by the Spirit into the desert for forty days, to be tempted by the devil. He ate nothing during those days, and when they were over he was hungry.
The devil said to him, "If you are the Son of God, command this stone to become bread."
Jesus answered him, "It is written,
  One does not live on bread alone."
Then he took him up and showed him all the kingdoms of the world in a single instant. The devil said to him, "I shall give to you all this power and glory; for it has been handed over to me, and I may give it to whomever I wish. All this will be yours, if you worship me." Jesus said to him in reply, "It is written:
  You shall worship the Lord, your God,
    and him alone shall you serve."
Then he led him to Jerusalem, made him stand on the parapet of the temple, and said to him, "If you are the Son of God, throw yourself down from here, for it is written:
  He will command his angels concerning you, to guard
    you,
and:
  With their hands they will support you,
    lest you dash your foot against a stone."
Jesus said to him in reply, "It also says,
  You shall not put the Lord, your God, to the test."
When the devil had finished every temptation, he departed from him for a time.

MUSIC CONNECTION

On this first Sunday of Lent, the Lucan pericope portrays Jesus' being led into the desert to be tempted. The words of the third temptation, "With their hands they will support you, lest you dash your foot against a stone," drawn from the responsorial, Psalm 91, strongly suggest Joncas's popular setting *On Eagle's Wings* at some point in today's service.

Other fine settings of Psalm 91 include those by Ferris, Gelineau, and Haugen. Since in many parishes catechumens will be leaving from church to go to their respective cathedrals for the Rite of Election, it would behoove the homilist to connect at least the readings to the journey of these men, women, and children to the waters of baptism. Deiss's *Grant to Us,* with its overlapping themes of renewal, repentance, and covenant

themes, is a wonderful hymn for this season. Ralph Finn's wonderful text *The Master Came to Bring Good News* blends traditional seasonal images into a forceful and attractive composition. Both James Chepponis's *This Is the Time of Fulfillment* and Alan Hommerding's *From Ashes to the Living Font,* with verses for each Sunday of the Lenten season, are great additions to the Lenten repertoire.

2ND SUNDAY OF LENT—YEAR C

First Reading: Genesis 15:5–12, 17–18

The Lord God took Abram outside and said, "Look up at the sky and count the stars, if you can. Just so, " he added, "shall your descendants be." Abram put his faith in the LORD, who credited it to him as an act of righteousness.

He then said to him, "I am the LORD who brought you from Ur of the Chaldeans to give you this land as a possession." "O Lord GOD, " he asked, "how am I to know that I shall possess it?" He answered him, "Bring me a three-year-old heifer, a three-year-old she-goat, a three-year-old ram, a turtledove, and a young pigeon." Abram brought him all these, split them in two, and placed each half opposite the other; but the birds he did not cut up. Birds of prey swooped down on the carcasses, but Abram stayed with them. As the sun was about to set, a trance fell upon Abram, and a deep, terrifying darkness enveloped him.

When the sun had set and it was dark, there appeared a smoking fire pot and a

SCRIPTURE COMMENTARY

The gospel of the transfiguration dominates the second Sunday of Lent for all three years of Lectionary readings. It is an example in the gospels of what scholars call in Old Testament books a "divine manifestation story" or an "epiphany," in which God appears to a human with some of the signs of divine glory and radiance. The Church pairs the story of the transfiguration today with the story of the divine appearance to Abraham in Genesis 15. Both contain the promise of future fulfillment in them. In Genesis 12, Abraham received the divine promise that he would have a son and heir, but nothing happened afterwards, so he prays to God to fulfill the promise and not let him die childless. In this reading, God appears in his majesty and renews the promise with Abraham while also extending the covenant relationship with a promise of prosperity and innumerable descendants to Abraham in the future. God's passing as fire through the middle of animals that have been cut in two reflects an ancient ritual for making covenants, one that we know of from other ancient treaties. The fire consuming the animals as a sacrifice signifies divine acceptance of the agreement. The smoke of the holocaust ascends to the

HOMILY HELPS

The three gospel accounts of the transfiguration present Moses and Elijah conversing with Jesus, but it is only Luke who tells us what they were speaking about. It was the "exodus" of Jesus, his forthcoming passage through suffering and death to glory. *Per aspera ad astra.* "Through trials to the stars." It is the story of the Christian life.

The Blanchard family celebrated a joyful fortieth anniversary for their parents, only to learn within a week that their mother had been diagnosed with Alzheimer's. Joe Talbot had a forty-fifth birthday party surrounded by family and friends and a month later was without a job as his company downsized. We cherish the golden moments and want to hold on to them, just as Peter did when gazing upon the transfigured Christ. But it was not meant to be. The cross and crown are inseparable.

Paul wrote his letter to the Philippians from a prison cell. In that letter he makes a rather surprising statement. "Be imitators of me." The injunction is hardly characteristic of Paul, who always insists that Christ alone is the exemplar of our lives. In him is found the one who truly heard the words of the Father: "Listen to him." Yet one has to understand the context in which Paul is writing. Within the congregation being addressed there were those who were abandoning Christ in pursuit of earthly interests; others, like Paul, were remaining faithful. Paul here simply makes an appeal for adhering to the truth, as he and other members of the community were doing.

In the midst of these trials, Paul wants his listeners to remember that their citizenship is in heaven, when their crosses will be transformed in glory. That is the meaning of the transfiguration: it is a glimpse of glory, a promise accepted on the word of God himself. In today's first reading, Abraham is promised

SCRIPTURE COMMENTARY, CONTINUED

heavens as a pleasing odor to God to confirm that the human party has given of the best of his animal possessions as a thanksgiving offering and is willing to submit himself to God.

flaming torch, which passed between those pieces. It was on that occasion that the LORD made a covenant with Abram, saying: "To your descendants I give this land, from the Wadi of Egypt to the Great River, the Euphrates."

PSALM REFLECTION

The highlight of the language in Psalm 27 is the constant imagery of light for God and the sense of our being in the divine favor because we stand in the light of his beaming face and presence and therefore in his protection. God often seems to be hidden from us and not to hear us when we pray, such as when disasters strike despite our cries or we don't seem to receive satisfaction in our requests. Moderns would say that our prayer is dry at such a time, but ancients would say that God had turned away his face from us. They would pray harder that God would hear them again and turn back toward them to listen to their pleas and answer them as in the past. When our prayer is heard and answered, God has looked down again, and the marvelous light of his look upon us dispels the darkness. The strength of this psalm is the sense of radiant confidence in the psalmist. He doesn't desperately seek God but declares his favor and light confidently and joyfully.

Psalm Response
Psalm 27:1, 7–8, 8–9, 13–14

Antiphon
The Lord is my light and my salvation.

Verse for Reflection
One thing I ask of the Lord...
To look on the beauty of the Lord
And stand in awe of his house! (v. 4)

the land of Canaan and countless descendants. Our promised destiny is eternity with God, something we cannot describe but which, we know in faith, is indescribable. Pain in this life is unavoidable, but we must never lose sight of the future. As Teresa of Avila tells us: "All things are passing; God alone is changeless." Our life is centered on listening to him. To do that is to recognize that our "exodus" too is inevitable. Suffering will come, but it will pass, for our "citizenship is in heaven." *Per aspera ad astra.* Hardship leads to the stars.

LITURGICAL NOTES

The Lenten journey continues as we hear that story of the transfiguration of Jesus. While both opening prayers provided in the Sacramentary are appropriate, the alternative prayer speaks more directly to the readings. The elect, the catechumens, and the candidates should be mentioned in the General Intercessions. The preface for the second Sunday of Lent situates the purpose of the transfiguration in the celebration of the paschal mystery. Both of the Eucharistic Prayers for Masses of Reconciliation are appropriate throughout the season of Lent.

The American adaptations to the RCIA provide on this Sunday a Penitential Rite for Candidates (RCIA, 459). This rite serves to mark the Lenten purification of those already baptized but uncatechized adults and those seeking admission into the full communion of the Catholic Church. This rite is intended only for the candidates; the rites on the next three Sundays are intended only for the catechumens, now called the elect.

**Second Reading: Philippians 3:17—4:1
(or Philippians 3:20—4:1)**

Join with others in being imitators of me, brothers and sisters, and observe those who thus conduct themselves according to the model you have in us. For many, as I have often told you and now tell you even in tears, conduct themselves as enemies of the cross of Christ. Their end is destruction. Their God is their stomach; their glory is in their "shame." Their minds are occupied with earthly things. But our citizenship is in heaven, and from it we also await a savior, the Lord Jesus Christ. He will change our lowly body to conform with his glorified body by the power that enables him also to bring all things into subjection to himself.

Therefore, my brothers and sisters, whom I love and long for, my joy and crown, in this way stand firm in the Lord.

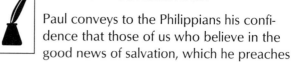

SCRIPTURE COMMENTARY

Paul conveys to the Philippians his confidence that those of us who believe in the good news of salvation, which he preaches through the cross and resurrection of Christ, expectantly await the coming of Christ again from heaven. Christ will transform us into the same glorified state he enjoys as the risen Lord, with bodies that are not tied to this world any longer but are open to being filled with divine grace and power and glory. What a contrast this is with those who live only for their own bodily satisfaction now ("Their god is their stomach"). They have no sense of a higher hope, and their conduct gradually leads them into ruin, since they live only at this lower level of the body and do not possess the great theological virtue of hope that sustains the Christian.

Today's liturgy, like all of the liturgies of Lent, should be marked by a stark simplicity.

In Luke's gospel, the voice from the cloud declares, "This is my chosen Son; listen to him." How we listen or how we are able to listen can provide a unique challenge to liturgy planners. Before the liturgy begins, do people have the opportunity to "listen" to what the Lord has to say? How can we better makes our churches places of prayer, quiet, and recollection before the liturgy begins? How do our liturgical ministers and, in a special way, music ministers model the kind of recollected silence we seek to create? Throughout the liturgy, do our presiders, deacons, music ministers, and readers speak so that they can be understood? Does the sound system help or hinder?

Here again, music ministers ought to look closely at how much amplification is actually needed to facilitate the full song of the assembly. This is a place where more is definitely not better.

CATECHETICAL SUGGESTIONS

Covenant renewal ceremonies
Prayers of petition
The Imitation of Christ (Thomas à Kempis)
Paul and the spiritual body
The Rosary and the mysteries of light
Ways in which we "listen to Christ"

SCRIPTURE COMMENTARY

Jesus has told his disciples in the previous verses that he must be rejected, die, and be raised again by his Father (9:18-22) and that his disciples must expect to also lose their lives for Jesus' sake (9:23-27). Now he allows the apostles, through their three representatives, Peter, James, and John, a foretaste of the rewards of heaven promised those who were poor in this world and suffered persecution for his sake (see the gospel on the beatitudes—sixth Sunday in Ordinary Time). The presence of Moses and Elijah are symbolic of the testimony of the whole of the scriptures (the "law and the prophets," i.e., the Old Testament) to God's prophetic plan for sending his Son as our Savior, to suffer rejection and death and then be raised for us. The entire scene is the only major "epiphany" of God presented in the New Testament before Jesus' day of resurrection. The apostolic witnesses have now heard God's own voice and seen with their own eyes confirmation of what Jesus has just told them. Like the promise of descendants made to Abraham in God's night epiphany of Genesis 15, God confirms he will bring about what he has promised, and presents a vision that provides a foretaste of Jesus' coming glory. The words the apostles hear ("This is my chosen son") actually come from Isaiah 42, the so-called Servant Song, and further specify that the way to glory for Jesus and for his disciples will be the way of the servant, not the king.

Gospel: Luke 9:28b–36

Jesus took Peter, John, and James and went up the mountain to pray. While he was praying his face changed in appearance and his clothing became dazzling white. And behold, two men were conversing with him, Moses and Elijah, who appeared in glory and spoke of his exodus that he was going to accomplish in Jerusalem. Peter and his companions had been overcome by sleep, but becoming fully awake, they saw his glory and the two men standing with him. As they were about to part from him, Peter said to Jesus, "Master, it is good that we are here; let us make three tents, one for you, one for Moses, and one for Elijah." But he did not know what he was saying. While he was still speaking, a cloud came and cast a shadow over them, and they became frightened when they entered the cloud. Then from the cloud came a voice that said, "This is my chosen Son; listen to him." After the voice had spoken, Jesus was found alone. They fell silent and did not at that time tell anyone what they had seen.

MUSIC CONNECTION

Each year, the transfiguration account anchors the second Sunday of Lent in the Roman Lectionary. Though written at different times and from different perspective, the three gospels show unusual similarity in detailing this pivotal New Testament event. The traditional 'Tis Good, Lord, to Be Here is a hymnic retelling of this story, as are Brian Wren's more recent Christ upon the Mountain Peak and Dunstan's text Transform Us. The dazzling description of the transfiguration in the gospel ties in with Paul's promise in Philippians that Jesus Christ "will change our lowly body to conform with his glorified body." With Psalm 27 emphasizing light imagery, several hymns come to mind, including Christ Be Our Light, Christ Is the World's Light, and O Sun of Justice. Psalm 27, today's responsorial psalm, has a wonderful treatment by Lillian Bouknight in GIA's Lead Me, Guide Me hymnal. Other settings include those of Gelineau, Haas, Hruby, and Alstott. Often used to dismiss children for the liturgy of the word and catechumens after the homily, Blessed Are They—with its emphasis on light—can be most useful during this Lenten season. "Blessed are they who hear God's word and keep it and live it all of their lives. They are a light that cannot be hidden. They are a light shining bright."

First Reading: Exodus 3:1–8a, 13–15

Moses was tending the flock of his father-in-law Jethro, the priest of Midian. Leading the flock across the desert, he came to Horeb, the mountain of God. There an angel of the LORD appeared to Moses in fire flaming out of a bush. As he looked on, he was surprised to see that the bush, though on fire, was not consumed. So Moses decided, "I must go over to look at this remarkable sight, and see why the bush is not burned."

When the LORD saw him coming over to look at it more closely, God called out to him from the bush, "Moses! Moses!" He answered, "Here I am." God said, "Come no nearer! Remove the sandals from your feet, for the place where you stand is holy ground. I am the God of your fathers, " he continued, "the God of Abraham, the God of Isaac, the God of Jacob." Moses hid his face, for he was afraid to look at God. But the LORD said, "I have witnessed the affliction of my people in Egypt and have heard their cry of complaint against their slave drivers, so I know well what they are suffering. Therefore I have come down to rescue them from the hands of

NOTE: *Because the gospels of Year A are of major importance in regard to Christian initiation, Year A readings (Exodus 17:3–7; Psalm 95:1–2, 6–7, 8–9; Romans 5:1–2, 5–8; John 4:5–42 or shorter form, John 4:5–15, 19b–26, 39a, 40–42) may be used in Year B and Year C, especially in places where there are catechumens (see Lectionary for Mass, Introduction, 97).*

SCRIPTURE COMMENTARY

The "call" of Moses is a key story in the book of Exodus. It begins dramatically enough by describing Moses as a threefold loser: he is a wanted murderer; he is scraping by in the remotest and most barren of deserts; and he is tending sheep, the lowest of all jobs in the ancient world. The passage describes three important acts God undertakes: (1) he calls this unpromising man to be his instrument; (2) God announces his plans for his greatest work of divine mercy in the Old Testament, the exodus; and (3) God reveals his name to Moses. The name Yahweh, "I am" or "He Who Is," is not a real name but conceals any idea of a personal name behind the work that God is going to do. The phrase really says that God's name is "The one who will be with

HOMILY HELPS

"I AM WHO AM." This is the single biblical instance in which God is asked about his identity. Moses wants to be able to carry his message of liberation to the enslaved Israelites with some measure of authority. In God's identifying himself as "I am," he is clearly distinguishing himself from the pagan gods, who "are not." As the God who truly is, he gives assurance to Moses that he will accompany him on his mission.

Most people in our world believe that God exists, but their response goes in different directions. The passage in Corinthians today reminds us that there were those who experienced the saving action of God in the exodus but did not remain faithful. The great impact of the event lost its significance with the passing of time. These people paid the price of their waywardness, for, as Paul says elsewhere, "God is not mocked."

How often do we start off on a new track with spiritual enthusiasm only to lose our way in a maze of underbrush? This is, at least partially, why our spiritual mentors approach a conversion experience with so much caution. The true fruit of newfound fervor is seen in the steady day-to-day adherence to faith, not in exceptional spiritual phenomena. What truly impresses us in life is that sense of commitment which

never fades with the passage of time.

People who are starting their faith life anew need time. And they need a measure of patience, since not everything goes right immediately. The owner of the fig tree who is willing to allow time for the tree to bear fruit is, in the Lucan parable, the God who presides over our lives. If another year will produce the desired results, then "so be it." After all, in the Christian life everything is gift. If God does not easily give up on us, why should we give up on ourselves or one another?

A church congregation in its makeup is as diverse as society itself. The name of God is surrounded by a sacred aura in the

SCRIPTURE COMMENTARY, CONTINUED

you." It is a pledge of intimacy, that God will accompany the people as a friend. The heart of this declaration of God is that he is the one who chose them and came down to them in their need—they did not choose him. He will free them and establish them as his people so that they will take him as their God. Further, he comes not as a stranger but as the God whom their ancestors, Abraham, Isaac, and Jacob, knew and depended on in their wanderings.

the Egyptians and lead them out of that land into a good and spacious land, a land flowing with milk and honey."

Moses said to God, "But when I go to the Israelites and say to them, 'The God of your fathers has sent me to you,' if they ask me, 'What is his name?' what am I to tell them?" God replied, "I am who am." Then he added, "This is what you shall tell the Israelites: I AM sent me to you."

God spoke further to Moses, "Thus shall you say to the Israelites: The LORD, the God of your fathers, the God of Abraham, the God of Isaac, the God of Jacob, has sent me to you.

"This is my name forever;
    thus am I to be remembered through all generations."

PSALM REFLECTION

We had the opening verses plus the second half of this psalm (verses 1–4 + 8,10, and 12–13) as the responsorial on the seventh Sunday in Ordinary Time only three weeks ago. It was noted there that this psalm is rich in the language of God's loving kindness, his *hesed*. The latter half of the psalm in verses 10–13 stressed divine forgiveness of sins. Today's selection repeats the opening verses again but continues instead with verses 6–7 and 11. The emphasis in these verses moves away from forgiveness and now focuses on how God rescued the oppressed Israelites in Egypt through Moses and proved his *hesed* in so doing.

**Psalm Response
Psalm 103:1–2, 3–4, 6–7, 8, 11**

Antiphon
The Lord is kind and merciful.

Verse for Reflection
[The Lord] made known his
    ways to Moses,
And his deeds to the children of
    Israel! (v. 7)

Judeo-Christian tradition. But while we all recognize that name, our responses vary, and admittedly, some of us do not live as a privileged people. Under this large tent, some have dramatic conversion experiences. Others have wandered far but, through care and solicitude, have found their way back. Some have never wavered in their commitment. Others seem lost in the mist and we pray to embrace them again. But the Church is always there, expressive of the loving Christ. Lent is a time to take stock of where we are. But through all our ups and downs, certainties and uncertainties, the patient owner of the vineyard, the true I AM, will never fail us.

LITURGICAL NOTES

The readings of cycle C call us to a more profound trust in the superabundant mercy of God. The alternative opening prayer speaks directly to the way we return to the font, "fasting, prayer, and sharing with our brothers and sisters." The General Intercessions should make mention of this journey, proclaiming our confident assurance in God's mercy. The preface for the third Sunday of Lent, used only when cycle A readings are proclaimed, give focus to the dialogue between Jesus and the Samaritan woman. When cycle C readings are used, the preface of

Lent I or Lent II would be appropriate. Both of the Eucharistic Prayers for Masses of Reconciliation are appropriate throughout the season of Lent.

Many parishes will find that there will be one Mass where the elect, the catechumens, and candidates are present. This Mass ought to use cycle A readings. Beginning with the third Sunday of Lent and continuing for the next two Sundays, the cycle A readings focus our attention on initiation. Although the elect and the candidates will figure prominently in our celebrations, it is useful to recall that this Lenten journey is also calling the faithful to return to their baptism. While the themes and images are par-

Second Reading:
1 Corinthians 10:1–6, 10–12

I do not want you to be unaware, brothers and sisters, that our ancestors were all under the cloud and all passed through the sea, and all of them were baptized into Moses in the cloud and in the sea. All ate the same spiritual food, and all drank the same spiritual drink, for they drank from a spiritual rock that followed them, and the rock was the Christ. Yet God was not pleased with most of them, for they were struck down in the desert.

These things happened as examples for us, so that we might not desire evil things, as they did. Do not grumble as some of them did, and suffered death by the destroyer. These things happened to them as an example, and they have been written down as a warning to us, upon whom the end of the ages has come. Therefore, whoever thinks he is standing secure should take care not to fall.

SCRIPTURE COMMENTARY

In this chapter, Paul also reminds his audience of the lessons of the exodus. God chooses the weak, even though they are sinners like everyone else. Paul draws a lesson for his Corinthians. Even though God freed the Israelites from the pharaoh's power, gave them food and drink in the wilderness, and provided clear guidance through Moses on how to behave, many of them failed and rebelled and disobeyed. They were not fully prepared to follow God in their hearts and wills. Yet they should have been able to read the signs in such acts of mercy and compassion. Because they did not, many of them died in the wilderness and lost the chance to reach the Promised Land. This lesson prepares us for the gospel that follows

CATECHETICAL SUGGESTIONS

The significance of God's name, I AM
What are the rights of the oppressed?
Our immediate ancestors in faith
Typology
Conversion and repentance: urgent or not?
Parable interpretation

---

ticularly appropriate for those involved in the RCIA, they should also speak to the entire worshiping assembly of our journey back to our baptism.

On the third Sunday of Lent, the First Scrutiny for the elect (RCIA, 150) is celebrated. The rite is presented clearly, but its celebration needs some choreography. It would be advisable to have the elect and their godparents face the assembly; the presider could stand at the head of the assembly. The invitation to prayer invites genuine silence. The intercessions provided in the rite are not the same as the General Intercessions of the Mass. While powerful, the intercessions in the rite can tend to be vague;

they can be easily adapted to be more specific to the sinfulness that a particular community might experience. The exorcism consists of two prayers and a ritual gesture, the laying on of hands. This gesture occurs between the prayers and should be done in an unhurried silence. After the final prayer, the elect, along with the catechumens (and candidates) are dismissed to go "reflect more deeply on the word of God."

Following the dismissal, the General Intercessions and the Profession of Faith are said. Note the reversal of the usual order. While the RCIA allows for the General Intercessions and the Profession of Faith to be omitted

(RCIA, 156), this would ordinarily not be done, since the both are a normative part of our Sunday Eucharist.

A remembrance of the elect and their godparents is made in the Eucharistic Prayer (see Ritual Mass, "Christian Initiation: The Scrutinies"). This remembrance can be made at all Masses, even if the Scrutiny has not taken place at a particular Mass.

During this week, the presentation of the Creed is celebrated with the elect (RCIA, 157).

If a parish chooses not to use the cycle A readings, care must be taken in the celebration of the Scrutinies to use the alternative text, which eliminates the references to the Samaritan woman.

SCRIPTURE COMMENTARY

The gospel for today is made up of three examples that Jesus gives about the need to wake up and change our ways before it is too late. The first two are actual historical events he uses as examples, and the third is taken from the lessons of nature. The first event was an act of Roman violence when the governor Pilate put down a protest on the temple grounds with great ferocity because the protest had to do with his seizure of the temple treasury to pay for public works. The second was a natural disaster that had taken place as a result of an earthquake perhaps or because of faulty construction methods. The first had happened in Judea, the second in Galilee. But did it matter, Jesus asks, where it happened, or to whom it happened, or for what reason it happened? The troubling aspect is that the people affected may not have ordered their lives and sought God so as to be ready for their unexpected deaths. The story of the fig tree makes the same point. Figs grow like weeds in stony fields and even in cracks of the wall and produce a fruit that leads the owners of vineyards to tolerate their presence between the vines or olive trees. But if they prove unproductive, they can be rooted out in a moment and replaced. So, unless they bear fruit, they are taken out quickly. God, however, in Jesus' parable, gives even these trees a second chance to pull their lives together and bear fruit. It is a story of God's gracious forgiveness.

Gospel: Luke 13:1–9

Some people told Jesus about the Galileans whose blood Pilate had mingled with the blood of their sacrifices. Jesus said to them in reply, "Do you think that because these Galileans suffered in this way they were greater sinners than all other Galileans? By no means! But I tell you, if you do not repent, you will all perish as they did! Or those eighteen people who were killed when the tower at Siloam fell on them— do you think they were more guilty than everyone else who lived in Jerusalem? By no means! But I tell you, if you do not repent, you will all perish as they did!"

And he told them this parable: "There once was a person who had a fig tree planted in his orchard, and when he came in search of fruit on it but found none, he said to the gardener, 'For three years now I have come in search of fruit on this fig tree but have found none. So cut it down. Why should it exhaust the soil?' He said to him in reply, 'Sir, leave it for this year also, and I shall cultivate the ground around it and fertilize it; it may bear fruit in the future. If not you can cut it down.'"

MUSIC CONNECTION

The theophany recounted in the first reading from Exodus and its discussion of the Israelites in Egypt's bondage connects more directly with the second reading from Corinthians than with the gospel. In the epistle, it is the subsequent history of the Israelites— their grumbling and surrender to "wicked desires"—that is at the heart of Paul's message. That message is rooted in Jesus' words underscoring the need to reform our lives and repent of our evil ways. Clearly, this is a central Lenten theme reiterated in hymns such as *Believe and Repent; Ashes; Lord, Who throughout These Forty Days; Forty Days and Forty Nights;* and *Beyond the Days.* Manalo's *In These Days of Lenten Journey* helps create a broad range of social-justice commitments as a backdrop against which we should measure our reform and repentance. These include our care for those who are homeless, hungry, poor, and oppressed. Hymns such as this provide a needed trajectory by which we can measure the social as well as the individual challenges of the Lenten journey. The responsorial Psalm 103 is well arranged by both Haugen and Cotter. It is recommended that parishes with *elect* preparing to be initiated make use of the A cycle readings, which are more intimately tied in with the Lenten Scrutinies. Music suggestions based on cycle A readings can be found in the first volume of the *Paulist Liturgy Planning Guide.*

First Reading:
Joshua 5:9a, 10–12

The LORD said to Joshua, "Today I have removed the reproach of Egypt from you."

While the Israelites were encamped at Gilgal on the plains of Jericho, they celebrated the Passover on the evening of the fourteenth of the month. On the day after the Passover, they ate of the produce of the land in the form of unleavened cakes and parched grain. On that same day after the Passover, on which they ate of the produce of the land, the manna ceased. No longer was there manna for the Israelites, who that year ate of the yield of the land of Canaan.

NOTE: Because the gospels of Year A are of major importance in regard to Christian initiation, Year A readings (1 Samuel 16:1b, 6–7, 10–13a; Psalm 23:1–3, 3–4, 5, 6; Ephesians 5:8–14; John 9:1–41 or shorter form, John 9:1, 6–9, 13–17, 34–38) may be used in Year B and Year C, especially in places where there are catechumens (see Lectionary for Mass, Introduction, 97).

SCRIPTURE COMMENTARY

Today's first reading is the narrative about the first Passover celebration celebrated after the exodus journey was completely over. It took place after Joshua had split the Jordan River into a dry pathway and led the people across the river into the Promised Land, just as Moses had led them through the sea. But it is a reversed pattern: Moses celebrates Passover and then leads the people through the waters; Joshua leads them through the waters and then celebrates Passover. The people had gone from slavery to freedom, but a freedom with no bounty to live by. God had to provide the food in the desert miraculously, and yet the people often tested God and rebelled and were unfaithful. But once God had brought them from the wilderness to the land of Israel, the miraculous food stopped and they ate of the produce of the land, making their own bread for Passover. Joshua notes that once God has blessed them with prosperity, they will now be faithful in their remembrance of God's goodness to them at the exodus by their careful observance of the Passovers to come.

HOMILY HELPS

Today's parable, one of the gospels' richest, is traditionally identified as that of the prodigal son. Yet that is something of a misnomer. It is not the ne'er-do-well son who is the centerpiece but rather the forgiving father, who towers over the figures of the two uncomprehending sons.

Every Christian profits by reading and pondering this touching story on a regular basis. In elegant prose and dramatic artistry, it depicts an all-forgiving God. It is worth taking a little time here to see how subtly the goodness of God is illustrated. In the first place, the father anticipates distribution of the inheritance by granting the selfish junior son what he asks for. Then, instead of putting the allotment to good use, the son squanders it in "dissolute living." Only when he has reached the depths—a Jewish lad feeding swine!—does he plan a return to his father. He has nowhere to go but up! It is hardly a perfect act of contrition.

The drama builds as he makes his way home. What sort of welcome will he receive? But then, climactically, the father breaks all the norms of propriety, runs to his son, completely reinstates him, and then calls for a major celebration to mark his return. And what was asked of the lad? Nothing more than "Father, I am sorry."

Is it any wonder that the older son feels treated unfairly in the face of this apparent inequality? This is the ever faithful one, the one who never left home, who worked assiduously for his father, and who had never been the recipient of such lavish favors. He never names his brother as such. In speaking to his father, he refers to his brother as "your son." It is the father who corrects him in speaking of "your brother," who "was dead and has come to life."

The point touches the very truth of God. There is no imaginable wrongdoing that cannot be overcome by the power of God. And the point of the story is that God does not need to be

PSALM REFLECTION

Today we are reading only the first six verses of a twenty-three-verse psalm. As a whole, Psalm 34 develops the theme of how God rescues the afflicted and powerless who call out to him. This is expressed most strongly in the first six verses, where the psalmist stresses God's free and compassionate response to the cry of the oppressed who turn to him. He lays down no conditions for his help but instead sends his angels to guard and protect those who call to him. The remaining verses that we do not read today shift the emphasis to the insistence on the upright behavior expected of all whom God rescues.

Psalm Response
Psalm 34:2–3, 4–5, 6–7

Antiphon
Taste and see the goodness of the Lord.

Verses for Reflection
Turn away from evil and do good,
Seek peace and pursue it;
For the Lord looks favorably on the
    just,
    and hears their cries. (vv. 15–16)

SCRIPTURE COMMENTARY

Paul says the true Christian is an ambassador of the reconciliation that Christ gave to us through his death. This passage echoes the theme of the Passover in the land as the moment when the people turn from the rebellion of the desert period to become reconciled to God in faithfulness, as well as the major theme of the parable of the prodigal son in our gospel today. Paul opened chapter 5 of his letter by reminding his hearers that they have no lasting home on earth. In this age they live in anxiety and long to be with the Lord in whom they have put their hope. He has rescued them from their sins and granted them an eternal

Second Reading:
2 Corinthians 5:17–21

Brothers and sisters: Whoever is in Christ is a new creation: the old things have passed away; behold, new things have come. And all this is from God, who has reconciled us to himself through Christ and given us the ministry of reconciliation, namely, God was reconciling the world to himself in Christ, not counting their trespasses against them and entrusting to us the

persuaded. He seeks out the sinner. A legalistic approach to reconciliation has frightened more than enough people in the history of the Church. And yet, if scripture teaches us anything, it is that this is the God who asks no questions, imposes no sanctions, and shuns rigidity and aloofness. Admission is free and the password is simply "I am sorry."

Paul today speaks of a "ministry of reconciliation." One might ask if that is not the whole meaning of the Christ event—bringing people home, making room at the table of the Lord.

Just as Joshua and his people ate the fruit of the land after the celebration of Passover, the incredible gifts of God in our own life are innumerable.

If the parable of the forgiving father encourages us and convinces us of God's total forgiveness, it has done its work. We pray that our own willingness to forgive may be the measure of what God extends to us. Belief in divine forgiveness always wards off discouragement or depression in the case of failure. The outcome will be felicitous. We are like the son who was dead and is now alive again.

LITURGICAL NOTES

The fourth Sunday of Lent, previously referred to as Laetare Sunday, signifies a midway point in our Lenten journey; rose vestments may be worn. When form C of the Penitential Rite is used, the fourth set of invocations makes mention of Christ as the one who reconciles, heals the wounds of sin, and intercedes for us. The first option for the opening prayer speaks directly to our position in mid-Lent: "Let us hasten toward Easter." The preface for the fourth Sunday of Lent, used only when cycle A readings

message of reconciliation. So we are ambassadors for Christ, as if God were appealing through us. We implore you on behalf of Christ, be reconciled to God. For our sake he made him to be sin who did not know sin, so that we might become the righteousness of God in him.

SCRIPTURE COMMENTARY, CONTINUED

destiny with the Father. But they must share this gift with others, so that we who were redeemed from our sins may in turn proclaim this good news to others. We did not deserve the gift we received, so we must allow others to hear of the gift and be freed by it. The steps are that we make it known, they convert, and they accept Christ, thus becoming reconciled to God. Then we and they will be joined as one holy people of God on earth, awaiting the master's return.

Gospel: Luke 15:1–3, 11–32

Tax collectors and sinners were all drawing near to listen to Jesus, but the Pharisees and scribes began to complain, saying, "This man welcomes sinners and eats with them." So to them Jesus addressed this parable: "A man had two sons, and the younger son said to his father, 'Father give me the share of your estate that should come to me.' So the father divided the property between them. After a few days, the younger son collected all his belongings and set off to a distant country where he squandered his inheritance on a life of dissipation. When he had freely spent everything, a severe famine struck that country, and he found himself in dire need. So he hired himself out to one of the local citizens who sent him to his farm to tend the swine. And he longed to eat his fill of the pods on which the swine fed, but nobody gave him any. Coming to his senses he thought, 'How many of my father's hired workers have more than enough food to eat, but here am I, dying from hunger. I shall get up and go to my father and I shall say to him, "Father, I have sinned against heaven and against you. I no

SCRIPTURE COMMENTARY

The story of the prodigal son is just about everybody's favorite parable. Its power lies in the unconditional love the father gives the son when he receives him back home. The son had been willful and headstrong, but not really evil in a special way. He is greedy for his wealth and wants his own way, he is stubborn and imprudent and careless—but would not most of us worry that we also share many of these faults? Jesus has emphasized the son's humanity by

---

are proclaimed, focus our attention on Jesus as the one who leads us "from darkness into the light of faith." When cycle C readings are used, the preface of Lent I or Lent II or one of the prefaces from Eucharistic Prayers for Masses of Reconciliation would be appropriate. The General Intercessions should make mention of those seeking reconciliation with God, with the Church, and with other people. Both of the Eucharistic Prayers for Masses of Reconciliation are appropriate throughout the season of Lent.

On the fourth Sunday of Lent, we celebrate the Second Scrutiny for the Elect (RCIA,

164). At Masses in which the Second Scrutiny is celebrated, cycle A readings should be used. See the notes on the Scrutiny for the third Sunday of Lent. If a parish chooses not to use the cycle A readings, care must be taken in the celebration of the Scrutinies to use the alternative text, which eliminates the references to the man born blind.

Following the dismissal of the elect, the catechumens (and the candidates), the General Intercessions and the Profession of Faith are said. Note the reversal of the usual order. While the RCIA allows for the General Intercessions and the Profession of Faith to be omitted (RCIA, 156), this

would ordinarily not be done, since the both are a normative part of our Sunday Eucharist.

A remembrance of the elect and their godparents is made in the Eucharistic Prayer (see Ritual Mass, "Christian Initiation: The Scrutinies"). This remembrance can be made at all Masses, even if the Scrutiny has not taken place at a particular Mass. For the Solemn Blessing, option six or seven from Prayers over the People would be appropriate. Option six recalls the care of God even when we stray; option seven asks God to send light upon us that we might continue to devote ourselves to doing good.

SCRIPTURE COMMENTARY, CONTINUED

letting him carry on his tortured inner dialogue about how to approach his father. The father does not even let him recite his confession but immediately accepts his return home and celebrates his son's goodness, not his sins. Only then does the son realize how gracious the father is and how he acts out of unconditional love. The older brother, on the other hand, is also like us in his humanity—jealousy and possessiveness block his acceptance of his younger brother's return and his recognition of the father's freely given love to both his brother and himself. Jesus draws the lesson that humility is required to dwell in the father's house. Like the younger brother, we are all sinners and undeserving of forgiveness—but God grants it anyway; and we are all like the older brother, who judges others but does not appreciate the gifts he himself enjoys in his father's house because of his father's love.

longer deserve to be called your son; treat me as you would treat one of your hired workers.'" So he got up and went back to his father. While he was still a long way off, his father caught sight of him, and was filled with compassion. He ran to his son, embraced him and kissed him. His son said to him, 'Father, I have sinned against heaven and against you; I no longer deserve to be called your son.' But his father ordered his servants, 'Quickly bring the finest robe and put it on him; put a ring on his finger and sandals on his feet. Take the fattened calf and slaughter it. Then let us celebrate with a feast, because this son of mine was dead, and has come to life again; he was lost, and has been found.' Then the celebration began. Now the older son had been out in the field and, on his way back, as he neared the house, he heard the sound of music and dancing. He called one of the servants and asked what this might mean. The servant said to him, 'Your brother has returned and your father has slaughtered the fattened calf because he has him back safe and sound.' He became angry, and when he refused to enter the house, his father came out and pleaded with him. He said to his father in reply, 'Look, all these years I served you and not once did I disobey your orders; yet you never gave me even a young goat to feast on with my friends. But when your son returns who swallowed up your property with prostitutes, for him you slaughter the fattened calf.' He said to him, 'My son, you are here with me always; everything I have is yours. But now we must celebrate and rejoice, because your brother was dead and has come to life again; he was lost and has been found.'"

MUSIC CONNECTION

Today's second reading contains the classic statement of Pauline atonement theology that "God was reconciling the world to himself in Christ." This leads to a ministry of reconciliation, which includes spreading the message of reconciliation to all. The familiar Lucan pericope of the forgiving father/prodigal son is a fitting complement to Corinthians. Together, they allow us to focus on the loving mercy and forgiveness that God shows to us. Deiss's *God Full of Mercy* and *Yes I Shall Arise* are both good choices for today. Other hymns that come to mind include *Our Father, We Have Wandered, There's a Wideness in God's Mercy, Forgive Our Sins, The Master Came to Bring Good News,* and Norbet's *Hosea.* Since mercy and forgiveness are central to this season, other hymns previously mentioned would also fit today's liturgy. There are many fine settings of Psalm 34, today's responsorial, including those of Moore, O'Brien, Dean, and Hommerding. Selecting one of these as the communion hymn would surely reinforce the message that God is bounteous in mercy and desires to bring all of us to the table of reconciliation.

CATECHETICAL SUGGESTIONS

The book of Joshua
The feast of Passover
Acrostic psalms
History of the sacrament of reconciliation
Ways in which we can be "ministers of reconciliation" in family, church, and community
Parables and allegories: what is the difference and how to interpret them

First Reading:
Isaiah 43:16–21

Thus says the LORD,
   who opens a way in the sea
   and a path in the mighty
      waters,
who leads out chariots and
      horsemen,
   a powerful army,
till they lie prostrate together,
      never to rise,
   snuffed out and quenched
      like a wick.
Remember not the events of
      the past,
   the things of long ago con-
      sider not;
see, I am doing something
      new!
   Now it springs forth, do
      you not perceive it?
In the desert I make a way,
   in the wasteland, rivers.
Wild beasts honor me,
   jackals and ostriches,

NOTE: *Because the gospels of Year A are of major importance in regard to Christian initiation, Year A readings (Ezekiel 37:12–14; Psalm 130:1–2, 3–4, 5–6, 7–8; Romans 8:8–11; John 11:1–45 or shorter form, John 11:3–7, 17, 20–27, 33b–45) may be used in Year B and Year C, especially in places where there are catechumens (see* Lectionary for Mass, *Introduction, 97).*

SCRIPTURE COMMENTARY

The one theme that runs through all the Sundays of Lent in cycle C is that of divine reconciliation and forgiveness in all of its New Testament manifestations. So, for example, in week three we heard about God leading the people to freedom in the exodus and in week four about Joshua directing the people to celebrate Passover in the land in gratitude for God's salvation. This week we turn to the prophet Isaiah, speaking in the Babylonian exile, who recalls God's deeds of rescue in the exodus so that he can convince his listeners eight hundred years later to expect God to come again as rescuer and savior. Isaiah tells them pointedly that they should not just dream the memories of the past but are to look

HOMILY HELPS

The preservation of the touching story of Jesus forgiving the sinful woman owes as much to St. Jerome as to anyone. He included it in his Latin translation of the Bible, known as the Vulgate, even though it was absent from the earlier Greek manuscripts and has a style quite different from that of the rest of John's gospel. Some authors attribute the story to Luke. However, its retention allows one of the most merciful and compassionate encounters of Jesus' ministry to unfold before us.

But let us first, for a moment, look at the teaching of Paul that appears today. Philippians carries our union with Christ to a new level. From the other writings of Paul we know that baptism is the touchstone here as the moment of our personal immersion into the death and resurrection of Jesus. It is this experience that gives us our "knowledge" of Christ. This "knowledge" is two-pronged and involves experiencing the death of Christ by sharing in his suffering and knowing the resurrection through the sharing in his Spirit. We all have sorrows and joys in life, but in our faith

life, there are sorrows and joys that are shared with Christ himself. The sorrows that come to us, especially in carrying out our Christian mission, become part of his total offering to the Father, just as our joys are derived from the gift of the Spirit. In Holy Week each year, we have days of joy and sorrow. The services are more than visual replay; our participation in them unites us with Christ's full gift to the Father.

For Paul this experience is central, compared with which everything worldly is so much "rubbish." Yet we have not

SCRIPTURE COMMENTARY, CONTINUED

ahead eagerly and confidently. They may well despair that they could ever get home again across five hundred miles of desert, but Isaiah says that if God did it before by leading them across the Sinai desert, he can do it again—and indeed, is already preparing the way to lead them in a new exodus in their own day!

> for I put water in the desert
>   and rivers in the wasteland
>   for my chosen people to
>   drink,
> the people whom I formed for
>   myself,
>   that they might announce my
>   praise.

PSALM REFLECTION

Using the powerful imagery of farming life—sowing and reaping—the psalmist speaks about the return from exile so confidently predicted in Isaiah 43. That return had taken place despite the doubts people had entertained. They could not have even hoped for such a miracle against the overwhelming power of Babylon, but God had guided Cyrus the Great of Persia to overthrow their captors and announce the policy of sending exiles back to their homelands. Now they rejoice, celebrating God's caring love for them. The special power of this psalm is that the miracle of God's act of salvation from Babylon is actually mirrored every day. God establishes the rhythm of the seasons to bring forth food for survival in the harvest of the grain we planted as mere seeds in fear and hope. We do what little we can, but God provides the bounty.

Psalm Response
Psalm 126:1–2, 2–3, 4–5, 6

Antiphon
The Lord has done great things for us;
  we are filled with joy.

Verses for Reflection
Restore our success, O Lord,
Like water in the southern desert:
Those that sow in tears shall reap in
  joy! (vv. 4–5)

reached the end of the journey. We keep moving forward.

Will there be fallout on the journey? Probably, but we keep moving. Our vision does get blurred at times; our "experience" is sometimes not too felt. We must realize that the Jesus of the gospel is ready to forgive and forget. Has the woman been presented to him to be stoned or not? It is a dilemma. An affirmative answer would pit Jesus against Rome, which did not allow the Jews to impose the death penalty. A negative response would disregard Moses and the Jewish law. No problem. The right response is God's: let the innocent cast the first stone. There are no takers. Left alone,

Jesus quietly addresses the humiliated woman with words of encouragement and an exhortation to walk a different path. It is finished. The case is closed. The climate is one of relief, calm, and persuasion. "My ways are not your ways," says the Lord.

A saintly priest who heard countless confessions over many years was asked what he remembered most. His answer was simple. "The goodness of people." Living now in the risen Christ, we all have within us the power to do better. The more we "know" him, the more we share in his death and resurrection. There can be no stronger motivation to "go and sin no more."

LITURGICAL NOTES

As we move into the fifth week of Lent, the emphasis begins to focus more on the passion of the Lord. Both opening prayers make explicit reference to the passion. The preface for the fifth Sunday of Lent, used only when cycle A readings are proclaimed, provides a pivotal link to the readings of the day: "Christ gives us the sacraments to lift us up to eternal life." When cycle C readings are used, the preface of Lent I or Lent II would be appropriate. The General Intercessions should make mention of those who seek to find the Lord, those unjustly accused, and those who seek

Second Reading: Philippians 3:8–14

Brothers and sisters: I consider everything as a loss because of the supreme good of knowing Christ Jesus my Lord. For his sake I have accepted the loss of all things and I consider them so much rubbish, that I may gain Christ and be found in him, not having any righteousness of my own based on the law but that which comes through faith in Christ, the righteousness from God, depending on faith to know him and the power of his resurrection and the sharing of his sufferings by being conformed to his death, if somehow I may attain the resurrection from the dead.

It is not that I have already taken hold of it or have already attained perfect maturity, but I continue my pursuit in hope that I may possess it, since I have indeed been taken possession of by Christ Jesus. Brothers and sisters, I for my part do not consider myself to have taken possession. Just one thing: forgetting what lies behind but straining forward to what lies ahead, I continue my pursuit toward the goal, the prize of God's upward calling, in Christ Jesus.

SCRIPTURE COMMENTARY

Paul makes the point forcefully that nothing matters to him now but participating in the life of Christ. Once Paul had realized that Christ, by his death and resurrection, had not only rescued him from the power that sin and death had exercised over his thinking and in driving his fears, but had also given him an inheritance as a son of God in union with Christ himself, nothing else mattered. Paul now lives the life of Christ daily, both in his interior union of heart and mind with Christ and in his external actions in imitation of Christ's own selfless and forgiving love for others. Not that Paul is perfect. He realizes his weakness in this bodily life and his inability to avoid sin on his own power. Paul has come to rely on Christ to empower him and help him on his earthly journey. But he is also filled with the certain hope of everlasting life. Thus he always keeps his eye on the goal—to complete this life and be fully united to God in Christ.

reconciliation. Both of the Eucharistic Prayers for Masses of Reconciliation are appropriate throughout the season of Lent.

The cycle C readings are powerful texts: the prophet Isaiah announced that God will "remember not the events of the past," nor will God consider the things of long ago. God is doing something new. The gospel proclaims that the "new thing" God is doing is the constant bestowal of his superabundant mercy and forgiveness.

On the fifth Sunday of Lent, we celebrate the Third Scrutiny for the Elect (RCIA, 171). Cycle A readings should be used. If a parish chooses not to use the cycle A readings, care must be taken in the celebration of the

Scrutinies to use the alternative text, which eliminates the references to the raising of Lazarus. See the notes on the Scrutiny for the third Sunday of Lent.

Following the dismissal of the elect, the catechumens (and the candidates), the General Intercessions and the Profession of Faith are said. Note the reversal of the usual order. While the RCIA allows for the General Intercessions and the Profession of Faith to be omitted (RCIA, 156), this would ordinarily not be done, since the both are a normative part of our Sunday Eucharist.

A remembrance of the elect and their godparents in the Eucharistic Prayer (see Ritual Mass, "Christian Initiation: The

Scrutinies") would be appropriate. This remembrance can be made at all Masses, even if the Scrutiny has not taken place at a particular Mass. If the Solemn Blessing is to be used, option five, the Passion of the Lord, with its reference to Christ destroying death forever, is appropriate.

During the week, the Presentation of the Lord's Prayer is celebrated with the elect (RCIA, 178).

Liturgy planners should make sure that this week's bulletin contains not only the schedule for the liturgies of Holy Week—and any changes in times, locations for gathering, and the like—but also information on opportunities for the celebration of the sacrament of penance.

SCRIPTURE COMMENTARY

The story of the woman accused of adultery has two lessons for hearers. We have no idea who this woman is, but suddenly the religious leaders have placed her before Jesus and demanded that he decide whether she should be stoned to death. Their motive no doubt is to show that Jesus does not believe in observing the law's requirements. So Jesus teaches the first lesson: "Judge not lest you be judged." By doing nothing but apparently idly passing time, he forces the accusers to wonder what to do next. Then he tells anyone who is sinless to begin the punishment. None can claim that they are sinless. They have been so judgmental of the sins of others, so lacking in mercy, that they have not realized they themselves could be condemned without mercy for their sins. Then Jesus teaches the second lesson. The real response to receiving mercy when you deserved to be punished is not just gratitude but conversion. Once forgiven, you must change your life and live the mercy, compassion, and goodness that you have received—you must act as God acted toward you. Although John's gospel does not contain the Our Father prayer, this story conveys its message: "Forgive us our sins as we forgive those that have sinned against us!"

Gospel: John 8:1–11

Jesus went to the Mount of Olives. But early in the morning he arrived again in the temple area, and all the people started coming to him, and he sat down and taught them. Then the scribes and the Pharisees brought a woman who had been caught in adultery and made her stand in the middle. They said to him, "Teacher, this woman was caught in the very act of committing adultery. Now in the law, Moses commanded us to stone such women. So what do you say?" They said this to test him, so that they could have some charge to bring against him. Jesus bent down and began to write on the ground with his finger. But when they continued asking him, he straightened up and said to them, "Let the one among you who is without sin be the first to throw a stone at her." Again he bent down and wrote on the ground. And in response, they went away one by one, beginning with the elders. So he was left alone with the woman before him. Then Jesus straightened up and said to her, "Woman, where are they? Has no one condemned you?" She replied, "No one, sir." Then Jesus said, "Neither do I condemn you. Go, and from now on do not sin any more."

MUSIC CONNECTION

The theme of forgiveness and reconciliation is continued this week, especially in the story of the woman caught in adultery and dragged before Jesus. His response, "Let the one among you who is without sin cast the first stone," underscores the fact that we are all sinners and we all have a need to turn to God for mercy and forgiveness. Hymns recommended for last week, such as *Our Father, We Have Wandered; There's a Wideness in God's Mercy;* and *Forgive Our Sins* are all good choices for today as well. Roc O'Connor's *Seek the Lord* and Bob Dufford's *Save Us, O Lord* are both rousing melodies with good texts, while *Turn to Me* and *Believe and Repent* are more subdued pieces for today. Psalm 126 is well expressed by Marchionda, Guimont, Stewart, and Gelineau. While some musicians shy away from chantlike hymns, many congregations, assisted by solid accompaniment, can rise to this challenge. The tenth-century text *Attende Domine* is one such piece worth reclaiming. Its English translation by Farrell reflects key Lenten themes, especially today as the readings lead us to reflect on sin, mercy, and forgiveness.

CATECHETICAL SUGGESTIONS

Morality of war: Old Testament; just-war theory; present debate

The purpose of suffering

Faith and good works

A Catholic response to the question "Have you been saved?"

What is sin? Old Testament, New Testament, *Catechism* insights

Justice and mercy: compatible or contradictory?

Processional Gospel: Luke 19:28–40

Jesus proceeded on his journey up to Jerusalem. As he drew near to Bethphage and Bethany at the place called the Mount of Olives, he sent two of his disciples. He said, "Go into the village opposite you, and as you enter it you will find a colt tethered on which no one has ever sat. Untie it and bring it here. And if anyone should ask you, 'Why are you untying it?' you will answer, 'The Master has need of it.'" So those who had been sent went off and found everything just as he had told them. And as they were untying the colt, its owners said to them, "Why are you untying this colt?" They answered, "The Master has need of it." So they brought it to Jesus, threw their cloaks over the colt, and helped Jesus to mount. As he rode along, the people were spreading their cloaks on the road; and now as he was approaching the slope of the Mount of Olives, the whole multitude of his disciples began to praise God aloud with joy for all the mighty deeds they had seen. They proclaimed:

"Blessed is the king who comes
  in the name of the Lord.
Peace in heaven
  and glory in the highest."
Some of the Pharisees in the crowd said to him, "Teacher, rebuke your disciples." He said in reply, "I tell you, if they keep silent, the stones will cry out!"

SCRIPTURE COMMENTARY

The story of how Jesus came from the Mount of Olives into Jerusalem to the cheers of the crowds occurs in all four gospels—a rare happening indeed! Matthew and Mark, whose versions are read in the other two cycle years, have the crowds proclaim that Jesus is *messiah*, in order to fulfill the prophetic hope of Zechariah 9:9 and 14:14 that God will come to the Mount of Olives to direct the battle against all of Israel's enemies and reestablish Israel in glory. He will then send his anointed king into Jerusalem on the back of an ass (a sign of royal dignity) in triumph, but without any army because God has won the victory himself. In the account we read today, Luke removes all of the military imagery and instead has the crowd proclaim Jesus as a *king* who comes to bring peace in the name of God. This echoes the earliest Lucan prophecy of Christ's coming as king, a prophecy spoken on the night of Jesus' birth when the angels announce to the shepherds the role of the messiah as that of one who brings peace to the earth (Luke 2:14).

HOMILY HELPS

The journey theme is one of the central features of Luke's gospel. Beginning in the ninth chapter, Jesus sets out for Jerusalem, the city that stands at the heart of the Jewish faith. His journey is both literal and figurative, with his teaching on the way containing the instruction that marks the Christian path to the heavenly Jerusalem.

The teaching of Jesus in Luke's gospel ends with his final breath on the cross, at the completion of his earthly mission. The final words of Jesus from the cross are a high point in the Lucan narrative.

To better understand the significance of this terminal teaching, let us look at the contrast between Jesus' teaching and the comportment of a number of the people who surround Jesus. A dispute arises among his disciples at their final supper with the Lord over which one of them is the greatest. There is an inescapable feeling that the teaching of Jesus on humility has simply been discarded. Judas, one of the most trusted, betrays his master to the Jewish authorities and then, in the garden, singles him out with a kiss.

Peter, who had sworn to stand by Jesus' side even unto death, denies to a servant girl that he even knows Jesus. Finally, there is the vacillating Pilate. He wanted desperately to free Jesus, finding him innocent of the alleged wrongdoing, but his convictions collapse before a crowd that demands Jesus' death.

SCRIPTURE COMMENTARY

Each year in Holy Week on Palm Sunday and on Good Friday we read the story of Jesus' passion and death. Before each reading of the passion narrative, the Church offers as a first reading one of the "Servant Songs" of the book of Isaiah. Since the inner spirituality of the story of Jesus' suffering and death is his humble obedience to the will of his Father, even to accepting rejection and death, the Old Testament parallels are best seen in the figure of Isaiah's servant figure. These four songs were composed at the time of the exile in Babylon to capture the role of the prophet to proclaim God's salvation and rescue of his people, not in power and might but in a lowly and humble spirit of the servant of the despairing and the weak and those without knowledge of God's mercy—namely, the exiles themselves and the pagan peoples who had no idea of such a good God. The Servant Songs move in order from Isaiah 42 to 49 to 50 to 53, all of them expanding on the role of the prophet in speaking and witnessing to God's saving message and describing the rejection and suffering the Servant must undergo. Jesus lived out the servant message in his life. In today's selection, the third of the four Servant Songs, the emphasis falls on the servant's acceptance of the persecution and rejection that will follow from his message. Yet he does not lose hope, he does not doubt that God will be his strength and see him through.

**First Reading:
Isaiah 50:4–7**

The Lord GOD has given me
  a well-trained tongue,
that I might know how to speak
    to the weary
  a word that will rouse them.
Morning after morning
  he opens my ear that I may
    hear;
and I have not rebelled,
  have not turned back.
I gave my back to those who
    beat me,
  my cheeks to those who
    plucked my beard;
my face I did not shield
  from buffets and spitting.

The Lord GOD is my help,
  therefore I am not disgraced;
I have set my face like flint,
  knowing that I shall not be
    put to shame.

In all of this, quite apart from the physical torment that Christ suffered, there is an added weight of disappointment in the human rejection that Jesus endured.

Yet, with it all, Jesus continues his teaching from the cross. And the great lesson he imparts, even as he fulfills the Father's will, is that of forgiveness. The religious leaders have rejected him and his teaching and have become accomplices in his suffering and death. The Romans are non-believers and foreign occupiers with little sympathy for the beliefs of the Jewish population. It makes little difference that Jesus has been condemned on trumped-up charges. Yet Jesus' death is an atoning death, and he is full of compassion for all human failing. It is not surprising that his major teaching from the cross is that of forgiveness. Praying for his persecutors and their sympathizers, he asks only that their sin not be held against them.

One of the criminals sentenced to die, hanging beside him, asks only a part in Christ's future, and he is assured by the dying Savior that they will be together in Paradise.

The lesson of forgiveness from the cross is overpowering. We ourselves find it easier to forgive at some times than at others, but the forgiveness of Jesus has no such qualifications. The death penalty is seen today as society's justifiable response to violence. Jesus experiences violence personally and still forgives. Moreover, the good criminal reminds us that conversion is always a possibility, and conversion calls for a spirit of forgiveness.

Before Jesus commends his spirit to God, he is compassionate. How like the Jesus of Luke's gospel, the Jesus of chapter fifteen, with its parables of the lost sheep, the lost coin, and the lost son. There are many lessons in today's passion narrative, but it would seem that forgiveness is the main one.

Psalm Response
Psalm 22:8–9, 17–18,
19–20, 23–24

Antiphon
My God, my God, why
   have you abandoned
   me?

Verse for Reflection
Do not be far from me, for
   I am suffering;
Stay close, for I have no
   other helper! (v. 12)

PSALM REFLECTION

No psalm expresses as well the rejection of a just person by scoffers and the sufferings they make him undergo as does Psalm 22. The Church selects just a few verses from this very long psalm to highlight the links to the sufferings of Jesus. There are four sets of verses today. The first three are each echoed in the gospel itself. The gospel writers clearly saw that the passion of Jesus fulfilled God's own prophecy, particularly that expressed in Psalm 22. The fourth set of verses sums up this sense of prophetic fulfillment: Jesus knew the psalm and knew that his passion therefore was not in vain, nor was it a defeat at the hands of his enemies; no, it was God's victory to be proclaimed as a message of good news to all: God's salvation has come through the suffering of his servant and Son!

LITURGICAL NOTES

The purple that has been seen throughout Lent is now replaced by red as the Church enters into the celebration of Holy Week. Palm Sunday will bring crowds, so planners should ensure that additional ministers of hospitality/ushers are both present and prepared. Palms are given to everyone. Those who do not participate in the procession are given palms as they enter church. Palms are a significant symbol of this day, and care should be taken that they be kept with some reasonable order. You might consider a visit to the local florist to obtain the kind of boxes that long-stemmed roses come in. These are just the right size to hold an ample amount of palm for those who will be distributing it.

The memorial of the Lord's entrance in Jerusalem is to be included at every Mass, with the procession or solemn entrance taking place at the principal Mass; at other Masses the second form, the solemn entrance is used. Although the second form does not require the introduction to the liturgy, it is worth including it, since it helps to situate our actions this day in the context of the Paschal Triduum.

After the greeting, introduction, and prayer of blessing, the palm branches are sprinkled with holy water. It would be helpful if the cantor or some other minister were to invite the assembly to hold their branches high so that the people will know that it is the palm that is being sprinkled. The gospel of the Lord's entrance into Jerusalem is proclaimed and may be followed by a brief homily. Following the invitation to the procession, all move into the church, accompanied by song. When the presider reaches the chair, the Mass begins with the opening prayer; there is no Penitential Rite. With a bit of imagination and rehearsal, the opening of this liturgy can be a very effective way to begin the celebration of Holy Week.

The gospel of the Lord's passion may be proclaimed by three

SCRIPTURE COMMENTARY

The great hymn that Paul cites here was no doubt recited by the earliest Christians at the Eucharist. It is in poetic meter and set to be sung. Paul points it out to the Philippians as proof that each disciple must live and act as Christ did. He tells them that the attitude of Jesus had been to let go of his divine glory and be humiliated in our estate, to suffer rejection by his fellow human beings, but that in the end God used this to exalt his status even higher so that all people would come to worship and acknowledge him as their Lord. The true follower of Jesus will follow in his master's way by living in humble awareness that we are sinners who have been forgiven by the death of the Lord and then exalted with the gift of his Holy Spirit. Thus we do not stand on our own but in the constant grace of God working in us and transforming us. We are constantly aware of God's goodness and give him exaltation and praise for what we have received.

Second Reading: Philippians 2:6–11

Christ Jesus, though he was in the form
   of God,
   did not regard equality with God
   something to be grasped.
Rather, he emptied himself,
   taking the form of a slave,
   coming in human likeness;
   and found human in appearance,
   he humbled himself,
   becoming obedient to the point of death,
   even death on a cross.
Because of this, God greatly exalted him
   and bestowed on him the name
   which is above every name,
   that at the name of Jesus
   every knee should bend,
   of those in heaven and on earth and
     under the earth,
   and every tongue confess that
Jesus Christ is Lord,
   to the glory of God the Father.

---

readers, with the part of Christ, if possible, reserved for the priest. A brief antiphon may be sung between each section of the passion narrative. If this is done, the antiphon should come at the natural breaks in the text. There are differing options on whether the assembly should take part in the reading of the passion narrative, proclaiming the texts reserved for the crowds. It might be more effective to provide your best readers to proclaim the entire text, with the assembly taking up the antiphon marking the changes of scene or movement. While the gospel of the Lord's passion is a long reading, it is not impossible for people to stand while it is being proclaimed. Those who, due to advanced age or other disabilities, cannot stand will take it upon themselves to sit.

Due to the length of the liturgy, there might be a temptation of omit the homily, but even a brief homily can be an important invitation to enter into the mystery of these coming days.

Catholic Household Blessings and Prayers contains an Order for the Placing of Palms Branches in the Home. You may want to reproduce this text in the bulletin.

CATECHETICAL SUGGESTIONS

Isaiah's Suffering Servant
   Songs
Psalm 22 in the Old Testament and in the gospels
High Christology hymns in
   the New Testament
The centrality of the cross
The significance of Jesus'
   words on the cross in
   Luke's gospel
Eucharist in Luke and in
   1 Corinthians

Gospel: Luke 22:14—23:56
Or Shorter Form—Luke 23:1–49:

The elders of the people, chief priests and scribes, arose and brought Jesus before Pilate. They brought charges against him, saying, "We found this man misleading our people; he opposes the payment of taxes to Caesar and maintains that he is the Christ, a king." Pilate asked him, "Are you the king of the Jews?" He said to him in reply, "You say so." Pilate then addressed the chief priests and the crowds, "I find this man not guilty." But they were adamant and said, "He is inciting the people with his teaching throughout all Judea, from Galilee where he began even to here."

On hearing this Pilate asked if the man was a Galilean; and upon learning that he was under Herod's jurisdiction, he sent him to Herod who was in Jerusalem at that time. Herod was very glad to see Jesus; he had been wanting to see him for a long time, for he had heard about him and had been hoping to see him perform some sign. He questioned him at length, but he gave him no answer. The chief priests and scribes, meanwhile, stood by accusing him harshly. Herod and his soldiers treated him contemptuously and mocked him, and after clothing him in resplendent garb, he sent him back to Pilate. Herod and Pilate became friends that very day, even though they had been enemies formerly. Pilate then summoned the chief priests, the rulers, and the people and said to them, "You brought this man to me and accused him of inciting the people to revolt. I have conducted my investigation in

SCRIPTURE COMMENTARY

Luke's account of the passion of Jesus differs somewhat from that in Mark and Matthew. For example, the long form of our reading today inserts into the Last Supper itself the argument among the disciples about who is the greatest. The other gospels present it as having taken place on another occasion. Luke, however, wants to underline the theme of servanthood for readers of the passion. Not only was Jesus the servant who gave his life for us; we must also follow in his path as servants. Luke is often identified closely with Isaian themes and with the thought of St. Paul. Luke's emphasis on servanthood as the primary definition of Jesus' ministry fits not only the Servant Songs of Isaiah but also Paul's advice to the Philippians that they must humble themselves as Jesus did. A disciple of

MUSIC CONNECTION

With Passion Sunday we enter into the richest and most stirring week of the Church's liturgical year. For the pastoral liturgist and musician, this is a most challenging and taxing time. The mood swing of Passion Sunday between the exuberant and triumphal recalling of Jesus' entry into Jerusalem and the somber realism of the Lucan passion challenges the musician to reproduce this ambience in his or her selections and arrangements. There are numerous traditional hymns that befit today's celebration, including *All Glory, Laud and Honor*; *All Hail the Power of Jesus' Name*; the Vaughan Williams *At the Name of Jesus* (inspired by the second reading from Philippians); *Lift High the Cross*; and *O Sacred Head Surrounded*. For a more contemporary feel, the spiritual *Ride On King Jesus*, Schutte's *Hosanna to the Son of David*, and Christopher Walker's enticing *At the Name of Jesus* are wonderful selections. The responsorial, Psalm 22, is well presented by Haugen as well as in the Schoen/Gelineau rendition. Richard Proulx's setting is also noteworthy. Finally, Dan Schutte's helpful collection *Glory in the Cross: Music for the Easter Triduum* is an excellent resource. His refrain *We Sing the Savior's Glory* works well within the passion narrative to punctuate and, at its end, to bring closure. It provides respites that help the congregation absorb and ponder the story of Christ's passion and death. Since this year's passion is from Luke, one should not ignore the popular Berthier piece *Jesus, Remember Me*.

SCRIPTURE COMMENTARY,
CONTINUED

Jesus brings good news to the poor not by lording it over them but by being one with them as Jesus was. A true "benefactor," the title used by the Roman emperors, was not a king with armies but a real "doer of good" (*bene facio* in Latin), one who acts in a truly humble manner in leading others to know Jesus.

The Women of Jerusalem.

This notice of the women who wept as Jesus carried the cross is only in Luke's gospel. It was customary for a group of pious women to go to all crucifixions and try to alleviate the suffering of the condemned person. They would bring drugged wine to help deaden his pain, and the soldiers apparently offered this type of wine to Jesus for them. Jesus refused it (see Matt 27:34), but he asked the women to help those who would die when Jerusalem was destroyed in the future.

your presence and have not found this man guilty of the charges you have brought against him, nor did Herod, for he sent him back to us. So no capital crime has been committed by him. Therefore I shall have him flogged and then release him."

But all together they shouted out, "Away with this man! Release Barabbas to us."—Now Barabbas had been imprisoned for a rebellion that had taken place in the city and for murder.— Again Pilate addressed them, still wishing to release Jesus, but they continued their shouting, "Crucify him! Crucify him!" Pilate addressed them a third time, "What evil has this man done? I found him guilty of no capital crime. Therefore I shall have him flogged and then release him." With loud shouts, however, they persisted in calling for his crucifixion, and their voices prevailed. The verdict of Pilate was that their demand should be granted. So he released the man who had been imprisoned for rebellion and murder, for whom they asked, and he handed Jesus over to them to deal with as they wished.

As they led him away they took hold of a certain Simon, a Cyrenian, who was coming in from the country; and after laying the cross on him, they made him carry it behind Jesus. A large crowd of people followed Jesus, including many women who mourned and lamented him. Jesus turned to them and said, "Daughters of Jerusalem, do not weep for me; weep instead for yourselves and for your children for indeed, the days are coming when people will say, 'Blessed are the barren, the wombs that never bore and the breasts that never nursed.' At that time people will say to the mountains, 'Fall upon us!' and to the hills, 'Cover us!' for if these things are done when the wood is green what will happen when it is dry?" Now two others, both criminals, were led away with him to be executed.

When they came to the place called the Skull, they crucified him and the criminals there, one on his right, the other on his left. Then Jesus said, "Father, forgive them, they know not what they do." They divided his garments by casting lots. The people stood by and watched; the rulers, meanwhile, sneered at him and said, "He saved others, let him save himself if he is the chosen one, the Christ of God." Even the soldiers jeered at him. As they approached to offer him wine they called out, "If you are King of the Jews, save yourself." Above him there was an inscription that read, "This is the King of the Jews."

Now one of the criminals hanging there reviled Jesus, saying, "Are you not the Christ? Save yourself and us." The other, however, rebuking him, said in reply, "Have you no fear of God, for you are subject to the same condemnation? And indeed, we have been condemned justly, for the sentence we received corresponds to our crimes, but this man has done nothing criminal." Then he said, "Jesus, remember me when you come into your kingdom." He replied to him, "Amen, I say to you, today you will be with me in Paradise."

It was now about noon and darkness came over the whole land until three in the afternoon because of an eclipse of the sun. Then the veil of the temple was torn down the middle. Jesus cried out in a loud voice, "Father, into your hands I commend my spirit"; and when he had said this he breathed his last.

Here all kneel and pause for a short time.

The centurion who witnessed what had happened glorified God and said, "This man was innocent beyond doubt." When all the people who had gathered for this spectacle saw what had happened, they returned home beating their breasts; but all his acquaintances stood at a distance, including the women who had followed him from Galilee and saw these events.

First Reading: Exodus 12:1–8, 11–14

The LORD said to Moses and Aaron in the land of Egypt, "This month shall stand at the head of your calendar; you shall reckon it the first month of the year. Tell the whole community of Israel: On the tenth of this month every one of your families must procure for itself a lamb, one apiece for each household. If a family is too small for a whole lamb, it shall join the nearest household in procuring one and shall share in the lamb in proportion to the number of persons who partake of it. The lamb must be a year-old male and without blemish. You may take it from either the sheep or the goats. You shall keep it until the fourteenth day of this month, and then, with the whole assembly of Israel present, it shall be slaughtered during the evening twilight. They shall take some of its blood and apply it to the two doorposts and the lintel of every house in which they partake of the lamb. That same night they shall eat its roasted flesh with unleavened bread and bitter herbs.

"This is how you are to eat it: with your loins girt, sandals on your feet and your staff in

SCRIPTURE COMMENTARY

The exodus story would not have been preserved in such detail as it is, the longest sustained narrative in scripture—extending over three books (Exodus to Numbers) and recapped in Deuteronomy—had it not been closely tied to the description and detailed ritual directions of Passover. We can note that the ancient authors announced that Passover was to stand as the beginning of the new year. Rescue and escape would mark the end of a past age and the beginning of a new one. The former relationship to God had been based on remembering his promises as future possibility. The exodus event from Egypt would inaugurate a new relationship based on the very real intervention of God that liberated the people from oppression. It allowed for the formation of a new community of Israel built on celebrating the great deeds of salvation performed by their God on their behalf. This community would honor God by obedience to his commands and directions and by sacrifice and the worship of thanksgiving—giving back to

HOMILY HELPS

The Holy Thursday liturgy of Holy Week brings a variety of themes to the fore, each of which merits our thought and reflection.

The keynote is Passover, which celebrates Israel's liberation from Egyptian slavery, with the killing of the young lamb whose blood was sprinkled on Hebrew door lintels as a protective measure.

Today it is still a major feast of the Jewish calendar.

Holy Thursday celebrates the Christian message of Passover. Christ has become the spotless lamb whose sacrificial death liberates us from sin and opens the way to eternal life. The three synoptic gospels place the Last Supper on the evening of Passover; John does not, reserving the feast for the evening of Jesus' death. Holy Thursday, then, signifies our own "passover," initiated in bap-

tism and continuing through our Christian life.

Passover also means food for the journey, as the Exodus account illustrates—and the connection with the Eucharist is clear. Christ is the paschal lamb, and we eat of the lamb during our earthly journey under the form of bread and wine. This sacrifice is renewed for us as a "pledge of future glory." It is incredible to think that this can be our daily food for the asking, a constant

SCRIPTURE COMMENTARY, CONTINUED

God some of the bounty with which he had blessed their fields and flocks. More than anything else, the Passover rites combined in one ceremony the *memory* of deliverance by God's power alone and the *offering of thanksgiving* for what he had done. The lamb was the ordinary animal of sacrifice for adoration, penitence, and thanksgiving in Israel's tradition, but now its blood would also symbolize rescue from death itself, since it had preserved them when the angel of death passed over. A separate narrative spoke of the need to take only unleavened bread when one went forth from Egypt in trust under Moses. The Eucharist established by Jesus would be built on both these elements: the unleavened bread also stands for the Passover lamb, and the cup of wine stands for its blood shed to give life.

hand, you shall eat like those who are in flight. It is the Passover of the LORD. For on this same night I will go through Egypt, striking down every firstborn of the land, both man and beast, and executing judgment on all the gods of Egypt—I, the LORD! But the blood will mark the houses where you are. Seeing the blood, I will pass over you; thus, when I strike the land of Egypt, no destructive blow will come upon you.

"This day shall be a memorial feast for you, which all your generations shall celebrate with pilgrimage to the LORD, as a perpetual institution."

CATECHETICAL SUGGESTIONS

Passover celebrations
The sacrament of the Eucharist
The history of ordination and the role of priests
Extraordinary ministers of Holy Comunion
Transubstantiation
The eucharistic prayer

---

reminder of Christ's incomparable love for us. It is a gift that never fails, whether in joy or in sorrow, at weddings or at funerals. Christ is with us in the Passover gift at every turn of our life.

A second theme today is the Catholic priesthood. We have reason for gratitude and concern: no priests, no Eucharist, something much on our mind in these times of priestly shortages. Today we are grateful for the many priests who have served us so generously over the years. We think of all the Sunday Masses that go on week after week without a hitch, or the unfailing presence of the

The Blood of the Lamb. Nomadic peoples in ancient times would sacrifice a newborn lamb in the spring, right after the ewes had all given birth, when the tribe needed to move from the winter pastures in valleys to the higher hills where there were summer grasses and it was cooler for the animals. They would put the blood on the animals' coats, seeing it as a magical protection, a prayer to the gods to protect the vulnerable lambs on the dangerous journey. The Jewish people adopted this ancient practice to symbolize a new theology of salvation in which God himself led and protected his people.

priest at early weekday Masses. We think of sick calls, hospital visits, funeral services, baptisms, and marriages. Deacons and others often assist in these regular ministries, but priesthood remains

essential in so many ways and is a serious consideration as we look to the future.

The impressive sculpture of *St. Teresa in Ecstasy* by Bernini captures in stone the saint's being

**Psalm Response
Psalm 116:12–13,
15–16, 17–18**

Antiphon
Our blessing-cup is a
communion
with the Blood
of Christ.

Verse for Reflection
I am your servant,
Lord;
I am your servant,
the child of your
servant,
You have freed me
from my bonds.
(v. 16)

PSALM REFLECTION

On this night dedicated to the events of the Last Supper, Psalm 116 is chosen because it contains the enigmatic and unusual expression that God provides a "cup of salvation," generally understood to be an offering of wine poured out before the altar to the Lord. This was a well-known practice in all ancient cultures, and although it is not specified by the laws of sacrifice in Leviticus 1–7, it was natural to accompany offerings of meat to God with those of drink, just as one would offer one's own guests both food and drink at a meal honoring them. This underlies the essence of such thanksgiving sacrifices, namely, that they are communion meals with God. Just as a human family celebrates with feasting, so one can both honor and be joined with God at a sacrificial meal shared with him. Psalm 116 is a plea for deliverance from death, a plea that ends in the promise of thanksgiving by the psalmist once he knows he has been rescued. It prepares us for the meaning of the Eucharist as a memorial of the death of the Lord that leads to life.

overcome by God's love. So much of Holy Thursday is expressive of that same love: the unblemished lamb led to slaughter, the Eucharist and foot washing mutually pointing to the self-emptying of Jesus, the boundlessness of the love of God. Could God have done more? The lesson is clear for all of us. The Eucharist should bring that same humility and spirit of service to life in all of us.

> *Drinking Cups in Religious Ceremonies.* The Hebrew Scriptures mention many occasions on which libations or drinking would occur in religious contexts beyond the one in Psalm 116. Jeremiah 16:7 mentions a "cup of solace" given to mourners at a funeral. At thanksgiving sacrifices, besides the animal and grain that were offered up, a cup of water or wine was often poured out at the foot of the altar (see Exod 25:29; Num 15:1–10). Fathers would symbolically fill the cup of each member of the family. Metaphorically, then, the cup came to mean the lot given to each person in life. Thus, when God punishes, the text can say that he holds a cup of wrath and makes many drink from it (see Isa 51:17; Jer 25:15–17; Lam 4:21; Ezek 23:31–32; Hab 2:16). The cup can also stand for our fate, as in Psalms 11:6; 16:5; 23:5; and Matthew 20:22.

SCRIPTURE COMMENTARY

We hear from Paul the account of the Last Supper that he had received from the preaching of the original apostles. He keeps quite close to the versions reported by Matthew, Mark, and Luke in their gospels with a few differences. The gospel accounts accent that the Last Supper took place in the context of celebrating Passover, but Paul does not mention this as significant. Instead he associates the Last Supper with Jesus' death. He notes that the meal took place *on the night he was betrayed*, not on Passover. His final phrase, "Every time you eat this bread and drink this cup, you proclaim the *death* of the Lord until he *comes again*," is not found in the synoptics but highlights the fact that the meaning of the Eucharist memorial will be to make present the saving power of the death of Jesus for us. Paul does tell us that the bread and cup represent the body and blood of Jesus, but he does not stress the connection to the figure of the Suffering Servant of Isaiah present in the gospel accounts, which add that the blood will be poured out for the many (see Isaiah 53:11–12). For the gospel writers, the link back to the prophetic words of Isaiah were very important; for Paul, the power of the cross for deliverance of the Gentiles from their alienation and sin and subjection to the despair of death was central.

Second Reading:
1 Corinthians 11:23–26

Brothers and sisters: I received from the Lord what I also handed on to you, that the Lord Jesus, on the night he was handed over, took bread, and, after he had given thanks, broke it and said, "This is my body that is for you. Do this in remembrance of me." In the same way also the cup, after supper, saying, "This cup is the new covenant in my blood. Do this, as often as you drink it, in remembrance of me." For as often as you eat this bread and drink the cup, you proclaim the death of the Lord until he comes.

LITURGICAL NOTES

Holy Thursday stands as the beginning of the Paschal Triduum. While it celebrates the institution of the Eucharist and the priesthood, its primary focus is the beginning of the celebration of the Lord's death and resurrection.

Before the Mass of the Lord's Supper begins, the tabernacle should be empty; a sufficient amount of bread should be consecrated at this Mass for the Communion of the clergy and laity today and tomorrow. White vestments are worn. The Gloria is sung, and the church bells are rung and then remain silent until the Easter Vigil.

The individuals whose feet are washed should represent a cross-section of the local community. The number is traditionally twelve, though there is no exact requirement. This action is not as much a historical reenactment of what the Lord did at the Last Supper as it is a demonstration of the Lord's injunction of Christian charity. The action also accentuates the humble service of the Lord who came to serve and not to be served and who calls his followers to do the same.

The 2004 *Sacramentary Supplement* provides a short Rite for the Reception of the Holy Oils Blessed at the Chrism Mass. This rite would take place during the procession of the gifts of bread

Gospel: John 13:1–15

Before the feast of Passover, Jesus knew that his hour had come to pass from this world to the Father. He loved his own in the world and he loved them to the end. The devil had already induced Judas, son of Simon the Iscariot, to hand him over. So, during supper, fully aware that the Father had put everything into his power and that he had come from God and was returning to God, he rose from supper and took off his outer garments. He took a towel and tied it around his waist. Then he poured water into a basin and began to wash the disciples' feet and dry them with the towel around his waist. He came to Simon Peter, who said to him, "Master, are you going to wash my feet?" Jesus answered and said to him, "What I am doing, you do not understand now, but you will understand later." Peter said to him, "You will never wash my feet." Jesus answered him, "Unless I wash you, you will have no inheritance with me." Simon Peter said to him, "Master, then not only my feet, but my hands and head as well." Jesus said to him, "Whoever has bathed has no need except to have his feet washed, for he is clean all over; so you

SCRIPTURE COMMENTARY

Since John has no Last Supper account of the bread and wine, he emphasizes that Jesus saw the meal as a preparation for the Passover. In John's calendar, the meal took place not on Passover itself, as in the synoptic gospels, but on the day *before* the Passover. This claim allows John to accent the meaning of Jesus' crucifixion as a *passover* from this life through death to a new life. Jesus would leave his disciples temporarily behind in this world, but they would not be of this world (John 13:36; 17:6–19). They would now belong to him through his saving death and he would be with them. They do not understand how he will do this, and they question him carefully on how they are to follow him (John 14:1–7). Jesus reassures them that they are chosen, that he will send his advocate the Spirit to help them, and that they are now one with the Father and him in his love, which they will also imitate (15:12–27). All of these are part of his

and wine. After each oil is presented, the bread and wine for the Eucharist are received and Mass continues in the usual way.

It is the custom in many parishes that the Eucharist be taken directly from the altar and brought to the sick. On Holy Thursday, it is fitting that at Communion time the Eucharist be taken directly from the altar by the deacons, acolytes, or extraordinary ministers of Holy Communion for the sick and infirm who

must receive Communion at home. After Communion, a ciborium with hosts for Good Friday is left on the altar. Following the Prayer after Communion, the procession with the Holy Eucharist to the place of reposition takes place.

When the celebration has ended, the altar is stripped privately. It is fitting that any crosses be covered with a red or purple cloth. Candles should not be lit before images of saints. Holy

water may be removed from the fonts. They will be refilled with the water blessed at the Easter Vigil.

The people of the parish should be encouraged to adore the Blessed Sacrament for a suitable period of time during the night. From midnight onward, however, the adoration is made without external solemnity, for the day of the Lord's passion has begun.

SCRIPTURE COMMENTARY, CONTINUED

farewell speech to his disciples. It is thus understandable why John begins this section with Jesus washing the feet of the disciples and commanding them to do likewise. They cannot be united to Jesus, or follow him, or share in his new life, unless they imitate him by serving one another. Jesus insists that no disciple is truly one with him until that person has fully understood the role of the Suffering Servant in his or her life.

are clean, but not all." For he knew who would betray him; for this reason, he said, "Not all of you are clean."

So when he had washed their feet and put his garments back on and reclined at table again, he said to them, "Do you realize what I have done for you? You call me 'teacher' and 'master,' and rightly so, for indeed I am. If I, therefore, the master and teacher, have washed your feet, you ought to wash one another's feet. I have given you a model to follow, so that as I have done for you, you should also do."

Other Symbolism in the Washing of the Feet. *Since Jesus takes off his cloak and lays it down, and then at the end of the footwashing, "takes it up again," there is a striking resemblance to John 10:11–18, where Jesus says that he as the Good Shepherd will lay down his life and take it up again for his sheep. This has led many commentators to understand that the washing of the feet here is not so much a lesson in humility as a symbol of Jesus' death for others and the humiliation he would undergo through that death.*

MUSIC CONNECTION

In the Roman calendar the celebration of Easter begins with the Evening Mass of the Lord's Supper on Holy Thursday. This underscores the liturgical understanding that Easter is a triduum, a three-day celebration of the Lord's dying and rising viewed from slightly different perspectives. While Holy Thursday is pregnant with several themes such as Eucharist, priesthood, and discipleship, the theme that most focuses the paschal mystery tonight is servanthood. "If I, therefore, the master and teacher, have washed your feet, you ought to wash one another's feet... as I have done for you, you should also do" (John 13:14–15). Hymns that stress service to others include Gillard's *The Servant Song, Jesus Took a Towel,* Alan Hommerding's *The Sacrament of Service, No Greater Love* by Schoenbachler, and *Jesu, Jesu.* Be sure to have a festive and vibrant Gloria, such as Chepponis's *Melodic Gloria* or David Haas's setting from his *Mass of Light,* ready for this evening's celebration. The responsorial, Psalm 116, is well presented either by Haas or the Peloquin/Gelineau collaboration. During the foot washing, consider Dan Schutte's *All I Have Done for You,* which is a perfect match for the ritual action. Other possibilities include *Where There Is Love* by Hughes and Larry Rosania's *Ubi Caritas.* For the transfer of the Eucharist to the chapel of repose, both the traditional *Pange Lingua* and the late Alex Peloquin's masterful *In Memory of You* are excellent choices.

GOOD FRIDAY

First Reading: Isaiah 52:13—53:12

See, my servant shall prosper,
  he shall be raised high and greatly exalted.
Even as many were amazed at him—
  so marred was his look beyond human
    semblance
  and his appearance beyond that of the sons
    of man—
so shall he startle many nations,
  because of him kings shall stand speech-
    less;
for those who have not been told shall see,
  those who have not heard shall ponder it.

Who would believe what we have heard?
  To whom has the arm of the LORD been
    revealed?
He grew up like a sapling before him,
  like a shoot from the parched earth;
there was in him no stately bearing to make
  us look at him,
  nor appearance that would attract us to
    him.
He was spurned and avoided by people,
  a man of suffering, accustomed to
    infirmity,

SCRIPTURE COMMENTARY

Scholars are often divided as to whether Jesus himself meditated on this powerful passage from Isaiah, which describes the prophet undergoing suffering to bring his message to all—even at the ends of the earth—who have never heard of hope or salvation. It seems highly likely that Jesus very early understood his work to be that of the servant. Jesus gave as much time to those outside Israel as to those within. He accepted suffering as his almost certain fate, and he remained faithful to his Father as his redeemer through every trial. It is unlikely he would have found such a model of ministry anywhere else except in the Servant Songs of Isaiah (chapters 42, 49, 50, and 53). Several things can be noted in Isaiah 53 that stand out as unique among the Old Testament prophets. The term "servant" is often found referring to the king who pledges obedience to his master, God. But it is rarely applied to a prophet. This servant-prophet is asked to die for his message, something that was not asked even of Jeremiah in the

HOMILY HELPS

No word comes more readily to mind on Good Friday than generosity. Our first reading today speaks of the servant of the Lord who suffers and atones not for his own sins but for those of others. For Christians, the servant is Christ himself, who, in the words of the epistle to the Hebrews, through what he endured became the source of our eternal life. Our hope rests in the generosity of a single man.

On Good Friday our passion narrative is from John's gospel. In each of Jesus' final words from the cross, there is profound meaning to be explored. It is worth the effort to consider each of these in turn.

"Woman, behold, your son... Behold, your mother." Two figures stand at the cross, the mother of Jesus and the unidentified disciple whom Jesus loved. The symbolism here is important. "Woman" was a respectful title, but not one ordinarily used in addressing one's mother. We are carried back to the "woman" in Genesis, who was called "woman" because she was taken "from man." Eve is also referred to as the "mother of the living." The same is true of the Johannine woman. Mary is here a symbol of the Church, the mother of those who live the new life in the Spirit.

Whoever the disciple may have been historically, he here stands for the faithful follower and intimate friend of Jesus—in short, for all of us. The Church here embraces the disciple and the disciple takes the Church to himself. The firstfruits of the cross unite Church and member in what Paul calls "the body of Christ."

"I thirst." Once again in John common expressions—bread, water, light, sight—take on a deeper meaning. More than referring to a physical need, Jesus speaks of another kind of thirst, the thirst to do his Father's will (18:11), which will then make of him a conduit of the water/Spirit of life (4:14). Jesus speaks here of

SCRIPTURE COMMENTARY,
CONTINUED

end, although he was often in danger of being killed for his preaching. Also, the death itself is an unjust death—the victim is innocent of any evil and is betrayed and abandoned even by his supporters. Finally, this death has a value beyond itself—that is, the servant accepts it to save others from their sins. It also confers divine salvation, since it is given for the life of others and God accepts this and as a result glorifies his servant.

one of those from whom people hide
their faces,
spurned, and we held him in no
esteem.

Yet it was our infirmities that he bore,
our sufferings that he endured,
while we thought of him as stricken,
as one smitten by God and afflicted.
But he was pierced for our offenses,
crushed for our sins;
upon him was the chastisement that
makes us whole,
by his stripes we were healed.
We had all gone astray like sheep,
each following his own way;
but the LORD laid upon him
the guilt of us all.

Though he was harshly treated, he
submitted
and opened not his mouth;
like a lamb led to the slaughter
or a sheep before the shearers,
he was silent and opened not his
mouth.
Oppressed and condemned, he was
taken away,
and who would have thought any
more of his destiny?
When he was cut off from the land of
the living,

and smitten for the sin of his people,
a grave was assigned him among the
wicked
and a burial place with evildoers,
though he had done no wrong
nor spoken any falsehood.
But the LORD was pleased
to crush him in infirmity.

If he gives his life as an offering for
sin,
he shall see his descendants in a long
life,
and the will of the LORD shall be
accomplished through him.

Because of his affliction
he shall see the light
in fullness of days;
through his suffering, my servant shall
justify many,
and their guilt he shall bear.
Therefore I will give him his portion
among the great,
and he shall divide the spoils with the
mighty,
because he surrendered himself to
death
and was counted among the wicked;
and he shall take away the sins of
many,
and win pardon for their offenses.

his thirst for souls. It is for this that he has become shepherd and guardian, the Savior of the world. This is the same master who, recognizing the woman's desire for water in chapter 4, gave her the water of faith, the Spirit of new life that bubbles up to eternal life.

"It is finished." Everything that the Father has given Jesus to do is accomplished. The plan that was inaugurated, even though

obliquely, centuries ago through the patriarchs and prophets has come to fulfillment. Indeed, Abraham desired to see this day, did so, and rejoiced. What occurred in a humble house in Nazareth some thirty years earlier was the beginning of the final moment. On the cross it was accomplished. "Bowing his head, he handed over the spirit." In John this is more than expiring. With Jesus' death he hands over the

Spirit of the living God, the first gift of the crucified Christ.

We all play a part in this final scene. As beloved disciples, we are sons and daughters of the Church, which, even with its human flaws, pulsates with the Spirit of Christ. And all this has come to pass because of the generosity, the goodness of a God who will never abandon us or leave us orphans.

Psalm Response
Psalm 31:2, 6, 12–13,
15–16, 17, 25

Antiphon
Father, into your hands I
commend my spirit.

Verse for Reflection
My fate is in your hands;
Rescue me from the grasp
of my enemies
and my persecutors. (v. 16)

PSALM REFLECTION

Psalm 31 expresses the depths of human trust in God. On the one hand, the psalmist prays for God's intervention to rescue him from his enemies. He compares the suffering at their hands to death itself. He needs God's intervention desperately in this hour of need and is willing to humble himself to ask for it. But at the same time he also trusts completely that God will stay beside him—he can even put his very life into God's hands without fear. This combination of begging divine help while believing completely in God's intention to save him forms a striking response to both the Isaiah reading and the gospel of the passion. Luke quotes the verse "Into your hands I commend my spirit" (Ps 31:5) as the final word of Jesus on the cross (Luke 23:46). It is Jesus' acceptance of his Father's will and the act of final and total obedience on his part to his Father. It fulfills the prayer he said in the garden of Gethsemane, "Not my will, but thy will be done" (Luke 22:44).

LITURGICAL NOTES

The Celebration of the Lord's Passion is a unique liturgy. The altar is bare, without candles, cloths, or cross. The liturgy begins in silence, and as the ministers arrive at the altar, they prostrate themselves, while the assembly kneels. Following the Opening Prayer, the liturgy of the word begins.

The gospel of the Lord's passion may be proclaimed by three readers, with the part of Christ, if possible, reserved for the priest.

A brief antiphon may be sung between each section of the passion. If this is done, the antiphon should come at the natural breaks in the text. There are differing opinions on whether the assembly should take part in the passion, proclaiming the texts reserved for the crowds. It might be more effective to provide your best readers to proclaim the entire text, with the assembly taking up the antiphon marking changes of scene or movement. While the passion gospel is long, it is not impossible for people to stand throughout the entire read-

ing. Those who due to advanced age or other disabilities cannot stand will take it upon themselves to sit.

While the reading of the passion is lengthy, homilists should avoid the temptation to reduce, minimize, or even omit the homily. After the homily, the General Intercessions begin. Each of the intercessions has two parts: the introduction, which states the intention, and a concluding prayer. After each introduction, there is a pause for silent prayer, and an acclamation

SCRIPTURE COMMENTARY

While the author of Hebrews is unknown to us, the letter reflects a particularly strong Jewish Hellenistic (i.e., from the Greek-speaking Jewish communities outside Palestine) way of arguing. It uses many of the typical methods of comparison and dialectical argument. In this passage the author compares the role of Jesus to that of the normal high priest of the Jewish temple. The earthly priest offers up prayers for his own sins as well as those of the people, and he proclaims the words of divine blessing over the people, not because of his own holiness or worthiness but because his role was to speak the sacred formulas in the temple liturgy. But Jesus, as high priest ascended into the divine realm, participates in God's own sinlessness and power to save. He can confer the divine blessing on us when we approach him. What makes this really possible is that he knows our situation firsthand. Moreover, God clearly answered Jesus' human call to God for deliverance (such as that expressed in Ps 31) by delivering him from death. This passage from Hebrews may seem to suggest Jesus never really died at all, but in light of the rest of the letter, we should take the words here as referring to the resurrection following Jesus' death. In dying, Jesus showed that his obedience to God was perfect and so he has now become the source of salvation by reason of his divine status with the Father.

Second Reading: Hebrews 4:14–16; 5:7–9

Brothers and sisters: Since we have a great high priest who has passed through the heavens, Jesus, the Son of God, let us hold fast to our confession. For we do not have a high priest who is unable to sympathize with our weaknesses, but one who has similarly been tested in every way, yet without sin. So let us confidently approach the throne of grace to receive mercy and to find grace for timely help.

In the days when Christ was in the flesh, he offered prayers and supplications with loud cries and tears to the one who was able to save him from death, and he was heard because of his reverence. Son though he was, he learned obedience from what he suffered; and when he was made perfect, he became the source of eternal salvation for all who obey him.

may then be sung before the concluding prayer. An option is to use the traditional "Let us kneel," followed by a period of silent prayer, along with "Let us stand" for the concluding prayer. If the assembly is invited to kneel, there should be a significant amount of time for silent prayer, lest the ritual become an exercise in gymnastics.

A collection for the Holy Land usually precedes the veneration of the cross.

There are two forms for the showing of the cross, unveiling or procession. There may be up to three stations for the veneration of the cross, but it is recommended that only one cross be used for veneration. While this might appear on the surface to be overly time-consuming, the veneration becomes a powerful individual and communal symbol as people approach the one cross and offer their act of veneration.

When the veneration of the cross has been concluded, the altar is covered and a deacon or priest brings the Blessed Sacrament to the altar. All stand for the Lord's Prayer and the other prayers as given in the Sacramentary. Communion is then distributed to the people.

Following the Prayer after Communion and the Prayer over the People, the ministers depart in silence. The altar is then stripped without ceremony.

Gospel: John 18:1—19:42

Jesus went out with his disciples across the Kidron valley to where there was a garden, into which he and his disciples entered. Judas his betrayer also knew the place, because Jesus had often met there with his disciples. So Judas got a band of soldiers and guards from the chief priests and the Pharisees and went there with lanterns, torches, and weapons. Jesus, knowing everything that was going to happen to him, went out and said to them, "Whom are you looking for?" They answered him, "Jesus the Nazorean." He said to them, "I AM." Judas his betrayer was also with them. When he said to them, "I AM," they turned away and fell to the ground. So he again asked them, "Whom are you looking for?" They said, "Jesus the Nazorean." Jesus answered, "I told you that I AM. So if you are looking for me, let these men go." This was to fulfill what he had said, "I have not lost any of those you gave me." Then Simon Peter, who had a sword, drew it, struck the high priest's slave, and cut off his right ear. The slave's name was Malchus. Jesus

SCRIPTURE COMMENTARY

The passion for Good Friday is always taken from John's gospel. For the most part, in the rest of his gospel, John takes a path different from that of the synoptics and has few stories in common with them. But in the passion narrative, John records most of the same series of events as do the other gospels. All four gospels have lengthy narratives of the passion, and it seems that they all draw on a long and fairly fixed tradition of how to present the passion story. It may have been the first part of the gospel tradition to be put into writing, and all four gospels drew on some earlier written story or outline of the events. John has two special emphases, however, not strongly presented in the

MUSIC CONNECTION

If Holy Thursday directed our gaze to the paschal mystery from the perspective of service to others, Good Friday views it from the trajectory of Jesus' suffering and physical death. As we well know, the liturgical year is not an exercise in historical "make believe" wherein we are transported back in time to relive Jesus' last hours. No, rooted in the present, we find in Jesus' suffering and death the mirror of our own *transitus* to

deeper life and glory. In his dying, Jesus has conquered death and been "lifted up" because John's cross is a cross of triumph and glory. Hymns today run the gamut from *O Sacred Head Surrounded, Sing My Tongue the Song of Triumph,* and Berthier's popular *Stay with Me* to the Watts classic *When I Survey the Wondrous Cross* and Dufford's *Behold the Lamb of God.* Psalm 31, the responsorial, is rendered well by Talbot, Schutte, and Howard Hughes. Frank Strahan and Nick Freund

also have a good setting (World Library). Dan Schutte has provided a wonderful strophe, *We Sing the Savior's Glory*, to punctuate the reading of the passion narrative. Finally, the veneration of the cross, the centerpiece of the Good Friday liturgy, requires good congregational singing. Hymns such as *Behold the Wood; Keep in Mind; Crucem Tuam; Shepherd Me, O God; Jesus, Remember Me;* and *My Song Is Love Unknown* can meet this need with beauty and pathos.

SCRIPTURE COMMENTARY,
CONTINUED

other gospels. One is the lengthy discussion with Pilate and the high priests over his kingship. Jesus shows a strong awareness that his death is not a defeat but the mysterious victory of God, who will validate that he is truly God's Son and at the same time establish him as a king whose kingdom is far beyond that of Herod or Pilate or the High Priest. The other is the

CATECHETICAL SUGGESTIONS

The Suffering Servant: Israel and Jesus
Ways others have given their lives for us
Ways we have given our lives for others
Ways we have suffered persecution
Ways we have persecuted others
Low and high Christology

said to Peter, "Put your sword into its scabbard. Shall I not drink the cup that the Father gave me?"

So the band of soldiers, the tribune, and the Jewish guards seized Jesus, bound him, and brought him to Annas first. He was the father-in-law of Caiaphas, who was high priest that year. It was Caiaphas who had counseled the Jews that it was better that one man should die rather than the people.

Simon Peter and another disciple followed Jesus. Now the other disciple was known to the high priest, and he entered the courtyard of the high priest with Jesus. But Peter stood at the gate outside. So the other disciple, the acquaintance of the high priest, went out and spoke to the gatekeeper and brought Peter in. Then the maid who was the gatekeeper said to Peter, "You are not one of this man's disciples, are you?" He said, "I am not." Now the slaves and the guards were standing around a charcoal fire that they had made, because it was cold, and were warming themselves. Peter was also standing there keeping warm.

The high priest questioned Jesus about his disciples and about his doctrine. Jesus answered him, "I have spoken publicly to the world. I have always taught in a synagogue or in the temple area where all the Jews gather, and in secret I have said nothing. Why ask me? Ask those who heard me what I said to them. They know what I said." When he had said this, one of the temple guards standing there struck Jesus and said, "Is this the way you answer the high priest?" Jesus answered him, "If I have spoken wrongly, testify to the wrong; but if I have spoken rightly, why do you strike me?" Then Annas sent him bound to Caiaphas the high priest.

Now Simon Peter was standing there keeping warm. And they said to him, "You are not one of his disciples, are you?" He denied it and said, "I am not." One of the slaves of the high priest, a relative of the one whose ear Peter had cut off, said, "Didn't I see you in the garden with him?" Again Peter denied it. And immediately the cock crowed.

Then they brought Jesus from Caiaphas to the praetorium. It was morning. And they themselves did not enter the praetorium, in order not to be defiled so that they could eat the Passover. So Pilate came out to them and said, "What charge do you bring against this man?" They answered and said to him, "If he were not a criminal, we would not have handed him over to you." At this, Pilate said to them, "Take him yourselves, and judge him according to your law." The Jews answered him, "We do not have the right to execute anyone," in order that the word of Jesus might be fulfilled that he said indicating the kind of death he would die. So Pilate went back into the praetorium and summoned Jesus and said to him, "Are you the King of the Jews?" Jesus answered, "Do you say this on your own or have others told you about me?" Pilate answered, "I am not a Jew, am I? Your own nation and the chief priests handed you over to me. What have you done?" Jesus answered, "My kingdom does not belong to this world. If my kingdom did belong to this world, my attendants would be fighting to keep me from being handed over to the Jews. But as it is, my kingdom is not here." So Pilate said to him, "Then you are a king?" Jesus answered, "You say I am a king. For this I was born and for this I came into the world, to testify to the truth. Everyone who belongs to the truth listens to my voice." Pilate said to him, "What is truth?"

When he had said this, he again went out to the Jews and said to them, "I find no guilt in him. But you have a custom that I release one prisoner to you at Passover. Do you want me to release to you the King of the Jews?" They cried out again, "Not this one but Barabbas!" Now Barabbas was a revolutionary.

Then Pilate took Jesus and had him scourged. And the soldiers wove a crown out of thorns and placed it on his head, and clothed him in a purple cloak, and they came to him and said, "Hail, King of the Jews!" And they struck him repeatedly. Once more Pilate went out and said to them, "Look, I am bringing him out to you, so that you may know that I find no guilt in him." So Jesus came out, wearing the crown of thorns and the purple cloak. And he said to them, "Behold, the man!" When the chief priests and the guards saw him they cried out, "Crucify him, crucify him!" Pilate said to them, "Take him yourselves and crucify him. I find no guilt in him." The Jews answered, "We have a law, and according to that law he ought to die, because he made himself the Son of God." Now when Pilate heard this statement, he became even more afraid, and went back into the praetorium and said to Jesus, "Where are you from?" Jesus did not answer him. So Pilate said to him, "Do you not speak to me? Do you not know that I have power to release you and I have power to crucify you?" Jesus answered him, "You would have no power over me if it had not been given to you from above. For this reason the one who handed me over to you has the greater sin." Consequently, Pilate tried to release him; but the Jews cried out, "If you release him, you are not a Friend of Caesar. Everyone who makes himself a king opposes Caesar."

When Pilate heard these words he brought Jesus out and seated him on the judge's bench in the place called Stone Pavement, in Hebrew, Gabbatha. It was preparation day for Passover, and it was about noon. And he said to the Jews, "Behold, your king!" They cried out, "Take him away, take him away! Crucify him!" Pilate said to them, "Shall I crucify your king?" The chief priests answered, "We have no king but Caesar." Then he handed him over to them to be crucified.

So they took Jesus, and, carrying the cross himself, he went out to what is called the Place of the Skull, in Hebrew, Golgotha. There they crucified him, and with him two others, one on either side, with Jesus in the middle. Pilate also had an inscription written and put on the cross. It read, "Jesus the Nazorean, the King of the Jews." Now many of the Jews read this inscription, because the place where Jesus was crucified was near the city; and it was written in Hebrew, Latin, and Greek. So the chief priests of the Jews said to Pilate, "Do not write 'The King of the Jews,' but that he said, 'I am the King of the Jews.'" Pilate answered, "What I have written, I have written."

When the soldiers had crucified Jesus, they took his clothes and divided them into four shares, a share for each soldier. They also took his tunic, but the tunic was seamless, woven in one piece from the top down. So they said to one another, "Let's not tear it, but cast lots for it to see whose it will be," in order that the passage of Scripture might be fulfilled that says:

SCRIPTURE COMMENTARY,
CONTINUED

presentation of Jesus as the "lamb of God," whose death fulfills his mission to deliver the people from slavery by his blood, as did the death of the Passover lamb, whose blood was smeared on the houses of Israelites in Egypt to preserve them from the angel of death. In this gospel, both themes have played a role from the very beginning. Already in chapter 1

The "Place of the Skull." The gospel speaks of the "Place of the Skull," but Matthew 27:33 and Mark 15:22 call it, technically, the place of "a skull." This leads to different theories of where Jesus was crucified. Executions took place outside the city walls but close enough so that people could watch from atop the city walls. One interpretation holds that the place was a small hill, just outside the walls, that resembled a human head or skull. Another is that it was the official execution grounds where skulls littered the ground. Another—and less likely—option is that it refers to a shrine to Adam, whose skull was supposed to have been buried in Jerusalem at the center of the universe. From the earliest centuries, the site has been identified with the location of the Church of the Holy Sepulchre, which is inside Jerusalem's walls today. But in ancient times, it may have stood outside the then current north wall. It was only in about AD 50 that the present line of walls on the north side of the city was completed.

SCRIPTURE COMMENTARY,
CONTINUED

John the Baptist had pointed to Jesus, saying, "Behold the Lamb of God" (John 1:36). In the same chapter, Nathanael announces that Jesus is both Son of God and king of Israel. The evangelist John expects us to follow how all three titles come to fulfillment throughout the gospel.

They divided my garments among them,
and for my vesture they cast lots.
This is what the soldiers did. Standing by the cross of Jesus were his mother and his mother's sister, Mary the wife of Clopas, and Mary of Magdala. When Jesus saw his mother and the disciple there whom he loved he said to his mother, "Woman, behold, your son." Then he said to the disciple, "Behold, your mother." And from that hour the disciple took her into his home.

After this, aware that everything was now finished, in order that the Scripture might be fulfilled, Jesus said, "I thirst." There was a vessel filled with common wine. So they put a sponge soaked in wine on a sprig of hyssop and put it up to his mouth. When Jesus had taken the wine, he said, "It is finished." And bowing his head, he handed over the spirit.

Here all kneel and pause for a short time.

Now since it was preparation day, in order that the bodies might not remain on the cross on the sabbath, for the sabbath day of that week was a solemn one, the Jews asked Pilate that their legs be broken and that they be taken down. So the soldiers came and broke the legs of the first and then of the other one who was crucified with Jesus. But when they came to Jesus and saw that he was already dead, they did not break his legs, but one soldier thrust his lance into his side, and immediately blood and water flowed out. An eyewitness has testified, and his testimony is true; he knows that he is speaking the truth, so that you also may come to believe. For this happened so that the Scripture passage might be fulfilled:
Not a bone of it will be broken.
And again another passage says:
They will look upon him whom they have pierced.

After this, Joseph of Arimathea, secretly a disciple of Jesus for fear of the Jews, asked Pilate if he could remove the body of Jesus. And Pilate permitted it. So he came and took his body. Nicodemus, the one who had first come to him at night, also came bringing a mixture of myrrh and aloes weighing about one hundred pounds. They took the body of Jesus and bound it with burial cloths along with the spices, according to the Jewish burial custom. Now in the place where he had been crucified there was a garden, and in the garden a new tomb, in which no one had yet been buried. So they laid Jesus there because of the Jewish preparation day; for the tomb was close by.

The Garden Tomb. Some modern scholars have identified a skull shape to the hill just north of the present wall of Jerusalem. It was first noticed by General Gordon, the English victor in the Sudanese war for Khartoum, in the 1880s, and soon Protestants concluded that it must have been the burial place of Jesus. There is even a tomb with a stone rolled over it nearby. It makes a wonderful scene to picture the ancient site but is unlikely to be the authentic place of burial, since no one ever mentioned or suggested that location before the nineteenth century and the excavations of the Antonia fortress and nearby areas in central Jerusalem around the Church of the Holy Sepulchre support the existence of a wall that stood there in the days of Pilate. Moreover, the Romans went to great trouble to build a temple of Athena over the present Holy Sepulchre site, and the only reason for such an unlikely temple location would have been to obliterate or cover over a place sacred to local Jews—in this case the Christians, who were seen by the Romans as a Jewish sect.

EASTER VIGIL—YEAR C

First Reading: Genesis 1:1—2:2
Or Shorter Form—Genesis 1:1, 26–31a:

In the beginning, when God created the heavens and the earth, God said: "Let us make man in our image, after our likeness. Let them have dominion over the fish of the sea, the birds of the air, and the cattle, and over all the wild animals and all the creatures that crawl on the ground.

God created man in his image;
in the image of God he created him;
male and female he created them.
God blessed them, saying: "Be fertile and multiply; fill the earth and subdue it. Have dominion over the fish of the sea, the birds of the air, and all the living things that move on the earth." God also said: "See, I give you every seed-bearing plant all over the earth and every tree that has seed-bearing fruit on it to be your food; and to all the animals of the land, all the birds of the air, and all the living creatures that crawl on the ground, I give all the green plants for food." And so it happened. God looked at everything he had made, and found it very good.

SCRIPTURE COMMENTARY

One of the most striking features of the story of God's loving creation of the world is that it takes place in an orderly manner on each day of a single week. The order in the first chapter of Genesis moves from the largest and most remote of physical processes, such as separating the realms of sky, earth, and sea from each other, down to the closest to home, asking why human beings are the way they are. To put it another way, God begins creation with light, a quality often associated with revealing the divine glory itself whenever God makes an appearance on earth, but ends with the gift of the truest image and likeness of divinity bestowed on the human being. Since God sees each stage of creation as good, then each day is described as leading into the next until it reaches a climax in the double blessing bestowed on the man and woman. Both blessings share in the very essence of God's relationship to his world: one confers the right to rule creatures as God himself does—with care and love—and the other grants partnership with God in creating new life itself. No wonder, then, that at the end of the final day of creation, God rests and beholds his entire work as "very good" indeed. When we read this magnificent account of the beginnings of our world, we realize how small we are before the goodness of God and how blessed indeed we are within his plan for that world.

HOMILY HELPS

If during Lent we have traveled a lengthy biblical journey describing God's activity in the world, in the Easter Vigil we see it all captured in one evening. The Vigil is a dramatic presentation geared especially to the catechumens to be baptized, showing their part in this salvation history, which carries us back to the very beginnings.

Initially there is the Genesis account, which illustrates the pre-eminence of man and woman in the order of creation. Abraham is then chosen to to be the conduit of salvation as the father of a new people; the honor, however, is not given without the challenge of unqualified obedience. The Exodus account of passing through the Red Sea presages the baptismal waters that will soon liberate new Christians from the clutches of sin and death.

There are readings from the prophets, notably Isaiah and Ezekiel, which speak encouragingly of God's covenant love and a new spirit that will guide and direct our lives.

The New Testament reading from Romans is clearly set in the context of the baptismal ceremony itself. In ancient times, candidates were fully immersed in a pool of water from which they emerged as new children of God. It was a reenactment of the burial of Christ, with his descent into the tomb and his resurrection on Easter morning. There are many ways for sin to be forgiven in the Christian experience, but none matches that of baptism. As the old is left behind, the new white garment of forgiveness and engagement envelops us.

PSALM REFLECTION

Psalm 104 makes a fitting response to the story of creation because it emphasizes the glory and greatness of God's wisdom and love in ordering all things according to his intention. Each and every part has a beauty that matches all the other parts. The psalmist extols all of creation as directed to the good of human beings, while humans in turn recognize the wisdom and intelligence of God's design for the world.

Psalm Response
Psalm 104:1–2, 5–6, 10, 12, 13–14, 24, 35
(or Psalm 33:4–5, 6–7, 12–13, 20–22)

Antiphon
Lord, send out your Spirit, and renew the face
of the earth.

Verse for Reflection
You set the earth on its foundations
not to be toppled forever. (Ps 104:5)

SCRIPTURE COMMENTARY

God's creatures may have been created good and human beings constituted in blessing to share God's work as partners, as Genesis 1 suggested, but the rest of the biblical story mostly tells of the human failure to obey God and retain his blessing. Still, God does not abandon these rebellious children but returns over and over to win them back to himself. The story of Abraham and his family is the first example of these extraordinary relationships where a person responds fully to the invitation of God to know and trust in him. The narratives about Abraham stress how he continues to believe in the promises of God that he will become the ancestor of a great nation, even when fulfillment of the promises seems impossible or improbable. Such complete trust in God is tested in

Second Reading: Genesis 22:1–18
Or Shorter Form—Genesis 22:1–2, 9a,
  10–13, 15–18:

God put Abraham to the test. He called to him, "Abraham!" "Here I am," he replied. Then God said: "Take your son Isaac, your only one, whom you love, and go to the land of Moriah. There you shall offer him up as a holocaust on a height that I will point out to you."

When they came to the place of which God had told him, Abraham built an altar there and arranged the wood on it. Then he reached out and took the knife to slaughter his son. But the LORD's messenger called to him from heaven, "Abraham, Abraham!" "Here I am," he answered.

Luke's account of the resurrection carries a slight note of disappointment. The first witnesses to the angels' announcement were Mary of Magdala, Joanna, and Mary, the mother of James. Their report of the happening to the disciples was considered "nonsense" and not worthy of belief. For many years women have been the carriers of truth, but we have been slow to accord them the recognition they deserve. And yet, for close to two centuries, they have been the backbone of the church in America.

But there is always the inescapable fact that at the empty tomb the faithful ones were the women who remained to watch and wait.

LITURGICAL NOTES

The Easter Vigil, the mother of all vigils, should not begin until approximately one hour after sunset, to ensure that the service begins in darkness. The Easter Vigil consists of four parts.

The first part includes the blessing of the new fire, the lighting of the candle, the procession into the church, and the singing of the Easter Proclamation. While a large fire presents its own set of problems, they are not insurmountable. Local troops of Scouts can be of great assistance, along with the local fire department. This new fire is significant, for from it will come the light that will illumine our church for the next fifty

days. The singing of the Easter Proclamation can be done by a deacon, a priest, or another minister. More important than who sings the Easter Proclamation is that it be sung, and sung well.

The second part of the liturgy is the liturgy of the word. While the Lectionary provides seven readings, their accompanying psalms and concluding collects, that number may be reduced to two; the reading from Exodus must always be read. Planners should exercise care when contemplating the reduction of the readings, since these readings unfold the whole of salvation history. After the vigil readings are completed, the Gloria is sung, the altar candles are lighted, and the church bells are rung. Following the Gloria, the

"Do not lay your hand on the boy," said the messenger. "Do not do the least thing to him. I know now how devoted you are to God, since you did not withhold from me your own beloved son." As Abraham looked about, he spied a ram caught by its horns in the thicket. So he went and took the ram and offered it up as a holocaust in place of his son.

Again the LORD's messenger called to Abraham from heaven and said: "I swear by myself, declares the LORD, that because you acted as you did in not withholding from me your beloved son, I will bless you abundantly and make your descendants as countless as the stars of the sky and the sands of the seashore; your descendants shall take possession of the gates of their enemies, and in your descendants all the nations of the earth shall find blessing—all this because you obeyed my command."

SCRIPTURE COMMENTARY, CONTINUED

this story of how God asks Abraham to sacrifice his only son and thus risk losing all hope of the promise being fulfilled. The key to the story is that "God will provide." Abraham does not know why he would be given such a seemingly cruel command as to kill his own child or what it might mean in God's plan, but he is willing to let God direct the future and to do as he is commanded. Of course, God never intends that Isaac be killed, for he will provide a new lesson for humans to learn—God is never pleased with human sacrifices but with an obedience of the spirit.

**Psalm Response
Psalm 16:5, 8, 9–10, 11**

Antiphon
You are my inheritance, O Lord.

Verses for Reflection
Guard me, O God, for I seek refuge in
    you;
I say to the Lord: "You are my Lord,
I have no good except for you." (vv. 1–2)

PSALM REFLECTION

As in the story of Abraham and Isaac, the psalmist here expresses a complete trust in God—it is he alone who is the psalmist's portion and inheritance in life. If we place our reliance on God, God will be there for us. This realization gives a deep peace that leads to joy both on the level of physical existence and in the realm of spiritual yearnings. For humans, the deepest of those yearnings is for enduring life. The psalmist seems to express a hope here for immortality. This is perhaps the earliest passage in scripture that moves in that direction.

presider prays the Opening Prayer. An epistle reading then follows. All rise as the priest or cantor intones the great Alleluia for the first time since Lent began. The gospel is then proclaimed. These readings require our best readers and adequate preparation.

The third part of the liturgy is the liturgy of baptism. If baptisms are to take place, it is easier to follow the ritual as it appears in the RCIA, 218–240. If baptisms, Reception into the Full Communion of the Catholic Church, and confirmations are to take place, it is easier to follow the ritual as it appears in the RCIA, 566–591. However, the RCIA encourages the celebration of the rites of initiation at the Vigil for the unbaptized; while candidates for

Reception into the Full Communion of the Catholic Church may be received at this time, it is preferable that they be received at another time, apart from the Vigil. If there are no baptisms, the Sacramentary provides the texts for the Blessing of Water, the Renewal of Baptismal Promises, and the Sprinkling of the Assembly. The General Intercessions then follow.

The fourth part of the liturgy is the liturgy of the Eucharist. Some of the newly baptized and their godparents ought to take part in the procession with the gifts of bread and wine. The preface of Easter I is used, with the text "on this Easter day." There are special interpolations for the newly baptized in the Eucharistic Prayer

(see Ritual Mass: Christian Initiation: Baptism). Before saying "This is the Lamb of God," it is fitting that the priest remind the newly baptized and the newly received of the preeminence of the Eucharist as the center of Christian life.

The Mass concludes with the double Alleluia added to the dismissal chant. It is worthwhile to have the newly baptized and their godparents as a part of the recessional.

The Easter Vigil stands as the mother of all vigils; it is the moment when the Church celebrates its very center. Careful planning, adequate preparation, and reasonable rehearsal will guarantee a wondrous conclusion to the Paschal Triduum.

SCRIPTURE COMMENTARY

The story of the exodus contains the major theme of God's relationship to Israel. It reveals a God who takes the initiative to deliver from danger and death his chosen people, small and unimportant as they are, and to stay with them no matter how often they rebel or forget him. Why should an eternal and all-powerful God care about such a difficult relationship at all? Biblical writers explore this question in all parts of the Bible without ever coming up with the kind of rational and intellectual answer that pleases philosophers. Instead, they conclude that God's ways are beyond our capacity to understand, even though they are shown in the concrete again and again. The central example is the rescue at the sea in this reading. Israel cannot see any possibility of escape, but miraculously God makes it happen. Not only does God rescue the people from the control of the most powerful nation on earth; he fights against this enemy and destroys its power completely. This event left such a powerful memory of God's true devotion to Israel that it became the basis for all future hopes of salvation.

Third Reading: Exodus 14:15—15:1

The LORD said to Moses, "Why are you crying out to me? Tell the Israelites to go forward. And you, lift up your staff and, with hand outstretched over the sea, split the sea in two, that the Israelites may pass through it on dry land. But I will make the Egyptians so obstinate that they will go in after them. Then I will receive glory through Pharaoh and all his army, his chariots and charioteers. The Egyptians shall know that I am the LORD, when I receive glory through Pharaoh and his chariots and charioteers."

The angel of God, who had been leading Israel's camp, now moved and went around behind them. The column of cloud also, leaving the front, took up its place behind them, so that it came between the camp of the Egyptians and that of Israel. But the cloud now became dark, and thus the night passed without the rival camps coming any closer together all night long. Then Moses stretched out his hand over the sea, and the LORD swept the sea with a strong east wind throughout the night and so turned it into dry land. When the water was thus divided, the Israelites marched into the midst of the sea on dry land, with the water like a wall to their right and to their left.

The Egyptians followed in pursuit; all Pharaoh's horses and chariots and charioteers went after them right into the midst of the sea. In the night watch just before dawn the LORD cast through the column of the fiery cloud upon the Egyptian force a glance that threw it into a panic; and he so clogged their chariot wheels that they could hardly drive. With that the Egyptians sounded the retreat before Israel, because the LORD was fighting for them against the Egyptians.

MUSIC CONNECTION

The Vigil is replete with primal imagery and energy. The musician needs to have a good grasp on the four component parts of the service and how and where hymns, psalms, and acclamations need to be integrated. Marty Haugen's *The Light of Christ* (GIA) is a melodic and engaging setting of the opening dialogue. The *Exultet,* sung with power and expression, then moves us into the celebration of the word. For the responsorial Exodus 15, be sure to check the Howard Hughes setting as well as that of Niamh O'Kelly-Fischer, both available from GIA. There are obviously numerous and fine settings of the Alleluia, including Haugen's *Let Us Rejoice* (GIA), with its resounding Alleluia and verses from Psalm 118. Be sure to consider Bernadette Farrell's Easter Vigil text to her popular hymn *Christ Be Our Light.*

Musicians should explore the musical options in the RCIA for the third part of the Vigil, namely, the Liturgy of Baptism/ Confirmation. The Litany of the Saints, which accompanies the procession of the candidates to the font, ought to be sung. As an alternative to the traditional setting of this ancient litany, be sure to consider John Becker's moving version from OCP. Also, have prepared a postbaptismal acclamation for each candidate who is baptized this night. Howard Hughes's setting, *You Have Put on Christ,* is one such possibility. A procession to the font for all to bless themselves in the water—far more robust than a mere "sprinkling"—can be accompanied by Foley's *Come to the Water,* Jaime Cortez's emotive *Rain Down,* and Dan Schutte's *River of Glory.* Tim Manion's *There is a River* is also a good piece to accompany this ritual action.

Communion songs abound, and noteworthy ones are Parker's *Praise the Lord, My Soul;* Walker's *One in Body, Mind and Heart;* and Peloquin's *Faith, Hope and Love.*

Then the LORD told Moses, "Stretch out your hand over the sea, that the water may flow back upon the Egyptians, upon their chariots and their charioteers." So Moses stretched out his hand over the sea, and at dawn the sea flowed back to its normal depth. The Egyptians were fleeing head on toward the sea, when the LORD hurled them into its midst. As the water flowed back, it covered the chariots and the charioteers of Pharaoh's whole army which had followed the Israelites into the sea. Not a single one of them escaped. But the Israelites had marched on dry land through the midst of the sea, with the water like a wall to their right and to their left. Thus the LORD saved Israel on that day from the power of the Egyptians. When Israel saw the Egyptians lying dead on the seashore and beheld the great power that the LORD had shown against the Egyptians, they feared the LORD and believed in him and in his servant Moses.

Then Moses and the Israelites sang this song to the LORD:
  I will sing to the LORD, for he is gloriously triumphant;
    horse and chariot he has cast into the sea.

Psalm Response
Exodus 15:1–2, 3–4, 5–6, 17–18

Antiphon
Let us sing to the Lord; he has covered
    himself in glory.

Verse for Reflection
I will chant praise to the Lord;
For he has triumphed in glory:
Horse and chariot he has hurled into the
    sea. (v. 1)

PSALM REFLECTION

The hymn presents the exodus not merely as divine rescue of God's people but as a war between the true God, and the pharaoh, who represents all the gods of Egypt. This is not a combat between earthly groups but a cosmic battle. The outcome, however, is never in doubt: the Lord is triumphant In the context of the night of Jesus' resurrection, this hymn highlights the fact that God himself has prophetically prepared us to understand that the death of Jesus was no ordinary death but a part of God's victory over the powers of sin and Satan.

Fourth Reading: Isaiah 54:5–14

The One who has become your husband is your Maker;
    his name is the LORD of hosts;
your redeemer is the Holy One of Israel,
    called God of all the earth.
The LORD calls you back,
    like a wife forsaken and grieved in spirit,
    a wife married in youth and then cast off,
    says your God.
For a brief moment I abandoned you,
    but with great tenderness I will take you back.
In an outburst of wrath, for a moment
    I hid my face from you;
but with enduring love I take pity on you,
    says the LORD, your redeemer.
This is for me like the days of Noah,
    when I swore that the waters of Noah
    should never again deluge the earth;
so I have sworn not to be angry with you,
    or to rebuke you.
Though the mountains leave their place
    and the hills be shaken,
my love shall never leave you
    nor my covenant of peace be shaken,
    says the LORD, who has mercy on you.
O afflicted one, storm-battered and unconsoled,

SCRIPTURE COMMENTARY

The readings from Isaiah 40–55 during Holy Week have emphasized the role of the servant who follows God's will in humble obedience combined with energetic proclamation of God's message of reconciliation and justice to all nations. This theme dominates chapters 40–48, but in chapters 49–55, it is combined with a second theme that begins to emerge on the restoration of Zion. Zion is the eastern hill in Jerusalem on which the temple stood. When the Babylonian armies devastated Zion and leveled the temple to the ground, it was as though God had abandoned a beloved wife. Using this imagery, the prophet longs for the day when God will return and embrace Zion once again, giving it peace and prosperity and healing the broken relationship. Since the temple was considered the house in which God made his residence in the midst of his people, the image used here is that of a separated husband and wife who return home to renew their intimate love for each other. Sin has caused the break on the part of Israel, but God has never failed in his love and is deeply committed to healing this break.

I lay your pavements in carnelians,
and your foundations in sapphires;
I will make your battlements of rubies,
your gates of carbuncles,
and all your walls of precious stones.

All your children shall be taught by the LORD,
and great shall be the peace of your children.
In justice shall you be established,
far from the fear of oppression,
where destruction cannot come near you.

PSALM REFLECTION

Psalm 30, a hymn of thanksgiving, is divided by the poet into two parts, verses 1–5 and 6–12, both of which follow the same development. Part two repeats and strengthens part one. Part one begins with the psalmist telling of how he faced the danger of death from his enemies, of how God rescued him from the "pit," the doorway to the underworld, and of how God lifted him out so that now he gives praise to God for his power and goodness. The second half of the psalm does not mention enemies but recounts how the psalmist despaired of life and how God restored his hope and confidence, changing him from hopelessness to rejoicing, even to dancing!

Psalm Response
Psalm 30:2, 4, 5–6, 11–12, 13

Antiphon
I will praise you, Lord, for you have
rescued me.

Verse for Reflection
You have changed my sorrow to
dancing;
You removed my mourning garb
And clothed me with joy. (v. 12)

SCRIPTURE COMMENTARY

Isaiah's theme of God's healing love for Zion continues in chapter 55. In the previous reading, the emphasis was on God's love for Zion and willingness to take her back as his beloved spouse. Now the prophet's attention turns to the other half of the Zion theme, namely, that the temple mountain is also the place of the palace of the Davidic king. The king, like the temple, had been taken captive and perhaps even killed by the Babylonians, so now the country has had no blessing through the promises made to David. God here reassures them that he has not forgotten his promise but will renew all the promises that had formerly come through the royal house of David. However, he does not promise to restore the kingship in Israel. Instead, he announces that all of the exiles will become the bearers of the promise and give witness to God's everlasting covenant to the entire world by their faithfulness. God's ways are not ours, and he does not need human rulers and institutions to instill his word in our hearts and bring forth love and fidelity.

Fifth Reading: Isaiah 55:1–11

Thus says the LORD:
All you who are thirsty,
come to the water!
You who have no money,
come, receive grain and eat;
come, without paying and without cost,
drink wine and milk!
Why spend your money for what is not bread,
your wages for what fails to satisfy?
Heed me, and you shall eat well,
you shall delight in rich fare.
Come to me heedfully,
listen, that you may have life.
I will renew with you the everlasting covenant,
the benefits assured to David.
As I made him a witness to the peoples,
a leader and commander of nations,
so shall you summon a nation you knew not,
and nations that knew you not shall run to you,
because of the LORD, your God,
the Holy One of Israel, who has glorified you.

Seek the LORD while he may be found,
call him while he is near.
Let the scoundrel forsake his way,
and the wicked man his thoughts;
let him turn to the LORD for mercy;
to our God, who is generous in forgiving.
For my thoughts are not your thoughts,
nor are your ways my ways, says the LORD.
As high as the heavens are above the earth,

so high are my ways above your ways
and my thoughts above your thoughts.

For just as from the heavens
the rain and snow come down
and do not return there
till they have watered the earth,
making it fertile and fruitful,

giving seed to the one who sows
and bread to the one who eats,
so shall my word be
that goes forth from my mouth;
my word shall not return to me void,
but shall do my will,
achieving the end for which I sent it.

Psalm Response
Isaiah 12:2–3, 4, 5–6

Antiphon
You will draw water joyfully from the springs
of salvation.

Verse for Reflection
With joy you shall draw out water
from the fountain of salvation. (v. 3)

PSALM REFLECTION

No passage in the book of Isaiah soars higher in its praise of God than does chapter 12. It is placed here as a response to the twofold promise spoken in the sixth-century Babylonian exile in Isaiah 54 and Isaiah 55 that God will restore Zion. Although the actual words of Isaiah 12 were uttered by the first Isaiah back in the eighth century, when God delivered Jerusalem from the attacks of the northern kingdom of Israel in 732, they apply just as well to the time of Babylon and to the death and resurrection of Jesus!

Sixth Reading: Baruch 3:9–15, 32—4:4

Hear, O Israel, the commandments of life:
listen, and know prudence!
How is it, Israel,
that you are in the land of your foes,
grown old in a foreign land,
defiled with the dead,
accounted with those destined for the netherworld?
You have forsaken the fountain of wisdom!
Had you walked in the way of God,
you would have dwelt in enduring peace.
Learn where prudence is,
where strength, where understanding;
that you may know also
where are length of days, and life,
where light of the eyes, and peace.
Who has found the place of wisdom,
who has entered into her treasuries?

The One who knows all things knows her;
he has probed her by his knowledge—
The One who established the earth for all time,
and filled it with four-footed beasts;
he who dismisses the light, and it departs,
calls it, and it obeys him trembling;
before whom the stars at their posts
shine and rejoice;
when he calls them, they answer, "Here we are!"
shining with joy for their Maker.
Such is our God;
no other is to be compared to him:

SCRIPTURE COMMENTARY

The book of Baruch is named after the secretary of the prophet Jeremiah, so we might expect that it carries the spirit of Jeremiah's words on the need for repentance and reform in order to be restored to God's favor. The book of Baruch was probably written several centuries after Jeremiah's death, however, and thus reflects back on why Israel ended up in exile in the first place. The author draws the lesson that Jeremiah was right—the people had abandoned the Lord and forgotten his ways. He makes use of the wisdom traditions of Israel to do so, a trend very strong during the postexilic centuries. God alone is the source of wisdom; he has in turn placed the lessons of wisdom in his Torah through Moses, and it is there that we find the true way to God's light and glory. Unlike our ancestors in the time of the exile, all faithful people can now live in understanding and confidence when they meditate on the law God has given to Israel. They should rejoice that they have been given a privilege not offered to others outside the faith, namely, to know the ways to union with God. This sixth reading thus takes another step forward in understanding the death of Jesus as the fulfillment of God's plan and the true way of wisdom.

CATECHETICAL SUGGESTIONS

Baptism
Right-to-life issues: seamless garment
Overview of the RCIA (Rite of Christian Initiation of Adults) process
Empty-tomb stories
Mary Magdalene in the gospels and in history
The role of women in Luke's gospel

He has traced out the whole way of understanding,
  and has given her to Jacob, his servant,
  to Israel, his beloved son.

Since then she has appeared on earth,
  and moved among people.
She is the book of the precepts of God,
  the law that endures forever;
all who cling to her will live,
  but those will die who forsake her.
Turn, O Jacob, and receive her:
  walk by her light toward splendor.
Give not your glory to another,
  your privileges to an alien race.
Blessed are we, O Israel;
  for what pleases God is known to us!

PSALM REFLECTION

Psalm 19 is the Psalm of the Law! It praises the life-giving power of God's Torah in our lives. In the early verses, it praised God's wisdom in making the universe according to an orderly plan that reveals God as the very source of all wisdom and goodness. But if God has done so much to reveal his wisdom in nature, how much the more is it made known when he speaks to us in person through the Torah given to Moses? When we contemplate the wisdom of the precepts of the law, we realize it is not really about legal obligations at all but a source of guidance and knowledge of the living God.

Psalm Response
Psalm 19:8, 9, 10–11

Antiphon
Lord, you have the words of everlasting life.

Verse for Reflection
But how many can discover their own faults?
Forgive me of my hidden sins! (v. 13)

SCRIPTURE COMMENTARY

The final Old Testament reading brings us to the most important insight needed to understand God's plan of salvation in the death and resurrection of Jesus. We have seen God's intention of goodness in creation in Genesis 1, his commitment to preserving human life in Genesis 22, his willingness to rescue us from our own evil in Exodus 14, his love and intention to restore his people to his favor in Isaiah 54 and 55, and his wisdom in restoring Israel's faithfulness to his word in Baruch. Now we see that he also renews the very covenant itself. When God saved the people from Egypt, he offered them a bond that would bind them together with him for all time. But this seemed to have been lost forever when Israel rebelled and was defeated by its enemies and led off into exile in 586 BC. Ezekiel, prophet of the exiles, announces that God fully intends to restore this covenant, but in a deeper and more intimate manner than before. Under Moses, it was written out for us to learn, but now it will be

Seventh Reading: Ezekiel 36:16–17a, 18–28

The word of the LORD came to me, saying: Son of man, when the house of Israel lived in their land, they defiled it by their conduct and deeds. Therefore I poured out my fury upon them because of the blood that they poured out on the ground, and because they defiled it with idols. I scattered them among the nations, dispersing them over foreign lands; according to their conduct and deeds I judged them. But when they came among the nations wherever they came, they served to profane my holy name, because it was said of them: "These are the people of the LORD, yet they had to leave their land." So I have relented because of my holy name which the house of Israel profaned among the nations where they came. Therefore say to the house of Israel: Thus says the Lord GOD: Not for your sakes do I act, house of Israel, but for the sake of my holy name, which you profaned among the nations to which you came. I will prove the holiness of my great name, profaned among the nations, in whose midst you have profaned it. Thus the nations shall know that I am the

LORD, says the Lord GOD, when in their sight I prove my holiness through you. For I will take you away from among the nations, gather you from all the foreign lands, and bring you back to your own land. I will sprinkle clean water upon you to cleanse you from all your impurities, and from all your idols I will cleanse you. I will give you a new heart and place a new spirit within you, taking from your bodies your stony hearts and giving you natural hearts. I will put my spirit within you and make you live by my statutes, careful to observe my decrees. You shall live in the land I gave your fathers; you shall be my people, and I will be your God.

SCRIPTURE COMMENTARY, CONTINUED

instilled by God into our very hearts and empowered by his own divine Spirit. This is the prophetic preparation for the final understanding of the early Church that the Last Supper meal and death and resurrection of Jesus were to be interpreted as the fulfillment of this promise. Jesus restores the covenant in a new way in his very act of love and obedience from the heart. He leaves us a new Passover meal to commemorate this salvation and sends his Spirit to guide us in the ages to come.

Psalm Response
Psalm 42:3, 5; 43:3, 4
(or Isaiah 12:2–3, 4bcd, 5–6)
(or Psalm 51:12–13, 14–15, 18–19)

Antiphon
Like a deer that longs for running streams,
  my soul longs for you, my God.

Verse for Reflection
Send forth your light and your faithfulness,
They shall lead me on. (Ps 43:3)

PSALM REFLECTION

Psalm 42 is a powerful liturgical song that expresses the congregation's desire to come near to God. It is written as the picture of a procession from the courts outside up to the temple altars, while the people sing and pray in thanksgiving. In a very fitting way, it is the last of the Old Testament passages we hear on this sacred night, and it seems to describe the Christian congregation gathered tonight, sharing in processions of the fire and paschal candle and new Christians ready to be baptized, as we draw closer to the eucharistic climax of the Vigil service.

Epistle: Romans 6:3–11

Brothers and sisters: Are you unaware that we who were baptized into Christ Jesus were baptized into his death? We were indeed buried with him through baptism into death, so that, just as Christ was raised from the dead by the glory of the Father, we too might live in newness of life.

For if we have grown into union with him through a death like his, we shall also be united with him in the resurrection. We know that our old self was crucified with him, so that our sinful body might be done away with, that we might no longer be in slavery to sin. For a dead person has been absolved from sin. If, then, we have died with Christ, we believe that we shall also live with him. We know that Christ, raised from the dead, dies no more; death no longer has power over him. As to his death, he died to sin once and for all; as to his life, he lives for God. Consequently, you too must think of yourselves as being dead to sin and living for God in Christ Jesus.

SCRIPTURE COMMENTARY

The Holy Saturday Vigil readings have centered on the saving will of God as a deliverer and liberator from the moment of creation through the years of slavery in Egypt to the exile in Babylon and beyond. But the key passage through which all other acts of deliverance are interpreted has been the exodus narrative. Out of that experience, Israel as a people was formed in the covenant of Mount Sinai. It is no surprise, then, that the earliest Christian preaching centered on the parallels between the exodus and the saving death of Jesus. As the people had gone from slavery to freedom, and from oppression to their own home with God in Zion, so Jesus had passed from subjection to the powers of this world to the glory of the Son in power. Moreover, as the Passover lamb had given its blood to preserve the Israelites from death and let them escape to life, so Jesus had shed his blood so that all humanity might be freed from sin and death. But Paul underlines the real lesson: Jesus did not do this for himself but that we might be with him in the journey from death to life, from sin to freedom, from alienation to reconciliation with the Father.

PSALM REFLECTION

What psalm would form a better response than the exhilarating words of Psalm 118? "Give thanks to God—His mercy endures *forever*—I shall not die but *live!*" The world searched for God before the coming of Jesus and had the guidance of the law to know God as a merciful God, but it did not yet know the power of redemption from sin and the fear of death. Now believers live in union with the master who died and lives once more for them. Our true home is life with God in union with the Risen One.

Psalm Response
Psalm 118:1–2, 16, 17, 22–23

Antiphon
Alleluia, alleluia, alleluia.

Verse for Reflection
I shall not die, but live!
And I will declare the deeds of the Lord!
   (v. 17)

SCRIPTURE COMMENTARY

Matthew says a mighty angel appeared in the presence of the women coming to the tomb and broke open the stone for Jesus to rise. Mark says that when the women arrived at the tomb, they found the stone rolled away and a young man there to speak to them. Luke differs yet again by saying two angels appear to the women after they have entered the tomb. The angels' garments are dazzling white, a sign of their glorified, heavenly status. Their message also highlights Luke's special emphasis: Jesus is now "the living one." We are not to look for him among the dead. Thus Luke addresses not the disciples of the past but his Christian communities of Gentile converts. Jesus is now with us, alive in the Spirit and in the community of faith, and is to be truly found here in the Eucharist. It is not accidental that the next event Luke adds after this moment is the story of the two disciples going to Emmaus who do not recognize the earthly form of Jesus when he walks with him but who immediately recognize him in the "breaking of the bread," that is, in the Eucharist of the Christian community.

Gospel: Luke 24:1–12

At daybreak on the first day of the week the women who had come from Galilee with Jesus took the spices they had prepared and went to the tomb. They found the stone rolled away from the tomb; but when they entered, they did not find the body of the Lord Jesus. While they were puzzling over this, behold, two men in dazzling garments appeared to them. They were terrified and bowed their faces to the ground. They said to them, "Why do you seek the living one among the dead? He is not here, but he has been raised. Remember what he said to you while he was still in Galilee, that the Son of Man must be handed over to sinners and be crucified, and rise on the third day." And they remembered his words. Then they returned from the tomb and announced all these things to the eleven and to all the others. The women were Mary Magdalene, Joanna, and Mary the mother of James; the others who accompanied them also told this to the apostles, but their story seemed like nonsense and they did not believe them. But Peter got up and ran to the tomb, bent down, and saw the burial cloths alone; then he went home amazed at what had happened.

First Reading:
Acts 10:34a, 37–43

Peter proceeded to speak and said: "You know what has happened all over Judea, beginning in Galilee after the baptism that John preached, how God anointed Jesus of Nazareth with the Holy Spirit and power. He went about doing good and healing all those oppressed by the devil, for God was with him. We are witnesses of all that he did both in the country of the Jews and in Jerusalem. They put him to death by hanging him on a tree. This man God raised on the third day and granted that he be visible, not to all the people, but to us, the witnesses chosen by God in advance, who ate and drank with him after he rose from the dead. He commissioned us to preach to the people and testify that he is the one appointed by God as judge of the living and the dead. To him all the prophets bear witness, that everyone who believes in him will receive forgiveness of sins through his name."

SCRIPTURE COMMENTARY

The first reading is selected from the last reported sermon in the Acts of Apostles that was given by Peter to win over converts. It summarizes the fundamental message of the good news. It begins with the news of the past: after the baptism that John preached, Jesus was anointed by the Spirit, healed and freed people from the power of Satan, and was betrayed and killed by his own, only to have God vindicate him by raising him from the dead. But it does not end there. The apostles were chosen as witnesses to bring the message to the world that the risen Lord is judge of the living and the dead—that is, he has power over death and can bestow life, and he has established forgiveness of all sins to all who believe in his name. The resurrection itself was not seen by anyone, but the Risen One is seen and known by the apostles, was named beforehand by the prophets, and lives now in the community of those who believe.

HOMILY HELPS

Our reflections here are based primarily on the readings for the afternoon or evening Mass. They include Luke's incredibly rich Emmaus story, one of the finest in the New Testament.

Pope John Paul II took as his motto the expression "*Totus tuus*," meaning "Everything is yours." It signifies one thing only, total surrender to God's will, the center of the Christian life. Yet, without Easter, it would have little meaning. Christ's resurrection is not simply an apologetic proof that he is God; it is a life-sharing experience, the life of the Spirit. It is in that Spirit that we can turn over our lives totally to him.

Colossians states it well in today's second reading. If we share Christ's resurrection in baptism, then our hearts are called to rise as well. We are directed toward our heavenly homeland, which is our true destiny. In the preface of the Latin Mass, one of the invocations reads: "*Sursum corda*," quite literally "Hearts up." It's good advice, since we are so easily ensnared in the affairs of the moment—those trivialities which are often the antithesis of everything we believe—and we are put off by, or indifferent to, that which is really of value.

Despite his violent death, Jesus was a man of peace. This is clearly seen in the first part of today's reading from Acts. Teaching, doing good, and healing: this was the call of Jesus, and it too had its "heavenly" quality, almost transcendent in character.

Daily we are given the opportunity to "lift up our hearts." The two disciples on the road to Emmaus were immersed in rambling thoughts and speculation. Their Jesus was a failure; they were left only with unfounded rumors of a bodily disappearance.

How did they come to faith? Through a "stranger" who interpreted the scriptures for them and then revealed himself completely in the "breaking of the bread." In a manner typical of Luke, a simple journey narrative, marked by bewilderment but elevated by a hospitable dinner invitation, is climaxed by a revelation of Christ himself.

PSALM REFLECTION

We hear the same responsorial psalm as was read after the New Testament reading during the Easter Vigil. Not only does the psalmist hope for life instead of death; he recognizes that being saved from death is not just a single act of mercy, it is part of God's salvation of all the world. In one of the most frequently quoted prophecies from the Old Testament, the psalm speaks of the cornerstone being rejected by its original builders and being chosen by God to be the foundation of a new building. The early Christians understood this to be the transforming change brought about by the death and resurrection of Jesus. The way for Christians was no longer centered on a temple in Jerusalem but on the risen Lord. It is not a rejection of Judaism with its faithful obedience to the way of the temple. Jews must remain faithful to the divine revelation of the First Testament. Christians, however, must live and believe through their knowledge of the risen Lord by faith.

Psalm Response
Psalm 118:1–2, 16–17, 22–23

Antiphon
This is the day the Lord has made; let us rejoice and be glad.
Or: Alleluia.

Verse for Reflection
I shall not die, but live! And I will declare the deeds of the Lord! (v. 17)

"Easter Water." You may want to consider reintroducing the custom of distributing "Easter water," which is simply the baptismal water blessed at the Easter Vigil. People could be encouraged to take home some of this blessed water to use throughout the season of Easter.

The Emmaus narrative is but a commentary on the Mass, made up as it is of the word of God and the sacrificial offering, the "breaking of the bread." Do our hearts burn within us as the word of God is read and explained? As we approach the altar, do we recognize him as "the bread is broken?"

The two disciples in the story were leaving Jerusalem, for Luke the center and heart of all salvation. As the story ends, they realize the truth and hasten back to the holy city. Christ is truly risen! Now "everything is his."

The heavenly homeland is in sight.

LITURGICAL NOTES

Our forty days of fasting have now led us to fifty days of feasting. "The fifty days from Easter Sunday to Pentecost are celebrated in joyful exultation as one feast day, or better as one 'great Sunday.' These above all others are the days for the singing of the *Alleluia*" (GNLYC, 22). The starkness of our Lenten liturgies gives way to the glorious excess of Easter. The paschal candle, shining brightly at every liturgy, stands in a prominent place near the ambo; the baptismal font is filled with water. Flowers, hangings, and other decorations adorn the whole worship environment.

Crowds will be at virtually every Mass this day. Ushers and ministers of hospitality, as well as the regular Sunday assembly, should be prepared to provide a gracious welcome to both visitors and the occasional churchgoers. Additional worship aids, bulletins, and other handouts should be available.

Music ministers might be exhausted from the liturgies of the Triduum, but this Easter day deserves their attention as well. Adequate planning will enable the parish to ensure that the magnificent music of Easter will be heard at every Mass.

Easter Sunday is one of the few occasions on which the

Second Reading:
Colossians 3:1–4

Brothers and sisters: If then you were raised with Christ, seek what is above, where Christ is seated at the right hand of God. Think of what is above, not of what is on earth. For you have died, and your life is hidden with Christ in God. When Christ your life appears, then you too will appear with him in glory.

Or 1 Corinthians 5:6b–8

Brothers and sisters: Do you not know that a little yeast leavens all the dough? Clear out the old yeast, so that you may become a fresh batch of dough, inasmuch as you are unleavened. For our paschal lamb, Christ, has been sacrificed. Therefore, let us celebrate the feast, not with the old yeast, the yeast of malice and wickedness, but with the unleavened bread of sincerity and truth.

SCRIPTURE COMMENTARY

The two choices for a New Testament reading that would echo the preaching of the apostles reported in Acts 10 both center on the changed status of our life in God as a result of the resurrection of Jesus. Colossians describes the change from being citizens of this world to being citizens of the heavenly world of the risen Lord. As Jesus has left the limitations imposed by sin and mortality in this life, so we are joined with him in the hope of everlasting life and in freedom from the penalties due our sins. In 1 Corinthians, Paul draws on the analogy with leavening bread. It is really a reference to the Passover, characteristic of the story of Jesus' Last Supper, death, and resurrection. Just as leaven takes dead dough and makes it into food for life, so Jesus by his death extended life-giving power to all humanity. It is a transformation that demands living in accord with the new life and forgoing the sins of the old. There is also a strong eucharistic reference here because we weekly eat the bread of life that has been made life-giving by the yeast of Christ's death, which it commemorates.

Sequence is prescribed before the Gospel Acclamation. Any number of musical settings will make this hymn of preparation before the gospel build the anticipation as the assembly waits to hear the story of the resurrection. The Profession of Faith is replaced by the Renewal of Baptismal Promises. Here we see our Lenten journey come full circle as we come back to the font, as we return to baptismal innocence. If possible, the presider should stand near the baptismal font for the renewal of promises and then take water from the font for the sprinkling of the assembly. Planners ought to consider the route to be taken by those involved in the sprinkling

CATECHETICAL SUGGESTIONS

The kerygma
The significance of Jesus' resurrection for Christians
The Beloved Disciple in John
Meaning of sacrifice in the Old Testament and in the New Testament
The primacy of love: Johanine scenes with Peter and the Beloved Disciple
The resurrection of the body: for Jesus and for us

so that, without unduly prolonging the ritual, as many people as possible can see and feel the baptismal water. Those who were baptized or received into the full communion of the

Church at the Easter Vigil and their godparents should be remembered in the General Intercessions. On this day, a double Alleluia is added to the dismissal.

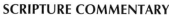

SCRIPTURE COMMENTARY

We hear the story of the discovery of the empty tomb in the other gospels read at the Holy Saturday Vigil Mass. All of them have an angel or angels announce to the women that the Lord is risen. This is not just a missing body but an act of the all-powerful God raising Jesus to life. John tells the story differently. There is no angelic announcement. Mary Magdalene alone comes to the tomb, sees it physically with her eyes that it is empty, and reports the shocking news to Peter and the Beloved Disciple. They in turn discover it with their normal senses, even observing small details, such as the rolled-up cloth that was put on the head of a corpse. The point John thus insists on is that with our natural faculties we cannot know much beyond the fact that Jesus was missing. It requires faith to know the risen Lord. This theme will dominate his later letters (1, 2, and 3 John). For now, the Beloved Disciple expresses a faith that this was somehow a work of God, but does not yet connect it to the prophetic words of the Old Testament Servant Songs of Isaiah or Psalm 118 or other messianic texts. Again, in a scene that follows this, it will be Mary Magdalene again who is the first to experience the risen Lord, not with human senses but by his voice calling her by name. Yet Jesus will tell her not to try to touch him in a normal manner—but to believe in and realize that he is now the Risen One who is with his Father.

Gospel: John 20:1–9
(or, at an afternoon or evening Mass, Luke 24:13–35; or, at any time of the day, Luke 24:1–12)

On the first day of the week, Mary of Magdala came to the tomb early in the morning, while it was still dark, and saw the stone removed from the tomb. So she ran and went to Simon Peter and to the other disciple whom Jesus loved, and told them, "They have taken the Lord from the tomb, and we don't know where they put him." So Peter and the other disciple went out and came to the tomb. They both ran, but the other disciple ran faster than Peter and arrived at the tomb first; he bent down and saw the burial cloths there, but did not go in. When Simon Peter arrived after him, he went into the tomb and saw the burial cloths there, and the cloth that had covered his head, not with the burial cloths but rolled up in a separate place. Then the other disciple also went in, the one who had arrived at the tomb first, and he saw and believed. For they did not yet understand the Scripture that he had to rise from the dead.

MUSIC CONNECTION

There is no dearth of hymnody to accompany this exuberant feast. *Hail Thee Festival Day, Jesus Christ Is Risen Today*, Sydney Carter's *Lord of the Dance,* and Dan Schutte's *Sing, O Sing* are always well received. For Sunday morning's responsorial, Psalm 118, look at Haugen's *Let Us Rejoice*, Michael Joncas's equally fervent *This Is the Day,* or Hommerding's rhythmic arrangement. Haugen's piece, with its rhythmic and joyful melody, can also function as the *Alleluia*.

Something that should stand out on Easter Sunday is the Church's Renewal of Baptismal

Bulletin Suggestion: Catholic Household Blessings and Prayers *provides two appropriate blessings that can be used this day: the Blessing of Easter Foods and the Blessing of Homes during Eastertime. These could be worthwhile additions to the parish bulletin.*

Promises and the subsequent sprinkling of the congregation. The renewal of these promises cries out for musical expression both in the priest's question and in the congregation's response. There are some unpublished versions available, but the skilled musician should be able to construct a simple chanted melody line for this. Many parishes, wanting a more robust and fulsome ritual, have substituted a procession to the font by everyone in attendance to the more anemic "sprinkling" we are used to. Paralleling the Communion procession as well as the procession to venerate the cross on Good Friday, it adds power to this ritual moment. Hymns such as *Come to the Water, Rain Down, River of Glory, Put on Christ,* and *There Is a River* all would enhance this communal ritual.

First Reading: Acts 5:12–16

Many signs and wonders were done among the people at the hands of the apostles. They were all together in Solomon's portico. None of the others dared to join them, but the people esteemed them. Yet more than ever, believers in the Lord, great numbers of men and women, were added to them. Thus they even carried the sick out into the streets and laid them on cots and mats so that when Peter came by, at least his shadow might fall on one or another of them. A large number of people from the towns in the vicinity of Jerusalem also gathered, bringing the sick and those disturbed by unclean spirits, and they were all cured.

SCRIPTURE COMMENTARY

In the two previous years, A and B, we have heard of the first preaching of the apostles on the day of Pentecost and immediately afterwards. In year C, we begin seven weeks of listening to further stories of the rapid growth of the early Church as people in Jerusalem and its surrounding area hear the preaching of the gospel and join the followers of Jesus. Our first selection this year gives a summary of that initial success by recounting the blessings people received through the apostles' efforts. Peter, especially, stands out as the leader of this group, the person through whom many miracles are performed. But for Luke he is also the symbol of all the apostles and everyone in the community. Luke's presentation of Peter's healing of the sick conforms very closely to his description of Jesus himself healing the sick, the possessed, and the unclean (see Luke 4:40–41; 5:17; 6:18–19; 7:18–23). Jesus may have ascended in bodily form to his Father's home in heaven, but there is no doubt that he is still alive and present in the power of the Holy Spirit acting in his followers.

HOMILY HELPS

In John's gospel, Easter, Ascension, and Pentecost become three aspects of a single event, united in their temporal expression. Jesus, once risen, is with the Father and thus in a position to confer the Spirit. These three features of a single mystery are not separated by forty or fifty days but occur on Easter Sunday itself.

In this first Easter meeting of Jesus with his disciples, the conferring of the Spirit has a threefold significance. First of all, it means peace. "Peace be with you" is a greeting repeated three times in today's gospel. Harmony is once again restored between heaven and earth. "Christ," Paul says succinctly, "is our peace." It is a harmony with both a vertical and a horizontal dimension, that is, peace with God and with humanity, in fact with all of creation. Sin is banished; grace restored. We are at one with God and the world.

The second expression of the Spirit's presence is the forgiveness of sins. "Whose sins you forgive are forgiven." Grace, for all its abundance, has to be appro-priated. It is available with a change of heart. In turning to God, we come to know what atonement means: at-one-ment. We can experience it in various ways, the sacrament of reconciliation being the foremost. But it requires no more than the sentiments of the man who was crucified with Jesus. "Remember me when you come into your kingdom." God's love is boundless, but it cannot be forced. With a change of heart, it is ours for the asking.

And, finally, Christ missions the apostles. "As the Father has sent me, so I send you." It is the

PSALM REFLECTION

Psalm 118 has two parts. The first, found at the beginning and the end in verses 1–4 and 14–29, is a joyous hymn of praise to God, and it wraps around the second and center part, in verses 5–13, which is a call for help from the depths of despair. Because the readings celebrate the resurrection, we hear only the joyful hymn today. The key refrain, "His mercy endures forever," is not just an abstract thought; it is always understood in terms of the very personal and concrete acts of God in relation to Israel and to the individual psalmist. God comes to the aid of, and gives protection to, anyone who worships his name and serves his will.

Psalm Response
Psalm 118:2–4, 13–15, 22–24

Antiphon
Give thanks to the Lord for he is
    good, his love is everlasting.
Or: Alleluia.

Verse for Reflection
Even though the Lord punished me,
He did not deliver me over to death!
    (v. 18)

SCRIPTURE COMMENTARY

This morning we hear selections from the opening chapter of the book of Revelation. The book begins in verses 1–8 with the claim to be prophecy given to the seer John (perhaps not the apostle of the gospels!) by Jesus for the sake of the seven churches of the Roman province of Asia. All of these communities are near the region of Ephesus in western Turkey. The vision announces that Jesus is coming again and his persecutors will behold his divine glory. Today's reading comes immediately after this passage, when John tells us of how he was called to be a prophet and what he saw in his initial vision. The seven gold lampstands stand for the seven churches of Asia, and the Son of Man is clearly the risen Christ, robed in the royal garments of his heavenly victory over

Second Reading:
Revelation 1:9–11a, 12–13, 17–19

I, John, your brother, who share with you the distress, the kingdom, and the endurance we have in Jesus, found myself on the island called Patmos because I proclaimed God's word and gave testimony to Jesus. I was caught up in spirit on the Lord's day and heard behind me a voice as loud as a trumpet, which said, "Write on a scroll what you see." Then I turned to see whose voice it was that spoke to me, and when I

Spirit who guides the Church; the Spirit is the principal actor in the Acts of the Apostles as the infant Church moves out into the world. This is simply a continuation of the work of Christ. In today's first reading, the very presence of Peter brings healing to the sick and despondent. Present in the temple setting, the apostles are agents of conversion and forgiveness. As the Father sent the Son, so the Son sends his disciples. They continue the work of Christ.

Thomas was absent that first Easter evening. But his absence is to our benefit. In later touching the hands and side of Jesus, he affirms the Lord's continued humanity. This is no vision or mental projection, a wishing that

it might be so. If it is his divinity that emerges strongly at Easter, Thomas has brought us into touch with his humanity. It is the oft-discredited "doubting" Thomas who makes the strongest faith affirmation to be found in the gospels: "My Lord and my God."

God and man. Both the Alpha and Omega of Revelation, the beginning and the end, but also the one totally human, the one who "died and now lives." The beauty of this Easter encounter lies in the fact that its primary features—peace, forgiveness, and mission—remain with us as much today, both as fact and as challenge, as they were in the upper room.

LITURGICAL NOTES

This Sunday's gospel presents both a resurrection appearance of the Lord and the story of Thomas, the one who doubted. Among the titles previously given to the second Sunday of Easter was *Dominica in albis*, the Sunday on which the neophytes, who had been wearing their baptismal garments all week, would now set them aside. The late Pope John Paul II added the title Divine Mercy Sunday to this day, although no liturgical texts have been added or changed. The Congregation for Divine Worship and the Discipline of the Sacraments decreed that "throughout the world, the Second Sunday of

turned, I saw seven gold lampstands and in the midst of the lampstands one like a son of man, wearing an ankle-length robe, with a gold sash around his chest.

When I caught sight of him, I fell down at his feet as though dead. He touched me with his right hand and said, "Do not be afraid. I am the first and the last, the one who lives. Once I was dead, but now I am alive forever and ever. I hold the keys to death and the netherworld. Write down, therefore, what you have seen, and what is happening, and what will happen afterwards."

SCRIPTURE COMMENTARY, CONTINUED

death. Although John falls down in fear, Jesus' message is one of reassurance: "Do not be afraid!" As Jesus died but now lives forever, so John must make the Christians who are suffering for their faith see what lies ahead for them—the one they believe in, the conqueror of death and liberator, is coming soon!

Gospel: John 20:19–31

On the evening of that first day of the week, when the doors were locked, where the disciples were, for fear of the Jews, Jesus came and stood in their midst and said to them, "Peace be with you." When he had said this, he showed them his hands and his side. The disciples rejoiced when they saw the Lord. Jesus said to them again, "Peace be with you. As the Father has sent me, so I send you." And when he had said this, he breathed on them and said to them, "Receive the Holy

SCRIPTURE COMMENTARY

The gospels of Matthew, Mark, and Luke all contain some scene of an ascension of Jesus in which he promises the Holy Spirit will come *after* he leaves. But John puts the first coming of the Spirit on the Apostles on Easter Sunday night, when Jesus appears to them in the upper room (presumably where he had shared the Last Supper with them three days before) and confers on them the Spirit. The key to the Spirit's work in them will be the power to forgive sins because it so centrally reflects the saving work of Jesus' cross and resurrection. But the Spirit also gives the deepest knowledge of Jesus possible for those who will live after Jesus' bodily presence is no longer with us. Thomas was missing on this occasion and did not see the Lord that first Easter night. So Jesus appears to the apostles a second time a week later (again on a Sunday—perhaps

Easter will receive the name Divine Mercy Sunday, a perennial invitation to the Christian world to face, with confidence in divine benevolence, the difficulties and trials that humankind will experience in the years to come." Celebrations of divine mercy take place on this day apart from the Sunday Eucharist.

On all the Sundays of Easter, the Rite of Blessing and Sprinkling with Holy Water is most appropriate. When this is done, the Penitential Rite is omitted. Both texts for the Opening Prayer make explicit reference to our rebirth in water and the Spirit. The Prayer over the Gifts makes reference to those born again in baptism. The reference is put in parentheses, presumably

> ***What Salvation Means.*** *Salvation is not a matter of feeling okay but an actually experienced change in our lives. If we have been saved, we have been rescued from some danger or fear or disease, and we now know we must act differently toward God. Sin cannot continue; we must live as people who praise and honor God with everything we do. As Christians, we realize by our faith in Christ that we have been forgiven and must act accordingly in our daily actions. A Christian lives in Christ, Paul loves to say, because he or she lives always in the reality of the mercy of forgiveness God has extended to us.*

to be omitted if there are no baptisms at the Vigil. However, in the wider Church, there were most certainly baptisms at the Vigil, so inclusion of the text will help to keep the connection between Easter and baptism before the prayer of the assembly. The preface of Easter I is prescribed on this day. The Solemn Blessing provided in the Sacra-

mentary continues to underscore the images of life and baptism.

It is useful for the planning team to recall that on all the Sundays of Easter we are celebrating Easter—the event is of such significance that it takes fifty days to celebrate! The music and the environment should reflect this fifty-day celebration of the Easter event.

SCRIPTURE COMMENTARY, CONTINUED

symbolic that it is at the Sunday Eucharist we later Christians most deeply meet the Lord). Thomas doubts what he has not seen for himself, and so Jesus offers him the chance to directly experience what his comrades know. Thomas suddenly reverses himself from the deepest doubt to the strongest statement of faith in the New Testament. In this gospel, Thomas is the symbol of all Christians who live by faith and not by personally meeting the earthly Jesus. God speaks to us as truly in the Church through the Holy Spirit now as he spoke to his apostles on earth. He taught them that he was the messiah and Son of God while he was with them, and he still makes himself known in both roles in the life of the Church, and especially in the Eucharist.

CATECHETICAL SUGGESTIONS

Acts of the Apostles: an overview
Apocalyptic literature
Peter's preeminence in the gospels and in Acts
The book of Revelation: setting, theme, and code
The gift (coming) of the Spirit in John and in Acts
In what ways can we say, "We have seen the Lord"?

Spirit. Whose sins you forgive are forgiven them, and whose sins you retain are retained."

Thomas, called Didymus, one of the Twelve, was not with them when Jesus came. So the other disciples said to him, "We have seen the Lord." But he said to them, "Unless I see the mark of the nails in his hands and put my finger into the nailmarks and put my hand into his side, I will not believe."

Now a week later his disciples were again inside and Thomas was with them. Jesus came, although the doors were locked, and stood in their midst and said, "Peace be with you." Then he said to Thomas, "Put your finger here and see my hands, and bring your hand and put it into my side, and do not be unbelieving, but believe." Thomas answered and said to him, "My Lord and my God!" Jesus said to him, "Have you come to believe because you have seen me? Blessed are those who have not seen and have believed."

Now Jesus did many other signs in the presence of his disciples that are not written in this book. But these are written that you may come to believe that Jesus is the Christ, the Son of God, and that through this belief you may have life in his name.

MUSIC CONNECTION

The Easter season, as we all know, extends fifty days to the great celebration of Pentecost, the fiftieth day. Most North Americans are more disposed to prepare for an event than to actually *prolong* the celebration (witness how much time we use to get ready for Christmas and how quickly we put away our lights and ornaments!). In terms of Easter, we are generally well tuned into Lent but find it far more difficult to sustain the celebration of Easter for these fifty days. In many

parishes, this season peters out and turns into a sequence of unrelated celebrations including baptisms, confirmation, First Eucharist, and Mother's Day, to mention but a few. A few seasonal motifs can help us celebrate through the full fifty days. Consider a sprinkling rite for each of these Sundays, including Pentecost itself. There are ample hymns to accompany this, including *Rain Down, There Is a River, Come to the Water,* and *Wade in the Water.* To eliminate the redundancy of an opening hymn followed by a sprinkling song,

consider combining the two so that the opening hymn includes the sprinkling of the congregation. Use the same festive setting of the Gloria that you employed at the Easter Vigil, and a seasonal Alleluia that erupts with joy, as, for example, Haugen's *Let Us Rejoice* or Deiss's *This Is the Day.* Hymns particularly appropriate today include *All You Nations, Without Seeing You, Peace,* Parker's *Praise the Lord, My Soul,* and *We Walk by Faith.* For the responsorial today, consider the settings by Alstott, Proulx, or Gelineau.

3RD SUNDAY OF EASTER—YEAR C

First Reading: Acts 5:27–32, 40b–41

When the captain and the court officers had brought the apostles in and made them stand before the Sanhedrin, the high priest questioned them, "We gave you strict orders, did we not, to stop teaching in that name? Yet you have filled Jerusalem with your teaching and want to bring this man's blood upon us." But Peter and the apostles said in reply, "We must obey God rather than men. The God of our ancestors raised Jesus, though you had him killed by hanging him on a tree. God exalted him at his right hand as leader and savior to grant Israel repentance and forgiveness of sins. We are witnesses of these things, as is the Holy Spirit whom God has given to those who obey him."

The Sanhedrin ordered the apostles to stop speaking in the name of Jesus, and dismissed them. So they left the presence of the Sanhedrin, rejoicing that they had been found worthy to suffer dishonor for the sake of the name.

SCRIPTURE COMMENTARY

The healing miracles and powerful preaching by the apostles soon led to their being persecuted by the religious leaders of the Jerusalem temple. Peter and the other apostles were accused of the same crime with which Jesus had been charged, namely, that of leading the people astray with *new* teachings not approved as orthodox by the leadership. Jesus had been condemned to death, but in this scene his followers do not suffer the same fate. Perhaps the leaders realize that the apostles are drawing huge numbers of followers precisely because they have made a martyr out of their leader. Instead, they now think that if they can only silence the voices, the movement will die out on its own. But as Luke notes, such persecution just strengthens the apostles all the more. They rejoice, knowing that they are now sharing in the sufferings endured by Jesus, just as he had told them they would. From this point onwards, apostolic preaching becomes only stronger day by day.

HOMILY HELPS

The power of the risen Christ encountering human frailty appears clearly in today's scriptures. In the reading from Revelation, universal acclaim and worship place God and Jesus on equal footing. Power, honor, glory, and might belong to the One seated on the throne and to the Lamb. It is this power of the Lamb which is seen in his activity on the human scene.

In today's reading from Acts, the apostles stand before the Jewish authorities, who were better educated and more accomplished than they. The apostles resolutely proclaim the lordship of Jesus and the obedience that they owe to God over any human authority. Their statement of obedience is as relevant today as it was then. Severely chastised because of their unwavering allegiance, the disciples, filled with joy, take their leave of the hearing. It was the power of the risen Lord that gave them the courage to face opposition with confidence.

With the disciples' failure to make a catch in today's gospel, they are told by Jesus to cast their net on the starboard side. The results surpass their wildest expectations. The teaching is clear. The mission entrusted to the apostles will not be successful because of human effort but because of God's direction. The weakened Peter, who thrice denied Jesus during his suffering, is now asked three times whether his repentance is authentic. "Does your love, Peter, surpass that of my other followers?" An affirmative response leads to his commission as pastor.

We are not called to accomplish great feats or receive honors or be given titles and positions. The injunction is simple and direct: "Follow me." Where there is true love, human frailty matters little. God makes great out of nothing.

We are asked only to remain faithful. Today this means obeying God rather than humans,

PSALM REFLECTION

In the Old Testament and in the ancient world in general, the abode of the dead was often pictured as a vast, dark, and damp hall or open field, deep under the earth, where those who had died would lie inert and powerless in neat rows of beds or sometimes would wander about aimlessly. The doorway to this gloomy future was a seen as a great pit, more like a quicksand trap, in which one who was dying would get caught and then sucked slowly down into the grip of the kingdom of death. In much of the Old Testament, God is recorded not as restoring already dead people to life but as stopping them from slipping further into death's hands or even as pulling them up from the doorway of the pit itself. God is pictured thus more as preventing death from finally taking the psalmist from this life and then restoring the psalmist back to health or acceptance by his community. In Psalm 30, the poet uses every device possible to show the tremendous reversal that happens when God comes to the rescue: night becomes day, mourning becomes dancing, a moment turns into a lifetime!

Psalm Response
Psalm 30:2, 4, 5–6, 11–12, 13

Antiphon
I will praise you, Lord, for you have rescued me.
Or: Alleluia.

Verse for Reflection
His anger lasts but an instant,
While his favor lasts a lifetime;
At nightfall there is weeping,
But at dawn, rejoicing.
(v. 6)

SCRIPTURE COMMENTARY

The book of Revelation is written around constant groups of seven that reveal the unfolding of coming events: seven angels, seven letters, seven seals, seven bowls, etc. But interspersed among these are short interludes when the reader suddenly gets a view into the heavenly realm, as though the skies parted and we get just a brief glimpse. The scene

Second Reading:
Revelation 5:11–14

I, John, looked and heard the voices of many angels who surrounded the throne and the living creatures and the

even government authorities. Nowhere is this more evident than in what are termed the life issues, the championing of human life at every turn. Governments may recognize abortion on demand, the justice of the death penalty, or assisted suicide. These trends are reflective of a "culture of death." A society that diminishes the value of human life is one that moves toward decay. War is admissible only when all efforts at peacemaking have been exhausted. That has long been the Catholic position. We may feel that we stand alone and isolated on any of these issues, but it is still better to obey God rather than men.

LITURGICAL NOTES

As we begin the third week of Easter, it may become difficult to maintain the Easter focus in preaching, music, and environment. Careful planning will allow the liturgy team to stretch both their imagination and the budget to extend it throughout the great fifty days.

While preparation for baptism permeated the Lenten liturgies, baptism, baptismal dignity, and the implications of baptism permeate our Easter liturgies. The Blessing and Sprinkling with Holy Water is appropriate on this Sunday and on all the Sundays of the Easter season. When this is done,

the Penitential Rite is omitted. Any of the prefaces for the Easter Season can be used. While the Sacramentary provides a Prayer over the People, the Solemn Blessing for the Easter Season will work well on all the Sundays of Easter.

Our baptism gives us clear assurance of the overwhelming love of God. And yet so often the dignity of baptism can be neglected. On these Sundays of Easter, with their baptismal emphasis, it might be helpful for planners to focus on the dignity of the baptized, those who stand in our assemblies as the holy people of God, and their "full, conscious, and active participation" in the celebration of the

elders. They were countless in number, and they cried out in a loud voice:
    "Worthy is the Lamb that was slain
        to receive power and riches, wisdom and strength,
        honor and glory and blessing."
Then I heard every creature in heaven and on earth and under the earth and in the sea, everything in the universe, cry out:
    "To the one who sits on the throne and to the Lamb
        be blessing and honor, glory and might, forever and ever."
The four living creatures answered, "Amen," and the elders fell down and worshiped.

SCRIPTURE COMMENTARY, CONTINUED

changes in today's passage from the stage on earth to the heavenly throne room of God. There the real citizens of God's kingdom, the angels and the saints who have completed their earthly journeys, form a heavenly choir that sits and stands and kneels and falls to the ground in praise and honor of God and of his Son the Savior. Jesus is portrayed in his risen victory as the "Lamb," that is, the Passover lamb who lives in glory because by giving his blood for us he rescued us from death, just as the original Passover lamb's blood was put on the doorposts in Egypt to save the Israelites from the angel of death. The vision is intended to give hope to the book's readers that our suffering is only for a moment that must be endured but our happiness and joy will be forever.

Gospel: John 21:1–19 (or John 21:1–14)

At that time, Jesus revealed himself again to his disciples at the Sea of Tiberias. He revealed himself in this way. Together were Simon Peter, Thomas called Didymus, Nathanael from Cana in Galilee, Zebedee's sons, and two others of his disciples. Simon Peter said to them, "I am going fishing." They said to him, "We also will come with you." So they went out and got into the boat, but that night they caught nothing. When it was already dawn, Jesus was standing on the shore; but the disciples did not realize that it was Jesus. Jesus said to them, "Children, have you caught anything to eat?" They answered him, "No." So he said to them, "Cast the

SCRIPTURE COMMENTARY

This is the final chapter of the Gospel of John and it is the climactic moment as well. This will be the last appearance of Jesus to his disciples in John's gospel, but he is no longer merely one with them. He stands in their midst as the risen Lord who now

liturgy. Students preparing for the priesthood or diaconate are often reminded of how helpful it is to occasionally sit among the members of the congregation to see and hear things as the assembly sees and hears them. It would be helpful for the planning team not only to observe the celebration from various parts of the church occupied by members of the assembly but also to elicit from some of those members observations about how they perceive the celebration and its strengths and weaknesses. Sometimes the wisdom of the body is both amazing and insightful. For example, some folks might be highly complimentary of the music ministry, but when pushed

a bit, they might suggest that the music amplification system might be turned down a notch or two. Or they might remark on the conscientiousness of the readers but also comment that some could use additional training. You might even receive comments concerning the environment, the cleanliness of the church building, or the accessibility of the facility for those with limited mobility. If you begin to ask the questions, you must be also willing to accept the challenges the answers offer.

CATECHETICAL SUGGESTIONS

The role of personal witness in evangelization
How to be a witness for Christ
Angels in Catholic belief
High Christology in the book of Revelation
The miraculous-catch story in John 21:1–8 and in Luke 5:1–11
Postresurrection appearance stories in John's gospel

SCRIPTURE COMMENTARY, CONTINUED

feeds them himself and commissions them to carry on his work of proclaiming the kingdom of God. He is revealed to them in the meal as a sign of his being with them and waiting for them. But he also provides a miraculous catch of fish in the waters beyond the shore. The apostles too will go forth and know the Lord is with them as they make converts by preaching the gospel. These they will bring to the meal as well. Finally, the apostles are to imitate the Lord in pasturing the flock as the Good Shepherd does. The words to Peter reveal this last commission. His failures had been the greatest, but he also experienced the greatest forgiveness and had always shown the most enthusiasm and loyalty. As a result, Jesus confirms him as the one who will show what it means to pastor and lead by love rather than by power and titles. Thus, in this final scene of the gospel, all the elements are now in place for the future, and with these final words to Peter, the Church is born!

net over the right side of the boat and you will find something." So they cast it, and were not able to pull it in because of the number of fish. So the disciple whom Jesus loved said to Peter, "It is the Lord." When Simon Peter heard that it was the Lord, he tucked in his garment, for he was lightly clad, and jumped into the sea. The other disciples came in the boat, for they were not far from shore, only about a hundred yards, dragging the net with the fish. When they climbed out on shore, they saw a charcoal fire with fish on it and bread. Jesus said to them, "Bring some of the fish you just caught." So Simon Peter went over and dragged the net ashore full of one hundred fifty-three large fish. Even though there were so many, the net was not torn. Jesus said to them, "Come, have breakfast." And none of the disciples dared to ask him, "Who are you?" because they realized it was the Lord. Jesus came over and took the bread and gave it to them, and in like manner the fish. This was now the third time Jesus was revealed to his disciples after being raised from the dead.

When they had finished breakfast, Jesus said to Simon Peter, "Simon, son of John, do you love me more than these?" Simon Peter answered him, "Yes, Lord, you know that I love you." Jesus said to him, "Feed my lambs." He then said to Simon Peter a second time, "Simon, son of John, do you love me?" Simon Peter answered him, "Yes, Lord, you know that I love you." Jesus said to him, "Tend my sheep." Jesus said to him the third time, "Simon, son of John, do you love me?" Peter was distressed that Jesus had said to him a third time, "Do you love me?" and he said to him, "Lord, you know everything; you know that I love you." Jesus said to him, "Feed my sheep. Amen, amen, I say to you, when you were younger, you used to dress yourself and go where you wanted; but when you grow old, you will stretch out your hands, and someone else will dress you and lead you where you do not want to go." He said this signifying by what kind of death he would glorify God. And when he had said this, he said to him, "Follow me."

MUSIC CONNECTION

Seeing Easter as a fifty-day celebration/season allows us to focus on the forest and not the individual trees, which, sometimes, like the somewhat polemical reading from Acts today, can skew the overall meaning of the season: life in the risen Lord. This season gives us the time and space to joyfully recall the great things God has done for us in the life, death, and resurrection of Jesus and to savor the ongoing meaning of the paschal mystery in our lives. The reading from Revelation recounts the celestial anthem "Worthy is the Lamb"— a text that is given powerful

Did you know?... The fish always symbolizes the Lord Jesus (even the Greek word ICHTHUS stands as an acronym for Iesus-Christos-Theou-Uios-Soter: "Jesus Christ, Son of God, Savior"). Thus, as the disciples in today's gospel consume the fish, they are united with Jesus, just as, when we receive the Eucharist, we meet the Lord coming to us.

expression in Dufford's anthem of the same name. Other hymns that come to mind today include *We Know That Christ Is Raised, Christ the Lord Is Risen Today,* and *Hymn of Joy.* Suzanne Toolan's *Two Fishermen* and Cesáreo Gabaráin's *Pescador de Hombres [Lord, When You Came]* aptly recount the scene in today's gospel where Jesus appears to the disciples on the shoreline. The latter is a favorite

in Spanish-speaking communities. In a manner reminiscent of Luke's Emmaus story, the disciples come to recognize Jesus in the sharing of the bread and the fish recently caught. Dunstan's *You Walk along Our Shoreline* carries through the narrative with a call to mission and working for God's justice. For today's responsorial, Psalm 30, be sure to check settings by Hillert, Guimont, and Inwood.

First Reading: Acts 13:14, 43–52

Paul and Barnabas continued on from Perga and reached Antioch in Pisidia. On the sabbath they entered the synagogue and took their seats. Many Jews and worshipers who were converts to Judaism followed Paul and Barnabas, who spoke to them and urged them to remain faithful to the grace of God.

On the following sabbath almost the whole city gathered to hear the word of the Lord. When the Jews saw the crowds, they were filled with jealousy and with violent abuse contradicted what Paul said. Both Paul and Barnabas spoke out boldly and said, "It was necessary that the word of God be spoken to you first, but since you reject it and condemn yourselves as unworthy of eternal life, we now turn to the Gentiles. For so the Lord has commanded us,

I have made you a light to the Gentiles,
that you may be an instrument of salvation
to the ends of the earth."

The Gentiles were delighted when they heard this and glorified the word of the Lord. All who were destined for eternal life came to believe, and the word of the Lord continued to spread through the whole region. The Jews, however, incited the women of prominence who were worshipers and the leading men of the city, stirred up a persecution against Paul

SCRIPTURE COMMENTARY

The story of the early Church jumps suddenly from the earliest Church in Jerusalem that we heard about last Sunday to the work of Paul on his first missionary journey through southwestern Turkey. Paul and Barnabas had been chosen by the Christian community at Antioch through signs by the Holy Spirit to set out and preach the good news for the first time to many other cities along the southern coastal area of Turkey. They moved inland to Perga and then to Antioch in Pisidia. The reading lingers here because it describes for us the primary method of Paul in his missionary work. He first went to synagogues to tell Jewish congregations about Jesus as their messiah and how his teaching extended even to welcoming Gentiles. When Gentiles responded together with many local Jews to the message of Jesus, the Jewish leaders would be angered and drive Paul (and

HOMILY HELPS

The theme for Good Shepherd Sunday is different for each year of the liturgical cycle. In year A, Christ is the sheepgate through which authentic pastors and sheep pass. In year B, he is the shepherd who guides, protects, and cares for his sheep. In year C, today's reading, the response of the sheep to the shepherd's lead is emphasized.

Today's gospel reminds us that the true followers of the Shepherd accept him with total assurance. They will never be torn away from him by predators or marauders. Adherence to him leads inevitably to eternal life; there is no need to

worry on the journey. Our trust rests in the solemn assurance of Christ himself.

What appears repeatedly in our Easter readings is the Church's universal mission. Today, for example, Revelation places at the center people of every race and nation who stand before the throne of God and the Lamb. God is clearly color blind, as people of every background, purified by the blood of the Lamb, form part of the heavenly court.

All of this may seem perfectly normal. However, when Christianity made its debut, it descended from a Judaism that had long expected a messiah. His appearance would usher in an era of

peace and deliverance from the oppressor's yoke. But it was not seen as a missionary chapter in the people's life. It was seen as a message that, while having repercussions in the broader world, was not primarily directed to a non-Jewish population. But the fact is that Christianity quickly made a radical departure from this earlier expectation.

Paul is often spoken of as the second founder of Christianity. The term may not be altogether felicitous, but it is expressive of an important reality. It was Paul, together with his early companions, who moved the Church away from Palestine and toward the West and the broader world. As we follow his journey, we see

SCRIPTURE COMMENTARY, CONTINUED

Barnabas) from the synagogue. But Gentile groups would welcome him to continue to preach to them about this Jesus and his work of salvation that even included them. Often, however, synagogue leaders went further and initiated local persecution of Paul because they had enough influence to have either the crowds or the officials drive Paul from the local area. But Paul would not be discouraged or stopped.

and Barnabas, and expelled them from their territory. So they shook the dust from their feet in protest against them, and went to Iconium. The disciples were filled with joy and the Holy Spirit.

PSALM REFLECTION

Psalm 100 is a hymn of praise to God's goodness to Israel. He is to receive honor and glory because they know his goodness and have received it. This is a frequent motif in many psalms, but Psalm 100 also mentions that Israel is God's flock, suggesting that the praise and gratitude comes from their recognition that he shepherds and guides them in every generation. Thus it will pick up Paul's message that all, whether Jew or Gentile, are called into God's flock, and it will prepare us for the gospel of the Good Shepherd that we hear each year on the fourth Sunday of Easter.

Psalm Response
Psalm 100:1–2, 3, 5

Antiphon
We are his people, the sheep of his flock.
Or: Alleluia.

Verse for Reflection
Know that the Lord is God;
He made us—we are his;
His people, the flock he tends.
(v. 3)

that, upon arriving in a city or town, he first visited the synagogue, where he generally encountered a mixed or negative reception. This was the case in Antioch of Pisidia. Then he would move toward the center of town and preach to the broader population a message of universal redemption. This was the beginning of the Gentile Church. It brought with it a large measure of accommodation to a worldview not steeped in Jewish tradition. There was tension, even struggle, within the Church in the face of this broader vision. But the change was eventually accepted.

The Church today is beset by serious problems and frightening questions. Yet, in hearing the voice of the Good Shepherd, it retains an inherent vibrancy and optimism. With the guidance of the Spirit, it must remain open to new possibilities and not surrender to a mind-set that sees change as a threat to the Church's fundamental beliefs. Like many human institutions, the Church wants to conserve and often seems to resist change, which it sees as unsettling. Yet, like every living organism, the Church must grow and develop.

The Spirit will call us out of our safe and sedentary posture. Christians do not relish the thought of being long-distance runners, but they should not be foot-draggers either.

Alexander Pope put it well: "Be not the first by whom the new is tried, nor be the last to turn the old aside." There are things in the Church that cannot change; there are other things that can. Modernity is not a virtue, but neither is intransigence. Be not afraid. The Good Shepherd will not abandon his sheep.

Second Reading: Revelation 7:9, 14b–17

I, John, had a vision of a great multitude, which no one could count, from every nation, race, people, and tongue. They stood before the throne and before the Lamb, wearing white robes and holding palm branches in their hands.

Then one of the elders said to me, "These are the ones who have survived the time of great distress; they have washed their robes and made them white in the blood of the Lamb.

"For this reason they stand before God's
   throne
   and worship him day and night in his
   temple.
The one who sits on the throne will shelter
   them.
They will not hunger or thirst anymore,
   nor will the sun or any heat strike them.
For the Lamb who is in the center of the
   throne
   will shepherd them
   and lead them to springs of life-giving
   water,
   and God will wipe away every tear from
   their eyes."

SCRIPTURE COMMENTARY

The image of God's flock that we have in Psalm 100 is magnified many times over by the vision of the Seer of Revelation. But this time the scene has shifted to the heavenly throne room of God. The purpose of Paul's missionary work, to bring the gospel to all peoples, is reflected in the vast multitude of people of every race and language who now enjoy the final fullness of the gospel's message of forgiveness and eternal life. The men and women hold palm branches and wear white robes symbolic of victorious soldiers in triumph. The elder notes, however, that each of them has achieved happiness with God only by enduring persecution and even martyrdom at the hands of those who opposed their faith on earth. We can see some parallels here between the trials of the Christian community as a whole and Paul's life story as an apostle.

LITURGICAL NOTES

The fourth Sunday of Easter, often referred to as Good Shepherd Sunday, is also the World Day of Prayer for Vocations. This day, designated as a day of prayer for vocations in 1964, was chosen to allow the texts of the Good Shepherd to speak to our need for vocations. Care should be exercised to allow the texts to speak. Mention should be made in the homily and in the General Intercessions about vocations. Our preaching and praying should not limit vocations to the priesthood alone but should also include the diaconate and the consecrated life. Many diocesan vocation offices provide print materials on vocations. These materials could be fittingly displayed in the vestibule or gathering space.

In many parishes, First Communions and the sacrament of confirmation are celebrated during the Easter Season. Those preparing for these sacraments should be included in the General Intercessions.

The Easter environment will no doubt need some tending, but it is important to maintain this festive environment for the entire span of fifty days.

The use of the Rite of Blessing and Sprinkling with Holy Water is appropriate. When this is done, the Penitential Rite is omitted. While both texts of the Opening Prayer make reference to the shepherd, the alternative prayer has richer imagery and invites us to "attune our minds to the sound of his voice."

The Day of Prayer for Vocations and the celebrations of First Communion and confirmation should not deter the planning

SCRIPTURE COMMENTARY

John devotes most of chapter 10 to reflections on Jesus as the Good Shepherd. In all, it takes up verses 1–30, so that today we read the final four verses. In the earlier sections Jesus had warned his disciples about false shepherds and showed them how the Good Shepherd knows each lamb, ewe, and ram by name, calls them to himself, and even, if necessary, gives his life to protect his flock. Moreover, his care extends out to bring in other sheep who have no shepherd, who are lost, or who belong to other masters, and to make of them all one flock. These concluding verses promise that this flock will have everlasting life because they remain faithful in following Jesus. And in doing this, they do not just follow their good rabbi; they are made part of God's own flock and thus merit his heavenly kingdom. John here uses language that recalls the great words of the prophet Ezekiel in chapter 34 that God will not tolerate evil shepherds over his people ever again but will himself watch over his people as their shepherd.

> **Gospel: John 10:27–30**
>
> Jesus said: "My sheep hear my voice; I know them, and they follow me. I give them eternal life, and they shall never perish. No one can take them out of my hand. My Father, who has given them to me, is greater than all, and no one can take them out of the Father's hand. The Father and I are one."

CATECHETICAL SUGGESTIONS

Nostra Aetate, Declaration on the Relation of the Church to Non-Christian Religions (Vatican II)
Catholic Evangelization in an Ecumenical and Interreligious Society (USCCB)
The Holy Spirit in Acts
The place of martyrs in Catholic belief
Eschatology: for the individual; for the human race
Meaning and ramification of our belief that Jesus *has* conquered evil

---

team from their reflection on the baptized and their dignity. When asked where she would be sitting in the church, a teacher once answered by saying that she would be found "in the best seat in the house—among the baptized!" If sitting among the baptized is "the best seat in the house," what do the sight lines look like? Can sanctuary, ministers, and other people be seen? Heard? How is the lighting in the morning? In the evening? Are there adequate hymnals/missalettes for singing? Are the kneelers in need of repair? These are but a few of the many questions that can be asked if we are going to take seriously the dignity of the baptized.

MUSIC CONNECTION

Abstracting from Acts, which continues the narrative of the early Church's conflicts with certain segments of the Jewish leadership, the central metaphor for today's liturgy is that of the Shepherd. The responsorial, Psalm 100, exultantly proclaims, "We are his people, the sheep of his flock." Settings from Haas, Bogdan, and Gelineau successfully deliver the text with joy and vigor. The book of Revelation tells of the Lamb on his throne who "will shepherd them and lead them to springs of life-giving water, and God will wipe away every tear from their eyes." The pithy passage from John 10 again gravitates to imagery of the Shepherd, whose sheep "hear my voice." Sylvia Dunstan's *Christus Paradox* artfully treats the images of Christ as sheep and shepherd as a paradigm for other Christological paradoxes such as the earthly Jesus and the cosmic Christ. In vogue are songs of pastoral imagery and meaning, such as *Shepherd Me, O God; Because the Lord Is My Shepherd; The King of Love My Shepherd Is;* and *Come, All You Blessed Ones.* The celestial and exalted imagery of the second reading suggests a robust rendition of Hillert's classic *Festival Canticle,* titled in some hymnals as *This Is the Feast of Victory.* In a similar vein, consider *At the Lamb's High Feast We Sing.*

First Reading: Acts 14:21–27

After Paul and Barnabas had proclaimed the good news to that city and made a considerable number of disciples, they returned to Lystra and to Iconium and to Antioch. They strengthened the spirits of the disciples and exhorted them to persevere in the faith, saying, "It is necessary for us to undergo many hardships to enter the kingdom of God." They appointed elders for them in each church and, with prayer and fasting, commended them to the Lord in whom they had put their faith. Then they traveled through Pisidia and reached Pamphylia. After proclaiming the word at Perga they went down to Attalia. From there they sailed to Antioch, where they had been commended to the grace of God for the work they had now accomplished. And when they arrived, they called the church together and reported what God had done with them and how he had opened the door of faith to the Gentiles.

SCRIPTURE COMMENTARY

We continue last week's account of the first missionary journey of St. Paul. In between the two readings, Paul and Barnabas had preached in Lystra, where Paul healed a crippled man and the pagans had tried to honor the two apostles as gods. They called Paul the god Hermes because he was the divine messenger of Zeus who brought God's words to humankind. But no sooner had they tried to give him divine honors than the Jews from Iconium came and denounced him and, as a result, the same people stoned him and left him for dead. Paul survived this and he and Barnabas apparently decided it was time to return home to Antioch. They revisited each group of converts, giving them strength to persevere in persecution, and also established leaders in each community to guarantee stability and survival. The gospel was beginning to take shape in individual church communities that were well structured and strengthened to endure opposition.

HOMILY HELPS

Life is played out on the uneven playing field of earth. It has its share of villains and heroes, immense pain and overwhelming joy. In the midst of all of this unevenness, the expressed intention of "making all things new" must mean having to begin from scratch. And so it is that Revelation's John of Patmos envisions a new heaven and a new earth. There is also a new Jerusalem, with people of all backgrounds forging a harmonious unity. Mourning and pain will be no more. It is a "consummation devoutly to be wished."

When the reality underlying that image will come about is something of which we are ignorant. But we have a program of life that anticipates that future day. In John's gospel, with the departure of Judas from the upper room, Jesus realizes that his own glorification is at hand. When he is taken from the cross and goes to the Father, his era of glory will have begun. God will be glorified in the death of his Son for the salvation of the world, and God will in turn elevate and glorify his Son. But it doesn't stop there. The love that binds and glorifies Father and Son is to be seen in the world in the love of his disciples. "All will know that you are my disciples if you have love for one another."

During this Easter season, many things have been recounted. The empty tomb, the weeping women, the empowered apostles, the converted Paul. But today's gospel gives meaning to it all. The living evidence that something bigger than life has happened is the love we have for one another. It is to be our sole distinguishing mark.

We need but stop and think of the ways in which this becomes evident. I need to think of that person whom I feel I cannot tolerate. That difference with a relative that has never been

PSALM REFLECTION

Psalm 145 repeats the covenant formula of Exodus 34, where God declared himself to be a God gracious and merciful, slow to anger, and rich in kindness. As a prayer of praise, it continues with glory and thanksgiving for all the works that God has done. And what are these great works? They are the saving deeds that brought his people out of Egypt in the events of the exodus. The Israelites were once enslaved to the power of Pharaoh's empire but are now freed to become members of the kingdom of God. This kingdom is an eternal kingdom living in praise of God's greatness. The psalm calls it a "glorious kingdom" and will thus prepare us for Jesus' word in the gospel about the true nature of his glory.

Psalm Response
Psalm 145:8–9, 10–11, 12–13

Antiphon
I will praise your name for ever, my king and my God.
Or: Alleluia.

Verse for Reflection
The Lord is near to all who call to him,
To all who call on him in sincerity. (v. 18)

CATECHETICAL SUGGESTIONS

Paul, his life and works in Acts
The passing on of leadership in Acts
Kingdom in the Old Testament and in the New Testament
Jerusalem: old and new; city and symbol
The relationship between Jesus and the Father in John's gospel
The relationship between the ten commandments and Jesus' "new commandment"

resolved. The rancor that characterizes my relationship with my spouse, whom I divorced. The feelings of hostility toward that person at work who received the promotion I wanted. The unfair accusations made against me at various moments of my life. The countless heartbreaks. The harsh words. The open wounds.

This cannot be the end. The risen Jesus calls the Christian to something more. Forgiveness and reconciliation are what Christianity is all about. "It is necessary for us to undergo many

hardships if we are to enter the kingdom of God," said Paul to newly converted Christians.

We were never told that the journey would be easy, only that it would be worthwhile. Surely, there is enough fallout along the way to make us wonder. But love overcomes all obstacles, and Easter love is unmatched. As the Father loves Jesus, so Jesus loves us. It is in sowing the seeds of love in this troubled world that we prepare the way for the "new heaven and the new earth."

LITURGICAL NOTES

The alternative prayer for the fifth Sunday of Easter prays that we might be given "voice to sing your praise throughout this season of joy." The Rite of Blessing and Sprinkling with Holy Water continues to be appropriate. When it is done, the Penitential Rite is omitted.

Today's first reading makes reference to the Church being built up and growing in numbers. That growth was accomplished

**Second Reading:
Revelation 21:1–5a**

Then I, John, saw a new heaven and a new earth. The former heaven and the former earth had passed away, and the sea was no more. I also saw the holy city, a new Jerusalem, coming down out of heaven from God, prepared as a bride adorned for her husband. I heard a loud voice from the throne saying, "Behold, God's dwelling is with the human race. He will dwell with them and they will be his people and God himself will always be with them as their God. He will wipe every tear from their eyes, and there shall be no more death or mourning, wailing or pain, for the old order has passed away."

The One who sat on the throne said, "Behold, I make all things new."

SCRIPTURE COMMENTARY

The book of Revelation nears its end in chapter 21. The battle for victory over Satan and the powers of this world is over, and now Christ returns to reign over his kingdom. It is not only a new heaven and earth, that is, a transformed universe, but it is also a new Jerusalem, thus signifying that this kingdom will be the successor, on the heavenly level, to the temple, where God had promised he would dwell in the midst of his people in the old city of Jerusalem. The Jerusalem of old had been the center of Israel's relationship with their God. The central covenant formula of the Old Testament was "I will be your God and you will be my people" (see Exodus 6; Ezekiel 36; and elsewhere) and was understood to be tied closely to God's dwelling with his people in the temple. But unlike the physical temple in Jerusalem, which had three times been torn down or destroyed and had often fallen under the control of oppressive conquerors, the new Jerusalem will offer its inhabitants joy, freedom from fear, and eternal life. God announces about it, "Behold, I make all things new!" It is a final word of hope to the suffering and persecuted Christians to whom John the Seer is writing.

through the living out of the words of the gospel, "As I have loved you, so you also should love one another." The scriptures speak boldly of what God has accomplished for us and of what God can accomplish in us.

Our baptism, renewed at Easter, binds us forever not only to Christ but also to each other. Acknowledging our baptism, we learn to live in peace and in love with one another. Acknowledging our own baptism, we recognize the bond that binds us to one another.

This might be a good Sunday for liturgical ministers to recognize and acknowledge the meaning of their service to the assembly of the baptized and the reverence that is due to all of the baptized. While this reverence is a part of our living within the context of the liturgy, it is also our obligation outside the doors of the church. Many find it easier to express reverence within the confines of the church building than outside the building. Gentle reminders can help keep our common baptismal dignity in focus.

There are three weeks until Pentecost. Plans for its celebration should be well under way, especially if the planning team intends to involve in the liturgies that weekend parishioners representing the diverse cultures and languages of the parish.

SCRIPTURE COMMENTARY

The gospel comes from the Last Supper discourse. Judas has left to finalize his betrayal of Jesus, and Jesus announces that the time of his glorification has come. In this he refers to the death he will undergo as Judas delivers him into the hands of the authorities. But this will not be a victory of those who attempt to stop his message by killing the messenger. It is instead the victory of God that will come about. Jesus is telling his disciples in a veiled manner that his death will not be final, and someday they will understand when he has been raised from the dead. But although it will also mean he must leave them, he will not leave them without the help they will need. His new commandment is not just to love but to love as he himself has shown them how to love one another. And what has he shown them that is so different? He has taught them that love will even give up life for the sake of the other. All his disciples must love with the same complete self-sacrifice as Jesus himself will reveal in the coming hours as he undergoes suffering and death for the sake of others. In this John is echoing for us the great message of the Suffering Servant of Isaiah, that the servant gives up his life the sake of the many and that God will glorify him for it.

**Gospel:
John 13:31–33a, 34–35**

When Judas had left them, Jesus said, "Now is the Son of Man glorified, and God is glorified in him. If God is glorified in him, God will also glorify him in himself, and God will glorify him at once. My children, I will be with you only a little while longer. I give you a new commandment: love one another. As I have loved you, so you also should love one another. This is how all will know that you are my disciples, if you have love for one another."

MUSIC CONNECTION

Paul's words of comfort in Acts that "we must undergo many hardships if we are to enter the kingdom of God" suggests hymns that encourage and console, such as *Be Not Afraid, Come to Me, Daylight Fades, We Walk by Faith,* and *Precious Lord*. This sentiment is echoed in Psalm 145, where the Lord is extolled as "gracious and merciful." Settings by Willcock, Gelineau, Hughes, and Haas would all work well for this, today's responsorial. John's celestial vision in Revelation is rich in imagery picked up in hymns such as *Jerusalem, My Happy Home; City of God, Jerusalem;* Parker's *Praise the Lord, My Soul;* and *I'll Be Singing Up There*. The gospel's brevity underscores the centrality of love in the message of Jesus from the Farewell Discourse in the fourth gospel. "I give you a new commandment: love one another.... This is how all will know that you are my disciples: if you have love for one another." Numerous hymns understandably take their lead from this central message, and all are fitting today. They include *Love Is His Word; Love Divine, All Loves Excelling; This Is My Commandment; A Simple Command;* and *The Summons*. The late Clarence Rivers's *God Is Love* would be especially fitting today, and Carl Nygard's *God So Loved the World* would make for a wonderful choir anthem.

First Reading: Acts 15:1–2, 22–29

Some who had come down from Judea were instructing the brothers, "Unless you are circumcised according to the Mosaic practice, you cannot be saved." Because there arose no little dissension and debate by Paul and Barnabas with them, it was decided that Paul, Barnabas, and some of the others should go up to Jerusalem to the apostles and elders about this question.

The apostles and elders, in agreement with the whole church, decided to choose representatives and to send them to Antioch with Paul and Barnabas. The ones chosen were Judas, who was called Barsabbas, and Silas, leaders among the brothers. This is the letter delivered by them:

"The apostles and the elders, your brothers, to the brothers in Antioch, Syria, and Cilicia of Gentile origin: greetings. Since we have heard that some of our number who went out without any mandate from us have upset you with their teachings and disturbed your peace of mind, we have with one accord decided to choose representatives and to send them to you along with our beloved Barnabas and Paul, who have dedicated their lives to the name of our Lord Jesus Christ. So we are sending Judas and Silas who will also convey this

SCRIPTURE COMMENTARY

The initial work of the apostolic Church comes to an end in Acts 15. The apostle Peter has brought the message of Christ's salvation and baptism out from Jerusalem to all of Palestine in chapters 2–12. The culminating moment comes when Peter himself announces that God has revealed to him in the case of the centurion Cornelius that Gentiles are to be included in the community along with Jews. The story of Paul's call and first missionary journey to Gentile lands of Turkey has taken up chapters 9–14, and his success has been notable. Luke's telling overlaps Paul's story with that of Peter in order to unite their work as though parallel and intertwined. But this has posed the most difficult question that faced the early Church. If Jesus has come to fulfill the covenant with God and the prophetic oracles of the Old Testament, are not new non-Jewish converts required to accept the regulations of the Old Testament law besides believing in Jesus as their messiah and Savior? A fierce battle breaks out between those who insist on every Christian being both fully Jewish and faithful to the way of Christ and those who insist that God has bestowed the Holy Spirit on the Gentiles and made them members of the Church even though they are not Jews and have not

HOMILY HELPS

There are two clear messages today: unity and continuity. These are values that appear clearly in the life of the early Church. The conflict over the place of the Jewish law was much more than a passing concern; it could easily have resulted in a major split in early Christianity. A more conservative Jewish Christian outlook in Jerusalem was interested in preserving the law, as symbolized primarily in the rite of circumcision. The Church at large, with no attachment to Jewish law and practice, did not want to see these things imposed on its members. Paul,

the leader of Gentile Christianity, was as adamant about freedom as some of his Jerusalem counterparts were about Jewish tradition.

What is worth highlighting is the way the issue was resolved. It was through dialogue, with prayer for the guidance of the Spirit. Humanly speaking, the process required flexibility on both sides, but the good of the Church was paramount. Therein lies the lesson. The ability to listen (and not just "hear") resulted in an understanding of what the Spirit wanted for the Church as a whole.

It may well be that today we are too partisan and too issue oriented. We should perhaps begin

with a true listening to the Church as a whole, especially the laity, as well as our leaders. How can the Church best meet the needs of these challenging times? These needs related to issues of authority, ministry, equality, and social justice. How, for example, do we view ministry? How can those needs best be met? What is our relationship to the needs of the world as a whole? Where there is respectful dialogue and a willingness to listen to the voice of the Spirit, we will be carried forward.

A second feature of Church life is continuity. This is strikingly seen in today's reading from Revelation. In the vision of the new Jerusalem descending from

SCRIPTURE COMMENTARY, CONTINUED

been circumcised into the covenant. Chapter 15 describes the critical meeting in Jerusalem that decided the question in favor of allowing two ways. Jews must continue to keep the law as they live Christ's way; the Gentiles can forego the rites and physical practices of being Jewish by receiving the Spirit in baptism. However, they should respect some practices of the law that would otherwise clearly divide Jews and Gentiles in their dealings with each other—not because they could not be in Christ without these practices but out of charity and the obligation of unity in Christ.

same message by word of mouth: 'It is the decision of the Holy Spirit and of us not to place on you any burden beyond these necessities, namely, to abstain from meat sacrificed to idols, from blood, from meats of strangled animals, and from unlawful marriage. If you keep free of these, you will be doing what is right. Farewell.'"

PSALM REFLECTION

Psalm 67 is especially appropriate for today's readings because it stresses the universal rule of God over all peoples and how all peoples will come to honor and worship God with praise. Above all, it emphasizes that God deals with and judges all nations equally in fairness. No one is outside God's care and saving power. One can imagine the very tense apostolic meeting in Jerusalem just described in Acts 15 ending with the embraces of acceptance by all its participants and the final singing of this psalm together!

Psalm Response
Psalm 67:2–3, 5, 6, 8

Antiphon
O God, let all the nations praise you!
Or: Alleluia.

Verse for Reflection
May the peoples praise you, O God;
May all the peoples praise you!
   (v. 4)

heaven, the city gates bear the names of the twelve tribes of Israel while the foundation stones are inscribed with the names of the twelve apostles. The Jewish and Christian traditions merge, the Old Testament and the New.

Regardless of what steps we take forward, we are part of a long history, and as the saying goes, "we stand on the shoulders of giants." Our history is one that carries us back four thousand years. We are deeply rooted in a tradition that is a source of

courage and strength for us. Every Mass we attend carries us back two thousand years and even further back to an ancient biblical tradition that foreshadowed the Eucharist.

In today's gospel, Jesus speaks at some length about the Holy Spirit, whom he is about to send. That Spirit will be a guide for the Church as well as a support in times of great difficulty. But the Spirit expresses itself in peace, that peace which the world cannot give. Christ speaks of it today before his departure and will give

it special emphasis when he appears on the night of his resurrection. This is a peace that re-establishes our ruptured relations with God, and it is also a peace that is meant to be extended to all humanity and all of creation.

Strident voices directed at one another accomplish little. Camps of division should be alien to Christians. But where there is conviction coupled with respect, as at the Jerusalem gathering, change will be accompanied by love.

Second Reading:
Revelation 21:10–14, 22–23

The angel took me in spirit to a great, high mountain and showed me the holy city Jerusalem coming down out of heaven from God. It gleamed with the splendor of God. Its radiance was like that of a precious stone, like jasper, clear as crystal. It had a massive, high wall, with twelve gates where twelve angels were stationed and on which names were inscribed, the names of the twelve tribes of the Israelites. There were three gates facing east, three north, three south, and three west. The wall of the city had twelve courses of stones as its foundation, on which were inscribed the twelve names of the twelve apostles of the Lamb.

I saw no temple in the city for its temple is the Lord God almighty and the Lamb. The city had no need of sun or moon to shine on it, for the glory of God gave it light, and its lamp was the Lamb.

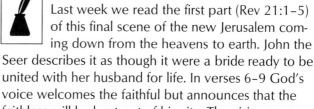

SCRIPTURE COMMENTARY

Last week we read the first part (Rev 21:1–5) of this final scene of the new Jerusalem coming down from the heavens to earth. John the Seer describes it as though it were a bride ready to be united with her husband for life. In verses 6–9 God's voice welcomes the faithful but announces that the faithless will be kept out of his city. The vision now turns to the physical depiction of the city, describing it as though made up of gold and radiant jewels. But once we hear of the twelve gates for the twelve tribes of Israel and twelve foundation stones for the twelve apostles, we realize the author is not describing bricks and paving stones but the *people* that make up the city. This city symbolically needs no walls because its citizens are its gates and walls and homes. Indeed, the Seer makes clear there will be no human temple of stone in the City of God, no more than it needs the sun or moon or other earthly bodies to make it livable. It will be lighted and sustained by the presence of God himself ruling with Christ in glory at his side. Christ, the Lamb of God, who gave his blood that all may live forever in this city!

LITURGICAL NOTES

As the celebration of Easter continues, we begin to move toward the coming of the Spirit at Pentecost. The scriptures also move our reflection to the coming of the Spirit and the work that the Spirit will accomplish in our midst. It is the Spirit who will keep the flame of our baptism alive in our hearts.

Today is also Mother's Day and can provide a host of challenges to liturgy planners. Mother's Day stands as an important secular holiday; however, we should not allow it to become a Marian feast. The Church celebrates Mary's motherhood on January 1; today is a day when we celebrate our own mothers, grandmothers, godmothers, and even some of the mother figures in our lives.

The *Book of Blessings* provides an Order for the Blessing of Mothers on Mother's Day (chapter 55). Sample intercessions are provided, and these are well done, mentioning mothers, mothers who have lost a child, and mothers who have died. Liturgy planners might consider expanding that scope to include single mothers, mothers-to-be, and godmothers. There is also a prayer of blessing for mothers, in the style of a Prayer over the People, which can be used at the end of Mass or at other liturgical services on Mother's Day. The theme of Mother's Day, however, should not overtake the General Intercessions or the liturgy of the seventh Sunday of Easter.

If Ascension Thursday is celebrated on Thursday as a holy day of obligation, the schedule of Masses should be announced.

SCRIPTURE COMMENTARY

John 14 comes from the farewell speech of Jesus to his disciples at the Last Supper. John has reported a very lengthy series of reflections by Jesus intended to strengthen the disciples for his departure from their midst. The speech takes up all of chapters 13–17 and has many of the characteristics typical of ancient examples of a father's deathbed advice to his children. Such talks typically stress what the father has tried to teach his children over the years and what he is leaving them as their inheritance and includes urgings to courage and continuation in his legacy. Reading this small section makes clear that the major legacy of Jesus is love. He has loved the Father and shown them the Father's love in turn; he has loved the disciples and taught his disciples how to love one another; and he encourages them to continue in that love, for it will be completely fulfilled only when Jesus is reunited with his Father. But this doesn't mean that Jesus will love his disciples less: he leaves them his teaching and the power of the Holy Spirit to help them understand his message; he leaves them a peace that the world cannot give; and he promises to return to them again. We are now prepared for the next step: his ascension into heaven.

Gospel: John 14:23–29

Jesus said to his disciples: "Whoever loves me will keep my word, and my Father will love him, and we will come to him and make our dwelling with him. Whoever does not love me does not keep my words; yet the word you hear is not mine but that of the Father who sent me. "I have told you this while I am with you. The Advocate, the Holy Spirit, whom the Father will send in my name, will teach you everything and remind you of all that I told you. Peace I leave with you; my peace I give to you. Not as the world gives do I give it to you. Do not let your hearts be troubled or afraid. You heard me tell you, 'I am going away and I will come back to you.' If you loved me, you would rejoice that I am going to the Father; for the Father is greater than I. And now I have told you this before it happens, so that when it happens you may believe."

MUSIC CONNECTION

The reading from Acts goes to the issue of what is necessary for non-Jewish followers of Jesus, what is essential if one is to be baptized and saved in Jesus' name. Peloquin's *A Simple Command* musically and textually sums up the answer in the command to love God and neighbor. Other hymns in this vein include *Come We That Love the Lord, Ubi Caritas, Love One Another,* and *Love Is His Word.* Revelation, with its images and numeric details, continues its graphic tour of the celestial Jerusalem. *O Holy City, Seen of John* is based on this visionary section of Revelation and would be most fitting today. The responsorial, Psalm 67, finds numerous good settings by Guimont, Proulx, and Gelineau. The gospel continues the treatment of love found in the Farewell Discourse. Hymns that touch on the themes of the first reading and the gospel include *Come Down, O Love Divine; Unless a Grain of Wheat; We Have Been Told; We Are Many Parts; Christians, Let Us Love One Another;* and *In Perfect Charity.*

CATECHETICAL SUGGESTIONS

The Jerusalem Council: purpose, decision, precedent
The teaching role of the Church
The role of ecumenical councils
The temple in the Old Testament and in the New Testament
Jesus' last meal with the disciples in John and in the synoptic gospels
The Trinity

First Reading: Acts 1:1–11

In the first book, Theophilus, I dealt with all that Jesus did and taught until the day he was taken up, after giving instructions through the Holy Spirit to the apostles whom he had chosen. He presented himself alive to them by many proofs after he had suffered, appearing to them during forty days and speaking about the kingdom of God. While meeting with them, he enjoined them not to depart from Jerusalem, but to wait for "the promise of the Father about which you have heard me speak; for John baptized with water, but in a few days you will be baptized with the Holy Spirit."

When they had gathered together they asked him, "Lord, are you at this time going to restore the kingdom to Israel?" He answered them, "It is not for you to know the times or seasons that the Father has established by his own authority. But you will receive power when the Holy Spirit comes upon you, and you will be my witnesses in Jerusalem, throughout Judea and Samaria, and to the ends of the earth." When he had said this, as they were looking on, he was lifted up, and a cloud took him from their sight. While they were looking intently at the sky as he was going, suddenly two men dressed in white garments stood beside them. They said, "Men of Galilee, why are

SCRIPTURE COMMENTARY

Luke provides a new introduction to the second volume of his two-volume work. It is similar in format to the introduction to his gospel. Both volumes are dedicated to the noble Theophilus. He may be a real person, a patron who commissioned Luke to write down his gospel, or he may be symbolic, a personification of all readers of Luke's gospel. The name means "One who loves God" and can easily be read to mean that this story is dedicated to "You who seek God's word." What stands out is that when Jesus chose the apostles, it was through the Holy Spirit; when he appeared to them after the resurrection, he taught them to rely on the coming Holy Spirit; and when he had departed, he would send the Spirit to empower them. The Acts of the Apostles unfolds the work of the Holy Spirit as it guided apostolic efforts to bring Jesus' message to Jerusalem, then to

HOMILY HELPS

Behind the imagery connected with this feast, there is one basic truth. This man Jesus who walked among us is now fully recognized as God, with all that divinity implies. Furthermore, we are destined to be with him one day. In today's reading from Ephesians, Paul speaks of "the hope that belongs to his call," and he prays that we will have the wisdom and insight to cherish it.

"Fuga mundi." "Flee the world." There is one type of spirituality that sees this as its fundamental truth. It calls us to leave the world behind and dedicate ourselves wholly to the things that are beyond. Another type of spirituality, more common today, would not adhere to such a dichotomous summons. When it comes to earth and heaven, it is not a question of "either/or" but rather "both/and." At Christ's ascension, the astonished apostles stood gazing up to heaven. They were enraptured and taken up by what they had seen. Then heavenly figures ask them quite bluntly why they are standing there gazing at the sky. In short, there is work to be done. There is no time for delay.

Certainly, there is a time for silence and contemplation in every Christian life. At the same time, there is a world out there awash in misplaced values and a loss of the transcendent. The first injunction given the apostles in today's gospel is to call people to conversion that their sins may be forgiven. Reconciliation was the primary aspect of Jesus' mission. Grace regained is friendship restored. And about all of this there is a certain urgency. There is little time for "sky gazing."

Today's feast has a clear note of joy, and the apostles' comportment reflects this. Despite all the pain and hardship, the story had ended well. Christ is with the Father, and the apostles are filled with happiness. Their relation to the temple is still intact and there they sing the praises of God.

Prayer and action are complementary, not exclusive. In fact,

SCRIPTURE COMMENTARY, CONTINUED

all of the country, and then even to the farthest ends of the world. At all stages, Luke assures us, Jesus is present. The Spirit inspires the apostles as witnesses to Jesus and instills the virtue of hope for his return. But they must not slacken in their efforts, for only God can determine when the apostolic mission is completed in order that Jesus may return.

you standing there looking at the sky? This Jesus who has been taken up from you into heaven will return in the same way as you have seen him going into heaven."

PSALM REFLECTION

The description of the ascension of Jesus to heaven in all three synoptic gospels (Matthew, Mark, and Luke) portrays him rising up above the clouds to heaven. This draws on a long tradition in the ancient Near East in which gods who come down to earth to act for the good of mankind return to their true residence in the heavens. There the god, whether Marduk or Baal or Zeus, is seated in royal splendor and glory in his divine throne room to govern the earth. Psalm 47 comes from a group of Psalms of the Sons of Korah (Psalms 42–49) that were originally associated with the annual celebration in the Jerusalem temple of the kingship of God. Such a feast also involved renewing the divine blessing on the earthly king, who was God's deputy on earth. The language of the psalm captures much of the magnificence of an ancient coronation rite when the whole people would acclaim the new king as he took his throne for the first time. But just as Jesus sent out his disciples to preach to the ends of the earth, so the divine king reigns not just over Israel but over the entire world.

**Psalm Response
Psalm 47:2–3, 6–7, 8–9**

Antiphon
God mounts his throne to shouts of joy: a blare of trumpets for the Lord.
Or: Alleluia.

Verse for Reflection
God ascends his throne to joyful shouts,
The Lord, with the blare of trumpets. (v. 6)

they are interwoven. As St. Vincent de Paul told the sisters whose nursing demands often limited their time for prayer: "To care for the sick is to pray." The risen Christ, now with the Father, sends us forth as "ambassadors of reconciliation." Where our feet travel, he can travel; where we go, he goes. Where our love reaches, his does as well.

CATECHETICAL SUGGESTIONS

The ascension in Luke and in Acts
The expectation of the second coming
Enthronement psalms
High Christology in Ephesians
The Church as the body of Christ
Fulfillment of Old Testament promises in New Testament events

**Second Reading: Ephesians 1:17–23
(or Hebrews 9:24–28; 10:19–23)**

Brothers and sisters: May the God of our Lord Jesus Christ, the Father of glory, give you a Spirit of wisdom and revelation resulting in knowledge of him. May the eyes of your hearts be enlightened, that you may know what is the hope that belongs to his call, what are the riches of glory in his inheritance among the holy ones, and what is the surpassing greatness of his power for us who believe, in accord with the exercise of his great might, which he worked in Christ, raising him from the dead and seating him at his right hand in the heavens, far above every principality, authority, power, and dominion, and every name that is named not only in this age but also in the one to come. And he put all things beneath his feet and gave him as head over all things to the church, which is his body, the fullness of the one who fills all things in every way.

SCRIPTURE COMMENTARY

The letter to the Ephesians is certainly the most universal of all the Pauline epistles. It speaks of the death and resurrection of Jesus as bringing about God's reign over the whole universe, including both people and every object of creation. God makes his rule known over all things through the exaltation of his Son, Jesus, who is now enthroned as equal to the Father himself in the heavenly throne room. The wonderful phrase "Seated at the right hand of the Father," which Paul uses here and which has been taken up in the words of the Nicene Creed, signifies the enthronement of Jesus as king of creation. Like a prime minister or, perhaps better, a crown prince, he enjoys the full authority of God himself to govern and receive the loyal obedience of all subjects of God's kingdom. Nowhere does Paul separate the rule of God the Father from that of Christ. Always they are as one in all decisions for us, and to know Christ is to come to know the Father. If Christ is the head of the Church as though it were his own body, then, in turn, Christ and his body are united to the Father as one. As Christ is the Son, so we become adopted as sons and daughters of God as well.

LITURGICAL NOTES

In many dioceses of the United States, the Solemnity of the Ascension is transferred to the seventh Sunday of Easter. When the celebration of the Ascension is celebrated on Thursday, it is a holy day of obligation. Although Mass attendance might be less than that on Sunday, this solemnity demands attention, for the ascension is "our glory and hope."

Depending on the time of day and the nature of the parish, some Masses may be celebrated under significant time constraints. Careful planning can allow the liturgy to be celebrated fully and well in a limited amount of time.

While the Sacramentary provides two prefaces of the Ascension, the first contains richer imagery. The practice of extinguishing the paschal candle this day has been abolished; the candle remains lit up until and including the celebration of Pentecost.

The weekdays after the Ascension until the Saturday before Pentecost inclusive are a preparation for the coming of the Holy Spirit (GNLYC, 26) The Spirit will pour out in abundance manifold gifts upon the Church. This might be a good time to reflect on the gifts of the Spirit and our response to those gifts. One suggestion is to distribute the prayer for confirmation, which lists the gifts of the Holy Spirit and places them in the context of the life of the Christian.

SCRIPTURE COMMENTARY

Luke's Gospel ends with the ascension scene, which he repeats in the opening to his Acts of the Apostles. By repeating the scene in this way, he ties the two books together as a single ongoing story of God's saving plan unfolding. It is not accidental, of course, that the ascension plays such a pivotal role in linking the time of Jesus to the time of the Church. It is at this critical moment when the Lord will no longer be present in the flesh that we rediscover that he is still present and made known by the work of the Holy Spirit. In both Acts and his gospel, Luke stresses that what begins in Jerusalem will reach to the ends of the known world. Until the moment of the ascension, the followers of Jesus are to be found worshiping God for his salvation in Jesus and honoring Jesus as their messiah in the temple courts, as very devout and faithful Jews. Luke is about to embark in his Acts on a story that will move away from the temple as the center of Christian practice, but never will the teaching of the apostles break the bond with the first covenant and its scriptures, which revealed the saving love of God for those he had chosen and which prophesied the work of Jesus as Savior.

Gospel: Luke 24:46–53

Jesus said to his disciples: "Thus it is written that the Christ would suffer and rise from the dead on the third day and that repentance, for the forgiveness of sins, would be preached in his name to all the nations, beginning from Jerusalem. You are witnesses of these things. And behold I am sending the promise of my Father upon you; but stay in the city until you are clothed with power from on high."

Then he led them out as far as Bethany, raised his hands, and blessed them. As he blessed them he parted from them and was taken up to heaven. They did him homage and then returned to Jerusalem with great joy, and they were continually in the temple praising God.

MUSIC CONNECTION

The Lucan chronology of Jesus' remaining on earth and appearing to the disciples for forty days after the resurrection suits the author's theological perspective. A new era has been inaugurated with Jesus' exaltation to the right hand of the Father. The rousing *Alleluia, Sing to Jesus* recounts this exaltation in its second verse, "Alleluia! Not as orphans are we left in sorrow now; Alleluia! He is near us, faith believes nor questions how: Though the cloud from sight received him when the forty days were o'er, shall our hearts forget his promise, 'I am with you evermore,'" The gospel mandate to the disciples in all three Lectionary cycles to "go, make disciples...baptize" (Matthew), to "go into the whole world and proclaim the good news" (Mark), and to be "witnesses of all this" (Luke) strongly suggests the ever popular *Lord, You Give the Great Commission* as well as the Wesley classic *Hail the Day That Sees Him Rise*. Sylvia Dunstam's text to *Sine Nomine*, the Vaughan Williams melody, entitled *Go to the World,* is a wonderful addition to the seasonal repertoire. The pastoral musician should not overlook Vaughan Williams's classic and powerful *Hail Thee, Festival Day* for this feast, whether it is celebrated on Thursday or Sunday. The responsorial Psalm 47 is well served both by Haugen and by the Proulx/Gelineau setting—both from GIA.

First Reading: Acts 7:55–60

Stephen, filled with the Holy Spirit, looked up intently to heaven and saw the glory of God and Jesus standing at the right hand of God, and Stephen said, "Behold, I see the heavens opened and the Son of Man standing at the right hand of God." But they cried out in a loud voice, covered their ears, and rushed upon him together. They threw him out of the city, and began to stone him. The witnesses laid down their cloaks at the feet of a young man named Saul. As they were stoning Stephen, he called out, "Lord Jesus, receive my spirit." Then he fell to his knees and cried out in a loud voice, "Lord, do not hold this sin against them;" and when he said this, he fell asleep.

SCRIPTURE COMMENTARY

On this Sunday that follows the Ascension, the church looks forward to the arrival of Pentecost next week, when the Holy Spirit will empower the apostles in their new task of going forth to spread the gospel of Jesus after his departure. So, we may ask, why do we jump ahead seven chapters to the story of Stephen, the first known martyr of the Church? In order to understand the difference the Holy Spirit will make, turning the frightened and timid apostles into the bold preachers of the good news who risk their lives to make Jesus' message known, we need some concrete example. It seems fitting enough to begin with such a practical example of the best that the power of the Spirit will bring—the courage to endure death itself rather than betray our fidelity to Christ. In such courage, the disciple is revealed as conformed to the example of the master, who gave his life for others. The very word "martyrdom" comes from the Latin for "giving witness." Martyrdom most completely fulfills the command of Jesus at his ascension that the disciples are to be witnesses to Christ to the ends of the earth. This, above all, is what the Spirit makes possible.

HOMILY HELPS

"Have this mind in you which was also in Christ Jesus." With these words Paul introduces his great hymn in the epistle to the Philippians. Each of us who bears the name Christian must deeply wish to have the "mind of Jesus." In the account of Stephen's death in today's reading from Acts, the martyr's words directly echo those of the dying Christ. The last are words of forgiveness for his persecutors. "Lord, do not hold their sin against them." And just as Christ expired with an expression of surrender to God, Stephen also exclaims: "Lord Jesus, receive my spirit."

What a difference it would make in our daily lives if we made an earnest effort to respond to events as Christ would respond. In the midst of confusion, it would mean calm; in a hostile environment, it would mean patience and understanding; in a world of egocentrism, it would mean self-giving and generous support.

It is a mistake to see Christ solely as our king and sovereign to whom worship and allegiance are due or to see him solely as the one who died for us and will deal with us mercifully in judgment. We are actually called to incorporate the life and teaching of Jesus at every turn. He is our model and exemplar. And it is his response to the events of daily life that are worthy of emulation. What a difference it would make in our world if what was said of the Church's first members could be said of us: "Behold how they love one another."

We spend a great deal of time criticizing secularism and worldly values. And all too often we allow ourselves to be shaped by those values. Having "the mind of Christ" is to live so as to make a difference, making Christian theory a reality.

The gospel today makes sense of all of this. We have the power to live what we believe. The Father lives in Jesus and Jesus lives in each of us. We are as close to Christ as he is to the

PSALM REFLECTION

Psalm 97 is part of the great body of hymns to God's kingship found in Psalms 93 and 95–99. It is particularly fitting in this period after the ascension, for it highlights God's reign over the entire universe and over all peoples. If the gospel is intended for all nations and peoples, then God's kingdom will come to fulfillment across the entire world. But this psalm has some special unique notes to it. After exalting the infinite power of God over the universe, it declares that the very foundations of the universe itself are the qualities of justice and judgment (this is the NAB Lectionary translation). These two words are usually rendered in other translations as "justice and righteousness." Justice is our just and fair behavior toward one another, what we usually refer to as social justice; righteousness refers to our right relationship in worship and obedience to God. The first term refers to our horizontal human relationships, the second to our vertical relationship with God. Both are necessary for membership in the covenant. But the psalmist goes further to say that these are the very attributes of God himself and are intrinsic to a world subject to God. In acting with justice and righteousness, we imitate the very love and fairness that God extends to every creature he has made.

Psalm Response
Psalm 97:1–2, 6–7, 9

Antiphon
The Lord is king, the
    most high over all
    the earth.
Or: Alleluia.

Verse for Reflection
The heavens proclaim
    his justice,
And all peoples will see
    his glory. (v. 6)

Father, in a spirit of unity and accord. That this divine unity be mirrored in the world is at the heart of Christ's prayer for his followers. Division is the antithesis of godliness. Yet, sadly, we see a sharply divided Christianity.

In recent times there has been a marked effort to overcome the obstacles to unity. Popes have met and prayed with leaders of other Christian churches on numerous occasions. The Lutheran–Roman Catholic joint agreement on justification, an issue that was one of the key causes of Reformation division, was a major step forward. But there still remain important areas of Christian separation, especially in the areas of authority, ministry, and the sacraments.

Nevertheless, nothing should stop us from recognizing our common baptism. It remains the great gift of Christ the redeemer, who has taken us all into his embrace. In every town and neighborhood, there are ways we can work together—in answering the needs of the poor, in promoting social justice, and in securing the common good.

CATECHETICAL SUGGESTIONS

Stephen: deacon and martyr
Paul before and after his conversion
The history of monotheism
Particular and general judgment
Encyclical *Ut Unum Sint,* On Commitment to Ecumenism (Pope John Paul II)
Ways in which Jesus has already come into our lives

Second Reading:
Revelation 22:12–14, 16–17, 20

I, John, heard a voice saying to me: "Behold, I am coming soon. I bring with me the recompense I will give to each according to his deeds. I am the Alpha and the Omega, the first and the last, the beginning and the end."

Blessed are they who wash their robes so as to have the right to the tree of life and enter the city through its gates.

"I, Jesus, sent my angel to give you this testimony for the churches. I am the root and offspring of David, the bright morning star."

The Spirit and the bride say, "Come." Let the hearer say, "Come." Let the one who thirsts come forward, and the one who wants it receive the gift of life-giving water.

The one who gives this testimony says, "Yes, I am coming soon." Amen! Come, Lord Jesus!

SCRIPTURE COMMENTARY

The final vision of the book of Revelation takes up chapters 21–22. On the sixth Sunday of Easter and the Solemnity of the Ascension we heard two sections on the coming of the new Jerusalem. The vision continues in chapter 22. The voice of God, or of Christ (they are considered the same here), that speaks to John the Seer declares at the beginning of the reading today that God is beginning and end, first and last. The sense, of course, is that God is the cause and origin of all things and of all events that unfold in history. What he has begun he also guides to its completion. Biblical scholars often talk about how the biblical story from Genesis to Revelation presents God's plan as parallel in beginning and end. God establishes a garden in Eden that has rivers at its center, jewels on its ground, bounteous fruit tress for all seasons of the year; and the new Jerusalem at the end has all the same qualities. What God intended as the harmonious world of *shalom,* or wholeness, at the beginning is now brought back into proper relationship at the end through the triumph of Jesus over sin and death. This city's walls and pavement are described as though gleaming with gold and jewels, but clearly this is only metaphorical. The twelve gates for the tribes of Israel and the twelve foundations built on the apostles reveal that it is the faithful who are the stones and pavement stones of this city. It needs no physical walls, just as it needs no temple of stone. God is its temple, and the people are its every stone.

LITURGICAL NOTES

In many dioceses in the United States, the Solemnity of the Ascension is transferred to this Sunday, replacing its texts and readings with those of the Ascension. If the Ascension is celebrated on this Sunday, see the liturgical notes for Ascension Thursday.

This Sunday, situated between the Ascension and Pentecost, prepares us for the coming of the Spirit. The weekdays after the Ascension until the Saturday before Pentecost inclusive are a preparation for the coming of the Holy Spirit (GNLYC, 26) While all the elements that have been part of our Sunday celebrations of Easter throughout this season continue, we are on the threshold of Pentecost, and our celebration of Easter is not so much drawing to a conclusion as it is rising to a culmination.

The gospel contains not only Jesus' priestly prayer for unity but also the mission of being sent forth into the world. The General Intercessions ought to make mention of unity among all the followers of Christ. The Intercessions should also contain prayers for those engaged in missionary work in our own country and throughout the world.

The baptized form the body of Christ, and it is Christ himself who prays for unity and single-heartedness among them. What are the words, gestures, and actions that unite our assemblies? And what are the words, gestures, and actions that divide our assemblies? A mere listing of these is insufficient. Planners can take the opportunity to examine those things that unite our assemblies, and both capitalize on them and expand them. Those things that divide our assemblies can be examined to discover ways in which, within the framework of the liturgy and the abilities of a given parish, that which divides the body can be minimized.

SCRIPTURE COMMENTARY

The final chapter of Jesus' farewell speech in John 13–17 centers on Jesus' prayer for the unity of the Church. As Jesus has full union with his Father, he has taught his disciples that they are one in him, and now he asks that they be given God's grace to be one with each other. Unity will always be the gravest test of the Church's faith. Humans are in love with their own ideas. Their disputes lead to breaks, which lead to competing centers of power and claims of truth. Jesus proposes to his disciples that they must overcome these tendencies to division by knowing and living in him. The unity of the Church depends on its unity with its head. The reward will be the glory of the risen Christ in which they will share someday. This is no ordinary glory won by hard work or human achievement; it is the very glory that belongs to Christ as the Son of God himself—it is the eternal glory of divine life now to be shared with us.

Gospel: John 17:20–26

Lifting up his eyes to heaven, Jesus prayed saying: "Holy Father, I pray not only for them, but also for those who will believe in me through their word, so that they may all be one, as you, Father, are in me and I in you, that they also may be in us, that the world may believe that you sent me. And I have given them the glory you gave me, so that they may be one, as we are one, I in them and you in me, that they may be brought to perfection as one, that the world may know that you sent me, and that you loved them even as you loved me. Father, they are your gift to me. I wish that where I am they also may be with me, that they may see my glory that you gave me, because you loved me before the foundation of the world. Righteous Father, the world also does not know you, but I know you, and they know that you sent me. I made known to them your name and I will make it known, that the love with which you loved me may be in them and I in them."

MUSIC CONNECTION

Luke's description of the proto-martyr Stephen's death in Acts is reminiscent of Jesus' words from the cross in the Lucan passion as Stephen prays, "Lord, do not hold this sin against them." The gospel of mercy and forgiveness does not end with the Master but, instead, becomes in Acts the road map for all disciples who are persecuted and may even suffer death. Stephens's strength and confidence is echoed in hymns such as *Be Not Afraid; Blest Be the Lord; Sing, My Tongue, the Song of Triumph; This Is the Day;* and *By All Your Saints Still Striving.* The responsorial, Psalm 97, is well expressed by Proulx's antiphon joined to the Gelineau arrangement. Revelation, continuing its tour of the heavenly realm, suggests Hansen's *Death Will Be No More* and Joncas's *When We Eat This Bread.* The latter author's skillful use of Revelation imagery, when joined with a good eucharistic antiphon, reinforces the fact that the Eucharist we share today is but a foretaste of the heavenly banquet. The traditional *Alleluia, Sing to Jesus* delivers the same message as does Parker's masterful *Praise the Lord, My Soul.* The gospel's testament for unity suggests hymns such as *Christ Is Made the Sure Foundation, In Christ There Is No East or West,* and *At That First Eucharist.*

First Reading: Acts 2:1–11

When the time for Pentecost was fulfilled, they were all in one place together. And suddenly there came from the sky a noise like a strong driving wind, and it filled the entire house in which they were. Then there appeared to them tongues as of fire, which parted and came to rest on each one of them. And they were all filled with the Holy Spirit and began to speak in different tongues, as the Spirit enabled them to proclaim.

Now there were devout Jews from every nation under heaven staying in Jerusalem. At this sound, they gathered in a large crowd, but they were confused because each one heard them speaking in his own language. They were astounded, and in amazement they asked, "Are not all these people who are speaking Galileans? Then how does each of us hear them in his native language? We are Parthians, Medes, and Elamites, inhabitants of Mesopotamia, Judea and Cappadocia,

SCRIPTURE COMMENTARY

Luke describes the day of Pentecost in two parts. In the first scene, the faithful remnant band gathered in the upper room await God's promise to them in trembling and fear of the same Jewish leaders who had put Jesus to death; in the second scene, the apostles boldly preach the gospel with such gifts of the Spirit that all nations and peoples can understand them. There are particular points to note about the descent of the Spirit. It comes in the form of fire. But note that it is one flame that divides and so touches each person differently and uniquely. The Spirit is always the same, but the gifts and the tasks it confers are given to us as individuals. Second, the image of fire is itself obviously important—we often say someone is on fire with an idea or conviction. This power is not passive or comforting; it will set the apostles a mission that it also impels them to do. We should understand, however, that this is not just a gift to the Twelve. Some verses earlier, in Acts 1:14, Luke has already told us that Mary the mother of Jesus, the women who had followed Jesus, and all his brethren were also present in the room with the apostles. The Spirit is the gift to the whole Church, and in some sense we all share in the role of apostles as a result. The second scene underscores the goal of the Spirit's presence in the Church—to bring the gospel to all people and to create the unity of all in accepting Christ's gospel of salvation. On the day of Pentecost people from every part of the

HOMILY HELPS

"I will not leave you orphans." This promise of Jesus, fulfilled in the Pentecost event, goes far beyond a simple historical remembrance or recollection of the past. Our national holidays often present for our edification the figure of one of our celebrated personalities of the past. But such is not the case with our religious recalling of the Christ event. The Christ who rose from the tomb actually lives today, in the Church and in each one of us, through the power of the Holy Spirit.

Again in today's feast the lesson is one of unity in diversity. As today's second reading makes

clear, we recognize in faith that Jesus is Lord, that is, God in the fullest sense of the word. As Corinthians states, this affirmation can be made only through the action of the Spirit. And it is this belief that is the lynchpin of our common unity. One Lord, one faith, one baptism. There are many human factors that distinguish and separate us as Christians—race, ethnicity, social standing, profession, and occupation. Formal education carries us in different directions; financial income puts us on different levels of society. Different languages create barriers to communication. Yet we are one in faith, with a unity that defies all boundaries. African, Asian, and

Caucasian Christians speak a common language, with the person of Christ at the center of our differences. We constitute the one body of Christ.

And yet we never cease to marvel at our diversity. The first Pentecost, recounted in Acts, found people of widely different cultural backgrounds gathered around Peter. This diversity will increase as the early Church moves out of Jerusalem into Samaria, then to Asia Minor, Greece, and Rome. The government was Roman; the common language, Greek. But in the Church there were different ministries and functions. There was no attempt to have everyone march to the same tune. The

SCRIPTURE COMMENTARY, CONTINUED

Mediterranean world hear the message as though it were directed especially to them. This first audience is made up of devout Jews, but it presages the movement of the gospel to every nation, a story that will be told in the rest of the story of the Acts of the Apostles.

Pontus and Asia, Phrygia and Pamphylia, Egypt and the districts of Libya near Cyrene, as well as travelers from Rome, both Jews and converts to Judaism, Cretans and Arabs, yet we hear them speaking in our own tongues of the mighty acts of God."

PSALM REFLECTION

Psalm 104 is one of the most beautiful of all biblical psalms because it describes every creature that God has made, from the great solar bodies to the animals and our human community, and acknowledges its dependence on the divine favor and blessing. Each one lives its individual "spirit" in the power of God's own Spirit. The psalmist describes this as God breathing his own divine life into each being to sustain it in existence and make it aware of its relationship to the creator. Today we would call this rather imaginative, noting that, in fact, most of creation is inanimate and without awareness of anything, much less a creator. But the ancients were convinced that in each being, whether stone or grass or the moon above, there was a law orienting it to follow the commands of God faithfully each day. It may not be what moderns call consciousness, but it was a clear relationship of obedience, in which each object in God's world said a kind of "Yes!" to God's commandments. Only human beings choose to say "No!" on occasion. But since we have a choice, how much more wonderful is our "Yes!" when we give it.

Psalm Response
Psalm 104:1, 24, 29–30, 31, 34

Antiphon
Lord, send out your Spirit, and
    renew the face of the earth.
Or: Alleluia.

Verse for Reflection
When you send out your spirit,
[all creatures] are given life,
And you renew the face of the
    earth! (v. 30)

---

commonality was found in faith; all believed in the one Lord and the empowering Spirit.

Presence at an international church event—the death or installation of a pope, a World Youth Congress, or some major church happening—instills a sense of pride in the Church's diversity. Yet when the Eucharist is offered at such events, in the presence of tens of thousands, we all stand on common ground. While championing our cultural heterogeneity, we realize that the safeguarding of our common faith is critically important.

Pentecost occasions our reflection on a precious heritage: one Lord and one faith together with a remarkable diversity. It is a heritage that never fails to inspire.

LITURGICAL NOTES

The Easter season reaches its culmination with the Solemnity of Pentecost. This is the day that the Father "sent the Holy Spirit on those marked out to be your children and so you brought the paschal mystery to its completion" (Pentecost preface). Since Pentecost brings the Easter season to its conclusion, it is appropriate to maintain the Easter colors that have graced the space for the past forty-nine days, and add the brilliant red of the Spirit to them. The paschal candle remains lit at all Pentecost Masses. At the conclusion of the final liturgy, the candle is placed near the bap-

tismal font, where it is displayed with honor.

Masses celebrated on Saturday evening use the texts of the Mass for the vigil of Pentecost, a prolonged celebration in the form of a vigil, focusing on prayer for the coming of the Holy Spirit. "Encouragement should be given to the prolonged celebration of Mass in the form of a vigil, whose character is not baptismal as in the Easter Vigil, but is one of urgent prayer, after the example of the apostles and disciples, who persevered together in prayer with Mary, the Mother of Jesus, as they awaited the Holy Spirit" (circular letter *On Preparing and Celebrating the Paschal Feasts,* 107). When the form of the vigil is used, Mass begins in the usual

Second Reading:
1 Corinthians 12:3b–7, 12–13
(or Romans 8:8–17)

Brothers and sisters: No one can say, "Jesus is Lord," except by the Holy Spirit. There are different kinds of spiritual gifts but the same Spirit; there are different forms of service but the same Lord; there are different workings but the same God who produces all of them in everyone. To each individual the manifestation of the Spirit is given for some benefit.

As a body is one though it has many parts, and all the parts of the body, though many, are one body, so also Christ. For in one Spirit we were all baptized into one body, whether Jews or Greeks, slaves or free persons, and we were all given to drink of one Spirit.

SCRIPTURE COMMENTARY

The Lucan account of the coming of the Holy Spirit on Pentecost clearly stated that one Spirit divided into many flames that came to each person separately. Theologically, this is similar to Paul's doctrine of the many gifts of the Spirit given to the Church. It leads him to the great spiritual insight that all of us are one in Christ, like a body that is made up of numerous different organs but always remains one. Thus, each of us is an organ of the Holy Spirit, bringing the Spirit's power into our individual situations according to the different gifts that the Spirit has bestowed on us. Above all, the doctrine of the Holy Spirit never permits the possessor of a gift to use it for himself or herself but only for the good of the entire body. If we are united to Christ as intimately as parts of the body are to one another, then we live in and for Christ as he dwells in every other member of the Church. Nor can we treat another person who is not Christian as though he or she were a stranger, but rather as one called to be part of the body of Christ as we are. Perhaps this helps us understand why every member of the Church is also charged with the apostolic task of bringing the gospel to those who have not yet heard it.

manner. After the Penitential Rite, the alternative opening prayer is sung or said. The presider then invites the assembly to join in prayerful reflection as we listen to God's word and await the coming of the Spirit. The readings follow, each with its own responsorial psalm and prayer, as at the Easter Vigil. After the prayer following the final reading, the Gloria is sung; then the Opening Prayer of the Mass is said. The epistle reading from Romans is then proclaimed, followed by the Gospel Acclamation and the gospel. Mass continues in the usual manner; a double Alleluia is added to the dismissal.

Masses celebrated on Pentecost Sunday would appropriately include the Rite of Blessing and Sprinkling with Holy Water. The Pentecost Sequence is a magnificent hymn invoking the Holy Spirit—"Shine within these hearts of yours, and our inmost being fill! Heal our wounds, our strength renew; on our dryness pour your dew." To realize the power of this hymn, it ought to be sung. A variety of chant, metrical, antiphonal, and responsorial settings are available. At the conclusion of the Sequence hymn, all stand for the gospel. Pentecost has its own proper preface; Eucharistic Prayer III is an excellent choice, with its emphasis on the action of the Holy Spirit. A double Alleluia is added to the dismissal.

CATECHETICAL SUGGESTIONS

Pentecost in the Old and New Testaments
The role of the Spirit in the Church
Missionary religious orders
Sacraments of baptism and confirmation
Gifts of the Spirit
The mission of the universal Church and of our parish

SCRIPTURE COMMENTARY

The Gospel of John has the Pentecost experience take place on Easter Sunday night rather than fifty days after the resurrection, the way Luke does (and, implicitly, Matthew and Mark do as well). A direct link is thus established between the resurrection and the bestowal of the Spirit. We share in the life of the risen Lord inasmuch as we also possess his Spirit. As soon as the apostles meet the risen Lord for the first time while huddled in their refuge, he gives them his Spirit. It is transforming—it gives a peace that will dispel their fearfulness; it sends them forth to proclaim Jesus; and it gives them the authority to confer divine forgiveness as the hallmark of the Church's message. The power to bind and to loose is not intended to accent the arbitrary power of an elite leadership but to express the role of faith. The apostles are empowered to welcome into the community those who receive God's grace of forgiveness; they are members of the community because of their faith. Membership in the kingdom of God, the Church, the Body of Christ, is by invitation but is not coercive. God has already forgiven all in accepting Jesus' death on people's behalf, but they too must reciprocate by assenting and living in Christ if they wish to be part of the Church.

> **Gospel: John 20:19–23 (or John 14:15–16, 23b–26)**
>
> On the evening of that first day of the week, when the doors were locked, where the disciples were, for fear of the Jews, Jesus came and stood in their midst and said to them, "Peace be with you." When he had said this, he showed them his hands and his side. The disciples rejoiced when they saw the Lord. Jesus said to them again, "Peace be with you. As the Father has sent me, so I send you." And when he had said this, he breathed on them and said to them, "Receive the Holy Spirit. Whose sins you forgive are forgiven them, and whose sins you retain are retained."

MUSIC CONNECTION

The Lucan chronology of events after the death of Jesus largely determines the contours of our liturgical year. Unlike John (cf. today's gospel pericope), where the Spirit is bestowed on "the evening of that first day of the week," that is, the very evening of the resurrection, Luke's theological chronology moves the gift of the Spirit into the future, fifty days from the day of Jesus' rising.

Clearly, music extolling the Spirit is fitting today, but the presence of Easter favorites will help avoid a theological wedge being driven between the resurrection and the giving of the Spirit—an avoidance crucial in John's gospel. Jesus' rising from the dead and his first appearance unleash the Spirit's ongoing presence in the hearts and minds of the disciples. Thus, a good rousing rendition of *Allleluia, Sing to Jesus; Hail Thee Festival Day; Hymn of Joy;* or *Jesus Christ Is Risen Today* can help reinforce the intimate theological connection between the resurrection and the outpouring of the Spirit. Neil Blunt's setting of Psalm 104, today's responsorial, with its buoyant spirit and melody, is sure to engage worshipers. The late Alex Peloquin's eerie *Lord, Send Out Your Spirit* fosters a feeling of the Pentecost event in musician and congregation alike.

Any hymnal will have numerous paeans to the Holy Spirit, but I call a few to your attention. *Come Down, O Love Divine* is wonderful poetry and wonderful music (Vaughan Williams). Dan Schutte's *Send Us Your Spirit* (OCP) is a good example of a contemporary text and melody. *One Spirit, One Church* by Kevin Keil (OCP) blends the traditional *Come Holy Ghost* with a newly composed refrain and time signature, and it really works well.

First Reading: Proverbs 8:22–31

Thus says the wisdom of God: "The LORD possessed me, the beginning of his ways, the forerunner of his prodigies of long ago; from of old I was poured forth, at the first, before the earth. When there were no depths I was brought forth, when there were no fountains or springs of water; before the mountains were settled into place, before the hills, I was brought forth; while as yet the earth and fields were not made, nor the first clods of the world.

"When the Lord established the heavens I was there, when he marked out the vault over the face of the deep; when he made firm the skies above, when he fixed fast the foundations of the earth; when he set for the sea its limit, so that the waters should not transgress his command; then was I beside him as his craftsman, and I was his delight day by day, playing before him all the while, playing on the surface of his earth; and I found delight in the human race."

SCRIPTURE COMMENTARY

In contemplating the mystery of the Trinity, the first question a finite human being always has is *why?* In our scientific age we have come to understand the idea of a single divine origin for all things, one God and not many, who set all of creation into being. Monotheism is the backbone of the great faiths of Judaism, Christianity, and Islam. But only Christianity has a doctrine of three "persons" in one divine nature. Of course, our fundamental answer is that Jesus taught us about this mystery in the way he spoke of his Father, himself as Son, and his Spirit that he would send. The Church always searches the whole of the scriptures for deeper understanding of this revelation. One of the important texts is Proverbs 8, where the author has God's Wisdom speak of its role in creation. Wisdom is described not only as existing before creation itself but as the architect or spirit that shapes that creation and gives it life and vitality. It is also described as God's child, playing at his feet and giving a joyful and playful quality to all that is created. This description of Wisdom as a person—and not an ordinary person but a part of the divine act of creation itself—has been understood as a forerunner to both roles of Son and Spirit in the Father's work as Creator.

HOMILY HELPS

The Trinity is a cornerstone belief for Christians, and we celebrate it solemnly on this Sunday each year. It is a mystery that in no way compromises our monotheistic faith yet finds distinct relationships in God seen as three persons. That God is one is at the root of the Judeo-Christian tradition, as the great *Shema* of Deuteronomy states: "The Lord is God, the Lord alone" (6:4). Yet God can be seen in distinctly different ways as the three persons who constitute the one God. These three separate relationships can be spoken of in terms of fatherhood, sonship, and a binding love. All of which is but to say that there is a family life in God, a Father and a Son united in Love.

The Hebrew scriptures are often seen as foreshadowing this mystery. In the reading from Proverbs today, Wisdom is depicted as a female companion of God; with him from the earliest moment of creation, she is present as God's blueprint in the whole process of the world's coming to be—with the mountains and hills, the seas and their depths. Wisdom is a loving and playful presence before God, a vital player in the fashioning and directing of the universe.

In the New Testament Jesus is often spoken of as God's wisdom, the concrete expression of God's plan to bring us home. He is that *Sophia* which is the way, the truth, and the life. He is our window on God. To know him is to know the Father.

And then there is the Spirit. Its role is to bind Father and Son together in a love that will never end. But that Spirit has been given to us as well, bringing us into the family life of God. This is an incredible thought. Our sacramental life gives us access to the bond that links Father and Son. We actually enter into the life of the Trinity.

Through a two-thousand-year history, often marked by disappointment and travail, the Church continues to proclaim

PSALM REFLECTION

Psalm 8 is a lofty hymn of praise for the wonderful status God has granted human beings as the high point of his creation. Only the human shares in God's task of guiding and steering what happens with nature. All other creatures act as nature dictates, but we can dream, and plan, and then work with at least some of it to establish new directions or to control its working. Control of river flooding is one example; redirecting waters to deserts and new fields to provide food is another. This psalm is clearly a reflection on the reading of Genesis 1, but it makes a fitting response to Proverbs 8 because it stresses the goodness of God in pouring forth life for all creatures and because it mentions the "son of man" in verse 5. The term is really simply a poetic phrase inside the psalm: "man" and "son of man" are the same thing and indicate a human being. But as a term of divine revelation, it is occasionally used by the Church as a prefigurement of the Incarnation itself. Not only is humanity given status little less than the angels; God will even send his own Son as fully human to be one with us and then to be exalted after the resurrection to the right hand of the Father in glory.

Psalm Response
Psalm 8:4–5, 6–7, 8–9

Antiphon
O Lord, our God, how
    wonderful your name
    in all the earth!

Verse for Reflection
O Lord, our God, how
    great is your name
Throughout the whole
    world. (v. 1)

the great good news of God's engagement with the world. We all know the meaning of weakness and inadequacy, a sinfulness that often deflects our good intentions. Yet the Spirit of truth, so prominently present in today's gospel, continues to guide us. As we grow older, we often reflect on the fads and fashions that cluttered our youth, and yet through it all, as our presence in church today indicates, we cherish that "hope of the glory of God" about which Paul speaks today. Our afflictions borne patiently lead to endurance, which is nothing more than the ability to remain faithful and is itself a virtue. Endurance only increases our hope in a God who will not disappoint.

The Trinity, then, is no abstraction. These are the relationships that constitute God himself. There is a Father who cares, a Son who responds, a Spirit who binds them in love. Trinity Sunday reminds us that we are also part of that picture. We belong to God's household. Ours is a family that will last forever.

LITURGICAL NOTES

Today's solemnity, celebrating our belief in one God revealed in three divine persons—Father, Son, and Spirit—was declared a feast of the universal Church in 1334. This day does not celebrate a theological dictum but the reality of God present and active in our lives. Today's solemnity proclaims God's love for us made known in Jesus Christ and sustained through the power of the Holy Spirit.

**Second Reading:
Romans 5:1–5**

Brothers and sisters: Therefore, since we have been
justified by faith, we have
peace with God through our
Lord Jesus Christ, through
whom we have gained
access by faith to this grace
in which we stand, and we
boast in hope of the glory of
God. Not only that, but we
even boast of our afflictions,
knowing that affliction produces endurance, and
endurance, proven charac-
ter, and proven character,
hope, and hope does not disappoint, because the love of
God has been poured out
into our hearts through the
Holy Spirit that has been
given to us.

SCRIPTURE COMMENTARY

This short passage makes an excellent reflection on the Trinity
because it mentions all three persons in one paragraph. They are
not listed side by side but described by the work of salvation each
divine person does for humankind. Jesus, the Son, has reconciled us to the
Father, who will glorify us. The Father in his love sent not just his Son but
also his Spirit so that it could dwell actively and effectively in our hearts. By
being in the love given through the Spirit of God, we are joined to the love
of Father and Son. Thus, for Paul, God has shown his love in a trinitarian
manner, and as a result we can endure the limits and sufferings of this
earthly life because we know in every way that God is with us until that
love is completed in union with God in his glory.

CATECHETICAL SUGGESTIONS

Wisdom literature in the Old Testament
Personified Wisdom in the Old Testament
The dignity of human beings and the right to life
Faith and works: Lutheran–Roman Catholic dialogues
The virtue of hope
The Trinity in the Creed

Hymns to the Trinity abound,
and care should be taken that
the shortening of a hymn or the
elimination of a verse not bring
us to the precipice of heresy!
While the Rite of Blessing and
Sprinkling with Holy Water could
be used, if it has been used
throughout the Easter season, it
might best be avoided on this
day. Trinity Sunday might tempt
us to compose trinitarian invocations for form C of the Penitential
Rite, but we must keep in mind
that the invocations are
addressed to Christ. Trinity Sun-

day has its own proper preface,
containing some of the most
ancient images of the Trinity.

The scriptures this day contain
rich imagery and warrant careful
proclamation. The delight that
God takes in Wisdom, "playing
before him . . . on the surface of
his earth" is the same delight that
God takes in his people. The
gospel appointed for this day
continues John's priestly prayer
of Jesus as we hear again of
God's continued presence and
action in our midst.

This Sunday provides an
opportunity to look at the focus
of our gathering and our celebration. Trinity Sunday is about God
revealed in relationship. Our relationships can mirror the creative,
the sacrificial, and the empowering love of God. Since God is
revealed through flesh and
blood, this would be a good Sunday to have a coffee hour after
each Mass, where men and
women of faith could come
together to rejoice in the gifts of
life and faith and celebrate those
gifts with each other.

SCRIPTURE COMMENTARY

Like Romans 5, our second reading, this short passage from the Gospel of John mentions all three persons of the Trinity in one short paragraph. Jesus is speaking to his disciples at the Last Supper. He is explaining to them that he must depart this world and they are dismayed. "What shall we do?" they ask. His answer is that he will send the Holy Spirit to guide them. This Spirit keeps them "in the truth," that is, keeps them faithful to what Jesus has taught them and shown them by his relationship to the Father. They will speak and lead people to Christ by the action of the Spirit, not by their own wisdom or eloquence. The passage ends with a wonderful expression of the unity of the three persons in the one God: All that the Father has belongs to me, and all that I have I send to you by the Spirit. Jesus talks about the Trinity not in philosophical or abstract language but in terms of God's grace and love poured out into human hearts. We know God as Trinity because we actually experience divine salvation as a change in our relationship to God that is manifested in God's fatherhood, his redeeming presence in his Son, and his power of forgiveness and eternal life in his Spirit.

**Gospel:
John 16:12–15**

Jesus said to his disciples: "I have much more to tell you, but you cannot bear it now. But when he comes, the Spirit of truth, he will guide you to all truth. He will not speak on his own, but he will speak what he hears, and will declare to you the things that are coming. He will glorify me, because he will take from what is mine and declare it to you. Everything that the Father has is mine; for this reason I told you that he will take from what is mine and declare it to you."

MUSIC CONNECTION

Today's readings yield a scriptural witness that our experience of God is differentiated and, for the Christian, trinitarian. The ineffable experience of God is, for the author of Proverbs, a sublime Wisdom begotten by God. "From of old I was poured forth, at the first, before the earth." The followers of Jesus would come to view him as this Wisdom, this Word, made incarnate. The later religious experience of the followers of Jesus, especially after his dying and rising, impart an insight into God whose Spirit is the source of the love of God poured out in our hearts. While the sophisticated trinitarian language of the Creed will have to wait for several centuries, the experience is present early on, embedded and described in the very pages of the New Testament.

Easter songs are still in vogue, especially since they tend, by nature, to be very trinitarian. A good example is *Hail Thee, Festival Day,* which addresses the Father in verse 2, the Son in verse 4, and the Spirit in verse 5. *I Know That My Redeemer Lives* primarily refers to Christ but can easily be put in tandem with *Come Holy Ghost* and *O God Our Help in Ages Past* to achieve a kind of trinitarian balance. The so-called Navy hymn *Eternal Father, Strong to Save* would be a wonderful choice for today's celebration. Today's assigned Psalm 8 is well expressed by Smith, Alstott, and Gelineau. Cooney's arrangement is both challenging and effective.

At some point, however, we all stand in a kind of cloud of unknowing where our theological axioms and trinitarian formulae seem inadequate to the task of naming our individual and collective experience of God. At such times, Bernadette Farrell's *God, beyond All Names* (OCP) helps us pierce that cloud.

**First Reading:
Genesis 14:18–20**

In those days,
Melchizedek, king
of Salem, brought
out bread and wine,
and being a priest
of God Most High,
he blessed Abram
with these words:
"Blessed be Abram
by God Most High,
the creator of
heaven and earth;
and blessed be God
Most High, who
delivered your foes
into your hand."
Then Abram gave
him a tenth of
everything.

SCRIPTURE COMMENTARY

Although Jesus used the Last Supper meal as the foundation for the Eucharist in the Church, the focus of Holy Week, including the Holy Thursday liturgy, had to remain on the dramatic telling of his coming passion, death, and resurrection. On that night, the Church remembered and celebrated that the Eucharist is a memorial of the death of Christ "until he comes again" (see the second reading today). So a second feast honoring just the sacrament of the Eucharist itself, Corpus Christi, has been set aside to meditate on its life-giving power *now*, not just at the hour of Jesus' death. The small and very unusual story of Melchizedek in Genesis 14 provides a good start. Here is a king and priest of Salem, a name which means "peace" and probably stood for the place where God would one day dwell in the temple, Jerusalem. Melchizedek gives to Abraham, the man of faith in God's promise, a blessing by sharing bread and wine with him. In ancient terms, he probably made an offering to God of bread and wine that was partly poured out and partly shared with the one honored. All of this is a foretaste of what we say about Eucharist: Jesus, priest and king, poured out himself for us to God and offered to share that self and the saving power of his death in the bread and wine of the Eucharist with all who, like Abraham, believe.

HOMILY HELPS

Jesus was a Jewish layman. He was not a member of the priestly tribe of Levi. Yet early in the life of the Church, Jesus' offering of himself to the Father was spoken of as a sacrifice. Since in Jewish terms sacrifice is identified with priesthood, how was this to be solved in Jesus' case?

The letter to the Hebrews found a solution to this problem. Jesus was a priest of a different order, related to a priest of the Old Testament who was not a Levite. The priest, also a king, was Melchizedek, a figure who makes a single brief appearance in the book of Genesis, as recounted in today's first reading.

On one occasion when Abraham was returning from battle, the pagan king-priest went out to meet him, offered him bread and wine, and blessed the patriarch.

By a free adaptation of this account, the author of Hebrews offers striking parallels between Melchizedek and Jesus and asserts that Jesus, the new and eternal High Priest, is a spiritual descendant of the priest-king in Genesis.

Paul tells the Corinthians that this priestly offering of Christ continues in the Eucharist. In this earliest written account of what transpired at the Last Supper, Paul indicates that with each repetition of the bread-and-wine offering, we "proclaim the death of the Lord until he comes." It is this sacrament of the Eucharist that we solemnly commemorate on this day each year.

The gospel narrative today speaks of Jesus' miraculous provision for the needs of the hungry multitude in the desert place. To read the narrative carefully is to see the eucharistic imprint woven into the text. Jesus takes the loaves and blesses, breaks, and gives them to the disciples. The words clearly echo those of the Last Supper and those repeated each time Mass is offered. We are reminded that we are more fortunate than the hungry people of the gospel story, for the Lord continues to provide spiritual food for us day after day, year after year. This is done with limitless generosity as we make our journey through life.

PSALM REFLECTION

Psalm 110 is chosen because it mentions Melchizedek by name in referring to the story of Genesis 14 that was just read. But in the psalm, Melchizedek has now become an eternal priest, not bound by this moment or by one lifetime. The psalmist is comparing Melchizedek to the Davidic king and praising God for having established the king in his authority "at his right hand" and as a "priest forever," as was Melchizedek. He adds, however, also that the king was the son of God. In ancient Israel, when a king was crowned, he was said to have been adopted by God as his son, and both ruled in God's name and led the worship in the temple on important occasions, saying a prayer over the sacrifices. An excellent example of this is found in Solomon's prayer in 1 Kings 8. These three qualities of kingship became elements of the hope for a messiah, a new David who would save his people: he would be ruler, priest, and God's son. In the sacrifice and sacrament of the Eucharist we see Jesus revealed in all three roles.

Psalm Response
Psalm 110:1, 2, 3, 4

Antiphon
You are a priest for ever,
    in the line of
    Melchizedek.

Verse for Reflection
Royal power is yours on
    the day of your
    birth;
In wondrous holiness,
    before there was the
    sun,
I begot you like the dew.
    (v. 3)

Since Christ is a priest, it is appropriate that those who are invested with the spiritual authority to offer the Eucharist are designated priests—and this despite the fact that no Christian individual or group in the New Testament is so designated. There was no desire to compromise the title "priest," seen as belonging to Christ alone. The fact is, however, that we have been served by priests throughout our Christian lives. In some cases our memories are not positive, clouded by the thought of priests whose conduct was incompatible with a sacred calling. Yet, on the other hand, all of us have been served by good and worthy priests, men marked by deep spirituality and generosity in the service of others.

We cannot end our reflections on this topic without mentioning the acute shortage of priests today. We are all witnessing the "graying" of the Catholic priesthood. There are parts of the United States where there are no longer regular Masses on Sunday. Prayer for an increase of priestly vocations is always commendable. At the same time, it may be that the Church is called to a broader solution. Providing Communion services or scripture services on Sunday is not a solution for a community that is essentially eucharistic. No local Catholic community can for long be deprived of Mass. On this solemnity of the body and blood of Christ, let us pray earnestly for the grace of the Holy Spirit.

CATECHETICAL SUGGESTIONS

Melchizedek in the Old Testament and in the New Testament

Priesthood in Judaism and in Christianity

The institution of the Eucharist in 1 Corinthians and in the gospels

Transubstantiation

Eucharist and ecumenism

Ways in which our parish/community feeds the hungry

Second Reading:
1 Corinthians 11:23–26

Brothers and sisters: I received from the Lord what I also handed on to you, that the Lord Jesus, on the night he was handed over, took bread, and, after he had given thanks, broke it and said, "This is my body that is for you. Do this in remembrance of me." In the same way also the cup, after supper, saying, "This cup is the new covenant in my blood. Do this, as often as you drink it, in remembrance of me." For as often as you eat this bread and drink the cup, you proclaim the death of the Lord until he comes.

SCRIPTURE COMMENTARY

The account of the Last Supper is so important to Paul that he tells the Corinthians that this is not his own gospel message but the one he has received to be handed on. Only one other time does he say this—when he narrates the witnesses to the risen Christ in chapter 15 of this same letter. Paul's version is similar to the account given by Luke's gospel. Perhaps the small difference between the versions of Paul and Luke and those of Matthew and Mark is that Paul's was a special form used for Gentile convert churches rather than for Jewish converts. The two commands to "do this in remembrance of me" are missing in Matthew and Mark, and Luke has only one of the two. Paul emphasizes this phrase because pagans often had memorial meals to remember the dead on anniversaries. Paul notes that the Eucharist is to recall the presence of Jesus, but he goes on to specify it very sharply—it is to proclaim the death of the Lord until he comes again. Thus Paul sees that this memorial is different from other memorials. Jesus' death is a saving death and one whose power remains in force for all ages until the end. It is not a simple remembering of a lost friend but the active presence of Christ in our midst.

LITURGICAL NOTES

The feast popularly referred to as Corpus Christi dates back to the late Middle Ages. The reform of the calendar has combined this feast with the feast of the Precious Blood and given it a new name: "The Solemnity of the Most Holy Body and Blood of Christ."

While both opening prayers in the Sacramentary are appropriate, the alternative prayer gives more explicit emphasis that our eucharistic life must be a life "poured out in loving service." This is another feast that provides a Sequence hymn (*Lauda, Sion*), although this time it is optional. Don't let its optional nature cause you to pass over it too quickly. It

is a text rich in imagery and theology. If it cannot be sung by all, maybe it can be used as a choral anthem during the liturgy.

Today is a day to ensure not only that the cup is offered at every Mass but that we provide our assemblies with renewed catechesis on the reception of Holy Communion and the reception of Communion from the cup.

Holy Communion and the Worship of the Eucharist outside Mass (101–108) provides the outline of the service when a eucharistic procession is to take place after Mass. If such a procession is to take place, adequate planning and rehearsal are necessary so that the procession route is clear, the places where the pro-

cession will stop are clearly marked, music ministers know what is expected of them, and ministers of hospitality and ushers are on hand to direct the people.

If no procession is to take place, it would be appropriate to have an extended period of eucharistic adoration that could conclude with Evening Prayer and Benediction of the Blessed Sacrament. The Blessed Sacrament could be exposed after the last Mass in the afternoon, and people could be invited to spend some time in prayer and adoration. Toward the end of the day, Evening Prayer would be celebrated, concluding with Benediction and the reposition of the Blessed Sacrament.

SCRIPTURE COMMENTARY

Luke sets the story of the feeding of the five thousand right after Jesus heals the ill. This is also true of Matthew's account. It may be true of Mark also, but he points out only that Jesus pitied the people because they were like sheep without a shepherd. But all of these are important for understanding the feeding as a preparation for the Eucharist. The sacrament does not just give spiritual nourishment, as food is given to the body; it also heals sin and thereby creates union with Christ when we are not worthy. The note in Luke that the men sat down in groups of fifty also suggests that they acted like a church community that has structure and is organized for being fed. Thus the incident may have happened once on a hillside in Galilee, but it is symbolic of what Christ would do for the Church always. Jesus challenges the disciples to feed the crowd from their own resources, and they rightly respond that they can at best provide some physical material for food but it will not be enough. The Church can supply physical bread and wine, but it cannot make these become the spiritual food of Christ except through the mystery of divine transformation of these elements into the very life of Christ. The Church insists on the actual statement that they become the body and the blood of Christ. The traditional term, "transubstantiation," explains this by saying the physical characteristics of bread and wine are unchanged but their essential nature has been totally changed into the life-giving presence of Christ united to us. That is why it is not simply a remembrance but is most properly called the mystery of the Real Presence.

Gospel: Luke 9:11b–17

Jesus spoke to the crowds about the kingdom of God, and he healed those who needed to be cured. As the day was drawing to a close, the Twelve approached him and said, "Dismiss the crowd so that they can go to the surrounding villages and farms and find lodging and provisions; for we are in a deserted place here." He said to them, "Give them some food yourselves." They replied, "Five loaves and two fish are all we have, unless we ourselves go and buy food for all these people." Now the men there numbered about five thousand. Then he said to his disciples, "Have them sit down in groups of about fifty." They did so and made them all sit down. Then taking the five loaves and the two fish, and looking up to heaven, he said the blessing over them, broke them, and gave them to the disciples to set before the crowd. They all ate and were satisfied. And when the leftover fragments were picked up, they filled twelve wicker baskets.

MUSIC CONNECTION

The feast of Corpus Christi, now known officially as the Solemnity of the Body and Blood of Christ, is a celebration rich in history, tradition, and meaning for generations of Roman Catholics. As a celebration it taps into two of the most primal feelings and needs of human beings: hunger and thirst. Over the past twenty-five years the Communion rite has spawned more new music than other parts of the Mass, and today's feast is the beneficiary of that creative outburst. One of the "older" compositions of this period, John Foley's *One Bread, One Body*, is still a moving and thought-provoking piece of music. Similarly, Marty Haugen's *We Are Many Parts* captures the flavor of the day and, especially, Paul's letter. The Omer Westendorf/Robert Kreutz collaboration *Gift of Finest Wheat* has incredible staying power and has blessed congregations with its beauty for many years. David Haas's *Song of The Body of Christ*, based on a native Hawaiian melody, can begin to wear thin by the end of the song but is still a very fitting song for today and other times throughout the year. Fran O'Brien's *Taste and See* pulsates with energy and, along with James Moore's song of the same name, brings Psalm 34 to life. Larry Rosania has contributed two wonderful pieces to the eucharistic repertoire—*As Grains of Wheat* and *The Supper of the Lord*. Both pieces reflect good eucharistic theology in the texts and moving melodies that fully bear the mystery they are depicting. Other possibilities include *At That First Eucharist; Father, We Thank Thee;* Peloquin's *In Memory of You;* and Joncas's *Our Blessing Cup*. This year's responsorial selection, Psalm 110, is well presented by both Guimont and the Bob Batastini/Gelineau arrangement.

First Reading:
2 Samuel 12:7–10, 13

Nathan said to David: "Thus says the Lord God of Israel: 'I anointed you king of Israel. I rescued you from the hand of Saul. I gave you your lord's house and your lord's wives for your own. I gave you the house of Israel and of Judah. And if this were not enough, I could count up for you still more. Why have you spurned the Lord and done evil in his sight? You have cut down Uriah the Hittite with the sword; you took his wife as your own, and him you killed with the sword of the Ammonites. Now, therefore, the sword shall never depart from your house, because you have despised me and have taken the wife of Uriah to be your wife.'" Then David said to Nathan, "I have sinned against the Lord." Nathan answered David: "The Lord on his part has forgiven your sin: you shall not die."

SCRIPTURE COMMENTARY

The theme of the readings for this Sunday is God's freely given forgiveness despite our evils. The first example is the great king David himself. Despite all of the praise he receives in the Bible as the author of the psalms and the one who made the monarchy truly great after Saul's rather pathetic efforts, he was capable of great personal sin as well. The episode of his lust for Bathsheba and subsequent cold-blooded manner of eliminating her husband is soundly condemned by God through the prophet Nathan. After recalling all that God has done for David, the prophet says that David has responded to God's goodness with a violation of his moral commandment, notably by the crime of murder. In typical ancient legal fashion, the punishment announced by Nathan is one-to-one. He announces the divine sentence: "You committed murder, now death will strike your household." David recognizes the justness of this punishment. In effect, he accepts the death sentence as right. God, however, accepts his repentance and generously gives David himself mercy by sparing his life. But God's justice, once decreed, must be completed because the word of God never fails to act. Although the subsequent passage is left out of today's Lectionary selection, Nathan decrees that the child whom David has conceived with Bathsheba will die instead.

HOMILY HELPS

In today's gospel, Jesus says to the woman, "Your sins are forgiven," and this within hearing of all the bystanders. But was she forgiven before her effusive expression of love or after it had taken place? In other words, what is the best translation from the Greek of Jesus' words: "Her many sins have been forgiven *because* (Greek: *hoti*) she has been shown great love" or "…sins…forgiven *with the result* that she has shown great love"? Either translation is possible; the latter seems preferable. It is due to the fact that the woman has been forgiven that she wants to do honor to the emissary of for-

giveness. Moreover, the context, including Jesus' parable of the two debtors, is consistent with this interpretation.

The woman violates several canons. Her reputation is such that she should not have approached the table of Jesus and his companions. Moreover, she uses a physical gesture to express her gratitude to a Jewish male, an act that could easily have been misconstrued.

But the story touches on one of the key teachings seen so frequently in Luke: religious observance as an expression of gratitude. As we have seen, this is basic in the Christian life. We are churchgoers not to gain God's favor but because it is already ours. We are generous with what we have because God

has been generous with us. We forgive because we have been forgiven. We show mercy because it has been shown to us. The woman's gratitude was so great that she overcame any feeling of humiliation. This is a story of humanity and divinity, the point where an all-powerful God and weak humanity intersect.

Another point of controversy centers on the woman's identity. She has often been identified with the woman disciple Mary Magdalene. This has been done solely on the basis of Mary's appearance in the subsequent narrative, where she is identified as the woman "from whom seven devils had gone out." Such an expression in Palestinian Judaism could well have meant

PSALM REFLECTION

Psalm 32 is one of the well-known "penitential psalms" of the Bible, which were popular in many Catholic cultures as an expression of penance in times of trouble and often recited as a regular litany by the very religious. Its emphasis on divine forgiveness stresses the connection between an honest confession of our sins and God's willingness to forgive our guilt completely. Moreover, it associates divine mercy to sinners with God's role as our refuge and protection in any time of trouble. This psalm expresses the same thoughts as those in the story of David's sin and God's forgiveness, and many commentators have thought it might truly have been one of the psalms that David himself composed after his repentance.

Psalm Response
Psalm 32:1–2, 5, 7, 11

Antiphon
Lord, forgive the wrong I
    have done.

Verse for Reflection
I said, "I confess my sin to
    the Lord!"
And you have forgiven the
    guilt of my wrong. (v. 5)

SCRIPTURE COMMENTARY

In the letter to the Galatians, Paul mounts his strongest defense of his ministry of the gospel to the Gentiles. Many devout Jewish converts to Christ had deep doubts about Paul's insistence that pagans did not have to first embrace Judaism and its religious beliefs and practices in order to be baptized Christians. They felt that Jesus came as a Jew and fulfilled his work as Savior within fidelity to the true meaning of the law. God had revealed the Torah, and all who believed in Jesus as messiah should be obligated to live it in order to know and follow Christ. Paul had been led by the Spirit, as had Peter in the case of Cornelius the Roman centurion in Acts 10, to see that the Spirit came to pagan believers in

Second Reading:
Galatians 2:16, 19–21

Brothers and sisters: We who know that a person is not justified by works of the law but through faith in Jesus Christ, even we have believed in Christ Jesus that we may be justified by faith in Christ and not by works of the law, because by works of the law no one will be justified. For

---

that she had been cured of a disabling sickness.

On such slim premises it seems unfair to have so labeled Magdalene for so much of Christian history. She was, in fact, a sterling example of fidelity to Jesus during his passion, at a time when most of his male companions were nowhere to be seen. In John's gospel, she is the first to announce the resurrection of Jesus to the disciples. Today she is spoken of as "the apostle to the apostles." We have all experienced some form of

mistaken identity, but not to the extent that Mary Magdalene has through the ages.

The issue of gratitude emerges again in today's second reading. We will never be saved because we are faithful servants, something we can hardly do anyway. It is because we have already tasted salvation that we try to do what is right. Faith is at the heart of the matter. It is because we have literally been loved to death that we, like the sinful woman, can only shed tears of thanks.

LITURGICAL NOTES

While the Easter season concluded two weeks ago with the celebration of Pentecost, the Sunday cycle of Ordinary Time was interrupted by the Solemnity of the Most Holy Trinity and the Solemnity of the Body and Blood of Christ. This, then, is the first Sunday since Lent began that the people will gather to celebrate the Eucharist on a Sunday during Ordinary Time.

Today Is Father's Day, *and in many places married deacons are frequently asked to preach. While this may be advantageous, liturgy planners should take care that a reflection on Father's Day does not become the primary subject of the homily.*

through the law I died to the law, that I might live for God. I have been crucified with Christ; yet I live, no longer I, but Christ lives in me; insofar as I now live in the flesh, I live by faith in the Son of God who has loved me and given himself up for me. I do not nullify the grace of God; for if justification comes through the law, then Christ died for nothing.

SCRIPTURE COMMENTARY, CONTINUED

Christ even when they were not circumcised or followers of the law. Paul is fierce and adamant: Jesus revealed salvation to the Gentiles not through observance of the law but by giving them the gift of faith. The cross made the difference. Jesus did not die and rise to establish the law more fully but to free human beings from sin and death. If that could be achieved by keeping the law, then Jesus died for no purpose. No, instead he bestowed everlasting life by offering life in himself through faith to all alike, Jew or Gentile.

Gospel: Luke 7:36—8:3 (or Luke 7:36–50)

A Pharisee invited Jesus to dine with him, and he entered the Pharisee's house and reclined at table. Now there was a sinful woman in the city who learned that he was at table in the house of the Pharisee. Bringing an alabaster flask of ointment, she stood behind him at his feet weeping and began to bathe his feet with her tears. Then she wiped them with her hair, kissed them, and anointed them with the ointment. When the Pharisee who had invited him saw this he said to himself, "If this man were a prophet, he would know who and what sort of woman this is who is touching him, that she is a sinner." Jesus said to him in reply, "Simon, I have something to say to you." "Tell me, teacher,"

SCRIPTURE COMMENTARY

Today's gospel points out several different aspects of forgiveness. In the simplest terms, a sinful woman decides to seek healing from Jesus through an act of weeping over her sins and then honoring him with an expensive oil. Because she clearly shows her desire for forgiveness, Jesus forgives her. But it is also a story of jealousy. The hosts are offended that Jesus would allow a person known as a sinner to be present in their company. They don't care about her interior conversion; they are concerned with the appearances. Jesus then challenges them as to who is the better person: one who sees little need for forgiveness or one who needs it badly and receives it. The

---

Many think of Ordinary Time as "returning to normal." In many ways we have returned to what will be a normal pattern of prayer for the next sixth months. This "Ordinary Time" provides liturgy planners with an opportunity not only to reflect on various aspects of the celebration of the liturgy but also to provide formational and catechetical connections for the entire assembly. The focus comes from the scriptural themes and images that emerge Sunday after Sunday.

The scriptures draw our attention to sin and reconciliation, acknowledging our sins and seeking forgiveness. The prophet Nathan tells King David that in spite of all that God has done for

him, he has sinned. Acknowledging his sin, David is forgiven. The responsorial psalm echoes this theme with its refrain, "Lord, forgive the wrong I have done." The gospel passage has Jesus at dinner in the home of a Pharisee. A "sinful woman in the city" hears where Jesus is and comes to bathe his feet with her tears. Jesus then tells a parable and draws the conclusion that this woman is forgiven because she has shown great love. St. John of the Cross many centuries later will echo this theme when he writes, "In the evening of our lives we will be judged on how we have loved."

Today's readings provide an excellent opportunity for reflec-

tion on reconciliation and the sacrament of penance. This sacrament continues to be one of the most misunderstood sacraments. Catechesis and even gentle reminders to the parish on when the sacrament of penance is celebrated, how it is celebrated, the nature of sin, how to examine one's conscience, and the like can assist those members of the parish who have lost touch with the sacrament or who are uncertain about particular aspects of the sacrament. Parishes throughout the country report that when additional or renewed catechesis is provided for the sacrament of penance, there is generally an increase in the numbers of people receiving it.

SCRIPTURE COMMENTARY
CONTINUED

parable reminds us of the parallel story of the Pharisee and the publican. There also, Jesus concludes that so-called terrible sinners actually discover the love and forgiveness of God far more deeply in their lives than those who feel good about their own righteousness. On a third level, today's gospel raises the question of how Jesus can forgive sins if forgiveness of sin is something that belongs only to God. The Pharisees and crowds cannot understand this now, but it is a foretaste of Jesus' power as the Son, which will be revealed at the resurrection.

he said. "Two people were in debt to a certain creditor; one owed five hundred days' wages and the other owed fifty. Since they were unable to repay the debt, he forgave it for both. Which of them will love him more?" Simon said in reply, "The one, I suppose, whose larger debt was forgiven." He said to him, "You have judged rightly."

Then he turned to the woman and said to Simon, "Do you see this woman? When I entered your house, you did not give me water for my feet, but she has bathed them with her tears and wiped them with her hair. You did not give me a kiss, but she has not ceased kissing my feet since the time I entered. You did not anoint my head with oil, but she anointed my feet with ointment. So I tell you, her many sins have been forgiven because she has shown great love. But the one to whom little is forgiven, loves little." He said to her, "Your sins are forgiven." The others at table said to themselves, "Who is this who even forgives sins?" But he said to the woman, "Your faith has saved you; go in peace."

Afterward he journeyed from one town and village to another, preaching and proclaiming the good news of the kingdom of God. Accompanying him were the Twelve and some women who had been cured of evil spirits and infirmities, Mary, called Magdalene, from whom seven demons had gone out, Joanna, the wife of Herod's steward Chuza, Susanna, and many others who provided for them out of their resources.

CATECHETICAL SUGGESTIONS

David: great king and great sinner

The role of the prophets in Israel

Beatitudes in the Old Testament and in the New Testament

The necessity of confession of sin

Grace

Forgiveness: received and given in our lives

MUSIC CONNECTION

Sin and forgiveness are central motifs of today's lessons. After Nathan confronts David with his sinfulness—almost a blind spot in the pivotal king's personality—the repentant David exclaims: "I have sinned against the Lord." His sincere confession is immediately met with Nathan's reassuring words of forgiveness: "The Lord on his part has forgiven your sin: you shall not die." Many hymns explore this richly human predicament and divine response. Examples are *God Full of Mercy, There's a Wideness In God's Mercy, Forgive Our Sins as We Forgive, Believe and Repent,* and *Father Mercy.* The responsorial, Psalm 32, is clearly in this mode, and settings by Kreutz, Stewart, and Alstott all convey the text with success. The gospel account of the sinful woman washing the feet of Jesus at the home of the Pharisee Simon reiterates the theme of the first lesson—that God is ready to forgive and that God's mercy knows no societal, cultural, or religious strictures. *Our Father, We Have Wandered,* a wonderful text wedded to the beautiful melody of the *Passion Chorale,* strikes at the heart of today's readings with its emphasis on God's prevenient mercy and forgiveness, which are the scriptural and theological a priori to our returning to the Lord and seeking God's mercy.

First Reading: Isaiah 49:1–6

Hear me, O coastlands
  listen, O distant peoples.
The LORD called me from birth,
  from my mother's womb he gave me my
    name.
He made of me a sharp-edged sword
  and concealed me in the shadow of his arm.
He made me a polished arrow,
  in his quiver he hid me.
You are my servant, he said to me,
  Israel, through whom I show my glory.

Though I thought I had toiled in vain,
  and for nothing, uselessly, spent my strength,
yet my reward is with the LORD,
  my recompense is with my God.
For now the LORD has spoken
  who formed me as his servant from the
    womb,
that Jacob may be brought back to him
  and Israel gathered to him;
and I am made glorious in the sight of the Lord,
  and my God is now my strength!
It is too little, he says, for you to be my servant,

SCRIPTURE COMMENTARY

This passage is the second of the great "Servant Songs" in the book of Isaiah. The first song in Isaiah 42:1–4 proposes a mission for the servant-prophet, one of bringing justice to the farthest corners of the world by the gentle witness of compassion to the wounded. This song adds some new aspects to the role of that servant: (1) He is called from birth to his role as the servant-prophet; (2) he will be given his name by God according to the special role he plays; (3) his ministry is described as that of a sharp sword or a finely honed arrow, suggesting that his words will generate opposition against which he will be eloquent; (4) his mission is directed to the reform or conversion of Israel itself. Like the first song in Isaiah 42, this song states that the servant's mission is directed to the farthest ends of the earth—that is, he will address his words to all nations, not just to Israel. This song describes the ministry of John the Baptist as portrayed in the gospels. It is closely associated with the ministry of Jesus himself, who is also described as the servant during his earthly ministry. As we shall see in Luke's

HOMILY HELPS

Despite all of the discussion in today's gospel concerning the child's name, the etymology of the name itself is not considered in the gospel narrative. For the child's parents, it was sufficient that the name had been determined by the angel who announced his future birth. The name John is derived from the Hebrew meaning "God has favored" or "God has shown mercy." This favor of God, of course, looks to the arrival of the messiah.

This is a point of more than passing interest. John the Baptist was an end-time prophet of considerable importance. In fact, the Jewish historian Josephus gives John more coverage than he gives Jesus. Yet John's single role in the gospels is to point toward Jesus. This is seen in today's second reading, from Acts, where John is remembered for two things: preaching conversion of life with its accompanying baptism and the superiority of the mission of Jesus. The final period in salvation history had arrived, and Jesus is its centerpiece.

This repeated subordination

of John to Jesus may reflect a conscious effort to offset a certain sectarianism, an effort to retain the baptism of John well into the Christian era. But irrespective of underlying reasons, the gospels clearly see John in a subordinate role.

A pundit once quipped: "There is nothing wrong with being in second place as long as you are remembered for it." No one would really have wanted to pinch-hit for Babe Ruth or do a substitution at the opera for Enrico Caruso. Who would relish the thought of writing a sequel to the Harry Potter stories? But the

SCRIPTURE COMMENTARY, CONTINUED

gospel below, the servant language about John the Baptist is made directly parallel to that of Jesus in order to identify John as the prophet Elijah preparing the way for the messiah. Each task of the forerunner to the messiah will fulfill the task of this Servant Song.

to raise up the tribes of Jacob,
   and restore the survivors of Israel;
I will make you a light to the
   nations,
   that my salvation may reach to
   the ends of the earth.

PSALM REFLECTION

Psalm 139 as a whole is a meditation on God as the one who bestows his spirit on humankind and then upholds the right use of that spirit. It includes in verses 19–24 an ending that threatens destruction and punishment for injustice against the wicked. But for the feast of John the Baptist, the sections of the psalm that are chosen highlight only John's mission as described in the gospels. God foreknows all that we will be called to do. He has chosen and destined the psalmist from his birth and knows his innermost thoughts and very being (vv. 14–15); but he also probes the psalmist's thoughts and actions as he develops in his life (vv. 2–3). Thus God watches over his ways at every stage of his life and guides the psalmist with his divine Spirit (vv. 5-7–not read today). The language of being formed in the depths of the earth is an ancient way of expressing the mystery of how God shapes a person in the womb for what that person will be in life.

Psalm Response
Psalm 139:1–3, 13–14, 14–15

Antiphon
I praise you for I am wonderfully
   made.

Verse for Reflection
You know when I sit and when I
   stand,
You discern my inner thoughts from
   afar. (v. 2)

place of John the Baptist is secure in Christian history, and it is a place based solely on his role as the forerunner of Jesus Christ. He has no independent status, yet he is remembered for who he was and what he did. And he lives in the memorable encomium of Jesus: "There is no greater man born of woman than John the Baptist."

Today's feast is a reminder that we don't have to end up "on top of the heap." It is quite enough to be who we are, to use our talents, to be faithful to our Christian calling as well as to our family and friends. The desire to surpass often ends in tragedy

and bitter disappointment; it may breed envy and a critical spirit. Considering that only a handful of names outlive a century, is all the frustration worth it?

It means much to live a life that points to Christ. Religious conviction is not a private matter. We may think our lives are private, but they are not. Our sense of honesty and decency, our concern for family values, our dedication to our parish and the broader Church, our love for the things of God—in all of these things, our attention is directed beyond, to Someone else. This is to live in the spirit of John the Baptist.

CATECHETICAL SUGGESTIONS

John's role in all four
   gospels
John, Elijah, and Malachi
Annunciation stories
Call stories
Baptism with water and
   baptism with the Spirit
   in the gospels and in
   Acts
Gospel scenes of John's
   disciples with Jesus

Second Reading: Acts 13:22–26

In those days, Paul said: "God raised up David as their king; of him he testified, 'I have found David, son of Jesse, a man after my own heart; he will carry out my every wish.' From this man's descendants God, according to his promise, has brought to Israel a savior, Jesus. John heralded his coming by proclaiming a baptism of repentance to all the people of Israel; and as John was completing his course, he would say, 'What do you suppose that I am? I am not he. Behold, one is coming after me; I am not worthy to unfasten the sandals of his feet.'

"My brothers, children of the family of Abraham, and those others among you who are God-fearing, to us this word of salvation has been sent."

SCRIPTURE COMMENTARY

This short passage comes from Paul's sermon at Antioch in Pisidia on his first missionary journey. He is addressing the Jewish congregation in the synagogue on the Sabbath. In this first recorded preaching of the great apostle, Paul stresses the history of the Old Testament promises for a messiah and how Jesus fulfilled all of those hopes despite not being accepted by the leaders in Jerusalem. As part of this argument for Jesus as the true messiah, Paul notes that John the Baptist, of whom his hearers have all heard and who many thought was the messiah himself, had refused the title of messiah, pointing instead to Jesus as the messiah for Israel. The key to Paul's interpretation was that God had intended this announcement of salvation by John equally for both Israel and all people who seek God with sincere hearts.

LITURGICAL NOTES

The Sundays of Ordinary Time are interrupted for the celebration of the Solemnity of the Nativity of St. John the Baptist. St. John the Baptist was highly regarded by the early Christians. His birthday is one of the earliest feasts in the Christian calendar and is an exception to the rule that martyrs are commemorated on the day of their death (their birth into eternal life.)

There are two sets of readings provided for this solemnity: a vigil Mass and a Mass during the day. The vigil Mass presupposes a genuine vigil, rather than our general practice of an anticipated Sunday Mass on Saturday evening. If there is no vigil, the readings from the Mass during the day ought to be used.

All three readings speak of John: from his naming (gospel) to his mission (Isaiah) to his particular ministry of preparing the way for the Lord (Acts). In a unique way, these readings also speak to the Christian assembly of their naming by God and of their ministry and mission. As God showed his glory through the prophet, so, too, the same God manifests his glory through each of us. How do we reflect that glory? How does our light shine?

For liturgical ministers, as for the whole liturgical assembly, the difficulty is generally not during the liturgy but before and after it. If liturgical ministers are to model the kind of behaviors that would be expected from the entire liturgical assembly, this might be a good Sunday to gently remind our ministers about the kinds of behaviors they should have: before the liturgy, by prayerful preparation; during the liturgy, by entering into the celebration fully, consciously, and actively; and after the celebration, by allowing what has been celebrated to affect their lives.

SCRIPTURE COMMENTARY

All the gospels relate that John the Baptist both preached a message of conversion to get ready for the coming of the messiah and announced that this messiah was coming soon. According to John's gospel, John the Baptist won over many disciples, including most of the men Jesus called to be his own apostles. Moreover, Jesus himself seemed to have wanted to see what John was doing, since in all four gospels we are told that he traveled to the Jordan River site in Judea where John was baptizing. Only Luke tells us that John was related to Jesus, born to Elizabeth, the cousin of Mary. Luke goes on to make the annunciation to John's father Zechariah parallel to the annunciation to Mary, and John's birth story parallel to the birth of Jesus. Scholars have often wondered on what historical basis Luke made this claim, and have concluded that Luke did not intend it literally but as a prophetic foretaste of God's plan of salvation. John was real and certainly acted as a prophet, but for Luke he symbolizes all the prophets of the Old Testament. By following the life of the prophet John, one would understand the special mission of Jesus as the messiah, who walked in their steps but went beyond them. The prophets provided the word of conversion and promise; Jesus brought both judgment on the world and the salvation and healing power of God that the prophets had announced.

Gospel: Luke 1:57–66, 80

When the time arrived for Elizabeth to have her child she gave birth to a son. Her neighbors and relatives heard that the Lord had shown his great mercy toward her, and they rejoiced with her. When they came on the eighth day to circumcise the child, they were going to call him Zechariah after his father, but his mother said in reply, "No. He will be called John." But they answered her, "There is no one among your relatives who has this name." So they made signs, asking his father what he wished him to be called. He asked for a tablet and wrote, "John is his name," and all were amazed. Immediately his mouth was opened, his tongue freed, and he spoke blessing God. Then fear came upon all their neighbors, and all these matters were discussed throughout the hill country of Judea. All who heard these things took them to heart, saying, "What, then, will this child be?" For surely the hand of the Lord was with him.

The child grew and became strong in spirit, and he was in the desert until the day of his manifestation to Israel.

MUSIC CONNECTION

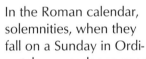

In the Roman calendar, solemnities, when they fall on a Sunday in Ordinary Time, take precedence over that Sunday's liturgy and readings. The birth of John the Baptist holds sway today, and it is, indeed, a very rich source for reflection. John is particularly revered in Latin countries, and in Puerto Rico he is the patron saint, the beloved San Juan Bautista. As a saint, John benefits from the corpus of music extolling the holy women and men revered by the Church in such hymns as *For All the Saints, Ye Watchers and Ye Holy Ones, Sing with All the Saints in Glory,* and *Jerusalem My Happy Home.* As a particular saint with a unique position in the New Testament and in the liturgical year, John also has hymns that are more unique to him, including *By All Your Saints Still Striving, When Jesus Came to Jordan* and *The Great Forerunner of the Morn.* Alan Hammering's *We Sing of the Saints,* with its specific verse for this feast, is also a good choice. Well placed in today's service would be the Canticle of Zechariah, the hymn of praise at the birth of Zechariah's son, John. Ruth Duck's *Benedictus* to the familiar melody *Forest Green* is both uplifting and accessible to most congregations. A variant translation to the same melody is that of James Quinn. In similar fashion, the Litany of the Saints could be a different and effective processional today, and Becker's setting is most singable. Psalm 139 is handled well by Guimont, Hughes, and Bogdan.

First Reading:
1 Kings 19:16b, 19–21

The Lord said to Elijah: "You shall anoint Elisha, son of Shaphat of Abelmeholah, as prophet to succeed you."

Elijah set out and came upon Elisha, son of Shaphat, as he was plowing with twelve yoke of oxen; he was following the twelfth. Elijah went over to him and threw his cloak over him. Elisha left the oxen, ran after Elijah, and said, "Please, let me kiss my father and mother goodbye, and I will follow you." Elijah answered, "Go back! Have I done anything to you?" Elisha left him, and taking the yoke of oxen, slaughtered them; he used the plowing equipment for fuel to boil their flesh, and gave it to his people to eat. Then Elisha left and followed Elijah as his attendant.

SCRIPTURE COMMENTARY

Elijah lived during the ninth century BC in the northern kingdom of Israel during the reign of King Ahab and his wife, Jezebel. The prophet was zealous in protecting the worship of Yahweh, the God of Israel, against royal efforts to introduce official recognition of the cult of Baal, the Canaanite God. Elijah's prophetic actions were dramatic and remembered in later tradition as spectacular for the miracles he was able to do. But God told him that he must pass on his role to another that the battle might continue. The reading today records the call of this successor, Elisha. The young man seemed to have been a successful farmer—it is not everyone who can own or use twelve oxen in plowing—when Elijah entered into his life. Elijah said nothing but put his cloak over Elisha's shoulders. Apparently prophets were known by this piece of dress, and Elisha understood the action as the call to become a prophet also. When, however, he wanted to delay by arranging things at home, Elijah pretended he had not meant anything. It was in fact a rejection of Elisha as unworthy because something meant more to him than the prophetic call. Elisha had to make a choice, and unhesitatingly gave up his own plan, immediately slaughtering his entire livelihood to indicate that his yes was unconditional. But even in this action he began his ministry by giving the benefits to others.

HOMILY HELPS

When the Israelites were led out of Egypt, a serious aspect of their later rebellion was the desire to return to Egypt. They had lived better, they said, in the bondage of Egypt. The gravity of their desire lay in their intention to reverse the direction of salvation history. On the other hand, the greatness of the figure of Abraham was his unwavering willingness to leave home and fortune for the land of promise, with a spirit of full acceptance of God's will.

This same positive spirit characterizes Elisha in today's first reading. The basic theme in today's readings is commitment.

Once Elisha learns of God's intent, he leaves behind his life as a farmer with all its appurtenances and gives the Lord his unwavering allegiance.

Jesus today makes clear to his disciples that, once the journey has begun, there can be no turning back. There is no time for, or interest in, punishing a hostile Samaria. True commitment takes little account of opposition. The runner in the marathon pays little attention to occasional hecklers on the sidelines. The finish line is always most important. Even domestic concerns, such as a final visit home or the burial of a dear relative, remain secondary. (In the gospel, an exaggerated Semitic emphasis rules out such things completely, but this direc-

tive need not be taken literally. It is simply a matter of priorities.)

The same point is made in Paul's admonition to the Galatians in speaking of the moral order. For years his hearers had groped and stumbled in moral darkness, but now they have been enlightened by God's Spirit. It makes no sense to retrace one's steps. Theirs is now a new-found freedom in Christ, and that freedom gives them only one precept—an unqualified love of neighbor. This summarizes everything. To pass from the flesh to the Spirit in baptism sets us on a trajectory that cannot be reversed. The thrust is forward; even "treading water" is impossible. We have once and for all set upon the task. We have the

PSALM REFLECTION

The phrase "My allotted portion and cup, you it is who hold fast my lot" in verse 5 of Psalm 16 is a favorite refrain of the Church, expressing the confidence that our true sustenance now and also our inheritance for the future is God alone. Every member in a covenant community who celebrates the thanksgiving sacrifices and participates in the feast day banquet offerings to God is entitled to a portion of the sacrificed animal or libation. Through the communion sacrifice, the Israelites were united with God and were thus secure in their close relationship with their God. But as they bound themselves in loyalty to God, God responded by promising security and protection for their welfare. The rest of the psalm verses express the psalmist's joy in the certainty of this relationship and in the confidence that God does indeed come to the aid of all who place their trust in him.

Psalm Response
Psalm 16:1–2, 5, 7–8,
9–10, 11

Antiphon
You are my inheritance, O Lord.

Verse for Reflection
I set the Lord always before me,
And I need not be afraid while he is at my side.
(v. 8)

CATECHETICAL SUGGESTIONS

Call stories
The passing on of authority in the Church
Meaning of freedom in a Christian context
Ways to "live by the Spirit"
James and John in the New Testament
What is required to be a disciple of Jesus Christ?

assurance of God that he will bring us home.

Commitment is not highly valued in today's world. We live in the midst of a sea of change, which makes permanence seem unrealistic. Yet our Christian call is constant and unequivocal. There is no turning back. In today's gospel, the Lucan Jesus begins his journey to Jerusalem, a journey that will bring him to his final hour, death by crucifixion. He cannot reject the Father's will and turn back. It is a journey without detour or reprieve. And he turns to each of us and says: "Come, follow me."

LITURGICAL NOTES

The alternative Opening Prayer for this Sunday asks that God "form our hearts in your truth, our hearts in your love." The scripture readings present the invitation to follow, along with the demands of discipleship. Any invitation to follow the Lord comes with its own set of demands as well as enormous benefits.

Since for many July and August are vacation months, there is sometimes a tendency to let things slip by, simply because it is summertime. A unique challenge is given to liturgy commit-

tees and liturgy planners to keep the enthusiasm of the liturgical ministers vital and alive and also to keep our expectations in focus, be they expectations about dress or attendance. Vacation time also brings home talent that might have been away at school. These months should provide ample opportunities for those members of the parish who are absent for the greater portion of the year to now exercise their ministries at home. Accommodation will not only need to be made to fit these people into the schedule; the year-round ministers should also be made aware of their presence and be invited to give these tem-

Second Reading: Galatians 5:1, 13–18

Brothers and sisters: For freedom Christ set us free; so stand firm and do not submit again to the yoke of slavery.

For you were called for freedom, brothers and sisters. But do not use this freedom as an opportunity for the flesh; rather, serve one another through love. For the whole law is fulfilled in one statement, namely, *You shall love your neighbor as yourself.* But if you go on biting and devouring one another, beware that you are not consumed by one another.

I say, then: live by the Spirit and you will certainly not gratify the desire of the flesh. For the flesh has desires against the Spirit, and the Spirit against the flesh; these are opposed to each other, so that you may not do what you want. But if you are guided by the Spirit, you are not under the law.

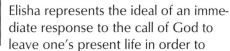

SCRIPTURE COMMENTARY

Elisha represents the ideal of an immediate response to the call of God to leave one's present life in order to serve God in a new way. In his case it was a full-time change of career to take on the role of professional prophet, but for most of us the call comes within our present jobs, family situations, and physical locations. Paul speaks to us of this call to live *new* lives in Christ wherever we are. Christ has freed us from the power of sin that has clouded our vision of a truly free life and chained us to the passions and lusts that drive sinful actions. In order to imitate and live as Christ lived, we must put into practice in our lives Jesus' teaching of love of God and neighbor. One cannot really be committed to being Christ's disciple in everything and continue in a life of sin.

porary parishioners a gracious welcome.

Summertime is also a time when people travel—to the next parish, or the next state, or another country. It would be interesting to ask them to jot down some of their "liturgical observations" while on vacation. They would be asked to share not only what they observed but also how they experienced these variations. If members of the liturgy committee were to review these comments in the fall, they would, without doubt, find some new twists on old ideas. They might also recognize some practices that should be avoided or, if they are currently in use, might need to be phased out. Such an opportunity for input not only broadens the horizons of the committee but also enables all those who participate in the gathering and sharing of information to have a new ownership and a deeper understanding of the liturgical action.

Independence Day is on Wednesday; this weekend is considered the Fourth of July weekend. Some people may be away; visitors may abound. Care should be taken that all the liturgical ministries are covered. Prayers for our nation and its leaders should be included in the General Intercessions.

An invitation to attend Mass on Independence Day is often met with a good response. If there are local parades or civic celebrations, the liturgy should be timed to augment them, not compete with them.

The Sacramentary provides special texts for this Mass, along with two options for the preface. While many have found the proper preface for Thanksgiving Day problematic, these texts tend more to acknowledge our present as an unfinished reality, a promise that brings us to tomorrow. While this is a day that celebrates our freedom, the purpose of today's liturgy is not simply patriotism. Our ultimate freedom is found in Christ.

SCRIPTURE COMMENTARY

The first nine chapters of Luke's gospel center on Jesus' ministry in Galilee and the surrounding regions. In 9:51, Luke announces that Jesus made a firm decision to leave Galilee and travel to Jerusalem because it was in Jerusalem that his task of salvation had to be fulfilled. Jerusalem was the home of the temple, and the important sacrifices demanded by the law had to be performed there. Moreover, in Jesus' time, it was also required that the Passover lambs be slain and prepared on the temple grounds. Jesus needed to give his life as the new Passover lamb only in Jerusalem. Even though his disciples could not contain their anger at the situation, the rejection by the Samaritans did not bother Jesus. He was fulfilling his Father's will, and no human resistance would deter him. This must also be the attitude of his followers. If they are not willing to give up everything and leave their concerns behind, they will not be able to share in his single-hearted mission. The kingdom of God Jesus proclaims is found only when we are fully united to the work of Jesus and his good news, and this means union with his suffering and death as well.

Gospel: Luke 9:51–62

When the days for Jesus' being taken up were fulfilled, he resolutely determined to journey to Jerusalem, and he sent messengers ahead of him. On the way they entered a Samaritan village to prepare for his reception there, but they would not welcome him because the destination of his journey was Jerusalem. When the disciples James and John saw this they asked, "Lord, do you want us to call down fire from heaven to consume them?" Jesus turned and rebuked them, and they journeyed to another village.

As they were proceeding on their journey someone said to him, "I will follow you wherever you go." Jesus answered him, "Foxes have dens and birds of the sky have nests, but the Son of Man has nowhere to rest his head."

And to another he said, "Follow me." But he replied, "Lord, let me go first and bury my father." But he answered him, "Let the dead bury *their* dead. But you, go and proclaim the kingdom of God." And another said, "I will follow you, Lord, but first let me say farewell to my family at home." To him Jesus said, "No one who sets a hand to the plow and looks to what was left behind is fit for the kingdom of God."

MUSIC CONNECTION

The reading from the Hebrew scriptures and the Lucan gospel are bound together in notions of discipleship and the demands it makes on us. For Elisha it involves leaving his father and mother and his main work up to this point in his life—plowing fields. Luke has a similar message in Jesus' unequivocal demand "No one who sets a hand to the plow and looks to what was left behind is fit for the kingdom of God." Hymns about discipleship and its demands are obvious pathways for the pastoral musician. They include *Jesus Lead the Way, Take Up Your Cross, The Servant Song, The Summons,* and *Here I Am Lord.* Sylvia Dunstan's text *You Walk along Our Shoreline,* set to music by Perry Nelson, convincingly beckons us to come and follow the Lord through the vicissitudes of storm and trial. The gospel piece *Lead Me, Guide Me,* in a more upbeat but no less serious fashion, urges us on to follow Jesus no matter what the cost. The talented Bernadette Farrell does the same in her insightful texts and inspiring melodies *Unless a Grain* and *All That Is Hidden.* Psalm 16, today's responsorial, has good arrangements by Paul Lisicky, John Foley, and Marty Haugen.

14TH SUNDAY IN ORDINARY TIME—YEAR C

First Reading: Isaiah 66:10–14c

Thus says the LORD:
Rejoice with Jerusalem and be glad because
    of her,
  all you who love her;
exult, exult with her,
  all you who were mourning over her!
Oh, that you may suck fully
  of the milk of her comfort,
that you may nurse with delight
  at her abundant breasts!
  For thus says the LORD:
Lo, I will spread prosperity over Jerusalem
    like a river,
  and the wealth of the nations like an over-
    flowing torrent.
As nurslings, you shall be carried in her
    arms,
  and fondled in her lap;
as a mother comforts her child,
  so will I comfort you;
  in Jerusalem you shall find your comfort.

When you see this, your heart shall rejoice
  and your bodies flourish like the grass;
the LORD's power shall be known to his
    servants.

SCRIPTURE COMMENTARY

The first reading comes from the final chapter of Isaiah and sums up the vision of the book as a whole. The book of Isaiah opens in chapter 1 with a call to return to the Lord and know him who is their source of nourishment and life. Israel has forgotten and their sins have become as red as blood, but they can be forgiven and return to the Lord and become the just and righteous people of Zion. The rest of the long book of Isaiah covers perhaps 250 years of crisis and military defeats and even 70 years of exile. At every key turning point, Isaiah announces a message of hope and restoration to come. Here, in the final vision, the prophet sees the future Zion (Jerusalem) restored and given both material prosperity and the spiritual treasure of security and peace in God's providential care. The image of motherly love is applied both to Jerusalem itself as a safe refuge and to God, who extends his tender care toward her citizens. Isaiah 66 is paired with the gospel reading that tells how the disciples were able to work effectively in Jesus' name. The connection is not just that both readings are about success; they are also about the kingdom of God that is coming. Isaiah's Jerusalem can be taken as a metaphor for the new Jerusalem, the heavenly kingdom; the proclamation of the kingdom by Jesus' disciples also brings God's promises to those who hear. Both readings proclaim that all who belong to God will find their true home.

HOMILY HELPS

Religion is often seen as a very somber affair. Some people oppose applause in church for any reason; others are still annoyed by the exchange of peace at Mass. But the fact is that there is much to rejoice about in our faith. It appears on the face of parents and relatives at a baptism, at First Communion, or at weddings.

Joy may be individual or collective. The latter was exemplified by the exuberant thousands gathered in Times Square at the end of World War II or in Germany with the fall of the Berlin Wall. For Catholics it is evident in a special way in St. Peter's Square on momentous spirited occasions.

Our scriptures today call for rejoicing. Isaiah tells a liberated Jewish people to rejoice in their homeland, especially Jerusalem. In poetic language that is arrestingly bold, Jerusalem becomes the mother nursing her children at her breast and carrying them in her arms. The children are the picture of complete contentment. It is a picture of beloved offspring, confident and secure.

Paul's joy arises from the Spirit of life, which has enabled him to overcome the sinful enticements of the world. The cross of Christ has effectively ended the world's power over him. The era of "peace and mercy" has begun.

The enthusiasm of Jesus' disciples in today's gospel arises from the message they bear, the great "good news" that the era of salvation is at hand. So urgent is their commitment that there is no time to pack provisions. No suitcases, no walking sticks, no sandals, no idle chatter. The time is short and there is much to do. They are to take lodging where it is offered. They are to be completely taken up with their message of peace and forgiveness. Their happiness is not to reside in their power to expel demons but in the fact that they are citizens of the heavenly realm.

We too have every reason to rejoice. It is within the Church, our own Jerusalem, that we find

PSALM REFLECTION

Psalm 66 is a good example of how the kind of poetry we find in the Psalter speaks strongly to modern readers. It opens with the call to the whole community to praise the God of might and goodness. The "tremendous deeds" refer to two separate things. One is God's creation. God has made all things in the universe and, in turn, all creatures reflect back his glory by being living witnesses to his wisdom and goodness. The psalmist pictures God's creatures beholding the beauty and pattern of all creation and singing God's praises. The second is the divine compassion to Israel. In today's selection, the psalmist calls on the people to give thanks and rejoice for the exodus, but the other verses will list other benefits God has given. Up to this point, experts call this a "psalm of communal praise." But the psalm ends with a sharp turn to the testimony of the psalmist himself giving thanks to God for what God has done for him. Many psalms show this same movement back and forth between the whole people and the individual.

> **Psalm Response**
> **Psalm 66:1–3, 4–5, 6–7, 16, 20**
>
> *Antiphon*
> Let all the earth cry out to God with joy.
>
> *Verse for Reflection*
> [The Lord] has given life to our souls, And has not let our feet slip. (v. 9)

SCRIPTURE COMMENTARY

This passage is the climactic moment in the letter to the Galatians. Paul has argued strenuously that salvation comes only through faith in Jesus. Jews should keep the law as Jews and Gentiles should keep their moral codes, but both need faith in Jesus as Savior to live in Christ. Paul preaches the crucifixion as the turning point of history. Everything before it was the old world under the power of sin, which ruled Jew and Gentile alike, but in the cross of Christ we have been freed from the power of sin and death to live as a new creation. The ways of the law are good, but they apply to Jews; Gentiles, outside the

> **Second Reading: Galatians 6:14–18**
>
> Brothers and sisters: May I never boast except in the cross of our Lord Jesus Christ, through which the world has been crucified to

word and sacrament, the message of a redeeming God. Perhaps there is too much said in the Church about our "excesses" and not enough about our deficits. Are we excited and enthused about our faith? We hear a great deal about the boiling pot that may overflow but little about the pot that won't come to a boil. Why is the term "boring" so often applied to our Sunday liturgy?

Paul waxed eloquent about his new life in God. That new life opens the doors of hope and assures us of Christ's love and God's goodness. Since we are on the track that leads to glory, we have reason to be joyful and enthusiastic. St. Margaret of Cortona used to shout this message from her rooftop in the middle of the night with enthusiasm—but probably to the chagrin of her fellow villagers! We too often bow to convention and live in the status quo. Yet we should rejoice that our names "are written in heaven."

CATECHETICAL SUGGESTIONS

Male and female images of God
Inclusive language
Personal witness: declaring what God has done for each of us
The centrality of the cross
The virtue of hospitality in the Old Testament and in the New Testament
Vows of poverty, chastity, and obedience

me, and I to the world. For neither does circumcision mean anything, nor does uncircumcision, but only a new creation. Peace and mercy be to all who follow this rule and to the Israel of God.

From now on, let no one make troubles for me; for I bear the marks of Jesus on my body.

The grace of our Lord Jesus Christ be with your spirit, brothers and sisters. Amen.

SCRIPTURE COMMENTARY, CONTINUED

demands of the law in the old order, certainly don't have to see them as required when they live in the new power of life in Christ. Thus Paul can give us his strongest personal statement yet on the central role of the cross in his preaching. Nothing matters but that he has Christ: the world and its ways, even his Jewish fidelity to the law—which he always maintained—become as nothing in light of Christ's gift of new life.

Gospel: Luke 10:1–12, 17–20 (or Luke 10:1–9)

At that time the Lord appointed seventy-two others whom he sent ahead of him in pairs to every town and place he intended to visit. He said to them, "The harvest is abundant but the laborers are few; so ask the master of the harvest to send out laborers for his harvest. Go on your way; behold, I am sending you like lambs among wolves. Carry no money bag, no sack, no sandals; and greet no one along the way. Into whatever house you enter, first say, 'Peace to this household.' If a peaceful person lives there, your peace will rest on him; but if not, it will return to you. Stay in the same house and eat and drink what is offered to you, for the laborer deserves his payment. Do not move about from one house to another. Whatever town you enter and they welcome

SCRIPTURE COMMENTARY

The incident of the seventy-two disciples being sent forth occurs only in the Gospel of Luke. Scholars often question whether it reflects a real situation in which Jesus would have such a large group of followers beyond the Twelve. Such a crowd is mentioned nowhere else in this or the other gospels. Moreover, the commands given to these disciples duplicate those given to the twelve apostles in Luke 9:1–9. Many think Luke added a second symbolic story

LITURGICAL NOTES

The alternative opening prayer for this Sunday asks that "our love may give life." The scriptures highlight the activity of God: in providing comfort and prosperity and in providing for the disciples sent out to announce the kingdom of God is at hand. It is all the activity of God, but an activity that is mediated through human hands. It is God's love flowing through us that will give life, God's words spoken through us that will announce the kingdom.

This Sunday invites us to look into not only what might be said directly but also what unspoken messages are presented at our celebrations. We need to take a look at things: from the physical environment of the church building, to the attitudes and dispositions of those who greet and ushers, to the deportment of the ministers in the sanctuary—do we look like we are about God's work?

The General Intercessions should certainly include intentions for vocations to the priesthood, the diaconate, and the consecrated life. But the Intercessions should also include an intention for an increase in the other ministries of the Church—liturgical ministries, outreach and social ministries, education and bereavement ministries. There are people who have remarked that they would consider the ordained or the vowed life but are not quite sure where they can obtain information. Is such information readily available? Is it visible? The same would hold true for the other ministries of the Church. Make certain that people can find out the who, what, when, where, why, and how of these ministries. God is acting to bring more and more people into service within the Church; if we do not provide information to assist them, we can be obstacles to God's activity.

SCRIPTURE COMMENTARY, CONTINUED

for his Gentile readers. There are three clues to this interpretation: (1) In Genesis 10, the total number of nations God has established for the whole world is seventy (or seventy-two). (2) In Numbers 11, when Moses was told to appoint elders to assist him in his work and on whom part of his own spirit would fall, he appointed seventy plus Medad and Eldad, who, although they were absent, were also to share in the Spirit; this would be symbolic of the mission of the apostles that was to be shared with others. (3) The Twelve are sent out in the part of Luke's gospel in which Jesus proclaims his message only to Jewish audiences, but this story takes place once he has begun to move through Gentile territory. Their mission is to announce that Jesus is about to come in person to these places but, even more, that his kingdom has arrived in their midst. They are to invite all who hear them to accept it. They are to rejoice that many have converted but to avoid glorying in their power, for their glory is that they too have been included in the kingdom.

you, eat what is set before you, cure the sick in it and say to them, 'The kingdom of God is at hand for you.' Whatever town you enter and they do not receive you, go out into the streets and say, 'The dust of your town that clings to our feet, even that we shake off against you.' Yet know this: the kingdom of God is at hand. I tell you, it will be more tolerable for Sodom on that day than for that town."

The seventy-two returned rejoicing, and said, "Lord, even the demons are subject to us because of your name." Jesus said, "I have observed Satan fall like lightning from the sky. Behold, I have given you the power to 'tread upon serpents' and scorpions and upon the full force of the enemy and nothing will harm you. Nevertheless, do not rejoice because the spirits are subject to you, but rejoice because your names are written in heaven."

 MUSIC CONNECTION

The first reading, from Isaiah, promising a return from exile to Jerusalem is replete with joy, bounty and the assurance that our ultimate home is one of comfort and jubilation. Hymns such as *Jerusalem My Happy Home, When from Our Exile, By the Babylonian Rivers, City of God, Jerusalem,* and *Alleluia, Song of Gladness* all build on the theme of exile and return. Paul's reference to the cross ["May I never boast except in the cross of our Lord Jesus Christ!] suggests hymns such as *Lift High the Cross, At the Name of Jesus, Take Up Your Cross,* and *When I Survey the Wondrous Cross,* all of which dwell on the image of the cross and its significance in the life of the disciple of Christ. This discipleship is further explored in the Lucan pericope, where Jesus appoints and sends forth the seventy-two to every town and place. *Lord, You Give the Great Commission,* whether sung to the *Abbot's Leigh* or the alternative melody *Hyfrydol,* is a clarion call to service in the name of the Lord. There are many newer pieces dealing with this theme. They include Inwood's *Take Christ to the World, The Spirit Sends Us Forth to Serve, The Summons,* and Farrell's *God Has Chosen Me.* Psalm 66 clearly picks up the joyful imagery from Isaiah, and settings by Strickland, Gelineau, and Haugen are recommended for today.

First Reading:
Deuteronomy 30:10–14

Moses said to the people: "If only you would heed the voice of the LORD, your God, and keep his commandments and statutes that are written in this book of the law, when you return to the LORD, your God, with all your heart and all your soul.

"For this command that I enjoin on you today is not too mysterious and remote for you. It is not up in the sky, that you should say, 'Who will go up in the sky to get it for us and tell us of it, that we may carry it out?' Nor is it across the sea, that you should say, 'Who will cross the sea to get it for us and tell us of it, that we may carry it out?' No, it is something very near to you, already in your mouths and in your hearts; you have only to carry it out."

SCRIPTURE COMMENTARY

The book of Deuteronomy sets out an agenda that is maintained throughout the entire book: if you obey the commandments of the Lord your God and remain faithful to him alone as God, you will find blessing; but if you disobey his commands and worship other gods, you will be punished by being thrown off the land God has given you. The book as a whole combines both a summary of the laws you are to obey (chapters 12–26) and urgent reminders of all that God has done for Israel and the need to remain faithful (chapters 1–9; 27–31). The book, drawing near its end, as in today's reading from chapter 30, *assumes* the people will not have obeyed and will have been exiled and punished. This is one piece of evidence that the book is not actually from the time of Moses but was written as a response to the Babylonian exile itself or the threatening period leading up to it, perhaps around 600 BC. Moses appeals here for the people to be very careful in keeping the commands of God after they have repented and been restored by God to their land again. This law of God is not some rare jewel that has to be found or a mysterious work in a foreign language to be deciphered. No, the law is already known to us in our hearts because it is the very way of the covenant that God established with our ancestors long ago.

HOMILY HELPS

As long as our faith remains theoretical, we are really "home safe." But when "the rubber hits the road" and it becomes a reality, it is then that we stumble and fall. I can find myself worshiping in church every Sunday while failing to realize that the woman on my block with a bedridden husband could use some time off and that I could offer my services to assist an ailing person.

This is the clear message of our scriptures this Sunday. Even Deuteronomy, written centuries before Christ, sees the practice of our faith to be as close as the homeless man on the park bench. God's will is not found in the stratosphere or at the far end of an ocean voyage. Rather, it is as close as a phone call or a knock on the door. It costs us little to echo the psalmist in today's responsorial: "The Lord hears the poor"; the rub comes when we realize that he hears them through our ears.

The story of the good Samaritan is very illustrative. The love of God and neighbor accurately summarizes the whole of the Christian life. Jesus' questioner has the answer right. But then the critical question is raised: "Who is my neighbor?" At that point we pass from the abstract to the real, from the general to the particular.

Notice that there are two questions raised in this gospel passage. The first is: "Who is my neighbor?" The parable makes the answer clear, as the Samaritan cares for the present and future needs of the injured victim. The Samaritan is more than generous in providing for the

PSALM REFLECTION

Psalm 69 stands in counterpoint to the words of Deuteronomy. There the stress was on our obedience and reforming our hearts to turn to God. The psalmist instead calls our attention to the great compassion and mercifulness of God toward us. In times of trouble he always hears and bestows his favor on those who call to him. The psalm begins with the personal cry of the psalmist himself about his own pain and need. He seems to be centered always on "I" in the selected verses, but by the end of the psalm we are reminded that God answers the prayers of the poor and all who are in need of his help. Like the words of Deuteronomy, this assurance is rooted in the covenant relationship with God on Mt. Sinai: "You will be our God, and we will be your people!"

Psalm Response
Psalm 69:14, 17, 30–31, 33–34, 36, 37
(Or Psalm 19:8, 9, 10, 11)

Antiphon
Turn to the Lord in your need,
and you will live.

Verse for Reflection
Hide not your face from your servant,
In my troubles, be quick to answer me! (Ps 69:18)

SCRIPTURE COMMENTARY

We begin the reading of the letter of St. Paul to the Colossians. It is different from most of Paul's letters because, while it is addressed to some issues in one church, it is really intended as an encouragement to a whole group of churches. The city of Colossae sits on the edge of a valley inland from Ephesus in western Turkey. Within sight lie Hierapolis and Aphrodisias and Laodicea, and nearby there are many other local churches. Paul concludes by saying that the Colossians are to share his letter with the Laodiceans and they are to share the letter

Second Reading:
Colossians 1:15–20

Christ Jesus is the image of the invisible God,
the firstborn of all creation.
For in him were created all things in heaven and on earth,
the visible and the invisible,

man's concerns. Our neighbor, then, is anyone in need.

The priest and the Levite pass by the stranger without approaching him. They are, of course, concerned about ritual uncleanness. If they were to come in contact with a dead man, they could not exercise their duties in worship. This for them was the important precept, which clearly here preempted love of neighbor. Today we would call it a matter of misplaced priorities.

At this point we come to the second question. Jesus does not repeat the initial question of the respondent. The answer to that question is clear. My neighbor is anyone in need. But Jesus poses another question: "Which . . . was neighbor to the robbers' victim?" The answer, of course, is "the Samaritan." But in those days the antipathy of Jews for Samaritans was virulent. The respondent now finds himself in a dilemma. He is hardly in a position to recognize a Samaritan, so he gives a neutral answer: "The one who treated him with mercy." But Jesus' point is well made. The neighbor is not only the person in need; it is also any person of good will who treats others with mercy.

In the splendid Colossians hymn, today's second reading, Christ holds primacy over the whole of creation as well as the Church. It is one of the texts that fueled the Franciscan school of theology in arguing that Christ exists independent of sin. The hymn is an outstanding expression of Christ's preeminence. But the fact remains that Christ is effectively and practically present when Christians bring his Spirit to life. We cannot bypass that final injunction of the gospel today: "Go and do likewise."

whether thrones or dominions or principalities or powers;
    all things were created through him and for him.
He is before all things,
    and in him all things hold together.
He is the head of the body, the church.
He is the beginning, the firstborn from the dead,
    that in all things he himself might be preeminent.
For in him all the fullness was pleased to dwell,
    and through him to reconcile all things for him,
    making peace by the blood of his cross
    through him, whether those on earth or those in heaven.

SCRIPTURE COMMENTARY, CONTINUED

he has written to them. The letter to the Colossians treats our unity in Christ and the need therefore for a Christian life based on Christ's word and risen life. Our reading is the beautiful hymn of Christ as head of his body, which is the Christian community. As God raised Jesus and made him receive the fullness of divine life, we as his Body will share in that divine life in a variety of ways, the first of which Paul mentions today: we will be reconciled with God from the alienation caused by our sins.

Gospel: Luke 10:25–37

There was a scholar of the law who stood up to test him and said, "Teacher, what must I do to inherit eternal life?" Jesus said to him, "What is written in the law? How do you read it?" He said in reply,
    "You shall love the Lord, your God,
    with all your heart,
    with all your being,
    with all your strength,
    and with all your mind,
    and your neighbor as yourself."

SCRIPTURE COMMENTARY

In our first reading, Deuteronomy could say that the law of God was not written somewhere outside us but resides in our hearts in the knowledge we have of God. It could also say that all Israelites must affirm every day that God is their God and is the only God and one must love him with all one's heart, and soul, and strength, and mind (Deut 6:4–5). For Deuteronomy, all laws or commandments depend on the covenant bond of love between God and Israel as their foundation. Jesus affirms this unconditionally and goes on to place next to it as a partner the love of neighbor, which is taught everywhere in the Pentateuch

LITURGICAL NOTES

The command to love God and love our neighbor resounds throughout the liturgy. Jesus, the teacher, provides an excellent example of just how the two sides of that same coin are put into action.

This Sunday provides an excellent opportunity for homilists to reflect on the mission of every Christian to treat every person with mercy. Too often the times we live in, as well as our own fears and worries regarding personal safety, may lead us to think that although we would like to help, we can't. We need to be reminded that we can and that there are opportunities within the liturgical assembly that can be a good starting point. How are compassion and mercy evidenced within our liturgical assembly?

What have been termed "distractions" in the liturgy are often parts of what it means to be human: a crying baby, a fidgety child, an elderly person who moves slowly, a person with a disability who breaks the pattern of seating or of the Communion procession. Without a doubt, each one of these presents an opportunity for us to display both mercy and compassion.

And if the challenge from the pulpit is not forthcoming, there could also be a few "points to ponder" in the parish bulletin. These points might provide people with some food for reflection; they could, for example, mention the father with the crying infant, and the middle-aged couple displaying their annoyance at the crying. We would not be giving specific directions; we would merely be inviting people to reflection—a reflection that might mean the difference between hearing the gospel and living the gospel.

SCRIPTURE COMMENTARY, CONTINUED

but especially stated in Leviticus 19:18. This did not surprise the lawyer who questioned Jesus, but he was nervous that by "neighbor" Jesus might mean someone beyond his fellow devout Jews. And sure enough, Jesus tells his wonderful parable of the good Samaritan, who put two so-called pious and devout Jews to shame by his love of a stranger. To make it worse, Jesus singled out priests and Levites, who knew the law backwards and forwards, as his examples of the type that can easily forget that the love of God cannot be restricted to those we know. We cannot exclude others or decide for ourselves just who is our neighbor or to whom we owe the dignity of a child of God. All are to be included.

He replied to him, "You have answered correctly; do this and you will live."

But because he wished to justify himself, he said to Jesus, "And who is my neighbor?" Jesus replied, "A man fell victim to robbers as he went down from Jerusalem to Jericho. They stripped and beat him and went off leaving him half-dead. A priest happened to be going down that road, but when he saw him, he passed by on the opposite side. Likewise a Levite came to the place, and when he saw him, he passed by on the opposite side. But a Samaritan traveler who came upon him was moved with compassion at the sight. He approached the victim, poured oil and wine over his wounds and bandaged them. Then he lifted him up on his own animal, took him to an inn, and cared for him. The next day he took out two silver coins and gave them to the innkeeper with the instruction, 'Take care of him. If you spend more than what I have given you, I shall repay you on my way back.' Which of these three, in your opinion, was neighbor to the robbers' victim?" He answered, "The one who treated him with mercy." Jesus said to him, "Go and do likewise."

MUSIC CONNECTION

Following the will of God as it is revealed and expressed in the law is at the heart of today's readings. Deuteronomy's admonition to heed the voice of the Lord and keep God's commandments should not be viewed through our usual Anglo-Saxon filters as restrictive of human freedom but rather in the more Jewish sense of liberating us to appreciate one of God's greatest gifts to his people. The law is "perfect, refreshing the soul...right, rejoicing the heart...true...just...more desirable than gold...sweeter also than honey" (Ps 19). Hymns such as *Love Is His Word, Let Me Sing*

of Your Law, This Is My Commandment, Your Words Are Spirit and Life, and *A Simple Command* are all good choices today. The Lucan story of the good Samaritan, a classic of biblical literature, points us to a faith in action that knows no ethnic, religious, social, or racial bounds. Thus, *In Christ There Is No East or West; Lord of All Nations; Grant Me Grace; How Long O Lord, How Long;* and *The Servant Song* all point us in the same direction. Bernadette Farrell's hymns *Community of Christ* and *God Has Chosen Me* broaden our notions of service rooted in love, as does Haas's popular *We Are Called.* The responsorial, Psalm 69, is well presented by Guimont and Alstott.

CATECHETICAL SUGGESTIONS

The Deuteronomist tradition

Prayers of petition in the eucharistic liturgy

Christ as the *firstborn* in the New Testament

The social context of first-century Judaism

Interpreting parables

Whom in our community do we fail to recognize as neighbor, and why?

First Reading: Genesis 18:1–10a

The LORD appeared to Abraham by the terebinth of Mamre, as he sat in the entrance of his tent, while the day was growing hot. Looking up, Abraham saw three men standing nearby. When he saw them, he ran from the entrance of the tent to greet them; and bowing to the ground, he said: "Sir, if I may ask you this favor, please do not go on past your servant. Let some water be brought, that you may bathe your feet, and then rest yourselves under the tree. Now that you have come this close to your servant, let me bring you a little food, that you may refresh yourselves; and afterward you may go on your way." The men replied, "Very well, do as you have said."

Abraham hastened into the tent and told Sarah, "Quick, three measures of fine flour! Knead it and make rolls." He ran to the herd, picked out a tender, choice steer, and gave it to a servant, who quickly prepared it. Then Abraham got some curds and milk, as well as the steer that had been prepared, and set these before the three men; and he waited on them under the tree while they ate.

They asked Abraham, "Where is your wife Sarah?" He replied, "There in the tent." One of them said, "I will surely return to you about this time next year, and Sarah will then have a son."

SCRIPTURE COMMENTARY

Both the scene in Genesis and the gospel passage deal with a situation of hospitality to guests who also bear important information for the hosts. Neither the three strangers who visit Abraham nor Jesus just happen to be passing by, desiring only a place to rest and receive food. They need to be heard attentively as well. The background to the Abraham story is the patriarch's disappointment that Sarah, his wife, has never been able to bear a child. God had promised that Abraham would be the father of a great people, but it seemed that soon there would be no hope. Sarah was already over the age of childbearing. Now three visitors arrive. But this incident is certainly more than an ordinary visit. The story opens with the statement that it was the Lord who visited Abraham. Then it turns out to be three men suddenly nearby. This is the ancient narrative way of saying that God was going to speak through these messengers. Yet in the final line, it is not all three who speak but one voice that says he will return next year after Sarah has given birth to a son. The promise is made despite the physical reality, and only God's divine intervention could lead to the birth of a son.

HOMILY HELPS

In our world of instant meaning and fast food service, we can lose sight of the significance of a dinner invitation. Ancient cultures did not, nor do some modern ones. We can wish people well in various ways, even through a simple greeting card. But food is necessary for life; without it, we perish. Therefore, to offer food to another is a significant and concrete way to wish them well on the journey of life.

In today's scriptures, Abraham and Sarah, as well as Martha and Mary, extend hospitality generously as hosts to their distinguished visitors. In the Genesis narrative, the three visitors are actually the Lord himself, who as God could not be seen by the naked eye. Abraham reverently addresses the three as "Lord" and offers them a meal. The story becomes a birth announcement of the child Isaac, with whom the aging Abraham and Sarah will be blessed.

The account of Jesus' visit to the home of Mary and Martha should not be seen as a put-down of Martha. The service she renders is praiseworthy and complements the listening posture of Mary. However, early in the Church's life, certain priorities had to be established. When a controversy arose about the unmet needs of Hellenist widows (Acts 6), seven men were selected to provide table ministry, leaving the apostles free for the ministry of the word. The word is always accorded priority, while social outreach is accorded subordinate but unquestionable importance. The same subordination obtains in the Mary-Martha story. Both sisters play a significant role in their attentiveness to Jesus, while meditation on the word is accorded an essential preference.

The balance between prayer and action has to be maintained in our life as well, but it is inter-

PSALM REFLECTION

Psalm 15 is a litany of the just person who prepares himself by examination of his behavior before approaching the altar of the temple with offerings. It is in part a positive description of the right attitude of one who acts faithfully before God, and partly a "negative confession," in which the psalmist lists what the just person has not been guilty of. The psalm is an appropriate response to the narrative about Abraham. In the incident we have just heard, Abraham is the example of the person who does not harm a fellow man or act harmfully against his neighbor. Above all, he honors those who fear the Lord. In fact, the book of Genesis always portrays Abraham throughout chapters 12–25 as a person who walks blamelessly before the Lord.

Psalm Response
Psalm 15:2–3, 3–4, 5

Antiphon
He who does justice will live in
the presence of the Lord.

Verses for Reflection
O Lord, who can rest in your
tent,
Or who can dwell on your holy
mountain?
The one who is blameless and
does what is right! (vv. 1–2)

CATECHETICAL SUGGESTIONS

God's covenant with Abraham
Entrance rites to the temple
The meaning of suffering
Ministry as stewardship
Marys in the gospels
Ways in which we "listen to Jesus speak"

---

esting to note the interplay between the two. A ministry of social outreach enriches our time spent at liturgy or in private prayer. And our prayer is sterile if it is detached from the needs of our neighbor and the world. As Church and as individuals we need both, while always seeing reflection on the word as our noblest endeavor.

In helping other Christians, it is the Christ-in-us that reaches out to the Christ-in-them. This is the great mystery about which Paul speaks in today's passage from Colossians. The life in the Spirit, which is the gift to all the baptized, was at the heart of Paul's

preaching. It was something for which he suffered; his hardship complemented that of Christ himself. And what is prayer except the ever-deepening awareness of what it means for Christ to live in us? And what is action except the reaching out to the Christ in others?

Luke's deep respect for women is again evident in this story of the two women who were part of Jesus' life. It is striking to see Mary as a true disciple of the word. In the Church, where it seems men are so much to the fore, we can only profit by reflection on women as ministers of word and charity.

LITURGICAL NOTES

The alternative Opening Prayer asks the Father to "keep us alive in Christ Jesus; keep us watchful in prayer." The scripture readings set before us prayer and action, or contemplative prayer and active prayer. The General Intercessions should certainly make mention of those who have responded to God's call and devoted their entire lives to contemplative prayer, along with those who are engaged in active prayer in the world.

If a person is to have a prayer life, the Sunday Eucharist cannot be the only time of prayer. Signifi-

**Second Reading:
Colossians 1:24–28**

Brothers and sisters: Now I rejoice in my sufferings for your sake, and in my flesh I am filling up what is lacking in the afflictions of Christ on behalf of his body, which is the church, of which I am a minister in accordance with God's stewardship given to me to bring to completion for you the word of God, the mystery hidden from ages and from generations past. But now it has been manifested to his holy ones, to whom God chose to make known the riches of the glory of this mystery among the Gentiles; it is Christ in you, the hope for glory. It is he whom we proclaim, admonishing everyone and teaching everyone with all wisdom, that we may present everyone perfect in Christ.

SCRIPTURE COMMENTARY

In last week's reading from the first chapter of Colossians, Paul described the union of the risen Christ with his Body, the Church. This union was made possible by Jesus' death on the cross, which erased our human alienation from God and made us one with Christ, who offered himself for us. But Paul in this following section goes further. He states that he, and every member of the Church, participates in reconciling the world to God. As Jesus acted on behalf of us all, we continue to be his Body living in time and space and sharing in his ministry of reconciliation. Since proclamation of the gospel brings to Gentiles and Jews alike the knowledge of that mystery of the cross by which God forgave our sins and restored us to everlasting life, we continue to carry that mystery to more and more fulfillment as people are brought into Christ. As Paul puts it, we ourselves are made more complete as we help make all people come to completion in knowing Christ.

---

cant numbers of people long for additional experiences and opportunities for prayer. Possibly one of the reasons we are seeing an influx in attendance at devotions is that they attempt to fill this void.

The Liturgy of the Hours stands as a treasure hidden in a field. It is one fruit of the liturgical reform of the Second Vatican Council that has yet to receive widespread implementation. Many reasons have been offered as to why this implementation has been so limited. Those parishes that have communal celebration of the Hours know the treasure they have uncovered. The *General Instruction of the Liturgy of the Hours* states:

The purpose of the liturgy of the hours is to sanctify the day and the whole range of human activity (11)....Those taking part in the liturgy of the hours have access to holiness of the richest kind through the life-giving word of God, which in this liturgy receives great emphasis. Its readings are drawn from sacred scripture; God's words in the psalms are sung in his presence, and the intercessions, prayers and hymns are inspired by scripture and steeped in its spirit (14)....When the people are invited to the

liturgy of the hours and come together in unity of heart and voice, they show forth the Church in its celebration of the mystery of Christ (22).

On a Sunday when the liturgy speaks so directly of prayer, liturgy committees ought to take the opportunity to consider how, where, and when parts of the Hours might be celebrated by the parish community. Resources abound, both of popular arrangements of the Hours and catechetical resources for learning more about them. Don't let another season go by without uncovering this treasure hidden in the field.

SCRIPTURE COMMENTARY

The story of Martha and Mary has become one of the most commonly used proverbial lessons in Christianity. Don't be a Martha, concerned too much with the external details of religion; be a Mary, who chooses prayer and meditation over accomplishments. It has been used as an argument for the superiority of contemplative religious orders over active orders and for religious life in general over a lay vocation. But we should read it in the context of Jesus' friendship with these two sisters. Martha reveals herself clearly to be a person who has come to know Jesus well and has deep faith in him, as shown in the story of Lazarus's death in John 11. In Luke, Martha is a worker and may well be depriving herself of the better part, which would mean that she needs to find the time to let go of other distractions in order to hear and understand Jesus' thoughts and insights more deeply. Jesus gently directs her to have fewer concerns and trust a little more that God will provide enough for us in all circumstances.

Gospel: Luke 10:38–42

Jesus entered a village where a woman whose name was Martha welcomed him. She had a sister named Mary who sat beside the Lord at his feet listening to him speak. Martha, burdened with much serving, came to him and said, "Lord, do you not care that my sister has left me by myself to do the serving? Tell her to help me." The Lord said to her in reply, "Martha, Martha, you are anxious and worried about many things. There is need of only one thing. Mary has chosen the better part and it will not be taken from her."

MUSIC CONNECTION

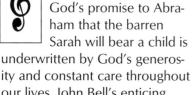

God's promise to Abraham that the barren Sarah will bear a child is underwritten by God's generosity and constant care throughout our lives. John Bell's enticing hymn *God It Was* connects this pivotal story of Abraham and Sarah with other tales of God's activity in human history, as in the stories of Moses and Miriam, Joseph and Mary, and Christ, Martha, and her sister, Mary. The undercurrent of hospitality in the Genesis account is explored more fully in the Lucan story of Martha and Mary. Caring for others is at the heart of discipleship, and as Mary's example reminds us, it is a care fully rooted in a personal relationship with the Lord. Several hymns help connect the dots between hospitality's table fellowship and service, notably *Here at This Table, Table of Plenty, Bless the Feast,* and *Gather Us In*. The second reading from Colossians is a classic statement of what it means to be a minister of the Church proclaiming the mystery of Christ to the world. Hymns such as Farrell's *Praise to You, O Christ, Our Savior; Your Words Are Spirit and Life;* Lynch's *In the Land There Is a Hunger;* and Manalo's *With One Voice* help elucidate that ministry for us disciples today. The responsorial, Psalm 15, is well done by Chepponis and Gelineau.

First Reading: Genesis 18:20–32

In those days, the LORD said: "The outcry against Sodom and Gomorrah is so great, and their sin so grave, that I must go down and see whether or not their actions fully correspond to the cry against them that comes to me. I mean to find out."

While Abraham's visitors walked on farther toward Sodom, the LORD remained standing before Abraham. Then Abraham drew nearer and said: "Will you sweep away the innocent with the guilty? Suppose there were fifty innocent people in the city; would you wipe out the place, rather than spare it for the sake of the fifty innocent people within it? Far be it from you to do such a thing, to make the innocent die with the guilty so that the innocent and the guilty would be treated alike! Should not the judge of all the world act with justice?" The LORD replied, "If I find fifty innocent people in the city of Sodom, I will spare the whole place for their sake." Abraham spoke up again: "See how I am presuming to speak to my Lord, though I am but dust and ashes! What if there are five less than fifty innocent people? Will you destroy the whole city because of those five?" He answered, "I will not destroy it, if I find forty-five there." But Abraham persisted, saying "What if only forty are found there?" He replied, "I will forbear doing it for the sake of the forty." Then Abraham said, "Let not my Lord grow impatient if I go on. What if only thirty

SCRIPTURE COMMENTARY

Last week we read the first half of Genesis 18 and its story of how God promised Abraham through the visit of three angels that a son would be born to him within a year. Abraham received the messengers joyfully and heard their message. The authors of Genesis now continue with a second example, for readers, of the uprightness of their ancestor Abraham. Once, the narrative tells us, Abraham even argued with God to obtain mercy and compassion for people who did not deserve to go unpunished. Reports have reached God that the sins of Sodom and Gomorrah are great, yet God does not act rashly but judges what is true and false. The authors never actually say that God intends to drastically punish the cities if they are guilty, but Abraham presumes that God will do so. From the point of view of the narrators, Abraham states the lesson with the first question about sparing the cities if God finds fifty innocent people in them: God does not punish the innocent along with the guilty but considers each person in terms of that individual's guilt or innocence. The dramatic sequence of

HOMILY HELPS

Prayer is not easy to explain. Is it possible that God does not know our needs? Is it possible to bring something to God's attention? To change his mind? The mystery of God is always before us, but the fact is that the scriptures are eminently clear on the importance of prayer. We are repeatedly told to bring our concerns to God, and nowhere more clearly than in today's readings.

Bartering is part and parcel of Middle Eastern buying and selling. An agent in a bazaar once commented on the astonishing conduct of American tourists. They would ask the cost, receive an answer, and then pay the price asked. They made no effort to barter, thus making the transaction a total bore!

In today's reading from Genesis, Abraham barters with God over the fate of the sinful cities of Sodom and Gomorrah. In what may strike us as an unusual form of prayer, the patriarch asks that the cities be saved if a determined number of innocent people can be found. Like a clever barterer, he brings the number down first by fives—fifty, forty-five, forty. And then, buoyed up by success, he drops by tens—thirty, twenty, ten. The story points up not only the justice of God, who will not punish the innocent with the wicked, but also God's concern and Abraham's persistence in prayer.

Persistence is to the fore in the parables connected with prayer in today's gospel. There is humor in the story of the man who causes a midnight ruckus for three loaves of bread. But his request is granted because he persists. Don't believe that God has abandoned you because the answer does not come at once. As the second parable states, no father is indifferent to the authentic concerns of his son. Continue to pray, knowing that a constant prayer is simply a measure of the depth of our faith.

A common feature of church life is what is termed "the prayer wheel," which is nothing more

SCRIPTURE COMMENTARY, CONTINUED

making the number lower and lower simply underlines the lesson further. But we can detect a second lesson as well: Abraham persists in his requests, relying on God's intimacy with him, to achieve even more. Abraham's persistence in prayer is an example for all of Israel to continue to call on God, confident that his mercy can be won even when their wickedness should justly condemn them.

are found there?" He replied, "I will forbear doing it if I can find but thirty there." Still Abraham went on, "Since I have thus dared to speak to my Lord, what if there are no more than twenty?" The LORD answered, "I will not destroy it, for the sake of the twenty." But he still persisted: "Please, let not my Lord grow angry if I speak up this last time. What if there are at least ten there?" He replied, "For the sake of those ten, I will not destroy it."

PSALM REFLECTION

Psalm 138 is first of all a prayer of thanksgiving to God for answering the prayer of the psalmist. Even though the psalmist had little to offer and was in trouble and among the lowly and unimportant, God responded by giving him strength and protecting him from the attacks of his enemies. But the effusive words of praise that the psalmist utters shows that he is confident that God considers him a friend and intimate. The psalmist is in God's very house, honoring and serving him. The repeated emphasis on the psalmist's humility reveals that God answers those who rely on him rather than on their own importance. God's kindness endures forever, the psalmist concludes, and so he praises God not just for this one time that the Lord has come to the rescue of his servant, but in full knowledge that God will do so throughout his life, for the "Lord will complete what he has done for me" (Ps 138:7).

Psalm Response
Psalm 138:1–2, 2–3, 6–7, 7–8

Antiphon
Lord, on the day I called for help, you answered me.

Verse for Reflection
When I called, you answered me;
You gave strength to my soul. (v. 3)

than the temptation to add more prayers to what was once a simple and direct invocation. Jesus did not multiply prayers. The single prayer that he left us, the Our Father, comes to us in two different forms, that of Matthew and Luke, and is surprisingly brief. The Lucan form of this singular prayer is given to us today. It contains five petitions. The first two are centered on God and pray that his sovereignty be recognized and his final kingdom be ushered in. The last three petitions look to us, as we ask for our material needs, God's forgiveness, and final deliverance. The Our Father, as we recite it daily, is a very simple but all-encompassing prayer.

Above all, it is an act of humble submission before a God of goodness and concern.

Prayer is universal. It is seen in the Hindu who takes his daily bath in the Ganges and in the Buddhist who makes his morning offering before the towering Buddha on the street. For us, it is a recognition, with Colossians today, that we have already been brought from death to life and, in this new Spirit, have ready access to our God. To contemplate that is a prayer in itself. God has already shown his readiness and concern. With the psalmist today we say: "Lord, when I called you answered me, you built up strength within me."

CATECHETICAL SUGGESTIONS

Anthropomorphic descriptions of God in Genesis
The mystery of innocent suffering
Psalms of thanksgiving
Divine mercy
Breaking open the Our Father
Personal witness: the power of prayer

**Second Reading:
Colossians 2:12–14**

Brothers and sisters: You were buried with him in baptism, in which you were also raised with him through faith in the power of God, who raised him from the dead. And even when you were dead in transgressions and the uncircumcision of your flesh, he brought you to life along with him, having forgiven us all our transgressions; obliterating the bond against us, with its legal claims, which was opposed to us, he also removed it from our midst, nailing it to the cross.

SCRIPTURE COMMENTARY

This is the third week of readings from the letter to the Colossians. Paul is expanding on what belonging to the body of Christ means for the Christian in light of the cross. He has emphasized that it means we are able to share in the merit of the sufferings of Christ in the proclamation of the gospel. Much has yet to be done to complete the salvation Christ won for us—it must be preached to all peoples so that they can hear of it and receive the salvation he bestows. Now Paul goes a step further and explains how Christ died and was raised in order to free us from the guilt of our sins and to restore us to life. To explain how Jesus' death could take away sin, he uses the metaphor of Jesus grabbing our deed of debt (from Satan perhaps?) and canceling it when he joined it to his death by crucifixion. Since we were taken up by Christ in his death, we are joined with him when the Father raises him to life. Sin made us dead to God; it was taken away by the dying Jesus, and now we live with Jesus, the risen Christ.

LITURGICAL NOTES

The first reading, taken from the book of Genesis, is the story of Abraham bargaining with God over the fate of Sodom and Gomorrah. Abraham speaks to God as a friend, as someone with whom he has an intimate relationship. The gospel presents the story of the disciples asking the Lord to teach them to pray. The kind of relationship that Abraham has with God is desired by so many people. The request posed to the Lord, "teach us to pray," is posed today by people of all ages, from all walks of life.

They earnestly seek that intimate relationship with God that can only come through prayer.

Communal prayer can bring us beyond our own limits, beyond our own needs and concerns, and unite us with the larger prayer and concern of the whole Church. The *General Instruction of the Liturgy of the Hours* states:

Those who take part in the liturgy of the hours bring growth to God's people in a hidden but fruitful apostolate, for the work of the apostolate is directed toward this end, "that all

who are made children of God by faith and baptism should come together to praise God in the midst of this Church." (18)

After study and prayer, the liturgy committee might embark on the regular public celebration of one or more of the Hours. There is a caution here: if the committee judges success by mere numbers, the celebration of the Hours might not be considered successful. However, numbers should not be the issue; prayer should be the issue. And when the Church prays, people come; people will pray.

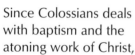

SCRIPTURE COMMENTARY

Luke places together several sayings of Jesus on the power of prayer. First he teaches the prayer we call the Our Father. At its heart is the presumption that we say it always and that hallowing God's name, seeking God's spiritual bread, and forgiving sins are daily activities of Jesus' followers. Luke complements this with the parable of the friend who will not take no for an answer. Persistence in seeking help from God will always win a hearing. In this, the lesson is similar to that of Abraham's petitions to God: in the matter of mercy and compassion, God always responds more than we could hope. No one who seeks and knocks at God's door with a request for a *good for another*, or for the gift of the Holy Spirit to aid us in *serving God better*, will be refused. But the examples of prayer here do not tell us how God would respond if we were to ask for more material goods for ourselves or seek honor or glory or even revenge against another.

Gospel: Luke 11:1–13

Jesus was praying in a certain place, and when he had finished, one of his disciples said to him, "Lord, teach us to pray just as John taught his disciples." He said to them, "When you pray, say:
> Father, hallowed be your name,
> your kingdom come.
> Give us each day our daily bread
> and forgive us our sins
> for we ourselves forgive everyone in debt to us,
> and do not subject us to the final test."

And he said to them, "Suppose one of you has a friend to whom he goes at midnight and says, 'Friend, lend me three loaves of bread, for a friend of mine has arrived at my house from a journey and I have nothing to offer him,' and he says in reply from within, 'Do not bother me; the door has already been locked and my children and I are already in bed. I cannot get up to give you anything.' I tell you, if he does not get up to give the visitor the loaves because of their friendship, he will get up to give him whatever he needs because of his persistence.

"And I tell you, ask and you will receive; seek and you will find; knock and the door will be opened to you. For everyone who asks, receives; and the one who seeks, finds; and to the one who knocks, the door will be opened. What father among you would hand his son a snake when he asks for a fish? Or hand him a scorpion when he asks for an egg? If you then, who are wicked, know how to give good gifts to your children, how much more will the Father in heaven give the Holy Spirit to those who ask him?"

MUSIC CONNECTION

Since Colossians deals with baptism and the atoning work of Christ, various Easter texts would be fitting today. These include *Alleluia, Sing to Jesus; Jesus Christ Is Risen Today;* and *This Is the Feast.* The story of Abraham bartering with God over the fate of Sodom and Gomorrah is matched with the Lucan version of the Lord's Prayer through notions of petition, perseverance in prayer, and God's benevolence and mercy toward his people. Hymns stressing these themes include *Hear Us, Almighty Lord; Amazing Grace; Surely It Is God Who Saves Me; Love Divine All Loves Excelling;* and *God Full of Mercy.* The classic Faber text *There's a Wideness in God's Mercy* well sums up the connection between God's prevenient mercy and our turning to God for forgiveness. Its reassuring melody *In Babilone* convincingly stresses that "there's a wideness in God's mercy like the wideness of the sea." This notion is reinforced in Psalm 138, which proclaims, "Lord, on the day I called for help, you answered me." Both the Lisicky and the Gelineau arrangements work well for this text. Since the Lucan text of the Lord's Prayer is embedded in the gospel, today would be a good day to chant this quintessential Christian prayer if you do not ordinarily do so.

First Reading:
Ecclesiastes 1:2; 2:21–23

Vanity of vanities, says Qoheleth, vanity of vanities! All things are vanity!

Here is one who has labored with wisdom and knowledge and skill, and yet to another who has not labored over it, he must leave property. This also is vanity and a great misfortune. For what profit comes to man from all the toil and anxiety of heart with which he has labored under the sun? All his days sorrow and grief are their occupation; even at night his mind is not at rest. This also is vanity.

SCRIPTURE COMMENTARY

The author of Qoheleth was heavily influenced by the Greek philosophical movements of the fifth and fourth centuries BC. Schools of Pythagoreans, Atomists, Aristotelians and others were interested in identifying the origins and structure of the physical world. They searched for the elemental building blocks of the universe, some identifying fire, air, water, and solids and others primeval atoms from which all things were made. They were very concerned with cause and effect, rational structures and purpose, and above all the ordered succession of things. Qoheleth is clearly aware of all these movements but is not himself interested in pursuing an abstract philosophical understanding of the world. He is more a *moral* philosopher, and he wishes to question Israel's similar traditions of certainties. He observes that the rules for the world do not work out predictably in human dealings. He states that all such speculation is vanity. If one assumes that hard work leads to prosperity and laziness leads to poverty, as the book of Proverbs does (e.g., Prov 6:6–11), it will not be proven in experience. Suffering is not the result of evil, nor is blessing a result of fidelity to God. In the end, Qoheleth will propose that all people should accept what God sends them and make the best of it instead of insisting that God has to act according to our certitudes.

HOMILY HELPS

A vintage Kaufmann and Hart comedy of decades ago was entitled "You Can't Take It with You." Actually the title contains a sobering thought, which is very much to the fore in today's scriptures. Jesus' parable, found only in Luke, speaks for itself and needs little or no explanation. In response to a person in the crowd, Jesus engagingly addresses the question of greed.

The central figure of the story has been blessed with such prosperity that he has had to enlarge his holdings to make provision for it. As he prepares to relax in his dotage and eat, drink, and be merry, sudden death ends his grandiose plans. He has no choice except to leave it all behind and move on. Those of us who have lived long enough have seen this scenario play itself out many times. There are those who are wealthy and do an immense amount of good through their philanthropy and benefactions. Others simply amass wealth and then have to face their final hours. The issue is not about being rich; it is what one does with riches. "Where your treasure is, there is your heart." It is all a question of values.

The gospel parable ends with a question. "The things you have prepared, to whom will they belong?" The answer to that question is found in the rather sardonic insight of Qoheleth in today's first reading. With a touch of cynicism, he states that the property amassed through a person's industry is left to someone who has contributed nothing to its acquisition. It still happens that many people are simply listed as heirs, and those who are left out will go to great lengths to effect their inclusion. The last

PSALM REFLECTION

In the spirit of Qoheleth, the psalmist sees life as fleeting and uncertain. We try to set limits and worry about how to shape the future, thinking that by careful planning we can control what happens. But God's thoughts are different from ours. He looks to the enduring obedience of all creation to his will and purpose. Our immediate goals and hopes for securing our world the way we want it pale in comparison to his plan. Indeed, the psalmist sees this completely, praying that God illuminate and straighten out our thoughts so that they conform to his will. The psalmist is also sure of how we will know God's will most fully: when we accept our limitations, our fragile existence as creatures, our sinfulness and failings, and turn in trust to God to support and sustain us with his compassion and kindness. The final verse of the psalm draws a firm conclusion: if we learn to rely on the mercy of God, then the gracious care of the Lord will be ours, and the work we do will prosper. There is no other plan that will succeed.

Psalm Response
Psalm 90:3–4, 5–6, 12–13, 14, 17

Antiphon
If today you hear his voice, harden not your hearts!

Verse for Reflection
Truly a thousand years in your sight
Seem like yesterday now that they are gone,
Or as a watch period of the night.
(v. 4)

chapter of a wealthy person's life is often the saddest, characterized by wrangling, animosity, and hostility.

And yet what does it all matter? Qoheleth calls it "vanity," a wisp of smoke, futility, and emptiness. Our values can easily be misplaced, especially in a world that is interested in competitiveness and human achievement. Yet Paul, in today's epistle, directs our attention elsewhere. If we now live in Christ, as the beneficiaries of his resurrection, then our gaze should follow his, to the things that are above, not those of the earth. The unseemly features of this passing world—

fornication, passion, and evil desires—really have no place. They are replaced by the things of God—justice, peace, compassion, and generosity.

Once the presumed heir of a wealthy merchant, the dying Francis of Assisi asked that he be placed naked on the ground. He then echoed the psalmist: "With my voice I have called to the Lord." Jesus reminds us today that if we truly live for God, we will be "rich in what matters to God." We pray that our gaze will be always directed to the things that are above. We want to "grow rich in the eyes of God," and everything else will be provided.

LITURGICAL NOTES

The scripture readings this Sunday invite us to look at what really matters. As the summer draws to a close, the liturgy committee could plan a day of prayer and reflection for its own members, asking this very question: What is really important?

The energy of many committees is seemingly boundless. In some parishes, there is no scrap of paper to be found in the vestibule, no dead leaf on a single plant. Every book is in place. Every intercession is crafted with care. Every schedule is mailed

**Second Reading:
Colossians 3:1–5, 9–11**

Brothers and sisters: If you were raised with Christ, seek what is above, where Christ is seated at the right hand of God. Think of what is above, not of what is on earth. For you have died, and your life is hidden with Christ in God. When Christ your life appears, then you too will appear with him in glory.

Put to death, then, the parts of you that are earthly: immorality, impurity, passion, evil desire, and the greed that is idolatry. Stop lying to one another, since you have taken off the old self with its practices and have put on the new self, which is being renewed, for knowledge, in the image of its creator. Here there is not Greek and Jew, circumcision and uncircumcision, barbarian, Scythian, slave, free; but Christ is all and in all.

SCRIPTURE COMMENTARY

In earlier chapters, Paul has led the Colossians through each stage of how they enjoy full union with the risen Christ as his body, both forgiven of sin and destined for everlasting life. If this is so, he says in today's continuation, then it must profoundly affect how we lead our lives as those who are in Christ. If the risen Lord now reigns with God in the full victory over the powers that rule this earthly world, namely, sin and death, then we too have been called to live for heavenly things instead of being enslaved to the powers of the flesh. If we hope to be raised to life with the Father like Jesus, then we must conform our lives to the life of Christ. This means being new persons who no longer allow passions and desires to drive our behavior, but seek to imitate Christ in all things. Even such fundamental characteristics as race or nationality are to be considered as nothing when we grow together as one in becoming God's image in Christ.

---

out well in advance. Every minister is given a copy of every bit of information pertaining to a particular liturgy. All of this is praiseworthy, but it is not enough.

In our attention to detail, we can easily lose sight of the bigger picture: we miss seeing the forest for the trees. The gospel tells us, "By their fruit you shall know them." Are all of our efforts, all of our attention to detail, helping to form people into the true image of the Church, the Body of Christ, God's holy people? We might be tempted to think of the "fruits" as phenomenal full, conscious, and active participation. Full, conscious, and active participation

certainly puts us on the right path, but it doesn't end there.

A wise old professor once asked his graduate students in liturgical studies to tell him what would make a "good liturgy." What would be so important that, if that particular element were present, you would just be able to touch the kingdom? The students, each depending on their particular bent, went through any number of answers: environment, singing, proclamation, ministries, preaching, and fellowship. Some rather heated debates ensued: was it the spoken word or the sung word? When all the students had

exhausted their arguments, the professor admitted that he had still not heard the correct answer. And so one brave student raised her hand and asked, "Then what is the answer?" The professor looked around, paused, and then began to speak. He said: "It is when the homeless are cared for, the naked clothed, the hungry fed, the prisoners visited, injustices rooted out."

As the liturgy committee looks ahead to another set of seasons of celebrating, preparing, recruiting, rehearsing, and evaluating, let the question "What is really important?" shape all their words and activities.

SCRIPTURE COMMENTARY

Luke emphasizes more than the other gospel writers that Jesus warned against desire for wealth among his disciples. He does not quote Jesus as saying, "Blessed are the poor in spirit," as does Matthew 5:3; he quotes him as saying, "Blessed are you poor, the kingdom of heaven is yours" (Luke 6:20). Luke adds a new saying to that, "Woe to you rich, for your consolation is now!" (Luke 6:24). Luke alone quotes the parable of Lazarus and the rich man in Luke 16:19–31. Today's short saying also occurs only in the Gospel of Luke. Jesus warns that human planning and certainties are not reliable because we cannot control the real circumstances of life and death. God gives us opportunity and blessing to be used wisely *now*, not to be stashed away to acquire even greater power and wealth. Like Qoheleth before him, Jesus strongly emphasizes that the action of God in our lives must be responded to in the present situation as God would wish us to act. True wealth is not goods and money that serve only this life, but our life with God that becomes everlasting life.

Gospel: Luke 12:13–21

Someone in the crowd said to Jesus, "Teacher, tell my brother to share the inheritance with me." He replied to him, "Friend, who appointed me as your judge and arbitrator?" Then he said to the crowd, "Take care to guard against all greed, for though one may be rich, one's life does not consist of possessions."

Then he told them a parable. "There was a rich man whose land produced a bountiful harvest. He asked himself, 'What shall I do, for I do not have space to store my harvest?' And he said, 'This is what I shall do: I shall tear down my barns and build larger ones. There I shall store all my grain and other goods and I shall say to myself, "Now as for you, you have so many good things stored up for many years, rest, eat, drink, be merry!"' But God said to him, 'You fool, this night your life will be demanded of you; and the things you have prepared, to whom will they belong?' Thus will it be for all who store up treasure for themselves but are not rich in what matters to God."

MUSIC CONNECTION

At first glance, the reading from Ecclesiastes seems problematic and a bit confusing. Some commentators have suggested that this message is meant to convey that all life, all success, all labor apart from God is vanity. Schutte's *If the Lord Does Not Build the House* and Hagan's *Unless the Lord* remind us that our labors need to be rooted in love of God, while Joncas's *The Love of the Lord*, based on the Philippians hymn, declares that all earthly gains and accomplishments fade in comparison to the love of the Lord. Luke reinforces this in the parable of the rich man with the good harvest. Jesus' punch line commenting on the death of the rich man says it all: "Thus it will be for all who store up treasure for themselves but are not rich in what matters to God." Hymns that acknowledge the primacy of God in our life—these tend to be hymns of praise—are most fitting. Examples include *Praise to Our God, Creation's Lord, All People That on Earth Do Dwell, Let Us Go to the Altar of God,* Tom Booth's rousing *Go Ye Out,* and Walker's *Great Is the Power We Proclaim.* Today's responsorial, Psalm 90, has numerous fine settings, including those of Gelineau, Alsott, and Johnson.

CATECHETICAL SUGGESTIONS

Overview of the book of Ecclesiastes
Development in the Old Testament of a belief in life after death
Beliefs about the end times
Multiculturalism in the Church and in our parish
Stewardship
Living wills

First Reading:
Wisdom 18:6–9

The night of the passover was
known beforehand to our
fathers,
that, with sure knowledge
of the oaths in which
they put their faith,
they might have courage.
Your people awaited the salvation of the just
and the destruction of their
foes.
For when you punished our
adversaries,
in this you glorified us
whom you had
summoned.
For in secret the holy children
of the good were offering
sacrifice
and putting into effect with
one accord the divine
institution.

SCRIPTURE COMMENTARY

Faithful readiness to answer the Lord in time of
danger is the theme of this Sunday's readings. In
the Old Testament, the great example of waiting
for the Lord and being ready to respond to his call is the
story of the Passover meal and exodus. The Israelites
girded themselves and prepared all the items for a journey.
They stood as they ate a roast lamb that symbolized the
type of meal taken in the field. The book of Wisdom is
largely an extended meditation on the miracle of the exodus and the nature of a God who showed his almighty
power in tenderness to such a small people. The author is
unknown, but he writes in the name of Solomon and his
wisdom to show that it is indeed wise and prudent to
know this God and worship him even in the midst of
pagan kingdoms that try to lure Jews to accept Greek religion. The book proposes as an example the Israelites of
old, a faithful, confident, ready, and even expectant people
who worshiped God even while their enemies sought to
destroy them, and as a result witnessed the destruction of
their foes instead, while offering the Passover to God in
true worship.

HOMILY HELPS

Tom lost his keys
and was looking for
them on the well-lit
street. Jack came along and
offered assistance in the search.
"Tom, where did you lose the
keys?" "Back by the house"
answered Tom. "Then, why are
you looking here?" "Because
there is more light here."

All too frequently, darkness is
man's nemesis. Many crimes are
committed at night because darkness lends itself to anonymity,
and the hours of sleep mean an
absence of vigilance. Like Tom,
most of us would rather work in
the light. The scriptures this Sunday have something to say on
the subject.

The deliverance of the
Hebrews from Egypt occurred in
the darkness of night. But it found
the Hebrews awake and attentive
as they celebrated the first
Passover. The brief reading from
the book of Wisdom today recalls
that awesome night. The people's
freedom would bring catastrophe
to their persecutors. But there
was light in that darkness, the
light of faith in God's promise.
The people who sat in darkness
had finally seen a great light.

In the gospel today, Jesus asks
vigilance of us. "Gird your loins
and light your lamps." Be vigilant
because you don't know when
the bridegroom will arrive home.
And what does vigilance mean?
The explanation of the parable
makes it very clear. Vigilance
means to keep busy looking after
the master's affairs. Indolence
will simply lead to dissipation
and all manner of carousing. As
the saying goes, "Idle hands are
the devil's workshop."

The vigilance shown by Abraham and Sarah was one of faith.
Despite the darkness of age and
incapacity, God's plan for a great
people would be fulfilled. That
faith was validated in the birth of
Isaac.

PSALM REFLECTION

This psalm was chosen because of verse 20, "Our soul waits for the Lord, who is our help and shield." It captures the expectant readiness of the exodus from the first reading and looks forward to Jesus' words on readiness in today's gospel. The psalm as a whole is in praise of God, who has always been faithful to his word to Israel. He alone has created all things, sees all things, and rules all things (vv. 6–15), and so all can have confidence that he looks down in kindness and protection on the people he has chosen and who in turn put their hope in him.

Psalm Response
Psalm 33:1, 12, 18–19, 20–22

Antiphon
Blessed the people the Lord has chosen
to be his own.

Verse for Reflection
Truly God looks favorably on those
who fear him,
On those who hope for his favor. (v. 18)

SCRIPTURE COMMENTARY

This Sunday we begin four weeks of readings from Hebrews 11–12. This section of the letter concentrates on the virtues necessary for Christian life: faith, perseverance, hope, and attentiveness to God's word. The selection for this first week focuses on the faith of Abraham, which made him obey God unquestioningly. Abraham had confidence in a promise that he would become the ancestor of a great nation, but most of the Genesis story of Abraham relates only to how he

Second Reading: Hebrews 11:1–2, 8–19
(or Hebrews 11:1–2, 8–12)

Brothers and sisters: Faith is the realization of what is hoped for and evidence of things not seen. Because of it the ancients were well attested.

By faith Abraham obeyed when he was called to go out to a place that he was to receive as an inheritance; he went out, not knowing where he was to go. By faith he sojourned in the promised land as in a foreign country, dwelling in tents with Isaac and Jacob, heirs of the same promise; for he was looking forward to the city with foundations, whose architect and maker is God. By faith he received power to generate, even though he was past the normal age—and Sarah herself was sterile—for he thought that the one who had

It is clear, then, that vigilance does not mean simply waiting for something to happen. It means continuing to go about the tasks of daily life, mastering the domestic virtues of kindness and consideration, being faithful to our responsibilities. It means not letting our guard down. If we put ourselves in compromising situations, we shall probably be compromised! Practically speaking, what might that mean? It means that I do not hold my finances so close to the vest that neither spouse nor confidant knows my transactions. When it comes to alcohol, I am careful about avoiding abuse. I take steps to avoid

places or situations where dalliance could lead to sexual misconduct.

Vigilance is not synonymous with a long-faced demeanor. There are many joys in life—family, friends, ball games, concerts, yes, even our jobs. Yet we are conscious of what it means to be baptized Christians, and we ask God's help daily to keep us mindful. With that type of vigilance, the Master, upon his arrival, will seat us at table and wait on us! As the psalmist says today: "May your kindness, O Lord, be upon us who have put our hope in you."

LITURGICAL NOTES

With images such as "await" and "prepare," one might think these scriptures would be more appropriately proclaimed toward the end of the church year. Not so, since we are always a Church that waits and prepares: we wait on the words our God will speak to us in our time, and we prepare our hearts and the hearts of others to receive these words.

But "prepare" also invites reflection on how we "get ready" for the celebration of the Eucharist. How do our ministers

made the promise was trustworthy. So it was that there came forth from one man, himself as good as dead, descendants as numerous as the stars in the sky and as countless as the sands on the seashore.

All these died in faith. They did not receive what had been promised but saw it and greeted it from afar and acknowledged themselves to be strangers and aliens on earth, for those who speak thus show that they are seeking a homeland. If they had been thinking of the land from which they had come, they would have had opportunity to return. But now they desire a better homeland, a heavenly one. Therefore, God is not ashamed to be called their God, for he has prepared a city for them.

By faith Abraham, when put to the test, offered up Isaac, and he who had received the promises was ready to offer his only son, of whom it was said, "Through Isaac descendants shall bear your name." He reasoned that God was able to raise even from the dead, and he received Isaac back as a symbol.

SCRIPTURE COMMENTARY, CONTINUED

got a single son to carry on his lineage. As the author points out, Abraham never saw the fulfillment of the promise but was steadfast in his trust anyhow. The author adds as a prime example of this complete faith the sacrifice of Isaac, which makes most moderns wonder how God could have commanded it and how any father could have obeyed it. The author to the Hebrews sees it as a prophetic sign of the death and resurrection of Jesus: even though he was ordered to kill his son Isaac, Abraham was confident that God would restore the boy to life, since he had promised that the future great nation would come through this son. In verse 1, the author defines that faith as hope and conviction about things we have not seen and concludes that fidelity to such hope leads to God's approval.

Gospel: Luke 12:32–48 (or Luke 12:35–40)

Jesus said to his disciples: "Do not be afraid any longer, little flock, for your Father is pleased to give you the kingdom. Sell your belongings and give alms. Provide money bags for yourselves that

SCRIPTURE COMMENTARY

In this series of sayings, Jesus teaches his followers the attitude they should have toward the future. But is he talking about the end of the world when Christ will come in glory to judge the living and the dead (as the Creed states it)? Matthew puts all of

prepare for the celebration of the Lord's paschal mystery?

All ministers should come to the celebration from their own prayer and their own prayerful reflection on this particular Sunday Eucharist. Ushers and ministers of hospitality should be reminded that they are preparing to meet Christ, who will come through the church doors in many a guise. Readers should be reminded that they are preparing to meet Christ, who will come to them in a word proclaimed by their lips: a word that needs to be proclaimed with clarity, with conviction, and with faith. Cantors and choir members should be reminded that they are preparing to meet Christ, who

will come to them in a word sung by their own voices as well as in a word sung by the gathered assembly. Extraordinary ministers of Holy Communion should be reminded that they are preparing to meet Christ, who will come to them under the appearance of bread and wine, as food and nourishment for their journey and for the journey of the world. They should be prepared to meet Christ in the eucharistic elements and in the faces of those who will form the Communion procession. Organists and other instrumentalists should be prepared to meet Christ as he comes in music without words, lifting our hearts and our minds to the promise of the

kingdom. They will also hear Christ's words in the song of the assembly. They need to be prepared through practice, that their notes might provide a fitting harmony for the Lord. Deacons should be reminded that they are preparing to meet Christ in the gospel proclaimed and also in the prayers for the suffering members of his Body. Presiders ought to be reminded that they are preparing to meet Christ when the Church gathers, in a word proclaimed, in a thoughtful and meaningful word preached, and in the Eucharist celebrated.

And all will then be prepared to meet Christ has he comes to us in the thousands of faces and thousands of places in our world.

SCRIPTURE COMMENTARY, CONTINUED

these sayings at the end of Jesus' ministry, when he is clearly talking about the return of the Son of Man in final victory But Luke separates these sayings from the end of Jesus' life and includes them among the general instructions on the proper behavior of disciples. The first piece of advice is to live in confidence and not fear—for their treasure is not subject to failure on earth. Is this a warning to be strong in time of persecution, to not lose faith in their heavenly goal? When joined to the next set of sayings about servants who are prepared for the master's unexpected return, it would seem that disciples must be ready for a coming crisis of great danger: not the master's returning after a long absence but the master's being taken and betrayed and crucified and then raised from the dead. Blessed are those who hold fast to faith through all this and are found ready to greet the risen Lord. Luke does not yet speak of the final end, for the next section, which is read next week, still speaks of conflicts with our families that result from serving the Lord.

do not wear out, an inexhaustible treasure in heaven that no thief can reach nor moth destroy. For where your treasure is, there also will your heart be.

"Gird your loins and light your lamps and be like servants who await their master's return from a wedding, ready to open immediately when he comes and knocks. Blessed are those servants whom the master finds vigilant on his arrival. Amen, I say to you, he will gird himself, have them recline at table, and proceed to wait on them. And should he come in the second or third watch and find them prepared in this way, blessed are those servants. Be sure of this: if the master of the house had known the hour when the thief was coming, he would not have let his house be broken into. You also must be prepared, for at an hour you do not expect, the Son of Man will come."

Then Peter said, "Lord, is this parable meant for us or for everyone?" And the Lord replied, "Who, then, is the faithful and prudent steward whom the master will put in charge of his servants to distribute the food allowance at the proper time? Blessed is that servant whom his master on arrival finds doing so. Truly, I say to you, the master will put the servant in charge of all his property. But if that servant says to himself, 'My master is delayed in coming,' and begins to beat the menservants and the maidservants, to eat and drink and get drunk, then that servant's master will come on an unexpected day and at an unknown hour and will punish the servant severely and assign him a place with the unfaithful. That servant who knew his master's will but did not make preparations nor act in accord with his will shall be beaten severely; and the servant who was ignorant of his master's will but acted in a way deserving of a severe beating shall be beaten only lightly. Much will be required of the person entrusted with much, and still more will be demanded of the person entrusted with more."

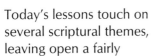

MUSIC CONNECTION

Today's lessons touch on several scriptural themes, leaving open a fairly wide musical playing field. Wisdom and Psalm 33 underline God's election and call, which led to the "salvation of the just and the destruction of their foes." Here consider such hymns as *O God, Our Help in Ages Past; How Firm a Foundation; How Can I Keep from Singing;* and *I Have Loved You.* Hebrews provides a scriptural excursus on faith—its meaning, its demands, its rewards. In this vein consider *We Walk by Faith; Faith of Our Fathers; Jesus, Lead the Way; Be Not Afraid; A Mighty Fortress; Set*

CATECHETICAL SUGGESTIONS

The book of Wisdom
Deuterocanonical books
The chosen people
Faith
The kingdom of God
What constitutes being ready for the coming of the Lord?

Your Hearts on Higher Gifts; and *There Is One Lord.* The gospel, colored with an Advent eschatological fervor, urges us to live our faith in eager anticipation of the Lord's return, since, "at the hour you do not expect, the Son of Man will come." In this mode

consider hymns such as *The King Shall Come, Soon and Very Soon, When He Comes, Somebody's Knockin' at My Door,* and *What Wondrous Love Is This.* Gelineau, Haugen, and Howard Hughes all have fine settings of the responsorial, Psalm 33.

ASSUMPTION OF THE BLESSED VIRGIN MARY

First Reading:
Revelation 11:19a; 12:1–6a, 10ab

God's temple in heaven was opened, and the ark of his covenant could be seen in the temple.

A great sign appeared in the sky, a woman clothed with the sun, with the moon beneath her feet, and on her head a crown of twelve stars. She was with child and wailed aloud in pain as she labored to give birth. Then another sign appeared in the sky; it was a huge red dragon, with seven heads and ten horns, and on its heads were seven diadems. Its tail swept away a third of the stars in the sky and hurled them down to the earth. Then the dragon stood before the woman about to give birth, to devour her child when she gave birth. She gave birth to a son, a male child, destined to rule all the nations with an iron rod. Her child was caught up to God and his throne. The woman herself fled into the desert where she had a place prepared by God.

Then I heard a loud voice in heaven say:
"Now have salvation and power come,
   and the Kingdom of our God
   and the authority of his Anointed One."

SCRIPTURE COMMENTARY

The Solemnity of the Assumption celebrates the fulfillment of Mary's role in salvation by her union with her son in his risen glory as she was united with him in his human journey. Jesus shared our human nature and the very physical genes and flesh of Mary while with us, but the greater role of his humanity is as the risen Lord who brings all humans over all millennia to reconciliation and immortal life with God as their destiny. If this is so, how much more should Mary be joined with the risen Lord. The New Testament, however, does not yet come to this insight. Instead, in passages such as Revelation 11, it uses the image of the mother and child to represent both Mary and her child and at the same time the whole Church in combat with Satan, who would attempt to defeat the mission of the son to save us by undermining our human ability to give up the power of sin over our lives and turn fully to God. But in today's reading God thwarts Satan's efforts to destroy the child by confirming his divine status and by protecting the Church in the desert of this world. Because John's vision sees the Church and Christ through the analogy of mother and son, we apply this same analogy to honor Mary as the mother to whom God will give special protection.

HOMILY HELPS

The poet speaks of Mary as "our tainted nature's solitary boast." Today's feast reminds us that Mary is now totally with God, body and soul. This ancient belief was solemnly declared an article of faith by Pius XII in 1950.

It is hard for us to do end-time thinking. While we believe that our future will be spent with God, what form that will take defies description. This has already transpired in the case of Christ, but even there our words fall short. Our first reading from Revelation speaks of the messiah's birth of the "woman," the figure of the faithful Israel. Christ, in the presence of the evil dragon, is then "snatched up to God and to his throne." This is what we ordinarily call the ascension.

In 1 Corinthians, we read that Christ has been awakened from his sleep and now stands ready to welcome us, his followers, to eternal life. Then Paul makes an interesting observation. The reign of Christ will eventually come to an end. At that point he will step aside and hand the kingdom back to the Father. Then God himself will permeate the whole created order.

Mary is the first creature to enter fully into life. She now makes our journey with us and guides us to our final goal. The gospel today highlights two important features of this guidance, charity and humility. Mary is a sterling example of concern and solicitude. Pregnant though she was, she made the journey to be with the elderly Elizabeth in her moment of need. It is not hard to make the application: The elderly person who needs our attention. The young woman about to give birth. The youth who suffers from depression, or a handicap, or Down's syndrome, or muscular dystrophy, or autism. All are common hardships of our time. They call us to inconvenience, personal presence, and a helping hand, to "visitation calls."

We are also faced with the central virtue of Mary's life—

PSALM REFLECTION

Psalm 45 is part of a series of visionary psalms attributed to the Sons of Korah (Pss 42–49). The psalm we read today celebrates the king who comes in honor from his military victories over his enemies to wed his queen in splendor. The imagery of the queen arrayed in the richest of clothes and jewelry signals God's blessings on the people. King and queen symbolize the whole people in harmony as they enjoy prosperity and blessing. It is a fitting responsorial for this feast day honoring the exaltation and coronation of Mary as the symbol of our human response to the salvation won by her son, the king.

Psalm Response
Psalm 45:10, 11, 12, 16

Antiphon
The queen stands at your right hand, arrayed in gold.

Verse for Reflection
All glorious is the king's daughter as she enters,
Her garments are as woven of golden thread! (v. 14)

SCRIPTURE COMMENTARY

Since the scriptures do not tell us when Mary died or where or even mention anything that would directly speak of her assumption, the Church uses texts that give us an analogy by which we can understand the meaning of the Church's faith that God intended the fulfillment of his plan for the redemption of humanity by giving a special place to the role of Mary. One such text is Paul's response in today's reading to questions about how the resurrection of the dead will occur. He suggests that God has an order he will follow: Christ first, then those who belong to him, then all others. If we take this a step further, then how fitting it is that Mary should be

Second Reading:
1 Corinthians 15:20–27

Brothers and sisters: Christ has been raised from the dead, the first-fruits of those who have fallen asleep. For since death came through man, the resurrection of the dead came also through man. For just as in Adam all die, so too in Christ shall all be brought to life, but each one in proper order: Christ the firstfruits; then, at his coming,

being humble enough to know that God is in charge. In the *Magnificat* we are told that all generations will call her blessed. And, indeed, her common title is Blessed Mother. But the line that follows these prophetic words has more than passing importance. "God who is mighty has done great things for me." How many worthwhile things might have occurred in our lives if we had let God take charge? And how many tragedies might have been avoided if we had been right with God?

The Psalms of Korah. Many scholars believe that the Psalms of Korah (Pss 42–49) were sung on New Year's Day. The feast was considered the annual remembrance of the day of coronation, and the ceremony was carried out exactly as it was done for the annual anniversary of the Davidic kings. Part of the coronation ritual was the renewal of the marriage ceremony of the king to his queen. Psalm 45 is a great love song of royalty, but it is really a song about God and his chosen people.

In the book of Tobit, Tobias decides to marry Sarah, even though she had buried seven husbands before they spent the first night together. But Tobias has a way of breaking this curse.

"Sarah, let's spend our first night in prayer." The message here is: if we put God first, things will be right.

This is a lesson that Mary teaches us as well.

those who belong to Christ; then comes the end, when he hands over the Kingdom to his God and Father, when he has destroyed every sovereignty and every authority and power. For he must reign until he has put all his enemies under his feet. The last enemy to be destroyed is death, for "he subjected everything under his feet."

SCRIPTURE COMMENTARY, CONTINUED

the first of those saved by Christ. As the mother of the one who saved us, she is at the very head of the line of faith. No disciple believed in her son before Mary did. This is a certainty of the Church's faith drawn from the annunciation story of Luke 1:26–38 and the visitation story of 1:39–56 (which is today's gospel). The key end point of Paul's thought is that all who are raised are brought to glory in heaven. Today's solemnity celebrates Mary's glorification as the first of her son's followers.

Gospel: Luke 1:39–56

Mary set out and traveled to the hill country in haste to a town of Judah, where she entered the house of Zechariah and greeted Elizabeth. When Elizabeth heard Mary's greeting, the infant leaped in her womb, and Elizabeth, filled with the Holy Spirit, cried out in a loud voice and said, "Blessed are you among women, and blessed is the fruit of your womb. And how does this happen to me, that the mother of my Lord should come to me? For at the moment the sound of your greeting reached my ears, the infant in my womb

SCRIPTURE COMMENTARY

For Luke, the scene of the visitation is an important middle point between the two scenes of annunciation to Zechariah of the birth of John the Baptist (1:5–25) and to Mary of the birth of Jesus (1:26–38), and the two scenes of their births, John in 1:57–80 and Jesus in 2:1–20. Luke has made the annunciation and birth of John parallel to that of Jesus to indicate strongly that the earlier mission of John and the fulfillment in the mission of Jesus were preordained in God's plan for salvation. Since John does not recognize Jesus at his baptism

LITURGICAL NOTES

This feast, celebrated since the fifth century, was defined as a dogma of the faith by Pius XII in 1950. Often referred to as the Dormition of Mary, this solemnity calls us to deeper devotion to Mary, a greater conviction of the value of human life devoted to God's will, and a strengthening of faith in our own resurrection.

The Lectionary and Sacramentary provide two sets of texts for this solemnity: one for the vigil Mass and the other for the Mass during the day. The vigil Mass tends to focus on Mary's participation in the victory of Christ over sin and death. The vigil Mass is presented for those places that will have an actual "vigil" in preparation for the celebration of the Solemnity of the Assumption. This is not the same as the anticipated Masses that can be celebrated the evening before the actual solemnity. If the Mass anticipates the solemnity, the readings and texts of the

solemnity ought to be used. The Mass during the day focuses on God's victory over evil and God's power at work in Mary.

Although it occurs during the week, this solemnity should be celebrated the same way Sunday is celebrated, and includes the Gloria and the Profession of Faith. It would be appropriate to place flowers in front of the image of Mary; she stands as Mother of the Church and as a sign of hope and comfort for us on our pilgrim journey.

SCRIPTURE COMMENTARY, CONTINUED

and later sends messengers to question who Jesus is (Luke 7:18), we should not take this scene as literal. Luke has brought the two mothers together to underline the divine nature of their destinies in God's plan. Both John and his mother, Elizabeth, respond to the Holy Spirit by recognizing the messiah from the womb, and in turn, Mary speaks the hopes of the Old Testament in her response to Elizabeth. Her words are largely based on the Song of Hannah in 1 Samuel 2. In form, it is very similar to the psalms, moving from personal thanksgiving to God for what he has done to the larger concerns of God's goodness to Israel and all humankind. It becomes a celebration of God's compassion in sending Jesus into the world for our salvation.

leaped for joy. Blessed are you who believed that what was spoken to you by the Lord would be fulfilled."

And Mary said:
"My soul proclaims the greatness of the Lord;
    my spirit rejoices in God my Savior
    for he has looked upon his lowly servant.
From this day all generations will call me blessed:
    the Almighty has done great things for me,
    and holy is his Name.
He has mercy on those who fear him
    in every generation.
He has shown the strength of his arm,
    and has scattered the proud in their conceit.
He has cast down the mighty from their thrones,
    and has lifted up the lowly.
He has filled the hungry with good things,
    and the rich he has sent away empty.
He has come to the help of his servant Israel
    for he has remembered his promise of mercy,
    the promise he made to our fathers,
    to Abraham and his children for ever."

Mary remained with her about three months and then returned to her home.

MUSIC CONNECTION

This solemnity is often overlooked and forgotten, falling as it does in the waning days of the North American summer. Nevertheless, its meaning and message are rich, stretching from the enigmatic "woman" in the book of Revelation to the oft-told story of Mary's visit to Elizabeth in the gospel of Luke and its centerpiece, the *Magnificat*. Alstott's setting of the responsorial psalm works well today, and David Haas's *Holy Is Your Name* from GIA is a good choice, too. Other Marian songs come to mind and include *Be Joyful, Mary; Hail Mary, Gentle Woman; Sing of Mary;* the Lourdes hymn, *Immaculate Mary;* and *Hail, Holy Queen.* On a feast of Mary such as this, one could sing the Litany of Loreto as an opening rite or conclude the service with the a cappella singing of the Gregorian *Ave Maria.* The latter has a timeless beauty and, once learned, can be a stalwart piece of your parish Marian repertoire.

CATECHETICAL SUGGESTIONS

Typology
The glorious mysteries of the Rosary
What makes Mary holy? What makes us holy?
The use of symbols in the book of Revelation
Our belief in the resurrection of the body
Mary as the preeminent disciple

First Reading: Jeremiah 38:4–6, 8–10

In those days, the princes said to the king: "Jeremiah ought to be put to death; he is demoralizing the soldiers who are left in this city, and all the people, by speaking such things to them; he is not interested in the welfare of our people, but in their ruin." King Zedekiah answered: "He is in your power"; for the king could do nothing with them. And so they took Jeremiah and threw him into the cistern of Prince Malchiah, which was in the quarters of the guard, letting him down with ropes. There was no water in the cistern, only mud, and Jeremiah sank into the mud.

Ebed-melech, a court official, went there from the palace and said to him: "My lord king, these men have been at fault in all they have done to the prophet Jeremiah, casting him into the cistern. He will die of famine on the spot, for there is no more food in the city." Then the king ordered Ebed-melech the Cushite to take three men along with him, and draw the prophet Jeremiah out of the cistern before he should die.

SCRIPTURE COMMENTARY

Jeremiah is the one prophet who, more than any other, suffered for the sake of the message that he carried. No matter how much he tried to soften the word or avoid condemning the people, God continued to press him to speak out warnings to the people before it was too late and the Babylonians destroyed the entire country. Jeremiah was treated with contempt by the political leaders who were intent on winning freedom from the power of Babylon. The king, Zedekiah, was weak and went back and forth in support of the princes and then in support of Jeremiah, so that in the end, while he was willing to save Jeremiah's life from the princes' hands, he went along with their plans for war. Jeremiah had failed in making God's word change Judah's mind, but the prophet was not to be killed by his enemies. King Zedekiah was worried that Jeremiah's word might come true, and he wanted to protect himself, just in case. He would go on consulting Jeremiah as the crisis deepened. And Jeremiah would live on to see all that he predicted come true, and yet he would still not be respected by the survivors! Truly he is the model for the gospel portrait of Jesus as the Suffering Servant, who gave himself for others without winning their hearts.

HOMILY HELPS

An unfortunate or unhealthy situation is often said to create a morale problem. This is precisely what Jeremiah is said to have created in today's first reading. His message of eventual doom had created a problem of morale. Yet morale remains always a bit elusive and at times is hard to discover. In 2001, after September 11, it was commonly said that morale was low among the New York clergy, with the attack on the twin towers and the clergy abuse scandal coming in rapid succession. But the clergy was so involved in bringing strength and solace to many who had lost loved ones that their own grief was submerged.

Still, one can truly wonder about the morale of Jeremiah and Jesus. The former was left in a dark and muddy cistern solely because he had spoken God's warning. In today's reading from Hebrews, Jesus is said to have endured the cross in the light of a greater good. As is ever the case in the Christian life, there is light at the end of the tunnel, a promise to be realized. But the present hardship always remains. Our morale is deeply affected by present circumstances. And to walk with Christ through his passion and to hear his cry of abandonment from the cross is to grasp what low morale must mean.

In today's gospel, Jesus calls for the burning light of faith to blaze forth. His is not a laissez-faire type of belief or the faith of the "comfortable pew." His is a faith that stirs things up and has unexpected consequences.

There is a seeming contradiction here. Jesus claims that he comes not for peace but for division. Yet elsewhere in the gospel, he is the prince of peace, who on Easter night confers his peace on the disciples. How can these two positions be reconciled? The answer is to be found in consequences, not intention. In the act of accepting Jesus, many people found themselves at odds with others, even family members. To accept Christ often meant rejection by one's own family. It happened in the early Church and it

PSALM REFLECTION

Psalm 40 is very unusual in its development. Typically, psalms begin with a complaint of despair and a petition to God for help; then they give thanks to God for his divine salvation and follow that with the promise to praise him all days to come. But Psalm 40 reverses this order. It begins with thanksgiving to God for having saved the psalmist's life. The psalmist had considered himself among those without hope, yet God paid attention to him when he put his trust in God ("I have waited, waited for the Lord"—v. 2). But our final verse (v. 18) is taken from the end of the psalm, which reports the psalmist still begging for divine assistance. Note the closing line: "Hold not back." By thanking God for his saving acts to the afflicted and then repeating the need for his help, the psalm becomes a powerful voice asserting that God is always there to answer our prayers.

Psalm Response
Psalm 40:2, 3, 4, 18

Antiphon
Lord, come to my
    aid!

Verse for Reflection
Let all be made
    ashamed and
    confounded
Who seek to take
    away my life!
    (v. 15)

CATECHETICAL SUGGESTIONS

The life and times of Jeremiah the prophet
The communion of saints
The Eucharistic Prayer
The cross: scandal and victory
Jesus' use of irony in Luke's gospel
The meaning of our professing that the Church is *one*

---

happens today. Christ desired peace, but a faith on fire often leads to division.

What does a convinced Christian do when family members turn their back on moral values? A young person decides to become a Christian and finds himself at odds with family members. A person pursues a dedicated Christian life, but her family offers no understanding or support. There can be very strong family reactions to one member's embrace of the faith. Then comes the realization that the following of Christ is not a

laid-back pursuit. It can and does produce division. Nevertheless, we must always strive for peace, understanding, and forgiveness. There are many virtues, says Paul, but the greatest is love.

Religious problems today are multiple. They come at us from various directions—the world at large, civil government, at times the Church itself. They can produce uncomfortable results and affect morale. The best solution is given us in our reading from Hebrews today: let us keep our eyes fixed on Jesus.

LITURGICAL NOTES

In our first reading we hear that the prophet Jeremiah must be put to death because he is steadfast in his mission from God. Jesus announces that he has come not for peace but for division. The disciple must be steadfast in following the Lord. The letter to the Hebrews reminds us that in spite of any burden or obstacle, we must "keep our eyes fixed on Jesus."

**Second Reading:
Hebrews 12:1–4**

Brothers and sisters: Since we are surrounded by so great a cloud of witnesses, let us rid ourselves of every burden and sin that clings to us and persevere in running the race that lies before us while keeping our eyes fixed on Jesus, the leader and perfecter of faith. For the sake of the joy that lay before him he endured the cross, despising its shame, and has taken his seat at the right of the throne of God. Consider how he endured such opposition from sinners, in order that you may not grow weary and lose heart. In your struggle against sin you have not yet resisted to the point of shedding blood.

SCRIPTURE COMMENTARY

Hebrews was not written by St. Paul. And yet, in this selection, the author highlights the major theme that Paul always preached: Jesus accepted the cross for our sins even though he was innocent, and as a result God raised him from the dead and enthroned him in divine power in heaven at God's right hand. This last expression, of course, means not a literal scene of two thrones side by side but that Jesus was restored to the fullness of his divine status in order to share that power with us because he had become human like ourselves. The "cloud of witnesses" in the first line refers to all the great heroes of the Old Testament, such as Abraham, about whom we read in last Sunday's selection. The author thus argues that the ancient saints showed us the example of a faith that persevered despite difficulties. Jesus did even more by dying on the cross for us, and so now we should have the courage learned from them to persevere ourselves. Suffering does not destroy our union with God; it only strengthens it.

For the liturgy committee or planning team, these scriptures provide an opportunity for reflection on goals. Frequently goals are set around the minutiae, around those little things that are easily taken care of, easily controlled. But such goal setting misses the bigger picture: celebrating the liturgy of the Church with God's holy people that we might become God's holy people; working toward the full, conscious, and active participation of the entire assembly in the liturgical action. This is the goal of the liturgical reform; this is the goal of the liturgy itself. While it is not an impossible goal, it is certainly not a goal that will be achieved in a year or two. It is not a goal that will be achieved by the mere renovation of the worship space or the addition of a new participation aid. And if we think that any such external changes will, in and of themselves, accomplish the goals of the liturgical renewal, we are bound to be disappointed.

The goals will be achieved maybe in a lifetime, maybe in several lifetimes. The present task is to labor toward the fulfillment of those goals. How do we labor? We labor through prayer, through celebration, through catechesis, through reflection on our celebrating, through listening, through studying, and then through more praying. Ultimately the goals of the liturgical reform are achieved by ensuring that we, together with all the baptized, "keep our eyes fixed on Jesus."

SCRIPTURE COMMENTARY

Jesus' use of fire for judgment reflects a common Old Testament image that God tests the people in the fire of the smelter, burning out all that is impure to leave only fine ore (see Isa 43:2; Pss 66:12; 69:2–3). Usually this metaphor means that God will punish the people through the attacks of their enemies or through natural disasters until the wicked are rooted out and the remnant faithful to God is left. But God may also test the good with trials and sufferings as the wicked seem to be triumphant, until God comes to defeat evil. The prophets and psalms never speak of "baptizing" anyone, however, in fire; in this, Jesus echoes the words of John the Baptist in Luke 3:16, "He [the messiah] will baptize you with the Holy Spirit and fire." Jesus is fully aware that he himself will be the one who must suffer the baptism of fire through rejection by some of his own people's religious leaders. Moreover, all who believe in him will also be tested in the time of persecution. To follow Jesus does not mean peace and security but constant opposition, even from within our families. Jesus knows that the victory against Satan cannot be won until he has undergone the ultimate baptism by fire, his cross, and he is more than willing to face it.

Gospel: Luke 12:49–53

Jesus said to his disciples: "I have come to set the earth on fire, and how I wish it were already blazing! There is a baptism with which I must be baptized, and how great is my anguish until it is accomplished! Do you think that I have come to establish peace on the earth? No, I tell you, but rather division. From now on a household of five will be divided, three against two and two against three; a father will be divided against his son and a son against his father, a mother against her daughter and a daughter against her mother, a mother-in-law against her daughter-in-law and a daughter-in-law against her mother-in-law."

MUSIC CONNECTION

Today's readings speak of the suffering and struggle we must face as followers of God's word. Jeremiah's rejection is an anticipation of Jesus' own rejection at the hands of some of his contemporaries while the reading from Hebrews exhorts us to face the struggle with patience and perseverance. The domestic divisions described in Luke's pericope remind us that we may face the costs of discipleship close to home as well as far away. Various hymns come to mind, including *Be Not Afraid, Unless a Grain of Wheat, As Grains of Wheat, The Church's One Foundation, Many and Great, On Eagle's Wings, Blest Be the Lord,* and *Go to the World.* The Quaker hymn *How Can I Keep From Singing* is a reassuring message to all who endure hardship, rejection, and pain in the cause of discipleship. "No storm can shake my inmost calm while to that rock I'm clinging. Since Love is Lord of heaven and earth, how can I keep from singing?" Another reassuring and consoling hymn is Lillian Bouknight's arrangement of Psalm 27, *The Lord Is My Light.* For today's responsorial, Psalm 40, a cry for God's help in time of trial, look to settings by Savoy, Gelineau, and Alstott.

First Reading: Isaiah 66:18–21

Thus says the LORD: I know their works and their thoughts, and I come to gather nations of every language; they shall come and see my glory. I will set a sign among them; from them I will send fugitives to the nations: to Tarshish, Put and Lud, Mosoch, Tubal and Javan, to the distant coastlands that have never heard of my fame, or seen my glory; and they shall proclaim my glory among the nations. They shall bring all your brothers and sisters from all the nations as an offering to the LORD, on horses and in chariots, in carts, upon mules and dromedaries, to Jerusalem, my holy mountain, says the LORD, just as the Israelites bring their offering to the house of the LORD in clean vessels. Some of these I will take as priests and Levites, says the LORD.

SCRIPTURE COMMENTARY

The book of Isaiah focuses particularly on the God of salvation who dwells in Jerusalem and will judge sinners to exclude them but protect the city if it is faithful to God and just in its behavior. Yet all through this message directed to the Judah of the eighth century BC, the theme of universal salvation regularly emerges. Isaiah 2:1–5 sets at the beginning of the book the theme statement that all nations will come to walk in the light of the Lord and that God's teaching will go forth from Zion to the ends of the earth, leading nations to seek a world of peace together. Here, in the final chapter of the book, the theme is sounded again as a summary of Isaiah's message: God will indeed draw all nations to the new Jerusalem and even include pagans among those who are able to become priests and Levites—something totally forbidden by the law. Isaiah 66:18–21 matches Isaiah 2:1–5 to form bookends of his vision: the beginning and the end of a revolutionary vision.

HOMILY HELPS

The Protestant theologian Dietrich Bonhoeffer once claimed: "When Christ calls a man, he bids him come and die." This was realized literally in his own case, since he died in a Nazi concentration camp in 1945, shortly before the liberation of Germany at the end of World War II. At the heart of his statement is the fact that Christianity is not an easy road. It is not sufficient to say "Lord, Lord."

There is a paradox in our readings today. They speak of both the broad expanse of Christian acceptance and the attentiveness needed to stay the course. Both Isaiah and the Lucan Jesus speak of the universal character of the faith. Isaiah sees converts to Judaism coming from distant lands. But even more than that, they themselves will become proclaimers of the one God in distant parts of the world. The path to Jerusalem, so sacred and segregated in times past, will be filled with an "unwashed" crowd, on various forms of transport, making their way to the holy mountain. This vision of people from east and west flocking to the reign of God was in fact realized. Within the first century after Christ, Christianity had become a largely Gentile faith.

But caution is advised. Today's gospel also speaks of the dangers of laxity and indifference. No one has the right to feel that he or she has it made. In employing the literary figures of the narrow entrance and the closed door, Jesus clearly advises us to take heed. The narrow entrance warns us against laxity and indifference. There can be no question of taking things for granted. Paul reminds us that we have been bought at a great price. We should be aware of the rocks over which we may stumble— worldly entrapment, human

PSALM REFLECTION

This is the entire Psalm 117. It is a pure hymn of praise of God in the classic two-line format: A:A′ + B:B′, with each line having matched elements within its two halves:

Praise	+	all nations	+	the Lord
Glorify	+	all peoples		

Steadfast	+	kindness to us		
Endures forever	+	fidelity	+	the Lord

Note that the name of the Lord is found only in the opening and closing lines in order to highlight its presence.

Psalm Response
Psalm 117:1, 2

Antiphon
Go out to all the world and
tell the Good News.
Or: Alleluia.

Verse for Reflection
Ever loyal is his kindness
toward us,
And the Lord's faithful-
ness endures forever.
(v. 2)

CATECHETICAL SUGGESTIONS

The meaning of our professing that the Church is *Catholic*
Israel after the exile
Missionary orders
Parish covenant relationships across nations
The Spiritual Exercises of St. Ignatius
The kingdom of God: present and future

---

weakness, a sleepy carelessness. The proper response is alertness and caution.

The closed door teaches us not to dally along the way, not to adopt an attitude of "I'll get it straightened out eventually." We all know of the "Catholic but don't practice," the "there is no other religion for me, even though I don't practice" frame of mind. Baptism is not synonymous with free admission, as is

evident in the parable about the man who was turned away from the wedding feast because he wasn't dressed for the occasion. We want to wear our garment with honor. Our baptismal commitment has to reflect itself in our conduct.

After hip or knee replacement, we don't run a marathon. Hebrews today speaks of the remedy. The trials of everyday life can strengthen us in the

Spirit. With proper rehabilitation, our weakened limbs will be healed. There will be no need to approach the kingdom with "droopy hands" or "weak knees."

Yes, there is room for everyone in this kingdom of ours, in this household of the faith we profess. No one is to be demeaned or deemed of lesser worth. But once we are included, there is still a race to be run toward the imperishable crown.

Second Reading:
Hebrews 12:5–7, 11–13

Brothers and sisters, You have forgotten the exhortation addressed to you as children:
"My son, do not disdain the discipline of the Lord
or lose heart when reproved by him;
for whom the Lord loves, he disciplines;
he scourges every son he acknowledges."
Endure your trials as "discipline"; God treats you as sons. For what "son" is there whom his father does not discipline? At the time, all discipline seems a cause not for joy but for pain, yet later it brings the peaceful fruit of righteousness to those who are trained by it.

So strengthen your drooping hands and your weak knees. Make straight paths for your feet, that what is lame may not be disjointed but healed.

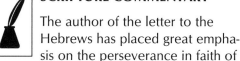

SCRIPTURE COMMENTARY

The author of the letter to the Hebrews has placed great emphasis on the perseverance in faith of the heroes of the Old Testament despite disappointments and trials and on how God fulfilled the promises made to them in the end, often at a much later time. He then urges his hearers to keep in mind the example of Jesus above all, for he endured even the cross in order to bring about the joyful achievement of our salvation. We ourselves must learn to accept trials and sufferings as Jesus did, and as the great ones of the Old Testament did, in order to be united to Christ. He proposes that his community view whatever sufferings they undergo as though it were discipline administered by a parent or teacher. It is painful for the present but later proves a very valuable lesson for life. Part of the writer's purpose, apparently, is to keep people from despair over persecution and give them enough courage to continue to live out their faith energetically.

LITURGICAL NOTES

The gospel appointed for this Sunday poses a difficult question: Who will be saved? Put another way, "Who will have a place at the table?" There are many Sundays where we are quite confident that our place is already reserved. But this reading gives us pause.

Those engaged in the work of preparing the liturgy, and even those who minister during the liturgy, can lose sight of just why they labor in this mission. There is often a tendency after the celebration of the liturgy to point out to the Almighty how lucky God is that we were here to do all these things that made the Almighty look so good. It may sound absurd, but over and over again people have made remarks that would make a person think that the success of the committee or planning team was the end result of the celebration of the liturgy.

The gospel also invites reflection on the way we welcome and treat those who do not appear like the other guests seated at the table: those whose language or color is different; those whose economic base is far below or far above the rest; those whose family structure is not like ours. It sometimes seems that the very people who think they are guaranteed a place at the table do, in fact, find the most welcome place at the table.

This Sunday invites us to check our focus and, if need be, to refocus on what is essential, on what is truly important.

SCRIPTURE COMMENTARY

Jesus regularly offered sayings that used paradox or reversal of fortune as their main point. The questioner wants to know if only a few can be saved. Jesus answers in such a way that it is certain that many—not just a few—will be invited to enter. But he also says that they will not come in as a crowd or be able to call on favors to pass inspection. No, each will have to manage to get through a narrow door and each will be given a test. The test is whether they know the master and the master knows them. There were certain Jews who believed that only they would be saved because of their special relationship to God as the chosen people. Jesus, like Isaiah in today's first reading, makes clear that people from pagan nations across the world will believe and find their way through the door of the kingdom. Jesus' inclusion of all people in the invitation to share in God's salvation is a key point in all his preaching.

Gospel: Luke 13:22–30

Jesus passed through towns and villages, teaching as he went and making his way to Jerusalem. Someone asked him, "Lord, will only a few people be saved?" He answered them, "Strive to enter through the narrow gate, for many, I tell you, will attempt to enter but will not be strong enough. After the master of the house has arisen and locked the door, then will you stand outside knocking and saying, 'Lord, open the door for us.' He will say to you in reply, 'I do not know where you are from.' And you will say, 'We ate and drank in your company and you taught in our streets.' Then he will say to you, 'I do not know where you are from. Depart from me, all you evildoers!' And there will be wailing and grinding of teeth when you see Abraham, Isaac, and Jacob and all the prophets in the kingdom of God and you yourselves cast out. And people will come from the east and the west and from the north and the south and will recline at table in the kingdom of God. For behold, some are last who will be first, and some are first who will be last."

MUSIC CONNECTION

Both Isaiah and Luke portray the universalism characteristic of God's saving activity. It is transnational, as noted by Isaiah: "I come to gather nations of every language; they shall come and see my glory." In the words of Luke, God's will to save extends to the powerless as well as the powerful: "Some are last who will be first and some are first who will be last." *There's a Wideness in God's Mercy* would make a wonderful opening song for today's liturgy. The principal metaphor for this universal inclusion is the heavenly banquet of which our Eucharist is a foretaste, and various hymns develop this connection. They include *Table of Plenty; In Christ There Is a Table Set for All; Come to the Feast; Praise the Lord, My Soul; This Bread That We Share; Gather Us In; All Are Welcome;* and *Shepherd Me, O God.* Ruth Duck's hymn *Diverse in Culture, Nation, Race* captures much of the meaning of today's lessons, that it is God who invites and extends mercy and healing to whomever God wills. Psalm 117 encapsulates that universality in its refrain: "Go out to all the world and tell the good news." Settings by Gelineau, Hruby, and Alstott are all workable.

First Reading:
Sirach 3:17–18, 20, 28–29

My child, conduct your
  affairs with humility,
  and you will be loved
    more than a giver of
    gifts.
Humble yourself the more,
  the greater you are,
  and you will find favor
  with God.
What is too sublime for you,
  seek not,
  into things beyond your
  strength search not.
The mind of a sage appreci-
  ates proverbs,
  and an attentive ear is the
  joy of the wise.
Water quenches a flaming
  fire,
  and alms atone for sins.

SCRIPTURE COMMENTARY

Sirach was a professional wisdom teacher in Jerusalem who lived in the second century BC. He prepared young men for careers as civil scribes or administrators and as teachers of the law. Throughout his book he stresses the value of life as a sage. Such a person has understanding and wisdom beyond the ordinary, and this could lead to pride and arrogance. But for Sirach, the true character of a wisdom teacher is humility. Not only does it not befit teachers to act superior to others; they should not inflate what they do know. True humility respects the learning ability and talents of other people and at the same time recognizes how little the sage himself really knows. Socrates' famous saying about the wise man could have also been spoken by Sirach: "The truly wise man knows what he does not know."

HOMILY HELPS

Place cards at a banquet help to avoid embarrassing situations such as that envisioned in today's gospel. But even without place cards, it is hard for us to imagine people advancing themselves to places of prominence without first being invited to do so. We must remember that to press a Semitic parable along literal lines is to miss the whole point. Today's gospel centers wholly on one of Christianity's most important virtues, that of humility.

There are two insights presented in today's gospel. One deals with our willingness to be in the last place. In the parable, the willingness of the guest to take the last place is wholly commendable, and that guest strongly merits advancement— determined by the host, not the guest! The second insight has to do with opening our hearts to those who, through no fault of their own, find themselves in the last place. Jesus' final words to the host speak of the importance of entertaining people of little or no status, the poor and the handicapped.

It is clear that the gospel is dealing not with questions of etiquette but with something much more profound. We have many examples of people who strive for advancement at any cost. It is sufficient to note the corruption that is present in government and business. Personal advancement takes precedence over all else, with the easy elimination of moral concerns. Climbing the

PSALM REFLECTION

Psalm 68 is not *exactly* about humility. It is about God's concern for the lowly and needy. It praises God for his care of those who are overlooked and forgotten: widows, orphans, the abandoned, and prisoners. God is a father to them all when no one else cares. God gives blessing to the earth when he pours forth his rain and restores prosperity to the land. In caring for the needs of nature, he also provides for the poor who need to live off the produce of the land. The psalm is directed to a society in which the ordinary person farmed for a living and starvation followed bad harvests or times of drought. Just as God returns with his rains after times of trouble, so God will come back to help those of the human family who are in need. We should stand in awe before such goodness. The humility of the psalm is before the goodness of God.

Psalm Response
Psalm 68:4–5, 6–7, 10–11

Antiphon
God, in your goodness, you
have made a home for
the poor.

Verse for Reflection
God makes a home for the
rejected,
And frees prisoners that they
might prosper. (v. 7)

CATECHETICAL SUGGESTIONS

Overview of the book of Sirach
Deuterocanonical books
The preferential option for the poor
Dorothy Day and the Catholic Worker Movement
Comparison in the letter to the Hebrews between the Old Testament
covenant and the New Testament covenant
Humility: What is it? Who models it?

ladder to success involves disdaining and demeaning competitors. It is also a feature of ambition within the Church that regrettably is not that uncommon.

There is something about being in the company of the rich and the powerful that affects many of us. It is not often that we open our doors to immigrants, day workers, or people for whom life is one long struggle. The gospels teach us that the dignity of the human person transcends social categories and draws us to be open to all people, especially the less fortunate.

There are human problems with aiming too high, which Sirach alludes to today. It may well happen that we find ourselves in over our heads. We all have certain gifts that we recognize and are grateful for, while acknowledging that our worth arises from the goodness of God. As Romans states, we have become God's friends not because we were worthy but because we were unworthy.

The antithesis of humility is pride, an expression of which is jealousy; the "green-eyed monster" always sees the good fortune of another as a threat. The only solution is to bring the other person down. This is not a question of *feeling* jealous; feelings have no moral consequences. It is what we do with our feelings—strong dislike, unkind criticism,

feeding on gossip. William Sloane Coffin writes: "Envy is the only one of the seven deadly sins that has no gratification at all. Lust and gluttony can claim some immediate gratification. But not envy. Yet that sin which can offer only endless self-torment can hold us faster than any other."

Humility is the honest awareness of who we are. We have our strengths and our weaknesses. We can easily exaggerate our strengths. And we can also glory in our weaknesses. Our weakness relies on God's strength, the God who can make great out of nothing. We are grateful for our gifts. We walk the sorry path of self-deception if we want to become what we are not.

Second Reading:
Hebrews 12:18–19, 22–24a

Brothers and sisters: You have not approached that which could be touched and a blazing fire and gloomy darkness and storm and a trumpet blast and a voice speaking words such that those who heard begged that no message be further addressed to them. No, you have approached Mount Zion and the city of the living God, the heavenly Jerusalem, and countless angels in festal gathering, and the assembly of the firstborn enrolled in heaven, and God the judge of all, and the spirits of the just made perfect, and Jesus, the mediator of a new covenant, and the sprinkled blood that speaks more eloquently than that of Abel.

SCRIPTURE COMMENTARY

This is the last of the four readings from Hebrews 11 and 12 that we have heard over the last four Sundays. The author is concluding his lengthy argument on how we need to persist in faith as did people of faith in the Old Testament and accept suffering now while persisting in the hope of obtaining God's life won by Jesus' enduring the suffering of the cross for us. God allows us to experience suffering in order to strengthen us as a father disciplines his children in order to make them stronger adults. But the author wants us to understand that this experience of God is different from the experience of hearing the voice of God on Mount Sinai. He portrays the meeting with God in Exodus 19 as awesome, with the Lord threatening judgment for people's sins in such a way that they were afraid to hear the voice of God a second time. But we encounter God in Christ and in his body, the saints of the Church. We encounter a God who thus allows us to know him intimately in his Son.

LITURGICAL NOTES

The scriptures invite us to embrace humility. It is a humility that is about not only what seat we take at the table but also our consciousness of whom we would invite to the table. We are to invite those who least expect an invitation. A humble heart has room to welcome all.

It has been said that liturgical ministers ought to model for the entire assembly the kind of behavior we ought to have. This does not mean only the kind of behavior in which we engage at the liturgy—full, conscious, and active participation. It also means the kind of behavior the follow-ers of Christ ought to have in the world. When people look at us, do they see lives consonant with what we celebrate in the liturgy?

Liturgical ministers should exercise their ministries not only with accuracy and care, knowledge and dignity, but also with the holiness that befits the sons and daughters of God. How is that lived within the liturgical assembly? Within the world?

The liturgical action is not an activity in which we find ourselves immersed for a hour each week apart from the rest of our lives but rather an activity that gives meaning and depth to the whole of our lives. It is because of the word proclaimed and the Eucharist celebrated that we can go out into the world to permeate it with the Spirit of Christ. Through our words, our acts of charity, our service to the poor, we begin to live the Eucharist we have celebrated. Because we fail, we neglect opportunities, and we sin, we are drawn back to our eucharistic gathering to once again remember the saving activity of God for us in Christ and to be refreshed and renewed to continue building God's reign.

This weekend is Labor Day weekend. Some people may be away; visitors might abound. Care should be taken that there are adequate liturgical ministers at each liturgy. The General Intercessions should include mention of all those who labor.

SCRIPTURE COMMENTARY

The reading in Luke 14:1-14 begins with Jesus curing a man of dropsy. This man has come to the table while Jesus is eating with Pharisees on the Sabbath. The Pharisees object to curing the man because it involves working on the Sabbath. But Jesus asks if any of them would lift his ox or ass out of a ditch on the Sabbath rather than let it die—and then goes on to ask why they would not be more concerned with healing a human being. It is this attitude of the Pharisees that leads Jesus to tell the parable we hear today. At a party, one who claims the best seat may be humiliated when asked to leave it open for another, while one who takes the lowest seat will often be honored when asked to come nearer to the host. It is a metaphor for the spiritual life—one does not obey God for honors and glory but humbly does only what he or she should, and God will take care of the rewards. Moreover, Pharisees were notorious for eating only with other Pharisees who were strict in keeping all the rules of purity. So Jesus adds a message to the host for all of them to hear: if all you care about is the satisfaction of being so elite, that is all you will get; if you were more generous and welcoming to all people, you would have a seat at the eternal banquet of heaven instead of just at your own party.

Gospel: Luke 14:1, 7–14

On a sabbath Jesus went to dine at the home of one of the leading Pharisees, and the people there were observing him carefully.

He told a parable to those who had been invited, noticing how they were choosing the places of honor at the table. "When you are invited by someone to a wedding banquet, do not recline at table in the place of honor. A more distinguished guest than you may have been invited by him, and the host who invited both of you may approach you and say, 'Give your place to this man,' and then you would proceed with embarrassment to take the lowest place. Rather, when you are invited, go and take the lowest place so that when the host comes to you he may say, 'My friend, move up to a higher position.' Then you will enjoy the esteem of your companions at the table. For every one who exalts himself will be humbled, but the one who humbles himself will be exalted." Then he said to the host who invited him, "When you hold a lunch or a dinner, do not invite your friends or your brothers or your relatives or your wealthy neighbors, in case they may invite you back and you have repayment. Rather, when you hold a banquet, invite the poor, the crippled, the lame, the blind; blessed indeed will you be because of their inability to repay you. For you will be repaid at the resurrection of the righteous."

MUSIC CONNECTION

Sirach and Luke both address humility, a virtue at the heart of today's readings. For the former it means "Humble yourself the more, the greater you are..." For the latter the meaning is encapsulated in the pithy saying "For everyone who exalts himself shall be humbled and he who humbles himself shall be exalted." This seminal Christian paradox is expressed in hymns such as *The Servant Song, Gather Us In, Christus Paradox, Shepherd of our Souls, Come to Me,* and *What Does the Lord Require.* The *Magnificat* comes to mind as the quintessential acknowledgement of humility's role in the life of the disciple, and settings by Joncas (*Mary's Song, Magnificat*) and Haas (*Holy Is Your Name*) are accessible and always well received. Since humility is rooted in our assessment of ourselves as creatures in the presence of the Uncreated, hymns of praise such as *How Great Thou Art, Holy God We Praise Thy Name, Earth and All Stars* would be fitting today. The references in Hebrews to Jerusalem and Mount Zion are suggestive of *Jerusalem My Happy Home;* Parker's *Praise the Lord, My Soul;* and Joncas's *When We Eat This Bread.* For today's responsorial, Psalm 68, look to settings by Cooney, Burns, and Gelineau.

First Reading:
Wisdom 9:13–18b

Who can know God's counsel,
> or who can conceive what the
> LORD intends?
For the deliberations of mortals are
> timid,
> and unsure are our plans.
For the corruptible body burdens the
> soul
> and the earthen shelter weighs
> down the mind that has many
> concerns.
And scarce do we guess the things
> on earth,
> and what is within our grasp we
> find with difficulty;
> but when things are in heaven,
> who can search them out?
Or who ever knew your counsel,
> except you had given wisdom
> and sent your holy spirit from on
> high?
And thus were the paths of those on
> earth made straight.

SCRIPTURE COMMENTARY

The nature of Old Testament wisdom was based on two principles: one was close examination of the lessons from human experience; the second was meditation on the nature of God as creator and sustainer of the universe. As to the first, the books of Proverbs, Qoheleth (Ecclesiastes), Sirach, and Wisdom are filled with proverbs and aphorisms based on examples drawn from nature and human behavior. As to the second, today's reading is an excellent sample. The author of the book of Wisdom wrote almost at the time of Jesus himself, perhaps in the decades just before Jesus was born. He was strongly influenced by the prevailing philosophies of the Greek world and may well have written this book in Alexandria, Egypt, the largest Jewish population center in the world in the first century. Still, it is truly biblical in its approach here, echoing the insights of the prophets that no one can fathom the plans in God's mind (see, e.g., Isa 40:12–31). Greek philosophy tended to see an impersonal first cause of all being and had deep skepticism about any personal divine care for the world. But the Jewish wisdom teacher sees the signs of divine personal governance of the world everywhere, even if we cannot understand the infinite master plan of God with our limited human intelligence. Yet God can bestow his Spirit and his wisdom on humans so that they can know his ways and his expectations. Thus he protects the philosophical infinity of God while believing in God's revelation to Israel.

HOMILY HELPS

In one of Dietrich Bonhoeffer's books, entitled *The Cost of Discipleship,* a key insight was the realization that there is no "cheap grace." Today's readings center on questions having to do with discipleship.

The first question deals with how much we are willing to spend. The Christian life requires a radical turnabout in our lives so that nothing takes precedence over Christ. That includes family and dear ones. To turn our backs on those dearest to us means, quite simply, that they are always subordinate to our religious commitment.

Our faith brings with it moments of true elation but also times when we are sorely tempted to say "Enough." We struggle with problems—insufficient funds to meet expenses, the unexpected critical illness, innocent victims of violence or vandalism. And the question arises: "Why me, Lord?"

The reading from Wisdom today tackles that question in a reflection not unlike that found in Job. Humans, in their mixture of clay and spirit, can never fully understand the ways of God. We even have difficulty in understanding the things that surround us—the mysteries of the sea and outer space. But one thing is certain. We have the light of faith

that guides us on a well-ordered path. There is also a life beyond, where light will be shed on many problems. The road on which we walk is well lit, not shrouded in darkness.

The second question asks us if we are willing to make a long-term commitment. Are we willing to stay in for the long haul? The parable speaks of the man who might lack the finances to complete construction and the king who may well lack the military force to complete his conquest. In both instances, initial calculations are indispensable. As the gospels were written, there were Christians who had made the initial commitment but then wavered or defected. The same

PSALM REFLECTION

Psalm 90 is a meditation on the fragility and shortness of human life and achievements. It notes divine qualities of eternal existence (a thousand years are as one day in your sight—v. 4) and divine governance of the world (v. 2 acknowledges that "before the mountains existed, from everlasting to everlasting you are God"). In contrast, humans are unable to control even the number of their days on earth and are just as uncertain and unreliable in their moral decisions. God judges our sins and punishes evildoers (vv. 8–11), but he also gives us wisdom and mercy to help us guide our behavior and the course of our life. The psalmist rightly acknowledges this as the care of a gracious God and prays that God will continue his goodness to Israel.

Psalm Response
Psalm 90:3–4, 5–6, 12–13,
14–17

Antiphon
In every age, O Lord, you
    have been our refuge.

Verse for Reflection
Teach us to propose our days
    rightly,
That we may possess wisdom
    of the heart. (v. 12)

CATECHETICAL SUGGESTIONS

The book of Wisdom
Laments
The New Testament and slavery
The Church and slavery through the centuries
The cost of discipleship
Priorities: how to establish them; how to live them

---

is true today. Various commitments make up the Christian undertaking, yet how often people step back when the going gets rough.

Imprisonment, especially when it is unjust, offers the occasion to measure the depth of faith commitment. Is it really worth it? Given the choice, would I do it all over again? But such was not Paul's attitude. He spent his time in prison living and preaching the word. Onesimus, a fellow prisoner, was the slave of one Philemon and was converted to Christianity. Paul sends Onesimus back to his master, asking that he be received no more as a slave but as a "beloved brother." Paul has been part of his rebirth in Christ.

Adversity can certainly lead us to question our deepest convictions. But it can also be a moment of grace and singular growth. It is a time when we share in the sufferings of Christ, sufferings that terminate in glory. Christianity is not a free pass, but it offers an unparalleled insight into God's plan as it touches each one of us and assures us of a future that will never end. The psalmist prays today: "Lord, teach us to number our days aright." There will be cloudy days and curves in the road. We pray for the grace to remain steadfast.

**Second Reading:
Philemon 9–10, 12–17**

I, Paul, an old man, and now also a prisoner for Christ Jesus, urge you on behalf of my child Onesimus, whose father I have become in my imprisonment; I am sending him, that is, my own heart, back to you. I should have liked to retain him for myself, so that he might serve me on your behalf in my imprisonment for the gospel, but I did not want to do anything without your consent, so that the good you do might not be forced but voluntary. Perhaps this is why he was away from you for a while, that you might have him back forever, no longer as a slave but more than a slave, a brother, beloved especially to me, but even more so to you, as a man and in the Lord. So if you regard me as a partner, welcome him as you would me.

SCRIPTURE COMMENTARY

The letter to Philemon, Paul's shortest letter, is written to a wealthy slave owner who has become a Christian, asking him to receive his slave Onesimus back into his household and to free him as a sign of gratitude for all that Onesimus has done to help Paul in his ministry. Paul tries to convince Philemon that he has already done Paul a great favor by allowing Onesimus to remain with Paul during his difficult trials in prison and that the completion of such generosity would be to see this slave no longer in terms of his political and social status but in terms of his Christian status as a brother in Christ to Paul and Philemon alike. Perhaps Philemon has thought that the slave has abused this time by staying far too long without his permission, but Paul begs forgiveness for this by insisting that Onesimus was fully occupied with the work of the gospel. There can be no better completion than to make him as fully free in civil status as he has become in Christ.

LITURGICAL NOTES

To be a disciple means that we must take up our cross and follow Jesus. Most of us like hearing the disciple part, and most of us are trying to follow. It's just the part about embracing the cross that causes us to doubt or to shrink back. The call to discipleship involves the cross. There is no escaping it. So, too, the call to ministry within the liturgical assembly will draw the minister not only into deeper discipleship, a more profound following of the Lord, but also to the experience of the cross.

Ministry is sometimes inconvenient; ministry is sometimes painful. Ministers experience the cross not only when they are assigned to nonprimetime liturgies but also when their service involves inconvenience in their personal schedules. And they experience the cross when their visits to the homebound include a few who appear to be unpleasant folks. They experience it when they are ministering at the same liturgy with the person they have just done battle with in the parking lot or on the soccer field. We need to help people find ways to carry their cross and continue to follow, discovering that the cross will not weigh them down but rather will bring them life.

SCRIPTURE COMMENTARY

Jesus seemed to draw great crowds often, but he knew that this did not mean they were all willing to follow him no matter what the cost. Many were no doubt curious, desirous of finding out what this fellow was proposing, and others were perhaps even hostile. Still others were enthusiastic but would never actually have the desire to do what Jesus taught. Luke has compiled here several warnings to those who would be Jesus' disciples. The first is that if you let family obligations or loyalties mean more to you than what discipleship requires, don't bother to come along. The second is that if you do choose Jesus, be prepared to share in his rejection and persecution and perhaps even his death on the cross. The third is that you should weigh this decision carefully, just as an architect would in constructing a tower or a king would in going to war. What resources do you have spiritually to accept and be able to live out the conditions of discipleship that you claim to want so badly? It is not a matter of following a crowd—it is the most important decision a person can make, and it should be done with full awareness of the cost. One must be willing to let go of all one's past possessions in order to possess the kingdom of God.

Gospel: Luke 14:25–33

Great crowds were traveling with Jesus, and he turned and addressed them, "If anyone comes to me without hating his father and mother, wife and children, brothers and sisters, and even his own life, he cannot be my disciple. Whoever does not carry his own cross and come after me cannot be my disciple. Which of you wishing to construct a tower does not first sit down and calculate the cost to see if there is enough for its completion? Otherwise, after laying the foundation and finding himself unable to finish the work the onlookers should laugh at him and say, 'This one began to build but did not have the resources to finish.' Or what king marching into battle would not first sit down and decide whether with ten thousand troops he can successfully oppose another king advancing upon him with twenty thousand troops? But if not, while he is still far away, he will send a delegation to ask for peace terms. In the same way, anyone of you who does not renounce all his possessions cannot be my disciple."

MUSIC CONNECTION

Central to Luke's message today is the centrality of the cross in the life of believers and the need of disciples to renounce themselves and their possessions. The nineteenth-century text *Take Up Your Cross* gets to the heart of this message. "Take up your cross, the Savior said, if you would my disciples be; Take up your cross with willing heart and humbly follow after me." Other songs depicting the cross, such as *Lift High the Cross, At the Name of Jesus, Wherever He Leads, Only This I Want,* and *Unless a Grain of Wheat* would also be most appropriate. Bernadette Farrell's *All That Is Hidden* convincingly dovetails the need to follow Christ in his suffering with our mission to care for those less fortunate. Temple's *Prayer of Saint Francis*, though many years old, helps convey the central message of today's readings, that it is in giving that we receive and in dying that we are given life. Paul's letter to Philemon, with its bid to welcome Onesimus no longer as a slave but as a brother, suggests hymns such as *All Are Welcome, Gather Us In,* and *What Is This Place.* Today's responsorial, Psalm 90, is deftly handled by Janco as well as in the Englert/Gelineau setting.

First Reading: Exodus 32:7–11, 13–14

The LORD said to Moses, "Go down at once to your people, whom you brought out of the land of Egypt, for they have become depraved. They have soon turned aside from the way I pointed out to them, making for themselves a molten calf and worshiping it, sacrificing to it and crying out, 'This is your God, O Israel, who brought you out of the land of Egypt!' "I see how stiff-necked this people is," continued the LORD to Moses. "Let me alone, then, that my wrath may blaze up against them to consume them. Then I will make of you a great nation."

But Moses implored the LORD, his God, saying, "Why, O LORD, should your wrath blaze up against your own people, whom you brought out of the land of Egypt with such great power and with so strong a hand? Remember your servants Abraham, Isaac, and Israel, and how you swore to them by your own self, saying, 'I will make your descendants as numerous as the stars in the sky; and all this land that I promised, I will give your descendants as their perpetual heritage.'" So the LORD relented in the punishment he had threatened to inflict on his people.

SCRIPTURE COMMENTARY

The gospel for this Sunday includes the story of the prodigal son, and the reading from Exodus is chosen to match the theme that one can stray from the house of one's father and still be taken back again. Of course, there are differences here. In Exodus 32, the people have become discouraged at Moses' absence and have reverted to pagan religious practices that they knew of in Egypt. These include making a statue of a bull, which suggests that the people had turned to the Canaanite god Baal, whose cult must have been popular among Semitic captives in Egypt. He was often represented standing on a bull. Such an action was a direct repudiation of the Lord, whose first commandment forbade loyalty to any other god. God is disposed to punish the people severely but yields to the appeals of Moses that God's own loyalty to this people should keep him from destroying those to whom he has pledged himself, and God agrees to spare them. If it is not exactly the same gracious mercy that the father shows in the parable of the prodigal son, it does reinforce Israel's conviction that prayer and petition to God can change his just anger to mercy in every case.

HOMILY HELPS

Without doubt, this Sunday's major theme is God's forgiveness. In the Exodus reading, God's willingness to forgive his people is obtained through Moses' intercession. The letter to Timothy speaks of Paul's former behavior and of how Paul's unbelief was overcome by God's mercy in abundance. Finally, chapter fifteen of Luke's gospel is a well-known classic that merits our frequent reflection, especially when we might be in doubt about God's willingness to let bygones be bygones.

If taken literally, the three gospel parables evidence a certain amount of hyperbole or measure of exaggeration. How reasonable is it to leave a flock of sheep unprotected to go after one? To do a thorough house-cleaning and then celebrate the finding of one rather insignificant coin? Yes, overstatement it may well be, but this is all in the service of illustrating God's forgiveness. That is the main point of the three parables. Righteous people have found the path that will bring them safely home. But the redirected sinner, who was completely off course, counts for more in God's sight.

In the third parable, the story of the prodigal son—or, as it might be better called, the forgiving father—we are looking at a three-legged stool, with each leg of literary importance to the story's dramatic impact. The three legs are the two sons and the father.

The younger son is a ne'er-do-well, totally self-absorbed, determined to satisfy his own desires. His story is one of an early and unwarranted claim on his inheritance, no plan for the future, a young life wasted in carousing and dissolution. With his means exhausted and nowhere else to turn, having descended to the despised occupation of feeding swine, he has only one hope left, his father's compassion.

The father possesses all the contrary virtues. A landowner with good insights and no small measure of success, he also has a great heart: he offers forgiveness beyond measure, with the risk of

PSALM REFLECTION

Psalm 51 is one of the seven penitential psalms of popular piety. The psalmist asks for forgiveness of his sins. Although the sins may be against one's neighbor, the psalm does not deal with reconciliation with the one sinned against. It recognizes that the sinful spirit is a rebellion against the commandments and guidance God has given to us and asks God to strengthen our spirit by giving us his own Spirit and allowing us to stay near to his presence.

**Psalm Response
Psalm 51:3–4, 12–13, 17, 19**

Antiphon
I will rise and go to my father.

Verse for Reflection
Wash me completely of my guilt,
And wipe away all my sin. (v. 4)

SCRIPTURE COMMENTARY

This is the first of a series of selections from the first and second letters to Timothy that we will be reading over the next few weeks. These letters contain many passages that are much more personal in tone than Paul's other letters. This has led many scholars to conclude that these may be actually reflections back on his life by disciples, reflections that have been produced in a letter form, similar to what Paul himself wrote. The letter to Timothy, like the letter to Titus, is directed not to a church but to Paul's closest associates. Whether by Paul or about Paul, this first chapter of the first letter to Timothy is an expression of Paul's humility and an admission of his many sins. But it is also a wonderful example of

**Second Reading:
1 Timothy 1:12–17**

Beloved: I am grateful to him who has strengthened me, Christ Jesus our Lord, because he considered me trustworthy in appointing me to the ministry. I was once a blasphemer and a persecutor and arrogant, but I have been mercifully treated because I acted out of ignorance in my unbelief. Indeed, the grace of our Lord has been abundant, along with the faith and love that are in Christ Jesus. This saying is trustworthy and deserves full acceptance: Christ Jesus came

being seen as overly generous, going beyond the restoration of his lost son's status, and finally, he celebrates the profligate son's return with an excess of merry-making. Isn't it all too much? There is someone who thinks so.

The older son comes upon the festive scene. He is the model son, of whom any father would be proud: always faithful, appreciative of family property, a laborer without complaint. But in the face of what he considers gross unfairness and inequality, he gives his father a surly retort. It is not *"my brother"* but rather *"your son"* who has returned, and the welcome he has received is "out of bounds." But the father has the final word:

"Your brother was dead and has come to life again; he was lost and has been found."

There is more than one lesson in this well-developed parable. The father is the prototype of God himself, who reaches out and embraces the sinner. It is a lesson to recall when our spirits are downcast because of our own personal failures. God is always there for us and asks only for sorrow, not explanations. Yet, looking at others, we often have the "older son complex," a bit too self-righteous and lacking in compassion. If we are among the righteous, let us be grateful, but let us never fail to appreciate the shepherd's joy in lifting up the lost sheep.

LITURGICAL NOTES

The issues of finding what was lost, of mercy, of justice, of forgiveness, of God's superabundant love permeate today's readings. We cannot help but think of the times we have been on the receiving end of undeserved mercy. We can also not help but think about those times we have been reluctant to forgive. We not only question how must we forgive; we question our own need of forgiveness.

Christ "loved the Church and gave himself up for her to maker her holy," and he united the Church to him-

into the world to save sinners. Of these I am the foremost. But for that reason I was mercifully treated, so that in me, as the foremost, Christ Jesus might display all his patience as an example for those who would come to believe in him for everlasting life. To the king of ages, incorruptible, invisible, the only God, honor and glory forever and ever. Amen.

Paul's faith in the power of divine forgiveness through Jesus Christ. Like the message of Paul heard so often in his major letters, this chapter relates God's forgiveness directly to the cross of Christ.

Gospel: Luke 15:1–32 (or Luke 15:1–10)

Tax collectors and sinners were all drawing near to listen to Jesus, but the Pharisees and scribes began to complain, saying, "This man welcomes sinners and eats with them." So to them he addressed this parable. "What man among you having a hundred sheep and losing one of them would not leave the ninety-nine in the desert and go after the lost one until he finds it? And when he does find it, he sets it on his shoulders with great joy and, upon his arrival home, he calls together his friends and neighbors and says to them, 'Rejoice with me because I have found my lost sheep.' I tell you, in just the same way there will be more joy in heaven over one sinner who repents than over ninety-nine righteous people who have no need of repentance.

"Or what woman having ten coins and losing one would not light a lamp and sweep the house, searching carefully until she finds it? And when she does find it, she calls together her friends and neighbors and says to them, 'Rejoice with me because I have found the coin that I lost.' In just the same way, I tell you, there will be rejoicing among the angels of God over one sinner who repents."

Then he said, "A man had two sons, and the younger son said to his father, 'Father give me the share of your estate that should come to me.' So the father divided the property between them. After a few days, the younger son collected all his belongings and set off to a distant country where he squandered his inheritance on a life of dissipation. When he had freely spent everything, a severe famine struck that

SCRIPTURE COMMENTARY

The combination of so many separate parables in one Sunday reading makes today's gospel passage very rich. Each of the three parables is well known and well loved by Christians: the man who had a hundred sheep and lost one; the woman who lost one of her ten valuable coins and searched for it diligently until she found it; and the prodigal son who left and returned home. In the first two parables, the owner did the searching himself or herself until the object was found. It is

self as his bride. He filled her with his divine gifts, because she is his body and fullness, and through her he spreads truth and grace to all.

The members of the Church, however, are exposed to temptation and unfortunately often fall into sin. As a result, "while Christ, holy, innocent and unstained," did not know sin, but came only to atone for the sins of the people, the Church, which includes within itself sinners and is at the same time holy and always in need of purification, constantly pursues

repentance and renewal. (Rite of Penance, 3)

The sacrament of penance is one of the treasures of the Church. In the sacrament of penance the people of God obtain mercy from God and are reconciled with the Church. God's Spirit moves our hearts to repentance and conversion; forgiveness is ours for the asking. People have not abandoned the sacrament of penance; they just seem to have forgotten about it.

Some people are not sure when the sacrament is celebrated in their parish. Others have forgotten how to celebrate it. This Sunday, as we hear the

message of mercy and forgiveness, would be an ideal time to provide some printed information on this sacrament. The Rite of Penance contains a wonderful theology of the sacrament, parts of which could be excerpted in the bulletin. In addition, it contains an outline of how to celebrate the sacrament, and several versions of an examination of conscience.

The sacrament of penance is not reserved for Lent. We Christians live each day as holy and sinful human beings, ever in need of the experience of God's mercy and reconciliation with our brothers and sisters.

SCRIPTURE COMMENTARY, CONTINUED

a sign of the loving concern of the shepherd or the woman to persevere in seeking out the lost item until it is found. In the story of the prodigal son, the son repents and returns to seek out the father. Thus it is on the surface the opposite situation, but we could readily surmise that Luke put these parables next to each other to show that the father too would have searched out that son, but he knew he would return, and his watching every day was his way of seeking diligently. In the combination of the three stories, however, the lesson is to be sure to understand both things about God our Father: he searches out the lost and he waits expectantly for the repentance of those who intentionally leave him. There are further lessons of how forgiveness is given out of love and does not require the sinner to explain himself to get it and how those who are faithful to God all along should welcome sinners back generously instead of complaining that it is unfair to them, the message taken from the elder son's attitude.

country, and he found himself in dire need. So he hired himself out to one of the local citizens who sent him to his farm to tend the swine. And he longed to eat his fill of the pods on which the swine fed, but nobody gave him any. Coming to his senses he thought, 'How many of my father's hired workers have more than enough food to eat, but here am I, dying from hunger. I shall get up and go to my father and I shall say to him, "Father, I have sinned against heaven and against you. I no longer deserve to be called your son; treat me as you would treat one of your hired workers."' So he got up and went back to his father. While he was still a long way off, his father caught sight of him, and was filled with compassion. He ran to his son, embraced him and kissed him. His son said to him, 'Father, I have sinned against heaven and against you; I no longer deserve to be called your son.' But his father ordered his servants, 'Quickly bring the finest robe and put it on him; put a ring on his finger and sandals on his feet. Take the fattened calf and slaughter it. Then let us celebrate with a feast, because this son of mine was dead, and has come to life again; he was lost, and has been found.' Then the celebration began. Now the older son had been out in the field and, on his way back, as he neared the house, he heard the sound of music and dancing. He called one of the servants and asked what this might mean. The servant said to him, 'Your brother has returned and your father has slaughtered the fattened calf because he has him back safe and sound.' He became angry, and when he refused to enter the house, his father came out and pleaded with him. He said to his father in reply, 'Look, all these years I served you and not once did I disobey your orders; yet you never gave me even a young goat to feast on with my friends. But when your son returns, who swallowed up your property with prostitutes, for him you slaughter the fattened calf.' He said to him, 'My son, you are here with me always; everything I have is yours. But now we must celebrate and rejoice, because your brother was dead and has come to life again; he was lost and has been found.'"

MUSIC CONNECTION

All three of today's readings speak of the mercy of God in the face of human sin and failure. In Exodus, Moses negotiates with God about the fate of the people, whom the Lord describes as "stiff-necked." The Lord's wrath is assuaged by Moses' mention of Abraham, Isaac and Israel, to whom God promised: "I will make your descendants as numerous as the stars in the sky." The ever-engaging and enlightening story of the prodigal son and forgiving father directs us to a God who is ever ready to welcome back and forgive his wayward children. The second reading reinforces this with its affirmation that "Jesus Christ came into the world to save sinners." Hymns abound, and include *There's a Wideness in God's Mercy; Amazing Grace; Our Father, We Have Wandered; Hosea; God Full of Mercy; Forgive Our Sins as We Forgive;* and *Turn to Me.* Rory Cooney's *Change Our Hearts* is a robust call for change fully grounded in the bounteous mercy and kindness of God, while Deiss's *Yes I Shall Arise,* based on the Lucan pericope, is more plaintive and soul searching. Both are good choices. The cardinal song of sorrow, Psalm 51, is today's responsorial, and one can find good settings by Thatcher, Gelineau, and Haugen.

CATECHETICAL SUGGESTIONS

Moses' role as God's chosen leader

Sacraments that effect and celebrate the forgiveness of sins

Ramifications in our lives of the fact that Jesus came to save sinners

In what ways does our Church community welcome sinners? In what ways do we fail to welcome sinners?

First Reading: Amos 8:4–7

Hear this, you who trample
　　upon the needy
　　and destroy the poor of the
　　　land!
"When will the new moon be
　　over," you ask,
　　"that we may sell our grain,
　　and the sabbath, that we may
　　　display the wheat?
We will diminish the ephah,
　　add to the shekel,
　　and fix our scales for cheat-
　　　ing!
We will buy the lowly for silver,
　　and the poor for a pair of san-
　　　dals;
　　even the refuse of the wheat
　　　we will sell!"
The LORD has sworn by the
　　pride of Jacob:
　　Never will I forget a thing
　　　they have done!

SCRIPTURE COMMENTARY

Amos provides a vivid picture of the social situation in the city of Samaria in about 750 BC. It is a city that lives on commercial trading—that is, it is a typical ancient market town, on whose merchants the local majority of the people, who were farmers, were dependent for the sale of their produce. Most land was owned by large landowners who took a large percentage of the annual crops in return for letting the farmers work the land. A small part was left to the farmers for their own needs and to sell for other products. Amos describes an atmosphere of widespread shortchanging of customers in payment for grain. It meant that the seller was cheated by the merchants and the poor of the town were overcharged for the resale of the same grain. God will not tolerate injustice toward, and abuse of, the poor and helpless. The book of Amos foresees disaster coming to Samaria.

HOMILY HELPS

We don't need fluency in French to know what an *entrepreneur* is. The word is closely related to our English word "enterprising," which is the key virtue of the manager in today's gospel. It was also a characteristic of many religious communities in the Church, at least in their beginnings. Frances Ward, the founder of the Sisters of Mercy in America, made the journey from Ireland in the nineteenth century with a few companions and little else. Trusting wholly in God and without any long-range planning, she established, in a matter of decades, many communities of sisters from New England to the Midwest. God provided the sisters, and she took on the commitments. Mother Teresa of Calcutta responded to human need spontaneously, and now there are Missionaries of Charity on every continent of the world. These were enterprising founders in the service of God.

When the manager in today's gospel is faced with unemployment, with no assets at his disposal, he acts with astuteness. He reduces the payment due his master for the benefit of various debtors. Recent discovery of Palestinian bills of sale from New Testament times suggests that the amount reduced may have been the manager's commission from the transaction. But regardless of the basic facts, he used his managerial skills to provide for his future. It is for this reason that his master commends him. He had acted wisely and prudently to ensure that friends would look upon him kindly in the future. We are asked to act as wisely for the kingdom of God.

The poor are frequently disadvantaged, as the reading from

PSALM REFLECTION

Psalm 113 as a whole is a soaring hymn of praise of how God rules the universe, directs nature, and determines the course of all the great heavenly bodies and yet has the tenderness to reach down to the lowly and the poor. The hymn is short—only nine verses—and we hear almost all of them today. Thus the psalm calls on the God who orders all creation rightly (one of the foundations of the idea of justice) to look after the lowly and poor. Verse 9, one of the two verses not heard today, adds to this sense of God's compassion: "God establishes in his home the barren wife as the joyful mother of children."

Psalm Response
Psalm 113:1–2, 4–6, 7–8

Antiphon
Praise the Lord who lifts
    up the poor.
Or: Alleluia.

Verse for Reflection
Praise, you servants of the
    Lord,
Praise the name of the
    Lord! (v. 1)

SCRIPTURE COMMENTARY

In the passage from the first chapter of 1 Timothy that was read last week, we heard Paul give thanks for the divine mercy that forgave him his sin through the cross of Jesus. Today the letter moves on to a further thought, that the salvation he experienced is offered to all human beings. We should regularly pray to God to bestow on those who have not heard of it this salvation by means of the preaching of the gospel, which is what Paul has committed his life to doing. The great truth, Paul says, is that God is one alone over all humans and his Son is the one mediator who brings forgiveness and salvation to humankind

Second Reading:
1 Timothy 2:1–8

Beloved: First of all, I ask that supplications, prayers, petitions, and thanksgivings be offered for everyone, for kings and for all in authority, that we may lead a quiet and tranquil life in all devotion and dignity. This

Amos illustrates. Buying and selling today are more sophisticated, but the poor are still left out. Entrepreneurs in other areas might well channel their efforts into religious equality. Several prominent New York businessmen in recent years pooled their resources to open a private school for underprivileged and poorly educated children. They were enterprising for the concerns of God.

Our enterprise today may take different forms. Parishioners organize themselves to provide services to the homebound. Oth-

ers provide periodic outings for the handicapped or look after the bereaved. There are small groups formed for book sharing or shared prayer, in the words of 1 Timothy read today, " lifting up holy hands, without anger or argument."

One can either sit back and lament the state of the world or realize that it is "better to light one candle than curse the darkness." When the inspiration comes and the cause is right, the entrepreneur says: "Let's go for it!"

LITURGICAL NOTES

"Seize the day." The scriptures this Sunday seem to challenge us not to miss any opportunity for doing good.

Liturgy planners and committees tend to look at the major feasts and celebrations of the church year and put great amounts of time and effort into their planning, preparation, and celebration. But we should also never miss the opportunities that the ordinary Sundays provide for us to allow the liturgy to touch

is good and pleasing to God our savior, who wills everyone to be saved and to come to knowledge of the truth.

For there is one God.

There is also one mediator between God and men,
the man Christ Jesus,
who gave himself as ransom for all.

This was the testimony at the proper time. For this I was appointed preacher and apostle—I am speaking the truth, I am not lying—, teacher of the Gentiles in faith and truth.

It is my wish, then, that in every place the men should pray, lifting up holy hands, without anger or argument.

SCRIPTURE COMMENTARY, CONTINUED

because he gave his life to redeem them. As a secondary thought, the mention of constant prayer leads Paul to remind his hearers that all prayer and petition should be extended to include all types of people, especially leaders, because the spread of the gospel is made easier when there is a peaceful and secure society and the leaders have goodwill.

Gospel: Luke 16:1–13 (or Luke 16:10–13)

Jesus said to his disciples, "A rich man had a steward who was reported to him for squandering his property. He summoned him and said, 'What is this I hear about you? Prepare a full account of your stewardship, because you can no longer be my steward.' The steward said to himself, 'What shall I do, now that my master is taking the position of steward away from me? I am not strong enough to dig and I am ashamed to beg. I know what I shall do so that, when I am removed from the stewardship, they may welcome me into their homes.' He called

SCRIPTURE COMMENTARY

The parable of the dishonest steward is very difficult to interpret. If the man is being fired for dishonest management, not just incompetence, then his further rewriting of the accounts to gain friends to help him after he has lost his position is just as dishonest. It is a thief's clever trick to get out of a difficult situation. But if so, an owner of the farm would hardly commend the steward for cheating him. So the owner must be Jesus (or God), who would like his disciples to be as resourceful and quick to take action for the sake of the kingdom of God as people hungry for money are in this world. The other possible

and transform the hearts and lives of the members of the assembly. The remaining Sundays of Ordinary Time might be a good opportunity to take a look not at the major celebrations but the ordinary Sunday celebrations. We consider not just the principal liturgies of the weekend but those that might be less well attended, those that don't take place at prime times. These liturgies and the exercise of liturgical ministries at them are often the ones that are neglected, if not overlooked. For example, many musicians claim that people do not sing or do not sing well at early-morning Masses. The issue might not be their lack of desire or inability to sing; maybe the keys are just too high for early morning. Trying hymns in a lower key might make all the difference in the world. The presence of the assigned number of liturgical ministers at such liturgies might bear some examination.

The scriptures also echo themes of stewardship. While we are certainly becoming more accustomed to this word and its meaning, we can be a bit narrow in eliciting gifts of time, treasure, and talent from our assemblies. Not everyone may be willing or able to function as a reader, cantor, extraordinary minister of Holy Communion, or minister of hospitality. But there are many folks out there who have valuable skills they could share. Look within your assembly for speech teachers and drama coaches, voice teachers, those who work in public relations or in the care of the sick. These people and what they have to offer our liturgical ministers is a treasure hidden in a field. All we need do is ask them.

SCRIPTURE COMMENTARY, CONTINUED

meaning is that the steward was being fired for dishonesty before but his changing of the debts afterwards was a legal act, since he had the authority to be the negotiator. In this case, Jesus is criticizing a practice of the Pharisees to get around the ban on lending money for interest. He tells them that they should stop cheating God and tells his disciples to be as energetic in doing what is right as the Pharisees are in getting around God's commands. Luke adds several other sayings of Jesus on just and responsible use of wealth and the temptation to value monetary wealth more than the kingdom of God. The overall lesson, then, is this: beware of being seduced by money for this life, but see your wealth as obtaining the kingdom of God and be as resourceful for that treasure as for earthly treasure.

in his master's debtors one by one. To the first he said, 'How much do you owe my master?' He replied, "One hundred measures of olive oil.' He said to him, 'Here is your promissory note. Sit down and quickly write one for fifty.' Then to another the steward said, 'And you, how much do you owe?' He replied, 'One hundred kors of wheat.' The steward said to him, 'Here is your promissory note; write one for eighty.' And the master commended that dishonest steward for acting prudently. "For the children of this world are more prudent in dealing with their own generation than are the children of light. I tell you, make friends for yourselves with dishonest wealth, so that when it fails, you will be welcomed into eternal dwellings. The person who is trustworthy in very small matters is also trustworthy in great ones; and the person who is dishonest in very small matters is also dishonest in great ones. If, therefore, you are not trustworthy with dishonest wealth, who will trust you with true wealth? If you are not trustworthy with what belongs to another, who will give you what is yours? No servant can serve two masters. He will either hate one and love the other, or be devoted to one and despise the other. You cannot serve both God and mammon."

CATECHETICAL SUGGESTIONS

Amos: life and times
Mendicant orders
Methods of prayer in the
   Catholic tradition
Stewardship
How can we live in this life
   to prepare for the next?
Our parish budget: are we
   serving the poor?

MUSIC CONNECTION

In the first lesson, Amos, the prophet *par excellence* of social justice and responsibility, criticizes those who trample on the poor and the oppressed. It may take a while to find the connective tissue with the gospel, but eventually we read that "the person who is dishonest in very small matters is also dishonest in greater." Justice and concern for others become a readable barometer of our faith and discipleship. Fortunately, many hymns composed in the past thirty years have fruitfully explored this connection between what we profess and how we live that out in lives of justice. Among these should be counted *I Say "Yes, Lord"; Bring Forth the Kingdom; The Kingdom of God; The Temple Rang with Golden Coins;* and *Good News.* David Haas's *We Are Called* is a clarion call to act with justice and compassion to all in our midst, while Bernadette Farrell's *Community of Christ* rightly directs our gaze beyond the doors of our churches to see the poor and dispossessed. The same author's *Alleluia, Raise the Gospel* as well as Soper's *God of the Hungry* are fine contemporary expressions of Amos's call for justice and compassion. Janco, Guimont, and Joncas all provide good settings of today's responsorial, Psalm 113.

First Reading: Amos 6:1a, 4–7

Thus says the Lord the God of
　　hosts:
Woe to the complacent in Zion!
Lying upon beds of ivory,
　　stretched comfortably on their
　　couches,
they eat lambs taken from the
　　flock,
　　and calves from the stall!
Improvising to the music of the
　　harp,
　　like David, they devise their
　　own accompaniment.
They drink wine from bowls
　　and anoint themselves with the
　　best oils;
　　yet they are not made ill by the
　　collapse of Joseph!
Therefore, now they shall be the
　　first to go into exile,
　　and their wanton revelry shall
　　be done away with.

SCRIPTURE COMMENTARY

The reading from chapter 8 of Amos last Sunday provided us a glimpse into the corrupt atmosphere of economic injustice in eighth-century Samaria. Today's reading from chapter 6 is another example of the wealthy having no concern except for their own pleasure and profit. They live luxurious lifestyles while their nation faces imminent disaster from its enemies. The prevailing political policies toward Assyria will lead to war and defeat while they strip the land of its strength and bounty to provide war materials and neglect the needs of the poor for the benefit of the upper classes. The people may think they prosper now, but their end will be reversed into defeat, exile, and death. The theme of the day is reversal of fortune, in particular that the rich who think that they have everything they will ever need will find themselves impoverished. Indeed, the gospel parable of Jesus goes on to say that the afterlife will be torment in the pains of Hades, the spiritual equivalent of Amos's prediction of the death and disaster to befall Samaria's leading citizens.

HOMILY HELPS

Luke has various parables and narratives that are found only in his gospel. The story of the rich man and Lazarus is one of them. Two lessons emerge quickly from the story. The first has to do with complacency, and the second with inverted values.

The rich man is the archetype of a complacent spirit. He is so lost in his own wealth and comfort that he scarcely notices the beggar at his doorstep, who asks only for leftovers from the table. The rich man is content with the status quo, with little thought as to what might come later.

The rich man reflects the attitudes of our modern society, absorbed, as we are, in financial status, our desire for the best for ourselves and our children, and the values of our consumer society. And all of this in the midst of a world where people live without the essentials for life and deprivation characterizes the day-to-day existence of millions.

When we learn of a death, we mourn the loss—but we somehow manage to keep death at a distance. "That is an illness that does not run in our family." "That is a dangerous road that I always avoid." We are determined to settle in for a long and happy life, or, in the words of William Sloan Coffin, "The trick is to die young as late as possible." Yet it is all paper thin and so uncertain. We simply do not know the day or the hour.

The letter to Timothy today speaks of the true riches in life: integrity, purity, devotion, patience, and gentleness. In the parable, these were evidently virtues that characterized the poor man more than his rich counterpart. The real truth, the inversion of values, appears only after death. The rich man suffers the poverty of eternal loss; the poor man is destined for the riches of eternity in Abraham's bosom. The poor man evidently found his treasure in God while

PSALM REFLECTION

Psalm 146 offers one of the most concentrated lists of those who are among the afflicted whom God looks after. It opens in the first six verses with the call not to trust in human leaders and human plans but to rely on God alone. It moves to praise humans who do rely on God, who have concern to work for justice and care for the hungry. And then it returns to praising God, who above all acts to both maintain justice and to show compassion. Rhetorically it expresses a wonderful partnership between God and his faithful people by using the literary device of chiasm, in which the thought ends where it begins and doubles the middle as well in the pattern A to B to B to A. It begins with relying on God, then turns to not trusting in humans, then praises those humans who do trust, and finally returns to praising God for his goodness. Such a pattern gives equal emphasis to both parts, A and B, by doubling them both.

**Psalm Response
Psalm 146:7, 8–9, 9–10**

Antiphon
Praise the Lord, my
   soul!
Or: Alleluia.

Verse for Reflection
[The Lord] assures justice for the
oppressed,
And gives food to the
hungry. (v. 7)

SCRIPTURE COMMENTARY

In this final chapter of the first letter to Timothy, the author, whether Paul or his disciple, comes to the conclusion of his arguments for basing the Christian life on the imitation of Christ and, in turn, on Paul's own example of doing so. Basically it is centered on the saving, forgiving role of Christ, which has united us to his Father by the cross and resurrection. As his final word, the author urges his readers to persevere in

**Second Reading:
1 Timothy 6:11–16**

But you, man of God, pursue righteousness, devotion, faith, love, patience, and gentleness. Compete well for the faith. Lay hold of eternal life, to which you were called when you made the noble

the man of wealth wallowed in his present abundance.

Perhaps things would be different if the rich man had been forewarned. But then again, probably not. The scriptures give sufficient warning. But are they simply sacred words on paper, readings to which we give little attention on Sunday morning?

Be it in the world or in the church, we can live in quiet complacency. However, each Sunday should be a wake-up call. We don't have it made until we breathe our last. In the meantime, we can be fully aware of the many signposts that dot the road of life.

LITURGICAL NOTES

The complacent find themselves in a rather difficult situation. Not able to look to the future, not even able to see beyond their own needs at the moment, they are sure to end up missing the promises of God unfolding in their midst.

Those involved in planning and preparing for the celebration of the liturgy can easily become complacent. Maybe all those involved in the liturgy seem to function like a well-oiled machine. Week after week it all happens, generally without incident. This

kind of complacency can enable planning teams to avoid looking at those places where there could be improvements, maybe some fine-tuning, maybe a complete overhaul. But complacency will blind them to thinking about any of these things.

Others might have become complacent because the bar has been so lowered that they believe they can do no better. The excuses are legion: we are just a small, little parish; we are a gigantic parish and doing the best we can. Then there is the worst possible excuse: what difference does it make anyway? The singing will never improve,

confession in the presence of many witnesses. I charge you before God, who gives life to all things, and before Christ Jesus, who gave testimony under Pontius Pilate for the noble confession, to keep the commandment without stain or reproach until the appearance of our Lord Jesus Christ that the blessed and only ruler will make manifest at the proper time, the King of kings and Lord of lords, who alone has immortality, who dwells in unapproachable light, and whom no human being has seen or can see. To him be honor and eternal power. Amen.

SCRIPTURE COMMENTARY, CONTINUED

the life of faith that they have learned as followers of Christ, and not to weaken. The spur to this perseverance is the hope of the coming again of Christ, who will offer us immortality when he is revealed as the very self of God in glory and majesty. This is as strong a statement about the unity of Jesus the Son with God the Father as we find in the New Testament. It is not as clear a definition as the Church would reach in the fourth century Council of Nicaea and after, but it clearly expresses that Jesus has complete divine power in heaven in all that he does for us.

Gospel: Luke 16:19–31

Jesus said to the Pharisees: "There was a rich man who dressed in purple garments and fine linen and dined sumptuously each day. And lying at his door was a poor man named Lazarus, covered with sores, who would gladly have eaten his fill of the scraps that fell from the rich man's table. Dogs even used to come and lick his sores. When the poor man died, he was carried away

SCRIPTURE COMMENTARY

This parable was a well-known folk tale told in Jewish circles about the reversal of fates between this life and the next. The idea of heaven as the bosom of Abraham, and of Hades as a place of torment, is common in apocalyptic works such as 2 Enoch 9:10 and elsewhere. Jesus does not praise Lazarus for his justice and piety; he just speaks of his helplessness and need of compassion. The real focus is the rich man, who had no compassion on the poor as demanded by

the preaching can never get any better, and so on.

Complacency is an enemy of good liturgy. Complacency does not allow one to ask the difficult questions or take on the difficult tasks. Complacency says, "This is all there is." If you have noticed some degree or another of complacency among your committee or among your ministers, what is the remedy? A suitable and effective remedy is to recapture the spirit of the liturgy. Invite your group, committee, ministry team into a prayerful reading of the opening chapters of the Constitution on the Sacred Liturgy and hear once again the voice of the

CATECHETICAL SUGGESTIONS

The history of the northern kingdom
Immigration law and practice in the United States
The universal call to holiness
What have we promised in the presence of witnesses? Are we keeping those promises?
The role and power of ritual
To whom do we listen? How do our lives reflect the values of those to whom we listen?

Holy Spirit speaking through the council fathers. Think about those areas where the vision has succeeded. Do not spend time thinking about the places where

it has failed. Think rather about those places where the vision has yet to be realized and what part each person might play in the full realization of that vision.

SCRIPTURE COMMENTARY, CONTINUED

the law of Moses in Exodus 22:20–26, Deuteronomy 15:7–8, and many other passages. Soon the rich man finds himself in need of compassion but discovers it is too late to change one's behavior in the afterlife. Jesus then adds a new point not known in the folktale: he has the rich man ask Abraham to warn his brothers not to follow his example, by sending the ghost of Lazarus to speak to them. Abraham's answer is that God has already sent the word to them through the law in ways they know well. But if they are as hardened against obedience to the law as the rich man was, they won't believe in a divine apparition either. By itself this would make a good sermon, and Christians understand that Jesus is also saying that many of his hearers will have lack of faith in his resurrection even though it was prophetically foretold in the Old Testament.

by angels to the bosom of Abraham. The rich man also died and was buried, and from the netherworld, where he was in torment, he raised his eyes and saw Abraham far off and Lazarus at his side. And he cried out, 'Father Abraham, have pity on me. Send Lazarus to dip the tip of his finger in water and cool my tongue, for I am suffering torment in these flames.' Abraham replied, 'My child, remember that you received what was good during your lifetime while Lazarus likewise received what was bad; but now he is comforted here, whereas you are tormented. Moreover, between us and you a great chasm is established to prevent anyone from crossing who might wish to go from our side to yours or from your side to ours.' He said, 'Then I beg you, father, send him to my father's house, for I have five brothers, so that he may warn them, lest they too come to this place of torment.' But Abraham replied, 'They have Moses and the prophets. Let them listen to them.' He said, 'Oh no, father Abraham, but if someone from the dead goes to them, they will repent.' Then Abraham said, 'If they will not listen to Moses and the prophets, neither will they be persuaded if someone should rise from the dead.'"

MUSIC CONNECTION

This week the social-justice thrust begun last week in Amos continues and ties in nicely with the memorable Lucan story of the rich man and Lazarus. Clearly, it is the lack of awareness and attention to the covenantal responsibility to care for the impoverished and less fortunate that puts the rich man in his current predicament. In this, there is a direct line from Amos to Luke. The psalm says it all: "Blessed those who keep faith forever, secure justice for the oppressed, give food to the hungry." Hymns that come to mind include Haas's popular *Blest Are They* as well as the same author's *We Are Called.* The Fred Kaan text *For the Healing of the Nations* is a classic of good theology and cogent writing and deserves consideration for today and other services throughout the year. In a similar vein, Haugen's singable and thought-provoking *God of Day and God of Darkness* helps us connect the dots between faith professed and faith lived. Susan Wente's engaging text *Make Us True Servants,* set to the traditional Irish melody *Slane,* offers an invitation to all of us to care for those in need. It is both subtle and convincing. While not new, Foley's *The Cry of the Poor* still elicits a fulsome response from congregations. Guimont, Joncas, and Lisicky all provide good settings for Psalm 146, today's responsorial.

First Reading:
Habakkuk 1:2–3; 2:2–4

How long, O LORD? I cry for help
  but you do not listen!
I cry out to you, "Violence!"
  but you do not intervene.
Why do you let me see ruin;
  why must I look at misery?
Destruction and violence are before
  me;
  there is strife, and clamorous
  discord.
Then the LORD answered me and
  said:
  Write down the vision clearly
  upon the tablets,
  so that one can read it readily.
For the vision still has its time,
  presses on to fulfillment, and will
  not disappoint;
if it delays, wait for it,
  it will surely come, it will not be
  late.
The rash one has no integrity;
  but the just one, because of his
  faith, shall live.

SCRIPTURE COMMENTARY

Habakkuk wrote his prophetic oracles to Judah in the disastrous days of the Babylonian attacks and capture of Jerusalem, perhaps between 598 and 586 BC. The situation already seems desperate, perhaps following the first capture and deportation of Jerusalemites in 598–597. But more likely he laments that a second and more total destruction has now come upon the city in 587–586, and where is God? "How long, O Lord" is a traditional cry to God in times of defeat by enemies (see Ps 89:47). The prophet calls to God to come to his aid as soon as possible and not to delay. The answer comes back that he is to write this message so large anyone can see it: Keep faith and do not waver! Whether I come soon or later, I will come to right the situation, and only the person who has faith enough to remain just and upright until that day will live.

HOMILY HELPS

One of the great tests of faith came in the Shoah, or Holocaust of World War II, when millions of people, many of them innocent women and children, were killed in Nazi death camps. The burning question remains with us: where was God in the Shoah? Death in combat is more easily explained, with the cause being more easily identified. This is particularly true if we can call the war "just," but then, who in history has ever waged war without claiming that it was "just"?

Still, the fact remains that massive deaths of the innocent sorely test our faith.

This is touched on by Habakkuk in today's first reading. Violence surrounds him, probably at the time of the Babylonian exile. He cannot explain the silence of God in the midst of such tragedy. Like the suffering Job, who boldly questioned the justice of God, or the exilic prophet Jeremiah, who went so far as to say that God had seduced him, Habakkuk seeks only an answer. And he receives a response—the assurance, in a vision, of a better day, the end of

destruction and deportation, the dawn of a new era. In the meantime it is faith that must carry the day. "The just one because of his faith shall live."

Faith is not mere acceptance of higher truths or unquestioning loyalty. Neither does it simply rest on doctrinal propositions drawn up by the church. Faith is a spark that, once enkindled, breaks forth in a flame of love. It is implanted in baptism and may remain dormant or even be smothered but, when stirred up and fostered, finds God even in suffering. Our inquiring minds will never have all the answers to

PSALM REFLECTION

The psalm response is similar in mood to Habakkuk's prophecy. Faith requires perseverance in good works and just behavior. God proves again by his saving deeds through the centuries that he does answer Israel's cries in time of need. But he doesn't promise that he will not let their enemies or natural disasters have their moment if it serves to discipline his people so that they learn to return and serve the Lord as they should. The psalmist calls for Israel to acknowledge God as the foundation and strength of their life as a community and nation. God has guided them and continues to shepherd them, and the proper attitude is one of worship in joyful thanksgiving for what he has done. They are to avoid the sin of their ancestors in the desert who, being ungrateful and forgetful, refused to obey God and thus never saw the Promised Land because they were kept for forty years in the desert until that generation had all died.

Psalm Response
Psalm 95:1–2, 6–7, 8–9

Antiphon
If today you hear his voice, harden not your hearts.

Verses for Reflection
Let us kneel before God our creator, For he is our God, and we the people he shepherds.
(vv. 6–7)

---

the puzzle of life, but faith tells us that God will have the final word. And if faith were not tested, of what worth would it be? A simple "I believe" says too little; but a faith that cries out, "My God, my God, why have you abandoned me?" says it all.

Jesus says today that faith can move mountains. But faith must be tested. The loss of a dear one's life is always painful, but less so with the belief in eternal life. It is hard to think of any memorable figure in the history of the Church whose faith was not sorely tried. And most striking is the One who, victimized by violence, asked forgiveness for the perpetrators.

We who have received so many good things must accept the misfortune as well. Like the servants in today's parable, our thanks for all we have received is never sufficient. When we have done all that we should do, we have only done our duty. The God who is all good will also bring us home. After the worst was over, our Master said simply: "Into your hands I commend my spirit."

O Lord, I do believe. Help thou my unbelief.

CATECHETICAL SUGGESTIONS

The fruits of the Holy Spirit
How did you "hear God's voice" this week? What did you hear?
The gifts of the Holy Spirit
Discernment of gifts
Faith
The role of service in the life of a Christian

Second Reading:
2 Timothy 1:6–8, 13–14

Beloved: I remind you, to stir into flame the gift of God that you have through the imposition of my hands. For God did not give us a spirit of cowardice but rather of power and love and self-control. So do not be ashamed of your testimony to our Lord, nor of me, a prisoner for his sake; but bear your share of hardship for the gospel with the strength that comes from God.

Take as your norm the sound words that you heard from me, in the faith and love that are in Christ Jesus. Guard this rich trust with the help of the Holy Spirit that dwells within us.

SCRIPTURE COMMENTARY

The second letter of Timothy continues some of the themes of the first letter that we have been listening to for the last three Sundays. Here Paul encourages Timothy to learn from his example. Occasionally in his major letters Paul will cite his own action as something to be imitated (see 2 Cor 13:1–6; Gal 2:20), but in the letters to Timothy and Titus he proposes that their ministry should be modeled on his own. Paul opens this second letter to Timothy by urging him to follow the lead of the Spirit that has been communicated to him to give him the courage to oppose without yielding those who try to stop his preaching and those who would change or corrupt the teaching he is to proclaim.

LITURGICAL NOTES

Last Sunday provided an opportunity to reflect on the complacency that can afflict the liturgy team. This week continues that reflection but provides words from Habakkuk and Luke that push us forward to a future filled with hope: "Write down the vision … for the vision still has its time, presses on to fulfillment, and will not disappoint," and "If only you have faith the size of a mustard seed…."

If the planning team or liturgy committee has engaged in prayerful and reflective reading of the Constitution on the Sacred Liturgy, this might be a good time to take an equally reflective look at some of the other liturgical documents. For the most part, many of these liturgical documents are referred to only to find out if something is permitted/forbidden or to attempt to get a handle on just how a particular aspect of the liturgical celebration ought to be carried out. But the opening chapters of all of these documents provide a magnificent vision of the Church's liturgy and its celebration in our time. Read opening sections of the *General Instruction of the Roman Missal* and discover anew the liturgy as the work of the Church. The Introduction to the *Lectionary for Mass* provides an excellent foundation for the role of God's word in the liturgical assembly. *Music in Catholic Worship* and *Liturgical Music Today* provide us with a rationale for why we sing when the Church comes together.

If complacency in one form or another has afflicted members of your team or if the vision has become blurry or distorted, spend these weeks seeking the remedy. You will come back to your work not only refreshed but renewed.

SCRIPTURE COMMENTARY

Matthew reports two similar sayings of Jesus: (1) that with enough faith one could throw a mountain into the sea (Matt 21:21; Mark 11:23) and (2) that with enough faith one could make a mountain move from this place to that (Matthew 17:20). Luke differs slightly in not having a mountain but a large sycamore tree being thrown into the sea. Both Matthew and Mark situate the saying in the context of the fig tree that seems barren; but Luke connects it to the attitude of the disciples as true servants. If they live by even minimal faith in Christ, as small as the mustard seed is among seeds, all things are possible. Jesus loved to use impossible hyperboles (see, e.g., his image of the camel getting through the eye of a needle in Mark 10:25) to challenge his followers to expect great things from God. The story of the servant who does not count his hours and demand overtime or a fitting reward for what he does belongs here because God acts entirely generously all the time for us, answering all our prayers and caring for our needs. In turn, true servants of God who recognize this live always for God without demanding anything, relying fully on God, who will give them everything they require.

Gospel: Luke 17:5–10

The apostles said to the Lord, "Increase our faith." The Lord replied, "If you have faith the size of a mustard seed, you would say to this mulberry tree, 'Be uprooted and planted in the sea,' and it would obey you.

"Who among you would say to your servant who has just come in from plowing or tending sheep in the field, 'Come here immediately and take your place at table'? Would he not rather say to him, 'Prepare something for me to eat. Put on your apron and wait on me while I eat and drink. You may eat and drink when I am finished'? Is he grateful to that servant because he did what was commanded? So should it be with you. When you have done all you have been commanded, say, 'We are unprofitable servants; we have done what we were obliged to do.'"

MUSIC CONNECTION

Each of today's readings deals with faith and its implications for our lives. According to Habakkuk, despite ruin, violence, and destruction all around, the just will survive through faith. The second letter to Timothy reminds us to guard the rich deposit of faith and assures us that the Spirit given us makes us strong, loving, and wise. The late Robert Hovda often said that the latter phrase was a wonderful description for all who preside at worship. Pastoral musicians may also find it a challenging job description. Finally, the gospel assures us that even small faith can lead to wondrous deeds. Look for hymns that explore the manifold dimensions of faith. These include *Faith, Hope and Love; We Walk by Faith; We Remember; A Living Faith; How Firm a Foundation; Precious Lord, Take My Hand;* and *Jesus Lead the Way.* Paul Tate's *God So Loved the World* restates John 3:16 in a hymnic form accessible to most congregations. Carl Nygard's choral setting of the same text is exceptionally moving and beautiful. Other hymns connecting faith and concern for neighbor that were recommended over the past two weeks are also appropriate today. Psalm 95, one of the most frequently used in the Roman Lectionary, has fine settings by Guimont, Haas, and Stewart.

First Reading: 2 Kings 5:14–17

Naaman went down and plunged into the Jordan seven times at the word of Elisha, the man of God. His flesh became again like the flesh of a little child, and he was clean of his leprosy.

Naaman returned with his whole retinue to the man of God. On his arrival he stood before Elisha and said, "Now I know that there is no God in all the earth, except in Israel. Please accept a gift from your servant."

Elisha replied, "As the Lord lives whom I serve, I will not take it;" and despite Naaman's urging, he still refused. Naaman said: "If you will not accept, please let me, your servant, have two mule-loads of earth, for I will no longer offer holocaust or sacrifice to any other god except to the Lord."

SCRIPTURE COMMENTARY

The cure of Naaman the Syrian general comes from a very ancient period in Israel's history. Elisha was the prophet who succeeded to the ministry of Elijah during the reigns of Ahab, Ahaziah, Jehoram, and Jehu, mainly in the years 850 to 840 BC. He mostly had to contend with the conflict between northern Israel and the kingdom of the Arameans in Damascus. Three times King Ben Hadad attacked Israel in those years, and victory in the battles often went back and forth (Ahab, for example, was killed in one of them and Ben Hadad captured in another). Elisha was certainly involved in the politics of war. In one period of peace, Elisha went to Damascus, where he incited the general Hazael to murder Ben Hadad and become king of Damascus himself. A second incident during a period of truce makes up today's reading. Naaman, a general of the enemy, feels free enough to search out Elisha for a cure of his leprosy. He is skeptical of the power of a god other than his own, and when Elisha doesn't do a spectacular act of curing, he goes away in disgust, but his servant convinces him to do what the prophet has commanded. The general is cured in the Jordan River and comes back to offer thanks to God for the cure. He even decides to become a subject of the God of Israel back in his foreign home.

HOMILY HELPS

Duty or gratitude—two different ways of looking at our faith life. Unfortunately for many of us, the emphasis is often on duty when it should be gratitude.

The Elisha story in our first reading highlights Naaman's gratitude on being cured of his leprosy. Once he plunged into the Jordan River, he was cleansed. When he tried to show his gratitude to the prophet, he was rebuffed; the latter wanted nothing and pointed to God as giver of the gift. Naaman then directed his thanks to God by deciding to offer sacrifice to the true Lord in his own land. Since sacrifice is acceptable only when offered on sacred soil, Naaman takes a load of dirt from Israel back to his country. Gratitude is clearly the underlying motif.

The gospel story is no different. Ten lepers were cleansed but only one returned to say "Thank you." And where were the other nine? Their faith expression went little further than their cure. Such was not the case with the man who returned. And he was, of all things, a Samaritan, a member of that renegade people despised by the Jews. Luke, always interested in broadening the spiritual horizon, does not hesitate to underscore a Samaritan's sense of gratitude.

The practice of our faith easily becomes a chore if it is simply duty-oriented. When sinful occasions present themselves, we may often turn away simply out of a sense of right and wrong. There is nothing wrong with that, of course, but it is only "half a loaf." We should want to do the right thing out of a sense of gratitude for God's goodness. This makes the burden much lighter.

Is this not what the letter to Timothy is addressing today? "The word of God is not chained." Paul bears "everything for the sake of those who are chosen" in order that salvation and eternal glory may be theirs. Even with all our infidelities,

PSALM REFLECTION

The royal songs of God's kingship, which include Psalm 98, always praise God for the marvelous deeds he does that stretch beyond Israel's own salvation. God is exalted as creator of all things and doer of wonders in the sight of foreign nations so that they will believe in him. Israel recognized that what-ever victories they enjoyed as a small nation pitted against the mighty powers of Mesopotamia or Egypt, they did so only because their God was the only God of all, Lord of history and all nations, whether known by them or not. Israel sang of his acts of salvation and attributed the defeat of their powerful attackers to the decision handed down by the ruler of the universe, who even directed the fates of pagan nations who worshiped other gods. Such claims that all nations recognize God's saving deeds go beyond the historical reality, of course. But it didn't matter if every nation actually acknowledged God: creation as a whole reflected his intentions and his ordering will and thus was there to be seen by all who were willing, like Naaman, to come to the Lord.

**Psalm Response
Psalm 98:1, 2–3, 3–4**

Antiphon
The Lord has revealed to the nations his saving power.

Verse for Reflection
[The Lord] rules the world with justice,
And treats all people with fairness.
(v. 9)

Christ remains faithful. Everything rests on God's favor. How can we possibly turn our backs on such goodness? Everything of worth that we do, every Mass that we attend, is a "Thank you" to God. It is the spirit of the Samaritan leper.

In Beethoven's single opera, *Fidelio,* the story finds an impris-oned husband, Florestan, sought after by his devoted wife Leonora. She obtains work in the prison, disguised as a man named Fidelio, overcomes major hurdles trying to reach her hus-band, and reaches his dungeon cell minutes before he is to be executed. Leonora willingly places herself between her hus-band and his killer. The execu-tion is averted only as the prison is liberated by the opposing forces. To Florestan's simple query, "Leonora, what have you done for me?" her answer is sim-ple and direct: "Nothing, Flo-restan, nothing."

Gratitude is the basic recogni-tion that we are loved beyond measure. For proof of that, we need but look at the cross. God has gone the full limit to bring us home. A grateful faith is noth-ing more than a response to this gift.

CATECHETICAL SUGGESTIONS

The life and times of the prophet Elisha
Boundaries and ethics for those in pastoral service
The letters of Timothy and pseudonymity
The Stephen Ministry
Healing ministries in our church and in our com-munity
The role of miracles in the Church today

**Second Reading:
2 Timothy 2:8–13**

Beloved: Remember Jesus Christ, raised from the dead, a descendant of David: such is my gospel, for which I am suffering, even to the point of chains, like a criminal. But the word of God is not chained. Therefore, I bear with everything for the sake of those who are chosen, so that they too may obtain the salvation that is in Christ Jesus, together with eternal glory. This saying is trustworthy:

If we have died with him
   we shall also live with him;
if we persevere
   we shall also reign with him.
But if we deny him
   he will deny us.
If we are unfaithful
   he remains faithful,
   for he cannot deny himself.

SCRIPTURE COMMENTARY

In chapter 1 of the second letter to Timothy, Paul had reminded Timothy to have courage to stand up to persecution and to remain steadfast in what he preached despite opposition. Paul follows this instruction with the reminder that he himself had always preached (the death and) the resurrection of Jesus without fear, despite the suffering he had borne in doing so. But Timothy should not be afraid, for the very message of the resurrection is far more powerful than those who oppose its messengers. It brings salvation to all whom God has chosen to hear and believe, and therefore it must be proclaimed fearlessly. Paul backs up his point by quoting a little hymn that sums up the gospel message of the cross and resurrection. The first half affirms that those who die with Christ to the old ways of sin will live with him in risen life. The second half warns that those who reject him will in turn be rejected and not find life with God. This is because God is faithful and must uphold the truth and cannot call a "no" a "yes" or turn rejection into faith. If we choose to remain in the power of sin and death, it is impossible for us to also live in the Lord.

LITURGICAL NOTES

The scriptures this Sunday speak of gratitude for gifts received. They speak to us of Eucharist, which means "thanksgiving."

Yet many in our Sunday assemblies do not fully enter into this thanksgiving. At the beginning of the Eucharistic Prayer, the presider proclaims, "Let us give thanks to the Lord our God." But what is the motive for our thanks? What is the motive for our thanks as a particular assembly gathered in prayer? What is the motive for our thanks as individual members of that assembly? Without a motive for our thanks, we can find ourselves offering a kind of "empty thanks"—thanksgiving for vague, unnamed gifts.

People have been taught to leave their problems, cares, and concerns at the church door. However, it seems that the very nature of the liturgy invites the opposite. The liturgy invites us to bring those cares and concerns to the table of word and sacrament and allow God to transform them. So, too, the liturgy invites us to bring our grateful hearts, our thanksgivings to the liturgy so that we can unite them with the great act of thanksgiving and worship that *is* the liturgy.

In our catechesis on the liturgy, liturgy committees can spend a good deal of time explaining things, pointing out changes and the reasons for those changes, and encouraging participation. It would be helpful to spend an equal amount of time on catechesis *for* the liturgy: on what attitudes and dispositions we can bring to the celebration and why. The committee, through its own catechesis, can assist people in naming the motives for their thanks and in expressing their thanks at the Sunday celebration.

SCRIPTURE COMMENTARY

The parable of the ten lepers seems somewhat unfair to the nine who did not return. After all, Jesus had commanded them to go to the priest to certify that they were cured, and they believed him despite the fact that he had not done anything to actually heal them at this point; they received healing on the road to the temple. They did what they had been told to do and presumably gave thanks to God in the temple after the priest had pronounced them healed, by offering the required thanksgiving sacrifice. But Jesus was noting that only a foreigner had gone beyond the law to recognize that God was acting in a new way through Jesus. That foreigner needed to thank the bringer of this new way of the kingdom, not to just simply fulfill the law's demands. The scene was a small event, but it reinforced the fact that many Gentiles were receiving Jesus' message with more faith in him and more desire to be his disciple than were many Jews. This story is unique to Luke's gospel. It prepares for Luke's second volume, the Acts of the Apostles, in which the apostles and disciples do indeed bring the gospel out more and more to the Gentile world.

Gospel: Luke 17:11–19

As Jesus continued his journey to Jerusalem, he traveled through Samaria and Galilee. As he was entering a village, ten lepers met him. They stood at a distance from him and raised their voices, saying, "Jesus, Master! Have pity on us!" And when he saw them, he said, "Go show yourselves to the priests." As they were going they were cleansed. And one of them, realizing he had been healed, returned, glorifying God in a loud voice; and he fell at the feet of Jesus and thanked him. He was a Samaritan. Jesus said in reply, "Ten were cleansed, were they not? Where are the other nine? Has none but this foreigner returned to give thanks to God?" Then he said to him, "Stand up and go; your faith has saved you."

MUSIC CONNECTION

The topic of faith introduced in last week's readings is continued today. In the first reading, Naaman the Syrian is cured of his leprosy and returns to Elisha to declare his faith in the God of Israel. Likewise, in the gospel's memorable story, the Samaritan leper, healed by Jesus, returns to render thanks to God. The notions of faith and gratitude for God's goodness and healing power are all intertwined in these passages, and the psalm is a wonderful summary statement of all these dimensions. *Your Hands, O Lord, in Days of Old,* with its enticing use of a Mozart melody, warmly invites us into the compassionate healing ministry of Jesus both in the past and today. The Ruth Duck hymn text *Out of the Depths* invokes God's healing power and ends in a rhapsody of praise—a dynamic paralleling the stories we contemplate today. Other possibilities include Fred Pratt Green's *O Christ the Healer, He Healed the Darkness of My Mind, There Is a Balm in Gilead, Song of Healing, Healing River of the Spirit,* and *Precious Lord, Take My Hand.* The second letter to Timothy calls to mind Deiss's early but still effective piece *Keep in Mind.* Finally, today's responsorial, Psalm 98, has numerous fine settings, including the popular Haas/Haugen version and that of Janco.

First Reading:
Exodus 17:8–13

In those days, Amalek came and waged war against Israel. Moses, therefore, said to Joshua, "Pick out certain men, and tomorrow go out and engage Amalek in battle. I will be standing on top of the hill with the staff of God in my hand." So Joshua did as Moses told him: he engaged Amalek in battle after Moses had climbed to the top of the hill with Aaron and Hur. As long as Moses kept his hands raised up, Israel had the better of the fight, but when he let his hands rest, Amalek had the better of the fight. Moses' hands, however, grew tired; so they put a rock in place for him to sit on. Meanwhile Aaron and Hur supported his hands, one on one side and one on the other, so that his hands remained steady till sunset. And Joshua mowed down Amalek and his people with the edge of the sword.

SCRIPTURE COMMENTARY

The story of Israel's defense against the attacks of the nomadic people of Amalek takes place in the midst of their desert journey from the place where they escaped through the Red Sea (chapters 14–15) to the place of their meeting with God at Mount Sinai (chapter 19). The various incidents that occur in these chapters include God providing water where there is no water (Exod 17:5–7), manna and quail when there is no food (Exod 16:13–14), judges and tribal organization where there had only been a crowd of escapees (Exod 18:14–24), and victory over enemies when attacked. Each of these incidents centers on turning to God when we are in desperate need or lack the basics of life. The desert symbolizes Israel's nakedness. Leaving the wealth of Egypt as well as its slavery behind, they trusted God's word enough to follow Moses into the wilderness, where they would have to depend entirely on God guiding them to his Promised Land. God provides our nourishment and our protection from evil. The strange and miraculous story of a victory that depends on whether Moses' hand stays raised in the air, and not on the military strategy or skills of Israel's generals, just confirms that only confidence in God will sustain Israel in its new relationship with God as his chosen people.

HOMILY HELPS

In early Christianity, after the resurrection and ascension of Jesus, the belief was strong that he would soon return for the full establishment of his reign. However, such was not the case. As we can see in Paul's letters to the Thessalonians and the Corinthians, the delay caused no small amount of concern and anxiety. John's gospel takes a positive approach in highlighting the fact that the end is already present in the Spirit life that Christians enjoy. Nonetheless, in those early days some people began to fall away from the faith, as is seen in the parable of the sower and the seed.

Perseverance is a virtue more easily addressed than practiced. It is hard enough to stand firm in our earthly aspirations; it is even harder to adhere to the promise of goods unseen.

If the Hebrews were to defeat the Amalekites, Moses had to keep his hands elevated. The battle was long, and it is not surprising that his arms began to drop. Since there was no substitute for victory to be obtained only with God's help, his hands had to remain raised. Help in keeping his arms aloft was given by trusted aides.

The gospel parable takes another approach to the matter. Perseverance can become persistence, which attains its goal by annoyance. The widow obtains recognition by repeated returns in pursuit of her request. It is finally in the interests of peace and quiet that the judge acquiesces and grants her request. Will God be less generous with a suppliant?

We all grow tired and weary when we believe our prayers are not being heard. Yet we fail to see the big picture and cannot foresee all the consequences. St. Monica prayed for years for the conversion of her pagan son,

PSALM REFLECTION

Psalm 121 expresses confidence in God as the source of our help, calls God the guardian of Israel, and mentions looking to the mountains for victory. These elements make it seem like an ideal response to the story of Moses' victory on the mountain in Exodus 17. In ancient thinking, including that of the Bible, God would dwell in his palace in heaven and rule the earth through his governance of nature and through sending the angels as his messengers to earth. But when God wanted to come down on his own, he would use the mountains as a ladder to step down to earth. Thus the psalmist is thinking both of God descending from his heavenly home to help him and also of the temple on its mountain in Jerusalem, Mount Zion. The idea was that God remains as ruler of the universe in heaven but makes himself present in a very special way in his earthly temple to see and hear and respond to the prayers of his people when they come to him.

Psalm Response
Psalm 121:1–2, 3–4, 5–6, 7–8

Antiphon
Our help is from the Lord, who made heaven and earth.

Verse for Reflection
May he not let your foot slip,
May he not sleep who stands guard over you.
(v. 3)

Augustine, only to see him finally take his leave of their home and journey to Italy. His mother could only believe that her prayer was fruitless. But in Milan Augustine met Ambrose, who was instrumental in his conversion to the faith.

Our scriptures today also underscore the great importance of the scriptures in the Christian life. There was a time, in the not too distant past, when Catholics were not encouraged to read the Bible. Fortunately, that day has passed. It is worth reflecting on the sterling examples of perseverance that the scriptures afford. The promise was made to the astonished Abraham that he would have progeny in his declin-

ing years, and his faith never wavered. Other examples include Esther's belief that national tragedy could be averted through a woman's efforts, Jeremiah's faith in the face of severe opposition and alienation, the undying allegiance of Paul in the face of a litany of misfortunes, and, of course, the example of Jesus himself, who never abandoned the Father's will.

We are all human and have our moments of "What's the use?" But then our spiritual energy returns and we persevere. With today's psalmist we lift up our eyes toward the mountain and say, "Our help is from the Lord, who made heaven and earth."

LITURGICAL NOTES

The scriptures today speak of constant and persistent prayer and the effects of such prayer. This Sunday invites the reflection of the liturgy team on their constant and persistent efforts at the planning and preparation for the prayer of the Church: the Sunday Eucharist.

These efforts remain a constant challenge because we can easily become discouraged when the fruits of these efforts are not evident. But while they might not always be evident, this does not mean our efforts are without fruits.

**Second Reading:
2 Timothy 3:14–4:2**

Beloved: Remain faithful to what you have learned and believed, because you know from whom you learned it, and that from infancy you have known the sacred Scriptures, which are capable of giving you wisdom for salvation through faith in Christ Jesus. All Scripture is inspired by God and is useful for teaching, for refutation, for correction, and for training in righteousness, so that one who belongs to God may be competent, equipped for every good work.

I charge you in the presence of God and of Christ Jesus, who will judge the living and the dead, and by his appearing and his kingly power: proclaim the word; be persistent whether it is convenient or inconvenient; convince, reprimand, encourage through all patience and teaching.

SCRIPTURE COMMENTARY

Paul continues his personal instructions to Timothy on how to be a good apostle by learning the lessons that Paul learned and by imitating Paul's own ministry. Paul gives special emphasis to knowledge of the scriptures, especially in church leaders. In particular he reminds Timothy that he was brought up in a Christian household to learn those passages of scripture that prophesized the salvation that would come in Jesus. Paul refers to knowing the type of scriptural prophesies that were spoken of by Jesus in the Emmaus story of Luke 24. But believing that Jesus is Savior is not enough. These same scriptures provide the commandments of God and the teaching of Jesus on moral living and behavior. In a special way, Jesus as judge of the living and the dead will demand accountability from his disciples for justice on earth.

In many of the nonliturgical churches, part of the regular Sunday service involves some kind of testimony on how God is clearly working one's life. The testimonies are designed to encourage the believers, to spur them on to deeper and more profound faith. This concept might well be used in our gatherings of liturgical ministers. In addition to the opportunities for enrichment and prayer, these gatherings provide opportunities for the various ministers to hear from one of their own what it means to be a proclaimer of God's word, or to be an extraordinary minister of Holy Communion, or to lead others in the sung praise of God. This kind of

CATECHETICAL SUGGESTIONS

The morality of war: Old Testament, New Testament, church teaching
Catholic tradition regarding guardian angels
Dei Verbum (Dogmatic Constitution on Divine Revelation)
The "Breaking Open the Word" process for faith sharing
Parables as distinct from allegories
New Testament teachings on prayer

witness, indicating that ministry is more than "just a job," serves to strengthen, encourage, and build up the other ministers. If you have a newsletter or a regular mailing to your liturgical ministers, consider adding a witness

piece to it. Initially this may sound strange to Roman Catholic ears, but you will surely be surprised at the delight many will experience in hearing or reading such witness, and how it will help to validate their own experience.

SCRIPTURE COMMENTARY

The Old Testament constantly returns to the theme of the importance of just judgments and decisions on the part of religious leaders, kings, and judges alike. The characteristic description of God is that of Exodus 34:5–6—that God is a God of mercy and compassion, slow to anger and rich in kindness, *but maintaining justice and right* against the wicked to the third and fourth generation. This is reflected also in the great prophetic passages, such as Amos 5:23-24: "Remove the noise of your hymns and liturgical instruments, and instead let justice flow down like a river, and righteousness like an unfailing stream." Jesus uses the example of a judge who has no such sense of God's fairness or mercy but is interested solely in career advancement. Still, even with the unjust, persistence pays off for petitioners. If this is so in the case of those who pay no attention to God's ways, then how much the more would God himself be the one who always fulfills his promise to hear and answer those in need. This is a warning to Jesus' disciples not to lose heart when it seems that Jesus has not returned when they have hoped, but to keep faith and trust that he will return at the end and that he certainly does hear and is answering their prayers in the meantime.

Gospel: Luke 18:1–8

Jesus told his disciples a parable about the necessity for them to pray always without becoming weary. He said, "There was a judge in a certain town who neither feared God nor respected any human being. And a widow in that town used to come to him and say, 'Render a just decision for me against my adversary.' For a long time the judge was unwilling, but eventually he thought, 'While it is true that I neither fear God nor respect any human being, because this widow keeps bothering me I shall deliver a just decision for her lest she finally come and strike me.'" The Lord said, "Pay attention to what the dishonest judge says. Will not God then secure the rights of his chosen ones who call out to him day and night? Will he be slow to answer them? I tell you, he will see to it that justice is done for them speedily. But when the Son of Man comes, will he find faith on earth?"

MUSIC CONNECTION

Both the first reading and gospel today speak of God's response to our cries for help. In Exodus, the gesture-prayer of Moses is answered by a victory over Israel's enemy, Amalek. Luke's story of the judge and the persistent widow sets the stage for assuring us that God responds to "his chosen ones who call out to him day and night." The overarching message that God hears us and cares for us is expressed in hymns such as *Remember Your Love; The Lord Is My Light; Sweet, Sweet Spirit; Shepherd Me, O God; God Whose Almighty Word; God beyond All Names;* and *Healing River.* A rousing rendition of *O God, Our Help in Ages Past* or *Lord of All Hopefulness* textually and melodically can reinforce the thrust of today's readings. Anne Quigley's moving *There Is a Longing* invokes a picture of God who is ever near and can be counted on to hear our prayers, and Joncas's lyrical *The Lord Is Near* paints a portrait of God in the same colors. Today's responsorial, Psalm 121, is given fine expression by Michael Joncas, Gelineau, and Alstott.

First Reading:
Sirach 35:12–14, 16–18

The LORD is a God of justice,
> who knows no favorites.
Though not unduly partial toward
> the weak,
> yet he hears the cry of the
> oppressed.
The LORD is not deaf to the wail of
> the orphan,
> nor to the widow when she pours
> out her complaint.
The one who serves God willingly
> is heard;
> his petition reaches the heavens.
The prayer of the lowly pierces the
> clouds;
> it does not rest till it reaches its
> goal,
nor will it withdraw till the Most
> High responds,
> judges justly and affirms the
> right,
and the Lord will not delay.

SCRIPTURE COMMENTARY

Since the parable of the Pharisee and the publican in today's gospel has to do with the right attitude of the heart toward God, the selection from Sirach is very appropriate. The wisdom teacher describes a God who judges fairly and wisely, upholding justice and right, while being compassionate and merciful at the same time. This is the ideal of the Old Testament teaching from the time of the earliest law code in Exodus 22, through the prophets, the Psalms, and down to the Wisdom books. God shows no favoritism to people because of their fortune or talents in this life. The mighty and the powerless are both called to obey the way of the Torah that God has revealed to Israel and at the same time to imitate God in his concern for the poor, the widow, the orphan, and all others who have no hope except to pour out their complaints and express their trust in God as their benefactor.

HOMILY HELPS

There is no question that insignificant people figure prominently and positively in the scriptures. In the Old Testament they were known as the *anawim*, which was originally a social category, the poor who were dependent upon others for the necessities of life. They were, in a sense, the dependents of God himself and therefore had a special claim on the people of Israel. From being a disenfranchised segment of society, their status gradually took on a spiritual significance as they came to represent the spiritual dependence to which we are all called. This is the "poor in spirit" of the beatitudes.

Sirach today addresses the question from two perspectives. The first is that of God's intent. He willingly hears the cry of the poor, even though he is not given to favoritism. The second is that of the poor themselves, who should be confident that God is open to their needs as the "have-nots" of society. The reason for this is that they recognize their need for God. Since they are not immersed in temporal preoccupations, they have a certain freedom to see God as the source of all good.

The gospel parable presents a rather startling comparison that illustrates clearly what Sirach is saying. The contrast is between a religious man, a Pharisee, and a public sinner, a tax collector in the employ of a foreign, pagan power. Both stand before God. The former litanies the good things that he is doing and gives thanks that, unlike many of his contemporaries, he is not a sinner. He personifies self-righteousness.

The other man is not pretentious and freely admits his sinfulness. He has no claim on goodness; he is simply a sinner in need of God's mercy. This is the man who wins God's favor.

There is always the danger of religion becoming religiosity. The externals, even good works, can become an obstacle to clear spiritual vision and our relationship with God. We assume that as long as we keep doing good things, we will reach our goal.

PSALM REFLECTION

Psalm 34 expresses in a very dramatic way the lesson that Sirach tries to teach his students. The psalmist announces his undying praise of God for his goodness to the lowly. He is confident that God always hears those who seek to live according to the way of God's commandments (the "just"). When it is most difficult to pray to God, as when one is afflicted by depression, suffering, or seemingly unfair treatment, the just person seeks God all the more. God will be close to those who are most broken and in need when they ask him; at the same time, God does not allow evildoers to go without punishment. God is a God of justice and mercy, and therefore we can rely on his help in any situation.

Psalm Response
Psalm 34:2–3, 17–18, 19, 23

Antiphon
The Lord hears the cry of the poor.

Verse for Reflection
When the afflicted called out, the Lord heard;
And saved him from all his troubles. (v. 7)

SCRIPTURE COMMENTARY

Saint Paul was certainly the most zealous of the disciples of Jesus whom we hear about in the New Testament. The second letter to Timothy is one of the latest Pauline writings in the New Testament and either comes from the very last days of Paul's life, perhaps even as he faced execution in Rome, or is the work of his disciples reflecting shortly after Paul's death on his overall attitude to his ministry. It has a very personal

Second Reading:
2 Timothy 4:6–8, 16–18

Beloved: I am already being poured out like a libation, and the time of my departure is at hand. I have competed well; I have finished the race; I have kept the faith. From now on the crown of righteousness awaits me, which the Lord, the just judge, will award to me on that

We use our good deeds to measure our progress, and with all the evil that surrounds us, we can easily place ourselves on a pedestal of self-justification. The sinner, on the other hand, has nothing on which to pride himself. He is in desperate need of God's outreach and freely admits it. It is the repentant sinner—not the man who justifies himself—who goes home justified. This brings to mind the story of the prodigal son. The older son was so convinced of his good conduct that he could not understand his father's willingness to reach out to his wayward brother.

Does the letter to Timothy today contradict this teaching? Paul says he has stayed the course and reached the finish line. Is this a matter of extolling personal accomplishment? Not really. We need but read on. "The Lord," he says, "stood by me and gave me strength."

Life holds many adversities for all of us. We often feel beaten and broken. But far from being abandoned, we are probably closer to God than we can imagine. "The Lord is close to the brokenhearted and those who are crushed in spirit he saves."

LITURGICAL NOTES

The scriptures tell us of the proper disposition we ought to have in prayer. It is the prayer of the humble that pierces the clouds.

Too often we can think that everyone is like we are. A Sunday like this can invite our reflection on how people with disabilities are welcomed into our liturgical celebrations. Liturgy committees should not presume to know the best locations for a wheelchair or the best spot for people to obtain a listening device. It would be well worth

day, and not only to me, but to all who have longed for his appearance.

At my first defense no one appeared on my behalf, but everyone deserted me. May it not be held against them! But the Lord stood by me and gave me strength, so that through me the proclamation might be completed and all the Gentiles might hear it. And I was rescued from the lion's mouth. The Lord will rescue me from every evil threat and will bring me safe to his heavenly kingdom. To him be glory forever and ever. Amen.

SCRIPTURE COMMENTARY, CONTINUED

tone to it, revealing much about Paul's sufferings. Paul clearly sees that the way of accepting lowliness and suffering for the gospel is what Jesus has taught him—and that he has sought to live in imitation of his master all during his ministry. Paul is confident that he will receive a reward—not fame or wealth or any other type of earthly reward but union with Christ in heaven. The whole of his life he has preached the message that we are united to Christ in his death and resurrection, and now he looks forward to the full completion of that hope in his own life.

Gospel: Luke 18:9–14

Jesus addressed this parable to those who were convinced of their own righteousness and despised everyone else. "Two people went up to the temple area to pray; one was a Pharisee and the other was a tax collector. The Pharisee took up his position and spoke this

SCRIPTURE COMMENTARY

There could hardly be a greater contrast than the two conversations with God presented by Jesus in this parable. The publican *prays in need to God*, asking God for mercy, seeking forgiveness, and acknowledging his need for God. The Pharisee *tells God in thanksgiving* how good he is and how much he deserves God's love and favor. Jesus portrays this as a fault. The Pharisee is rightly thankful for his situation as a student of Torah who has mastered living it. But he is proud of this in his own eyes and has forgotten whatever his sins have been and his consequent need of God's mercy for himself. Pharisees were a reform

the effort to consult with those who work with persons with disabilities as well as the very people themselves. The information gathered in consultation can be placed within the context of what the parish can do at this time and what plans it might make for the future to make both the worship space and the celebration itself more accommodating to those with disabilities.

This is also a Sunday on which we can consider both a renewed and additional catechesis on the sacrament of the sick. People still continued to be amazed that this is not the sacrament of the dying but of the sick. This might be a

good Sunday to consider a communal celebration of the sacrament of the sick. The Rite of Pastoral Care of the Sick outlines this communal rite in great detail.

During the coming week the Church will celebrate the Solemnity of All Saints (November 1) and, on November 2, the Commemoration of All the Faithful Departed (All Souls Day). All Saints Day is a holy day of obligation. All Souls Day invites the parish to remember and pray for those who have gone before us in faith. The liturgy committee ought to find some ways of having people submit the names of those family members and friends

they wish to have remembered in the All Souls Day liturgies.

In little more than a month, the church year will conclude with the Solemnity of Christ the King, and then a new liturgical year will begin with the first Sunday of Advent. In addition to attending to the preparations needed for Advent, liturgy committees would do well to review the entire year: planning, ministries, music, environment, scheduling, and so on. Such a review provides an ideal opportunity to capitalize on the strengths of the past year and to identify and improve those areas that might need correction or additional attention.

SCRIPTURE COMMENTARY, CONTINUED

movement in Judaism that began about a century before Jesus to keep the law of God and root out the political compromises and manipulations of religious institutions such as the temple priesthood for the gains of a few. Pharisees made a difference and attracted many ordinary Jews to a deeper life of faith, but the more rigid were their expectations that someone should be perfect, the greater was the danger of pride. Jesus warns that all observance of prayer and worship is to recognize our dependence on God, not to make our case for divine reward or recognition. Even more, there is a suggestion the Pharisee may have done much of this for the recognition of his goodness by others, and this is why he looks down on those who have not had the same opportunity or made a commitment to the same observant life. The Talmud records other examples of this kind of prayer. Thus Rabbi Nehunia used to pray as he left his rabbinic academy: "Thank you, O Lord, that you set my destiny to sit in the house of learning and have not set my portion with those who sit on the street corners....I rise early to the words of the law and they rise early to vain things." Jesus refuses this if it does not include awareness of our own sinfulness and compassion to those who are in need of it.

> prayer to himself, 'O God, I thank you that I am not like the rest of humanity — greedy, dishonest, adulterous—or even like this tax collector. I fast twice a week, and I pay tithes on my whole income.' But the tax collector stood off at a distance and would not even raise his eyes to heaven but beat his breast and prayed, 'O God, be merciful to me a sinner.' I tell you, the latter went home justified, not the former; for whoever exalts himself will be humbled, and the one who humbles himself will be exalted."

MUSIC CONNECTION

Once again this week the readings speak of God's answering our prayer. Both Sirach and Luke stress God's partiality to the oppressed and poor while, at the same time, underscoring the importance of humility in our relationship with God. For Sirach, "the prayer of the lowly pierces the clouds" while Luke declares that "whoever exalts himself will be humbled; but whoever humbles himself will be exalted." Possible hymns include *My Soul Is Longing, Anthem, I Lift Up My Soul, The Cry of the Poor, What Does the Lord Require, The Summons,* and *Jesus Shepherd of Our Souls.* Jim Marchionda's *Make Us One,* with its stress on humility and care for others, is a fine expression of what it means to be a disciple. The *Magnificat,* a focal point of Christian humility in the face of God's help and blessing, has many fine settings, including those by Alstott, Haas, and Joncas. Any of these would certainly be fitting today. Michael Joncas's *The Lord Is Near,* an arrangement of Psalm 27, strikes a textual balance between God's answering our prayers and the virtuous humility that is a sign of true discipleship. Today's responsorial, Psalm 34, finds good settings by Foley, Kasbohm, and Gelineau.

CATECHETICAL SUGGESTIONS

Catholic social-justice teachings
Parish bereavement ministries
Individual and general judgment
Go and Make Disciples (USCC document)
Forms of private prayer
The seven deadly sins

ALL SAINTS

First Reading: Revelation 7:2–4, 9–14

I, John, saw another angel come up from the East, holding the seal of the living God. He cried out in a loud voice to the four angels who were given power to damage the land and the sea, "Do not damage the land or the sea or the trees until we put the seal on the foreheads of the servants of our God." I heard the number of those who had been marked with the seal, one hundred and forty-four thousand marked from every tribe of the children of Israel.

After this I had a vision of a great multitude, which no one could count, from every nation, race, people, and tongue. They stood before the throne and before the Lamb, wearing white robes and holding palm branches in their hands. They cried out in a loud voice:
"Salvation comes from our God, who is
seated on the throne,
and from the Lamb."

All the angels stood around the throne and around the elders and the four living creatures. They prostrated themselves before the throne, worshiped God, and exclaimed:

SCRIPTURE COMMENTARY

The book of Revelation combines graphic scenes of the battle on earth between the forces of evil and the judgment of God with inspiring visions in the heavens of those who have died in Christ and live now in eternal happiness and glory with Christ himself in their midst. The scene in chapter 7 is built on the narrative of the prophet Ezekiel in his chapter 9 when, just before the destruction of Jerusalem, God marks with a cross (which stands for the letter T in Hebrew) the heads of all who are to be saved. John the Seer here prepares his readers for the great battle with Satan by noting that God marks *all* who might be saved, not just a mere one hundred and forty-four thousand. The twelve times twelve times one thousand symbolizes a vast number beyond counting—it represents all of the Old Testament people (the twelve tribes), all the Christian faithful (the twelve apostles), extended a thousand times over! Literalism has no place in the interpretation of this book! Moreover, when we see through the crack into the heavens, it is a symbol of hope for the persecuted and suffering readers of the book here on earth—don't lose hope! God has fixed a reward for all who remain faithful, and it is a union with all of the prophets

HOMILY HELPS

Today we celebrate the arrival at their final destiny of the baptized who have fought the good fight and have finished the course. At the same time, we are reminded that this state exists not only in the future but also in the present as well.

In the striking panorama presented to us in Revelation, we see the elect or saved, formerly sealed in baptism, now sealed by the angel in anticipation of full redemption. They include the full complement of Israel (one hundred and forty-four thousand from the twelve tribes) and the world at large (the crowd from every nation, race, and people). Theirs is the glory that is the inheritance of us all, not by reason of our own merit but because we "have washed our robes and made them white in the blood of the Lamb."

The Church gives us today's feast not simply to congratulate and commend those who have attained their appointed destiny. We are also reminded that we already enjoy their company and will be fully united with them if we but stay the course. They are the role models of the way we should live. And our program of life is outlined for us in today's

SCRIPTURE COMMENTARY, CONTINUED
and leaders of the Bible, the Christian saints and martyrs who came before us, and the angelic choirs praising God. And in the center is Jesus the Christ, who died as our Passover lamb on the cross to save us by his blood just as the lamb at the Exodus did for Israel of old.

"Amen. Blessing and glory, wisdom and thanksgiving, honor, power, and might be to our God forever and ever. Amen."

Then one of the elders spoke up and said to me, "Who are these wearing white robes, and where did they come from?" I said to him, "My lord, you are the one who knows." He said to me, "These are the ones who have survived the time of great distress; they have washed their robes and made them white in the Blood of the Lamb."

PSALM REFLECTION

Scholars view Psalm 24 as a processional psalm from the liturgy of the temple. In the parts that are not read today, the psalm pictures the priests and people bringing the Ark of the Covenant into the temple, probably on New Year's Day, when Israel celebrated God's rule over the universe as king of creation. Two characteristics of faith are presented to us in the responses today: (1) God has control over all events in the universe and nothing is beyond his purpose and rule, so we need to have confidence that no evil can overcome God's plans. (2) God comes with judgment to reward all who are faithful and keep his commandments. He will not neglect or overlook anyone who turns to him for help in time of trouble. He looks upon and bestows his light and favor on all who would turn their faces toward his!

Psalm Response
Psalm 24:1bc–2, 3–4ab, 5–6

Antiphon
Lord, this is the people that
   longs to see your face.

Verses for Reflection
Who can stand in his holy
   place?
He whose hands are sinless,
   whose heart is pure.
(vv. 3–4)

gospel, in the beatitudes that open the Sermon on the Mount and constitute the Magna Carta of the Christian life.

The beatitudes have to do with our spiritual posture in life, a basic state of being. Poor in spirit, sorrowing, lowly, transparent (pure of heart), persecuted, and insulted. In a certain sense, the first of them encompasses the others. The poor in spirit are those who realize their dependence on God in the face of whatever difficulties they may encounter. With Job, the poor in spirit say: "Naked I have come into this world and naked I shall leave. Blessed be the name of the Lord." Our human existence is but an expression of God's goodness.

Two of the beatitudes are more assertive in character; they are blessed who show mercy and work for peace. These beatitudes spring from the aforementioned basic dispositions but often bring us into controversy. Showing mercy today may mean opposing the death penalty or cruel and inhuman punishment. The Church's position has been clearly stated, yet many are not in agreement. Those who oppose the death penalty are often labeled "soft on crime" or "socially unrealistic." Peacemakers oppose war except in legitimate defense. This would mean a "just war," but the problem is that almost all modern wars have

been claimed to be "just." There is, however, one overriding truth. War brings in its wake death and devastation, especially for the poor and innocent. A stand against war or the death penalty is not always popular and brings more than a share of rejection and alienation, even from other Christians. It is proof that living the beatitudes was never meant to be easy.

The letter of John today looks to the future, the heavenly state that awaits us. But even now we are joined to God. "We are God's children now; . . . [later] we shall see him as he is." It is consoling to know that heaven and earth are joined.

**Second Reading:
1 John 3:1–3**

Beloved: See what love the Father has bestowed on us that we may be called the children of God. Yet so we are. The reason the world does not know us is that it did not know him. Beloved, we are God's children now; what we shall be has not yet been revealed. We do know that when it is revealed we shall be like him, for we shall see him as he is. Everyone who has this hope based on him makes himself pure, as he is pure.

SCRIPTURE COMMENTARY

The early Church often called the Christian converts "saints" (see Rom 1:7; 1 Cor 1:2). They are *holy* in the Lord because they imitate and live the holiness of God revealed by his Old Testament commandments and teaching and by Jesus Christ, the very Son of the Father, who shared his sonship with us through his death and resurrection. But today we celebrate the feast of the saints who have completed their Christian lives and now reside in heaven with God forever. This double focus on sainthood as partly now and partly in fulfillment after death is kept before us in the reading from the letter of John. We must cultivate the deep and vibrant gift of hope that sustains us in this life to live as though we were already fully with Christ in heaven. What stands out about the canonized saints we know is their eagerness to be with Christ and in Christ—now in our imperfect struggle to live the grace of Christ and in hope of that fullness in heaven. John captures that tension and joy in this passage.

LITURGICAL NOTES

This solemnity commemorates all those who have gone before us—the named and unnamed saints—who now stand in glory, singing the praises of the Lamb. The liturgy is celebrated in the same manner as a Sunday Mass and includes the Gloria and Profession of Faith. A proper preface is given in the Sacramentary for All Saints Day.

It would be appropriate to adorn with flowers the shrines of the saints within the church building or within the gathering space. Surrounded by the images of the saints, we, the pilgrim church, are reminded that

CATECHETICAL SUGGESTIONS

The communion of saints
The saints after whom we are named
The saint after whom our church is named
Martyrology in the book of Revelation
The beatitudes
The models of holiness we have had in our lives

we are called not just to imitate them but to become saints ourselves.

Vigil Masses can find themselves in competition with local Halloween traditions. Rather than compete, liturgy planners would do well to consider ways of including children in the celebra-

tion of these vigil Masses. For example, children might be encouraged to wear Halloween costumes representing their patron saint or their favorite saint, clearly adding a new level of meaning to the Halloween celebrations and the celebration of All Saints Day.

SCRIPTURE COMMENTARY

The eight beatitudes are part of the Sermon on the Mount, which in Matthew gathers the first teachings of Jesus on discipleship into one place. Indeed, the eight beatitudes open this sermon and thus are the formal beginning of all of Jesus' teaching in the gospel. The form of eight beatitudes arranged into two groups of four creates a summary of what discipleship is to be. Note that the first and last both end with the promise that the "kingdom of God is theirs." The middle ones suggest that those who live out these commands will be rewarded in this life itself, at least in part. But the opening and closing promises make the reader think immediately of that kingdom in its victory and fullness as portrayed in the first reading today from Revelation 7. Thus the beatitudes serve to teach us how to live in this life, but also look forward to the last sermon of Jesus in Matthew 25, where, *at the end of time*, God will gather all the sheep and goats together for judgment and welcome into his eternal kingdom only those who lived the kind of discipleship described by the beatitudes.

Gospel: Matthew 5:1–12a

When Jesus saw the crowds, he went up the mountain, and after he had sat down, his disciples came to him. He began to teach them, saying:

"Blessed are the poor in spirit,
for theirs is the Kingdom of heaven.
Blessed are they who mourn,
for they will be comforted.
Blessed are the meek,
for they will inherit the land.
Blessed are they who hunger and thirst
for righteousness,
for they will be satisfied.
Blessed are the merciful,
for they will be shown mercy.
Blessed are the clean of heart,
for they will see God.
Blessed are the peacemakers,
for they will be called children of God.
Blessed are they who are persecuted for
the sake of righteousness,
for theirs is the Kingdom of heaven.

Blessed are you when they insult you and persecute you and utter every kind of evil against you falsely because of me. Rejoice and be glad, for your reward will be great in heaven."

MUSIC CONNECTION

One of the most popular holy days in the United States, All Saints is rich both scripturally and musically. Revelation's imaginative vision sets the tone for the feast with an otherworldly vision of the one hundred and forty-four thousand from every tribe of Israel and another large crowd of people dressed in long white robes. Psalm 24 names them. "Lord, this is the people that longs to see your face." Either Kevin Keil's setting from GIA or Owen Alstott's from OCP would work well today. The lesson from 1 John points us to the heavenly existence that will be ours. Reginald Heber's classic text *Holy, Holy, Holy! Lord God Almighty* catches the feel and imagery of these first two readings. The gospel is Matthew's version of the beatitudes, one of the most beloved texts in the New Testament. David Haas's *Blest Are They* is a musical restatement of this central Christian text, and John Becker's *Lead Me, Lord* is an equally moving arrangement of this text. Other saints' texts abound, including the Vaughan Williams' classic *For All the Saints, Lift High the Cross,* and *Ye Watchers and Ye Holy Ones.* Two Dan Schutte songs merit special attention today: his *Table of Plenty* reminds us that saints and sinners share the heavenly banquet, while his setting of *For the Beauty of the Earth* unites in a moving and emotive phrase those of us still on earth and those who have found their rightful place in heaven.

First Reading: Wisdom 11:22—12:2

Before the LORD the whole universe is as a grain
from a balance
or a drop of morning dew come down upon the
earth.
But you have mercy on all, because you can do
all things;
and you overlook people's sins that they may
repent.
For you love all things that are
and loathe nothing that you have made;
for what you hated, you would not have fash-
ioned.
And how could a thing remain, unless you willed
it;
or be preserved, had it not been called forth by
you?
But you spare all things, because they are yours,
O LORD and lover of souls,
for your imperishable spirit is in all things!
Therefore you rebuke offenders little by little,
warn them and remind them of the sins they
are committing,
that they may abandon their wickedness and
believe in you, O LORD!

SCRIPTURE COMMENTARY

The reading from Wisdom centers on the wonderful paradox that God is the almighty ruler of all creation and controls even the smallest particles of dust in the universe but at the same time can find room to treat every single person with compassion and mercy. This is because God does not just make and rule creation; he loves it as the reflection of his own goodness and wishes to bring everything that has been alienated back into harmony and unity with himself. Because it is only humans who consciously reject God and who sin, God's mercy is especially directed to all who have turned away from God in sin or rebellion to seek them out and bring them to conversion. His gentle forgiveness reflects his love of all whom he has made in his image and likeness by putting his spirit into us in a way that no other creature shares (Gen 2:7). The author of Wisdom expresses total wonder at the generosity of God's forgiving love.

HOMILY HELPS

When it comes to forgiveness, there is often a wide gap between God and ourselves. In our daily life we are so quick to judge and so slow to forgive. With the slightest suspicion that we have been betrayed, we become hostile and aloof. Even our body language is revelatory. In our more sober moments, however, we know that as disciples of Christ we are to mirror Christ in the world. Our conduct should be commensurate with our calling.

The universe is immense, yet God's mercy extends to the most insignificant creature. Such is clear in the message of Wisdom in today's first reading. There is nothing in God's creation that is not loved—least of all, the human person. This is true especially of those who are most overlooked— the refugee in the Sudan, the migrant worker approaching our borders, the Islamic fundamentalist we have such difficulty understanding. No one is a candidate for our disdain; all are precious in God's sight.

Think of the divine qualities that roll off our psalmist's lips today—mercy, grace, kindness, compassion. All of them find concrete expression in the Zacchaeus story. What he wants is an unobstructed view of Jesus passing by, and so he climbs a sycamore tree. Unfortunately, he has a rather unsavory occupation. As a tax collector, he is in the employ of a foreign power and is consequently excluded from the company of his coreligionists,

PSALM REFLECTION

Psalm 145 is the perfect response to the reflection of the author of Wisdom. God is to be extolled because his compassion and mercy are so great. The psalmist praises God not just for his graciousness to human beings but also for the loving care extending down into the most distant of God's creatures, as small and hidden as they may be in his universe. Above all, God's "works" refer in a special way to the acts of deliverance and salvation God extends to Israel when it calls to him for help. The great narratives of Exodus and Numbers in the period of the escape from Egypt and God's rescue of the tribes from their enemies in Joshua and Judges are in the psalmist's mind. Reciting these acts of salvation in the liturgy and recalling them to each new generation is the constant theme of the Psalms.

**Psalm Response
Psalm 145:1–2, 8–9,
10–11, 13, 14**

Antiphon
I will praise your name
    for ever, my king
    and my God.

Verse for Reflection
The Lord is good to all
    creatures,
And compassionate to
    all his works.
    (v. 9)

CATECHETICAL SUGGESTIONS

Wisdom literature in the Old Testament
The role of reason in religion
An examination of conscience
Acrostic psalms
1, 2 Thessalonians and the end times
Jesus and the marginalized in Luke's gospel

whether at table or elsewhere. But once again Jesus breaks with convention and reaches out to the man. He calls him down from his perch and invites himself to dinner!

It is in private conversation that the real Zacchaeus emerges. He is willing to change, to give half of his possessions to the poor, and to offer to those he has cheated restitution that far exceeds what is required. Jesus commends him and says that he is on the road to salvation.

The story is illustrative of the biblical dictum "Humans see appearances; God looks at the heart."

Thessalonians reminds us today that the time of the second coming will not be anticipated or delayed for our worrying about it. Paul suggests that now is the time for "good purpose" and the "work of faith." Instead of being critical and judgmental and expecting everyone to come to us, we should be speaking the

word of salvation. Where our feet go, Christ can go; where our ears hear and our eyes see, Christ can hear and see.

When a wealthy man in the comfort of his home considered the plight of the starving and homeless, he berated God. "Why do you let these things happen? Why don't you do something about it?" The response was clear and unequivocal. "I did something about it. I created you."

Second Reading:
2 Thessalonians 1:11—2:2

Brothers and sisters: We always pray for you, that our God may make you worthy of his calling and powerfully bring to fulfillment every good purpose and every effort of faith, that the name of our Lord Jesus may be glorified in you, and you in him, in accord with the grace of our God and Lord Jesus Christ.

We ask you, brothers and sisters, with regard to the coming of our Lord Jesus Christ and our assembling with him, not to be shaken out of your minds suddenly, or to be alarmed either by a "spirit," or by an oral statement, or by a letter allegedly from us to the effect that the day of the Lord is at hand.

SCRIPTURE COMMENTARY

As the end of the liturgical year draws near, the Church turns to the second letter of Paul to the Thessalonians because in it Paul answers people's worried questions about the end of the world itself. Many scholars think this letter must be a later addition to the regular collection of Paul because it is so apocalyptic in tone. But on the other hand, there is just as good a reason to believe it is authentic, since it follows from Paul's initial thoughts found in the first letter to Thessalonica. These two letters, then, are the earliest of Paul's letters, and they show that in about the year 50, he still believed Jesus might come very soon. In later letters he cautions about such immediate expectations. He is strongly opposed to the dire warnings produced by many people seeing signs of the end everywhere. The hysterical prophecies of the end have led even to false letters attributed to him, and Paul fears that people's commitment to forming and living true Christian community may be affected. He calls here for faithful living in Jesus as he has taught them, so that they will be ready for the end, regardless of when it comes.

LITURGICAL NOTES

The scriptures clearly proclaim the Church's mission to seek out the lost and bring them home. But there is always one more difficult question: what kind of welcome will they find once they come home?

The kind of welcome we would hope that people will find is both physical and personal. Entering the church building, what does the physical space look like? How many weeks of past bulletins can be located in the vestibule? Is it well lighted? Are exits and restrooms clearly marked? Does the entry or gathering space look like a place that invites people into something greater?

How does our personal welcome reflect our desire to bring people home? Are there sufficient numbers of ushers or ministers of hospitality? Are they clearly identified? Do they know the location of the restrooms, water fountains, first-aid kits, and the like? Do they understand that theirs is a ministry of welcome, and of particular welcome to the unfamiliar or timid person? When is the last time these folks have gathered for prayer, for instruction, for reflection?

If we are to welcome the lost home and if they are to recognize that indeed they are home, let us ensure that they are provided with the same kind of welcome we would give people entering our own personal homes.

SCRIPTURE COMMENTARY

Zacchaeus is the "chief tax collector," but there is no known position under that title in Roman or Jewish records. He may have bought the contract that the Romans put out for bids to collect taxes for the Jericho region. Since this would imply that he could get more tax money from his region than others could, it would make him very unpopular for his use of legal force to do so. Under normal circumstances, he would have avoided crowds because they would have mocked and booed him. If Zacchaeus went out of his way to climb a tree to see Jesus, he did so because something drove him to discover who this man was. Understanding this, Jesus summons Zacchaeus to his side and honors him with a visit to his home. The experience confirms for Zacchaeus his desire to reform and change, and he converts dramatically, promising to those he has cheated restitution far beyond what Moses demanded (see Exod 22:4, 7; Num 5:7) and even giving up the legitimate profits he is entitled to keep in his job. The compassion of God that Jesus offers extends even to someone considered a traitor to the faith by his service to Rome, and that compassion is so strong that even the hardest heart can be turned back to God.

Gospel: Luke 19:1–10

At that time, Jesus came to Jericho and intended to pass through the town. Now a man there named Zacchaeus, who was a chief tax collector and also a wealthy man, was seeking to see who Jesus was; but he could not see him because of the crowd, for he was short in stature. So he ran ahead and climbed a sycamore tree in order to see Jesus, who was about to pass that way. When he reached the place, Jesus looked up and said, "Zacchaeus, come down quickly, for today I must stay at your house." And he came down quickly and received him with joy. When they all saw this, they began to grumble, saying, "He has gone to stay at the house of a sinner." But Zacchaeus stood there and said to the Lord, "Behold, half of my possessions, Lord, I shall give to the poor, and if I have extorted anything from anyone I shall repay it four times over." And Jesus said to him, "Today salvation has come to this house because this man too is a descendant of Abraham. For the Son of Man has come to seek and to save what was lost."

MUSIC CONNECTION

Today's liturgy stresses the wideness of God's mercy, which extends to all creation. As the story of Zacchaeus in the gospel makes clear, this mercy is bestowed on all, even those considered outcasts and undesirables. This stress is firmly rooted in the assertion of the Hebrew scriptures: "But you have mercy on all, because you can do all things." This is a good corrective to our sectarian and limiting perspectives on God's graciousness, kindness, and salvation. Hymns appropriate for today include *Gift of Finest Wheat, All Are Welcome, Come to Me, There's a Wideness in God's Mercy, I Heard the Voice of Jesus Say, Great God of Mercy, Love Divine All Loves Excelling, Softly and Tenderly Jesus Is Calling,* and *Our Father We Have Wandered.* Dan Schutte's *Give Thanks to the Lord* is a paean of praise and thanksgiving to the God who is merciful and does wondrous deeds, while Manibusan's *With All Our Hearts* reminds us that God's love is "unrelenting," a notion fully in accord with the thrust of today's readings. Settings by Jordan, Haas, and Gelineau would work well for today's responsorial, Psalm 145. A rousing setting of *From All That Dwell below the Skies,* with its hymnic claim "eternal thy mercies, Lord," would be a fitting conclusion to today's celebration.

First Reading:
2 Maccabees 7:1–2, 9–14

It happened that seven brothers with their mother were arrested and tortured with whips and scourges by the king, to force them to eat pork in violation of God's law. One of the brothers, speaking for the others, said: "What do you expect to achieve by questioning us? We are ready to die rather than transgress the laws of our ancestors."

At the point of death he said: "You accursed fiend, you are depriving us of this present life, but the King of the world will raise us up to live again forever. It is for his laws that we are dying."

After him the third suffered their cruel sport. He put out his tongue at once when told to do so, and bravely held out his hands, as he spoke these noble words: "It was from Heaven that I received these; for the sake of his laws I disdain them; from him I hope to receive them again." Even the king and

SCRIPTURE COMMENTARY

There is hardly a more poignant passage in all of the Bible than the story of the mother and her seven sons from chapter 7 of the second book of Maccabees. The story is set in the persecution by the Seleucid king Antiochus Epiphanes, who ruled Palestine from his capital in Antioch in Syria from 175 to 164 BC. Antiochus Epiphanes ruled over a variety of Semitic nations and wanted to make all of them conform to Greek values and submit their different religious practices to the cult of Zeus. Since most of these peoples had polytheistic religions in which any one of their gods could be identified with another one like it in some other religion, it was not considered such a radical demand. But alone of these nations, the Jews refused to give up their faith because the God of the Bible did not accept other gods. The king began to enforce his rules by making the Jews give up circumcision, offer meat to idols, and eat pork against the kosher laws. As the persecution grew worse, the Jews rebelled under Judas Maccabeus and gradually defeated the Greeks to win

HOMILY HELPS

Life is indeed precious. The documentary film *March of the Penguins* depicts the tenacious hold on life of the penguins in Antarctica. In the winter months they walk seventy miles in blizzards and blinding snow to reach the water where they can nourish themselves on the abundant sea life and then make the return trip to feed their mates and their young. It is a fierce battle for survival, all in the name of life.

St. Irenaeus speaks of the glory of God as the human person fully alive. It is this gift of life, both present and eternal, which

comes to the fore in today's readings. The life of the young sons in the Maccabees narrative was as precious to them as it is to any young person today. Their best years were still ahead of them and were cherished for whatever they might hold. But rather than tread on their consciences and act against their religious convictions, they were willing to suffer death. By then, close to the dawn of the Christian era, belief in the afterlife was gaining ground. The widow's sons go to their death fully confident that their lives will not be extinguished.

Jesus turns to belief in the afterlife in rebutting the Sad-

ducees, who vehemently deny its possibility. In response to their rather ludicrous casuistry, Jesus prescinds from the example presented, wherein they cite the Old Testament law calling for fraternal substitution in the case of a childless marriage punctuated by the death of the male spouse. Jesus transposes the discussion to a new key. He leaves no doubt about life beyond the grave but sees it as totally different from any earthly experience. No more need be said.

All of us speculate on life after death, but we do so with the language and the images at hand. What will our relationship be to loved ones and family? What will

SCRIPTURE COMMENTARY, CONTINUED

some freedom for themselves. But many gave their lives before that day—among them the family in this story. Above all, the brothers and their mother affirm a faith in the afterlife that will be theirs if they remain faithful. Therefore they do not value rewards in this world as worth anything compared with the hope for everlasting life.

his attendants marveled at the young man's courage, because he regarded his sufferings as nothing.

After he had died, they tortured and maltreated the fourth brother in the same way. When he was near death, he said, "It is my choice to die at the hands of men with the hope God gives of being raised up by him; but for you, there will be no resurrection to life."

PSALM REFLECTION

Several of the verses in Psalm 17 echo themes that were found in the speeches of the brothers in the Maccabees reading. God always hears the cry of those who call to him, because they are faithful and just and have not strayed from his commandments. They are steadfast in the paths of the Lord. These paths are the teachings of the Torah of Moses. The very word *torah* is from the Hebrew word for a way of teaching for life. One walks in the ways of the Lord's teaching. Like the seven brothers, the psalmist is sure that God will not let one of those who keep faith from being destroyed by his or her enemies. Instead, God will protect and hide such a person from harm and show him favor. To be the apple of the eye is to have God look on us in delight and keep us always in his sight. In turn, we will look on his face and be content in his presence on waking. This last verse can foreshadow the hope of resurrection that the brothers all express.

Psalm Response
Psalm 17:1, 5–6, 8, 15

Antiphon
Lord, when your glory appears, my joy will be full.

Verses for Reflection
Hide me in the shadow of your wings
From the wicked who do violence against me!
(vv. 8–9)

it mean to have a completely untroubled life? What is the significance of a "heavenly chorus"? All that we can say is that our honest desires will be fulfilled but in a manner that defies description. Life is the single reality that we can truly affirm, a life now enjoyed by "Abraham, Isaac, and Jacob." In faith, we leave the future to God.

But we do know what life means in the here and now, and it is a life that we champion and defend. To kill a child in the

womb is to deprive it of the richness of experience that we all cherish. To demand the life of one who has taken life is to descend to the same disregard for divine proprietorship as the killer himself. To launch into war is to bring to an untimely death combatants and noncombatants alike for what is claimed to be a just cause and the only solution to an impasse, a claim that leaves many questions unanswered. Finally, to fail to value the lives of

the elderly is to disregard the contributions they have made to the life we all cherish.

Paul says today that ours is an "everlasting encouragement." A deeper life of blessedness has been attained for us by a loving God and his generous Son. The Christian life builds on our natural life. On celebrating someone's birthday, our wish for that person is "long life and happiness." Both in the here and hereafter, it is our greatest gift.

Second Reading:
2 Thessalonians 2:16—3:5

Brothers and sisters: May our Lord Jesus Christ himself and God our Father, who has loved us and given us everlasting encouragement and good hope through his grace, encourage your hearts and strengthen them in every good deed and word.

Finally, brothers and sisters, pray for us, so that the word of the Lord may speed forward and be glorified, as it did among you, and that we may be delivered from perverse and wicked people, for not all have faith. But the Lord is faithful; he will strengthen you and guard you from the evil one. We are confident of you in the Lord that what we instruct you, you are doing and will continue to do. May the Lord direct your hearts to the love of God and to the endurance of Christ.

SCRIPTURE COMMENTARY

In last week's reading, Paul warned the Thessalonians not to be concerned about rumors of the end of the world, not to run after every voice warning of doom and destruction ahead. Today he continues that lesson by counseling them to have confidence in God and continue to work in the Lord. There is still much work ahead because the gospel needs to reach many others who have not heard the good news of salvation. In hoping for Christ's second coming, we must be patient and keep faith as we avoid the temptations of the evil one, Satan. God will continue to strengthen our efforts and keep us constant in love for both himself and his Son. When God rules the heart, one can live in this world and hope for the next world without fear or contradiction.

LITURGICAL NOTES

The scriptures today are not about martyrdom or marriage but about resurrection to new life. There can be no reflection on resurrection without a reflection on the dignity of the human body and the dignity of the human person. How do we reverence one another out of love for Christ?

From the parking lot, to the gathering space, to the seating, to our being sent into the world, it is through very human signs and very human hands that God's presence is mediated to those who have gathered for the liturgy. This Sunday might provide the occasion for reflection on how well we allow our liturgical signs and our human hands to mediate God's presence.

Among the aspects that merit the consideration of the liturgy committee might be the seating space for the baptized; the books for the proclamation, spoken and sung, of the word of God; ample bread for those who will receive Communion; ample wine for those will receive under both kinds. The committee should also consider the attitudes and deportment of the liturgical ministers: their preparation before arriving in church, their attitude of prayer before the liturgy begins, their full, conscious, and active participation in every aspect of the liturgy. All of these signs point to our belief in a life beyond this life, a life filled with the utter fullness of God.

SCRIPTURE COMMENTARY

The question of the resurrection of the dead was a major dividing line between Sadducees and Pharisees. The former believed that only those things that are explicitly affirmed by the Pentateuch are matters of faith. They found no claim to everlasting life in the Torah. The Pharisees, however, took the wider view that all of scripture is an extension of Torah legislation and, beyond that, there is an oral Torah that contains teachings from Moses not found written in the law. The resurrection had become a standard hope of Jews by the time of the book of Daniel in 160 BC and after. It is affirmed in Daniel 12:3 and in non-biblical writings such as the first book of Enoch. Here the Sadducees think they can trap Jesus with an impossible situation for the doctrine of an afterlife. In Deuteronomy 25:5–6, the law said if a man died childless, his brother was to conceive a child with the widow and bring it up as his brother's heir. Jesus is not trapped but changes the grounds for why an afterlife is sure. There can be no marriage in the afterlife because raising new children will not be needed where there is no death. On the contrary, God did affirm an afterlife in another text: in Exodus 3 God said that he was the God of living ancestors long after they had died, which shows that they must still be alive with God in the afterlife.

**Gospel: Luke 20:27–38
(or Luke 20:27, 34–38)**

Some Sadducees, those who deny that there is a resurrection, came forward and put this question to Jesus, saying, "Teacher, Moses wrote for us,

*If someone's brother dies leaving a wife but
no child,
his brother must take the wife
and raise up descendants for his brother.*

Now there were seven brothers; the first married a woman but died childless. Then the second and the third married her, and likewise all the seven died childless. Finally the woman also died. Now at the resurrection whose wife will that woman be? For all seven had been married to her." Jesus said to them, "The children of this age marry and remarry; but those who are deemed worthy to attain to the coming age and to the resurrection of the dead neither marry nor are given in marriage. They can no longer die, for they are like angels; and they are the children of God because they are the ones who will rise. That the dead will rise even Moses made known in the passage about the bush, when he called out 'Lord,' the God of Abraham, the God of Isaac, and the God of Jacob; and he is not God of the dead, but of the living, for to him all are alive."

MUSIC CONNECTION

While there are *hints* of a promise of eternal life in the Hebrew scriptures (witness today's gruesome but hopeful lesson from Maccabees), it is really in the New Testament that a fully developed notion of life beyond the grave fully blossoms. This follows, of course, in the wake of the pivotal event of Christian belief and self-understanding—the resurrection of Jesus from the dead. Thus, Luke's almost creedal affirmation "God is not the God of the dead, but of the living, for to him all are alive" needs be seen in the light of this pivotal event. Easter hymns are certainly appropriate and include *I Am the Bread of Life, Alleluia Sing to Jesus, Lord of the Dance, I Know That My Redeemer Lives, Hail Thee Festival Day, Darkness Is Gone, Death Will Be No More,* and *Sing O Sing.* Several Communion songs, such as *Eat This Bread; Praise the Lord, My Soul;* and *Pan de Vida,* reinforce this theme. The Quinn/Joncas collaboration *Take and Eat* is particularly skillful at blending eucharistic and resurrection imagery in its numerous verses. Hughes, Stewart, Alstott, and Gelineau all have fine settings for today's responsorial, Psalm 17.

CATECHETICAL SUGGESTIONS

The time of the Maccabees in Jewish history
The development of a belief in life after death in the Old Testament
Laments
Intercessory prayer
What does "resurrection of the body" mean?
Jewish society in the time of Jesus

First Reading:
Malachi 3:19–20a

Lo, the day is com-
ing, blazing like
an oven,
when all the proud
and all evildoers
will be stubble,
and the day that is
coming will set
them on fire,
leaving them nei-
ther root nor
branch,
says the LORD of
hosts.
But for you who fear
my name, there
will arise
the sun of justice
with its healing
rays.

SCRIPTURE COMMENTARY

The dire warning of the prophet Malachi was issued about the year 520 BC as the former exiles from Babylon were struggling to rebuild Jerusalem and the temple out of the rubble and total destruction that they found at the site when they returned. Malachi spoke out against a malaise and sense of despair that had gripped these returnees when they saw how impossible the task seemed. The prophet blamed a lack of enthusiasm for the Lord as the source of their seeming failure in getting crops to succeed and walls to be built. If they first put up the temple and reinstated the proper worship of the Lord, blessing would follow. Malachi's frightening language in his prophetic oracles was not due to any threat of war or enemy attack because the Persian Empire had the area under full control. No, the images of the blazing oven and wildfires that sweep all sinners away were borrowed from a long tradition of words used by prophets for judgment. Once fire has smelted raw ore, there is fine metal; once a fire has gone through the stubble of a harvested field, the new crop begins to find room to sprout. In contrast to the purifying fire, the blessing is described in the solar images of God's bright rays bringing healing and warmth to a society living justly and rightly with God.

HOMILY HELPS

There is never a shortage of speculation regarding the end of the world, which always includes predictions as to when it will come. The truth of the matter is that we simply do not know. After the resurrection and ascension of Jesus, the first Christians believed that the return of Christ and the final summing up were close at hand. This sense of imminence centered on the predicted destruction of Jerusalem, about which Jesus had spoken. This actually occurred when the Romans leveled the city in AD 70. But the return of Christ did not occur.

The gospels sometimes reflect this pervasive belief in connecting the end with the destruction of the temple. Luke, however, does not. He writes well after the events of the year 70 and has reconciled himself to a longer interim period in the life of the Church. This is clear in today's gospel, wherein the predicted destruction of the temple is "de-eschatologized" and seen as simply a part of history. It was an important event, but there was still much to come, including a period of trial and persecution for Christ's followers. But it was a period to be accompanied by the abiding presence of Christ.

Thus, the call of the Lucan Jesus today is for patient endurance, a key virtue at any time in the Christian life. We can think of many examples. The trials of a prolonged illness; the precarious situation of employment; a world beset by problems; people who are hungry, or homeless, or sick with AIDS; the corrupt government leaders in many countries who prevent well-intentioned help from reaching people in need.

Then there are the grave problems that face the Church. Clerical misconduct, the growing

PSALM REFLECTION

The joyous tones of Psalm 98 may seem strangely out of synch with the threatening tones of Malachi's warnings. The psalm itself is a song of praise for God as the creator and benefactor of all creatures in the universe. It celebrates God as king of creation. However, one characteristic of God's divine reign over the world is that every creature obeys the laws of nature God has established and fulfills its proper role for the good of all. Thus the world is well ordered and "just." This sense of universal obedience to God's purposes is the meaning of justice here. Thus, Malachi expected that the day when God will return in blessing will be the day of justice among humans, and it is because of this that we turn in obedience to God's will, giving him our proper worship and fidelity.

Psalm Response
Psalm 98:5–6, 7–8, 9

Antiphon
The Lord comes to rule the earth with justice.

Verse for Reflection
The Lord has made his salvation known. He has revealed his justice before the nations. (v. 2)

SCRIPTURE COMMENTARY

This is the third and last of the readings from 2 Thessalonians to prepare us for the end of the world. As Jesus will caution his disciples to prepare for a period of persecution and suffering if they are to see the day of the Lord's coming with victory for them, so Paul opposes the apocalyptic and terrifying efforts of some to picture disaster here or there and everywhere. Paul, like Jesus, declares that such wars and disasters are with us in all ages of this world but our task is to order our lives for the good of the whole community each day

Second Reading:
2 Thessalonians 3:7–12

Brothers and sisters: You know how one must imitate us. For we did not act in a disorderly way among you, nor did we eat food received free from anyone. On the contrary, in toil and drudgery,

---

number of people who do not practice their faith, children moving toward maturity with very little knowledge of their faith.

Finally, there are the realities of society today: divorce, same-sex and premarital relationships. None of these issues is uncomplicated or easily resolved. Yet they do affect our lives.

But Paul once again today offers the practical solution. Do not grow depressed or weary. But do not be a bystander either. Lend your efforts to the task at hand. Paul preached the gospel tirelessly and supported himself at the same time. As he suggests today, he kept busy and had little time for busybodies.

When the Lord does come, will he find faith on the earth? It

is a question that Jesus himself raises. The psalmist today states that the Lord will come to rule the world with justice.

Of one thing we can be certain. If peace is the final gift of Christ, the dictum of the Church makes sense: "If you want peace, work for justice." We have limited possibilities in this interim period, but the opportunities are there. We may care for one impoverished child in Africa. We may provide an education for one person to whom it is denied. When the hungry eat, and the thirsty drink, and the naked are clothed and a house is constructed for a homeless family, then the kingdom becomes a reality. It is already in our midst.

LITURGICAL NOTES

As Ordinary Time comes to a conclusion, our attention is drawn to the end times, to the time when the world as we know it will pass away. It also calls us to reflect on our own mortality. Virtually all the members of our assembly have experienced the death of a family member, friend, or coworker. And while we stand speechless when confronted with the mystery of death, our faith provides both support and comfort because we know that for God's faithful people "life is changed, not ended."

In the face of death, the Church confidently pro-

night and day we worked, so as not to burden any of you. Not that we do not have the right. Rather, we wanted to present ourselves as a model for you, so that you might imitate us. In fact, when we were with you, we instructed you that if anyone was unwilling to work, neither should that one eat. We hear that some are conducting themselves among you in a disorderly way, by not keeping busy but minding the business of others. Such people we instruct and urge in the Lord Jesus Christ to work quietly and to eat their own food.

SCRIPTURE COMMENTARY, CONTINUED

and to work in a spirit of patience and trust that God has control of his plan and will unfold it in his time line, not ours. Busybodies, as Paul points out, do not just create annoying disturbances by their interference and offensive curiosity. They also do not set themselves to be productive for any good. Instead, they start rumors and create fear about all kinds of absurd possibilities that quickly break down the spirit and the order of the community.

Gospel: Luke 21:5–19

While some people were speaking about how the temple was adorned with costly stones and votive offerings, Jesus said, "All that you see here—the days will come when there will not be left a stone upon another stone that will not be thrown down."

Then they asked him, "Teacher, when will this happen? And what sign will there be when all these

SCRIPTURE COMMENTARY

Much of this passage is found in the Gospel of Mark, chapter 13, but there it is not clear whether Jesus was speaking of the future of the temple and Jerusalem or of the greater judgment on the whole world when Christ will come again. Luke, however, distinguishes the two moments very clearly. In today's gospel, all the words of Jesus center on what will happen to his followers in the decades after he has risen and left them. In particular, some of the language may refer to the coming

claims that God has created each person for eternal life and that Jesus, the Son of God, by his death and resurrection, has broken the chains of sin and death that bound humanity. Christ achieved his task of redeeming humanity and giving perfect glory to God, principally by the paschal mystery of his blessed passion, resurrection from the dead, and glorious ascension. [The Church] recognizes the spiritual bond that still exists between the living and the dead and proclaims its belief that all the faithful will be raised up and reunited in the new heavens and a new earth,

where death will be no more. (*Order of Christian Funerals*, 1, 6)

This Sunday can provide an ideal opportunity for renewed catechesis concerning not only what the community believes about the death of a Christian but also how the Church's funeral rites express in sign and symbol, word, and song these profound truths.

Excerpts from the *Order of Christian Funerals* and from parish or diocesan guidelines on the funeral rites as well as information concerning the ministry of consolation can provide both catechesis and information to parishioners. Parishes that have done this kind of catechesis often

report that parishioners tend to keep this information and tuck it in with wills and other items related to funerals. This is a project that is well worth the effort.

Thursday is Thanksgiving Day, a day on which many Catholics will attend Mass. Ministers should be scheduled and on hand at all the Masses that will be celebrated, not just the principal Mass. The *Book of Blessings* (chapter 58) contains an order for the Blessing of Food on Thanksgiving Day. *Catholic Household Blessings and Prayers* also contains several prayers for use on Thanksgiving. Excerpts of these prayers could very appropriately be printed in the bulletin for people to use at their Thanksgiving table.

SCRIPTURE COMMENTARY, CONTINUED
destruction of Jerusalem by the Romans in AD 66–70, which culminated in the total destruction of the temple and the city. Luke is writing this passage after that event had already happened, so he is probably collecting a variety of sayings of Jesus warning that the city would be destroyed because of the people's lack of faith and also warning his disciples that they must expect persecution and suffering for the sake of his name. His assurance is that even when he is not present among them physically, he will provide them with the strength and the words needed to defend themselves. But even if they suffer death for his name, they will not suffer the loss of their lives. This follows upon his words last week to the Sadducees that the afterlife was a certainty because God remains faithful in his relationship to his just ones.

things are about to happen?" He answered, "See that you not be deceived, for many will come in my name, saying, 'I am he,'" and 'The time has come.' Do not follow them! When you hear of wars and insurrections, do not be terrified; for such things must happen first, but it will not immediately be the end." Then he said to them, "Nation will rise against nation, and kingdom against kingdom. There will be powerful earthquakes, famines, and plagues from place to place; and awesome sights and mighty signs will come from the sky.

"Before all this happens, however, they will seize and persecute you, they will hand you over to the synagogues and to prisons, and they will have you led before kings and governors because of my name. It will lead to your giving testimony. Remember, you are not to prepare your defense beforehand, for I myself shall give you a wisdom in speaking that all your adversaries will be powerless to resist or refute. You will even be handed over by parents, brothers, relatives, and friends, and they will put some of you to death. You will be hated by all because of my name, but not a hair on your head will be destroyed. By your perseverance you will secure your lives."

 MUSIC CONNECTION

Apocalyptic detail accompanies this last Sunday of the year before the solemnity of Christ the King and the impending season of Advent. It is the liturgy's way of helping us to shift gears and to attune our religious imaginations to the imagery of the upcoming season. The nature of this type of literature is not to frighten us into submission but, rather, to invite us into a trusting faith in God, who can rescue us from the darkest night. For Malachi it means "there will arise the sun of justice with its healing rays," while Luke assures us that "by your perseverance you will

secure your lives." Appropriate hymns include *Be Not Afraid, How Can I Keep from Singing, Though the Mountains May Fall, Patience People, Only in God, Now the Day of the Lord Is at Hand, On Eagle's Wings, We Will Rise Again, Precious Lord, The Lord Is My Light,* and *A Mighty Fortress.* Grayson Brown's sway-inducing *Don't Be Worried* reinforces the feeling that, no matter what may befall us or impede our life's journey, trusting in the Lord, as described in today's readings, is our primary vocation as disciples. Psalm 98, the responsorial, has fine settings by Haas/Haugen, Guimont, Gelineau, and Kreutz.

CATECHETICAL SUGGESTIONS

Setting and message of the book of Malachi
The twelve minor prophets
Rerum Novarum (Leo XIII's encyclical)
The role of the temple in the history of Israel
Jesus' end-time statements in the synoptic gospels
Catholic beliefs about the end times

**First Reading:
2 Samuel 5:1–3**

In those days, all the tribes of Israel came to David in Hebron and said: "Here we are, your bone and your flesh. In days past, when Saul was our king, it was you who led the Israelites out and brought them back. And the LORD said to you, 'You shall shepherd my people Israel and shall be commander of Israel.'" When all the elders of Israel came to David in Hebron, King David made an agreement with them there before the LORD, and they anointed him king of Israel.

SCRIPTURE COMMENTARY

In the gospel today, Luke reports that Jesus declared his kingship was over those who ask forgiveness and suffer innocently. He is of the family of David but not a king of power and conquest as David had been. Yet that was the David who was a skilled and wily political leader. There was also the David whose heart was faithful to God's will for him, who sang God's praises in the psalms and sought to establish the temple as a worthy home of the God of Israel. The first reading today is from the moment when even the northern tribes who had been holding out against David as king came to him and accepted his rule. God declares that David will indeed have military power and success, but also announces that David will be the shepherd of God's people. In this role, the king stood in the place of the true shepherd, God himself, who had led his flock to freedom in the Exodus and watched over them all the years before David became king. Now David will be God's deputy in caring for his people as the shepherd looks after his sheep.

HOMILY HELPS

Christ's is indeed a different type of kingship. None of the trappings of royalty, no obeisance of the courtiers, no unapproachable grandeur. In response to Pilate's question, Jesus admitted that he was a king but not a king of this world. The inscription on the cross that read "This is the King of the Jews" hung over One who was nailed to wood and suspended between earth and heaven. This was a king who followed a single path, the royal road of the cross.

One of this king's subjects turns to him from an adjacent cross. A common criminal sentenced to death for his felonies directly asks for admission to the kingdom. His request is immediately granted. Full citizenship is accorded with a simple admission of wrongdoing and a heartfelt turning to the Lord.

Shades of this different type of kingship are implied in the mission given to David. The religious dimension of his calling is seen in his commission, not to govern or dominate but to shepherd his people. This image, used so frequently in both Testaments, conveys an idea of solicitude and concern, qualities much to the fore in the ministry of Jesus.

The Colossians hymn, read on this last Sunday of the church year, summarizes the primacy of Christ under two headings. The first is related to the eternal Son, and the second to his redemptive role in the Church.

Christ is first as the image of God, present to the Father from all eternity. At the moment of creation, he is God's blueprint in bringing all things into being. In his incarnate person, he is the juncture between heaven and earth, the center of all that is

PSALM REFLECTION

The commentary on the first reading pointed out that David is glorified for both his piety and his interest in glorifying God with a magnificent temple. It is this second aspect of David's real kingship before God that the psalm accents. The true glory of Jerusalem is its role as the site of the house of God. In a joyous hymn that was probably sung by pilgrims coming to Jerusalem to celebrate a major feast, the psalmist describes the beauty of the city that is totally centered on God's house. It is the source of all the people's hopes because God dwells there in his majesty, and his presence confirms that he is their protector and help. The psalm also refers to the seats of the house of David, where judgment takes place. The Davidic dynasty does indeed maintain justice and order for the community, but its role is clearly subordinated to the rule of God. God—not David—is the heart of the meaning of the city of Jerusalem.

Psalm Response
Psalm 122:1–2,
3–4, 4–5

Antiphon
Let us go rejoicing
 to the house of
 the Lord.

Verse for Reflection
I rejoiced when I
 heard them say,
"Let us go up to the
 house of the
 Lord!"
(v. 1)

created. Through him God sees all that has been made, while all creation sees in Christ the image of the Father. In our faith, then, Christ is pivotal; nothing in heaven or on earth has meaning independent of him.

Christ's role is also primary in the order of redemption. He has given birth to the Church in his dying and rising through the Spirit, which he confers. Thus he is the head of the Church. Also, as the first to rise from the dead, he has a primacy in the new life. Not only are all Christians related to him; the same is true of the whole created order, the animate and the inanimate. All are touched by redemption. With

the poet, we can "see his blood upon the rose."

Clearly, the title "king" is accorded Christ in an analogous sense. It is a title that approximates his unique role but in no way exhausts it. Everything in our spiritual life—Church, sacraments, scripture—centers on his person. Our daily lives in work, rest, and recreation find their focal point in him. Titles are multiple in professions, in the corporate world, in government, and in the military. They all represent clear marks of demarcation. On this concluding Sunday of the year, it is important to remember that when all is said and done, the title "Christian" is at the center of our life.

CATECHETICAL SUGGESTIONS

Kingship in Israel
"God's anointed" (messianism) in Israel
Pilgrim feasts and songs of ascent in Israel
High Christology in Colossians
The kingdom of God
In what ways is Christ the *King* in each of our lives?

Second Reading: Colossians 1:12–20

Brothers and sisters: Let us give thanks to the Father, who has made you fit to share in the inheritance of the holy ones in light. He delivered us from the power of darkness and transferred us to the kingdom of his beloved Son, in whom we have redemption, the forgiveness of sins.

He is the image of the invisible God,
    the firstborn of all creation.
For in him were created all things in heaven and
      on earth,
    the visible and the invisible,
    whether thrones or dominions or principalities
      or powers;
    all things were created through him and for
      him.
He is before all things,
    and in him all things hold together.
He is the head of the body, the church.
He is the beginning, the firstborn from the dead,
    that in all things he himself might be preemi-
      nent.
For in him all the fullness was pleased to dwell,
    and through him to reconcile all things for him,
    making peace by the blood of his cross
    through him, whether those on earth or those in
      heaven.

SCRIPTURE COMMENTARY

Colossians states that we are citizens of God's kingdom. It is the opposite of a kingdom of darkness. That is where we were subjects, but now forgiveness of sins has brought us out of that kingdom into a kingdom of light. If the kingdom of darkness is the power of sin that ruled over our lives and dictated a hopelessness of ever escaping its control, then the kingdom of light is union with Christ, who reconciled the world to God by his resurrection from the dead. Paul talks of Christ in his preexistent state as the divine model for the universe, containing the fullness of all that God intended to create. As God sent Christ down to us in human form and then glorified him with the divine fulfillment that brought all things back into oneness in God, so we now have the complete assurance that we are united to him as a body is to its head. Jesus frees us from the power of sin and death by his cross and carries us with him into glory with the Father.

LITURGICAL NOTES

The church year finds its conclusion in the Solemnity of Christ the King. The feast was instituted in 1925 by Pope Pius XI and moved to the last Sunday of the church year in the new calendar brought about by the liturgical reform of the Second Vatican Council. Most Catholics live their lives based on a school year calendar and see the conclusion of another school year as the end of the year. Others think of the end of December as the end of their year. Few will experience this solemnity as an ending. This is not meant to downplay today's celebration but rather to recognize that the notion of "conclusion" or "ending" will probably not resonate with most members of our assemblies.

While the images of "king" and "kingdom" are difficult for most Americans, the gospel asks us to consider a different way of seeing kingship. The kingdom is about truth and justice; the king reigns not from a royal throne but from the wood of the cross.

The alternative Opening Prayer asks that we might rejoice in the peace of Christ the King, "glory in his justice, live in his love." The proper preface given for this feast speaks of the kingdom that Christ establishes: "a kingdom of truth and life, a kingdom of holiness and grace, a kingdom of justice, love, and peace."

The environment should look festive, with the finest vestments, hangings, and floral arrangements, for next Sunday we will return to the stark simplicity of our Advent waiting. The cross and even the processional cross should figure prominently in today's liturgy. The processional cross might be adorned with flowers or streamers.

SCRIPTURE COMMENTARY

The gospel writers all report the details of the passion and crucifixion of Jesus in great detail. It is certainly the most developed part of the gospel tradition and probably the earliest to have been given in written form. But none of the four great narratives are simply a report of the historical facts. They have several significant differences in the things they report. What they have in common is that they go out of their way to identify all parts of the passion steps with the predictions of the prophetic writings. In today's short section of the passion story, the crowds mock Jesus' claim to be God's chosen one (Isa 42), the soldiers give him vinegar to drink (Ps 69:21), and he is asked to fulfill the royal hopes of a messiah (various passages, such as Pss 2, 89, and 110). But Luke follows the report of their cynical sign affixed to the cross over Jesus, the condemned criminal, saying that he was a king, with the story of what his kingship really means: when the thief asks Jesus to include him in his kingdom, Jesus promises that he will indeed be in that kingdom. Jesus is no king in the worldly sense but ruler of the humble of heart, the contrite who ask forgiveness, and those who put all their hope in God alone.

Gospel: Luke 23:35–43

The rulers sneered at Jesus and said, "He saved others, let him save himself if he is the chosen one, the Christ of God." Even the soldiers jeered at him. As they approached to offer him wine they called out, "If you are King of the Jews, save yourself." Above him there was an inscription that read, "This is the King of the Jews."

Now one of the criminals hanging there reviled Jesus, saying, "Are you not the Christ? Save yourself and us." The other, however, rebuking him, said in reply, "Have you no fear of God, for you are subject to the same condemnation? And indeed, we have been condemned justly, for the sentence we received corresponds to our crimes, but this man has done nothing criminal." Then he said, "Jesus, remember me when you come into your kingdom." He replied to him, "Amen, I say to you, today you will be with me in Paradise."

MUSIC CONNECTION

On this final Sunday of the year, we turn our gaze to the theological symbol of the kingdom or reign of God. The reading from the second book of Samuel portrays David as the shepherd of Israel as well as their king. The Colossians hymn praises God, who "delivered us from the power of darkness and transferred us to the kingdom of his beloved Son." Luke's Jesus, hanging under the ignominious sign "This is the King of the Jews," is the Lord of mercy who, even in his dying breaths, reassures the repentant criminal with the words "Amen I say to you: today you will be with me in paradise." Given this Lucan gospel, *Jesus, Remember Me* is an obvious choice. The standards—*Alleluia, Sing to Jesus; Rejoice the Lord Is King; Jesus Christ Is Risen Today; To Jesus Christ Our Sovereign King; At the Lamb's High Feast; Crown Him with Many Crowns;* and *All Creatures of Our God and King*—are all appropriate. These regal images ought to be balanced with the less hierarchic and more biblical "shepherd" imagery as found in wonderful pieces such as *Like a Shepherd, Because the Lord Is My Shepherd, Shepherd of Souls, Gift of Finest Wheat, Shepherd Me O God* and *We Will Rise Again.* Particularly attractive are the two Irish melodies, *My Shepherd, Lord* and *The King of Love My Shepherd Is.* The responsorial, Psalm 122, finds good expression in Gelineau, Haas, and Joncas.

INDEX OF SCRIPTURE PASSAGES